CONFLICT AND COMPROMISE

How Congress Makes the Law

Ronald D. Elving

A TOUCHSTONE BOOK
Published by Simon & Schuster

TOUCHSTONE
Rockefeller Center
1230 Avenue of the Americas
New York, NY 10020

First Touchstone Edition 1996

TOUCHSTONE and colophon are registered trademarks
of Simon & Schuster Inc.

Designed by Levavi & Levavi

Manufactured in the United States of America

1 2 3 4 5 6 7 8 9 10

Library of Congress Cataloging-in-Publication Data
Elving, Ronald D.
Conflict and compromise : how Congress makes the law /
Ronald D. Elving.
p. cm.
Includes index.
1. United States. Family and Medical Leave Act of 1993.
2. Parental leave—Law and legislation—United States.
3. Maternity leave—Law and legislation—United States.
4. Sick leave—Law and legislation—United States.
I. Title.
KF3531.E45 1995
344.73'0125763—dc20
[347.304125763]   95-5572
CIP
ISBN 0-684-80195-7
0-684-82416-7
(Pbk)

Acknowledgments

AMONG THOSE WHO ENCOURAGED THE writing of this book was Eric Redman, who wrote his own *(The Dance of Legislation)* in the early 1970s. Redman's account of the creation of the National Health Services Corps remains a vivid evocation of the legislative life, even after more than two decades. And while this book was conceived as an update— recognizing the changes in congressional process and personalities since the Nixon era—it is intended also as a tribute.

Redman noted that the NHSC bill he chronicled was the vehicle of his story but that Congress itself was the subject. Similarly, here, the issue of family leave performs much the same function. For help in guiding me toward this particular vehicle (and away from other prospects) I am indebted to former Congressman Bill Frenzel, Republican of Minnesota; Professor James Thurber, director of the Center for the Study of Congress and the Presidency at the American University; Dr. Catherine Rudder, executive director of the American Political Science Association; and Alan Ehrenhalt, executive editor of *Governing* magazine.

Ehrenhalt also favored the manuscript with his critical skills, tempering and refining the end product. Another source of expert consultative advice was Walter J. Oleszek, senior specialist in American national government and public administration for the Congressional Research Service, whose own book on congressional procedure is the standard text.

I wish to thank all of the *Congressional Quarterly* reporters whose careful coverage of family leave over five Congresses helped inform this narrative, especially Julie Rovner and Jill Zuckman, who each followed the bill through more than one Congress and shared generously what they had learned. Rovner, one of the leading experts in Washington's social policy debates of the 1980s and 1990s, was not only full of insights into the subject matter but a willing commentator on the text as well. Any errors are solely my responsibility.

At Simon & Schuster, it was Alice Mayhew who felt the need for a book of this kind and who was willing to entrust the project to me. Senior editor Bob Bender saw me through not only the uncertainties at the outset but also the anxieties at the end. Special thanks must go to Edwin R. Bayley, first dean of the Graduate School of Journalism at the University of California at Berkeley, who encouraged my interest in words and politics. I am greatly indebted to Robert W. Merry, executive editor of *Congressional Quarterly*, who was at once a model and a patron for this enterprise. Also essential from beginning to end were Gail Ross, a literary agent willing to tackle tough projects, and Belle Elving of *The Washington Post*, always my first and most forthright critic, for her patience and forbearance and for squaring it with our daughter, Kelsey.

For Esther Holmlund Elving (1916–1988), who began school in Opportunity, Montana, in 1921, graduated first in her high school class and pursued careers as teacher, wife and mother. She finished her college degree in 1971. She would have liked to hold this book in her hands.

Contents

Introduction   11

Part One • Beginnings:
The 98th and 99th Congresses (1984–1986)   15

1. *The First Months of Life*   17
2. *To the Hill*   35
3. *Testing the Track*   53

Part Two • Revision:
The 100th Congress (1987–1988)   73

4. *Back Up on the Horse*   75
5. *A Breakthrough in Committee*   92
6. *Hitting the Wall*   110

Part Three • "So Near, and Yet":
The 101st Congress (1989–1990)   *127*

7. *New Beginnings*   *129*
8. *A Year of Living Dangerously*   *145*
9. *A Vote in the House*   *161*
10. *The Veto*   *183*

Part Four • Forcing the Issue:
The 102nd Congress (1991–1992)   *199*

11. *Testing the Mettle*   *201*
12. *The Penny Affair*   *219*
13. *To the White House Once Again*   *236*

Part Five • Enactment:
The 103rd Congress (1993)   *253*

14. *A New Day*   *255*
15. *The Final Act*   *272*

Epilogue   *291*
Glossary   *297*
A Note on Sources   *302*
Index   *305*

Introduction

ON FEBRUARY 5, 1993, BILL CLINTON staged his first bill-signing ceremony as president of the United States. The midwinter day was remarkably warm and sunny, with a high near sixty degrees, so the event was held outdoors in the Rose Garden. There were chuckles as Clinton tried his hand at signing parts of his name with different pens. He then handed out the pens to the congressional worthies arrayed behind him, applauding and beaming for the cameras.

The celebration seemed in order, not only because the Family and Medical Leave Act of 1993 would be the first law of the new presidency but also because it had shot through both chambers of Congress in a month. Just sixteen days after taking his oath of office, Clinton could claim to have enacted a significant change in social policy in keeping with the "People First" theme of his campaign.

But this ceremony, intended to be rich in political symbolism, was also rife with irony. Family leave was the furthest thing from an overnight success. Before its swift passage at the outset of the 103rd Congress, it had been through painstaking consideration in each Congress since the 99th. Reintroduced every two years, it had hacked its way again and again through the thicket of Capitol Hill hearings, markups, cloakrooms and pitched battles on the House and Senate floors. One participant compared the bill's fitful progress to the myth of Sisyphus, others thought it closer to *The Perils of Pauline*. To read family leave's journal of survival is to realize how ingeniously frustrating the mechanisms of Congress can be.

Rarely has a piece of social legislation been as simple and succinct. Its gist could be summed up in a sentence: *Employers would be required to grant leaves of absence for employees who were seriously ill, who had newborn or newly adopted children, or who had to care for sick children, spouses or parents.*

But if the new law was short, its history was extensive. The basic idea had come to Congress from disparate channels that seemed to converge all at once in the mid-1980s. But as far back as the turn of the century there had been talk among various social reformers and labor organizers of the need to recognize temporary disabilities—including those originating with family obligations—as legitimate workplace issues.

The idea took hold in Europe after World War II, where severe shortages of male workers kept women in the labor force. But it did not find favor in America's baby-boom years of nuclear families and *Father Knows Best.* The demography of it all began to change in the later 1960s, when recession and inflation ended the relatively easy prosperity the nation had enjoyed for most of two decades. Women began going back to work to supplement the earnings of husbands who could no longer earn enough to cover the bills.

Soon, working women were no longer a minority and women's rights were no longer a campus theory. As part of this change, family leave became a concept, then a proposal and then a bill. It was not proposed by the president or the executive branch, and it was not a favorite of the congressional leadership until its latter days. It arose from real-life situations, and it moved through Congress largely on the lobbying, organizing and pressure-building skills of outsider groups.

As a political cause family leave began with feminists. But from the beginning, common cause was made with advocates of traditional family life such as the Association of Junior Leagues and the U.S. Catholic Conference. By setting aside its fundamental disagreement with feminists over abortion for the sake of this issue, the Catholic Conference made it possible for Bella Abzug and John Cardinal O'Connor to soldier together in a shared crusade. In time, this coalition added organized labor and senior citizen groups. The coalition would prove resilient through the years of frustration, widening its base both outside and inside the institution of Congress. It made friends in both parties and in both chambers, among women and men, among ancient committee chairmen and brash newcomers alike.

And yet, powerful as this array became, it was checked year after year by the equally effective tactics and strategies of a business-lobbying coalition. These men and women and the members with whom they were allied saw family leave not as a labor standard but as the first in a new generation of government mandates on business. They saw an underfunded and largely unpopular federal government trying to impose a social agenda using private employers as its agents.

This corresponding and adversarial coalition not only delayed the bill but also managed to amend it substantially along the way. Even when the opposition had been worn down by years of compromise, family leave was obstructed by the workings of Congress itself and the realities of divided government. Twice passed in the early 1990s by both chambers of Congress, family leave was twice vetoed by Republican President George Bush. Both times the Democrat-controlled House failed to muster enough votes to override.

That was why the election of a new, Democratic president made the difference for family leave. In his own remarks in the Rose Garden in February 1993, Clinton hailed the "end of gridlock." The new administration and the Congress had shown they could work together and accomplish something, after all. "With the passage of this bill, we hear the sound of cracking ice as the iceberg breaks away," said Congressman Pat Williams, a Democrat from Montana.

Some believed family leave would raise the curtain on a new era of social legislation. Welfare and health care would be reformed, government reinvented. But nearly two years later Clinton would still be citing family leave as his showcase social achievement because his administration would have nothing to top it. While the new administration was pleased to sign family leave and claim some measure of credit for its enactment, it was not able to replicate that success on other social issues.

In the end, family leave never belonged to any White House. It was a bill that emerged from Congress and the forces that work upon it. That is why it reveals so well the ways of Congress in their natural place and time, the internal workings and relations between officeholders and those who serve or seek to influence them. The purpose in telling this story is to demonstrate how these elements interact with that system of rules, procedures, traditions and customs by which Congress makes the law.

Part One

BEGINNINGS: THE 98TH AND 99TH CONGRESSES (1984–1986)

1.

The First Months
of Life

IN 1981, THE YEAR SHE BECAME pregnant, Lillian Garland was in her early
twenties and in her fifth year as a receptionist at the headquarters of
the California Federal Savings and Loan Association in downtown Los
Angeles. Her supervisor asked repeatedly about when the baby was due
and when Garland could be back at work. The baby girl came in February 1982 by caesarean section. After two months of convalescence under
doctor's orders, Garland returned to her office to be told her job had
been given to the woman she herself had trained as her temporary replacement.

Garland's experience was anything but unprecedented. For most of
the twentieth century, American women who worked outside the home
still expected to quit when they had children. Typically, they were expected to leave work as soon as they were visibly pregnant. But in the
1980s nearly half the nation's workforce was composed of women. And
more than half the nation's women were working outside the home. And
most of those women were, or still expected to be, mothers.

Garland herself had not thought that having a baby would mean giving
up her job—much less that her situation would soon entangle the state,
the courts and the Congress and become a turning point in labor relations and national social policy. But after weeks of looking for another

job, Garland took her story to the state Department of Fair Employment and Housing. Lawyers there told her that her job at Cal Fed should have been waiting for her when she returned. They said her employer had broken a 1978 state law requiring companies to allow not just two but four months of leave for a temporary disability related to pregnancy or childbirth.

Garland's was just one of three hundred complaints filed against employers under that state law in 1982, but it was the one on which California business chose to make its stand. Buttressed by the Merchants and Manufacturing Association and the California Chamber of Commerce, Cal Fed filed a federal lawsuit challenging the leave law and defending a company's right to set its own personnel policies and benefits.

Among those taking a sudden, personal interest in Lillian Garland in mid-1982 was Howard Berman, a Democratic state legislator from the San Fernando Valley suburbs northwest of Los Angeles. Berman had quickly become a highly visible player in the state Assembly of the 1970s, becoming majority floor leader in his second term at the age of thirty-three. Among his achievements had been the 1978 law that created the four-month disability leave for new mothers. When Cal Fed filed its suit, Berman was running for Congress and touting his leave law in his campaign. Naturally, he told reporters and activists that he believed his state statute would hold up in court. But just in case, Berman would add, he hoped to go to Washington and write the right-to-leave into federal law.

The outcome of Berman's congressional race was not much in doubt. He was running in a newly drawn district with borders tailored expressly for him by Phil Burton, the San Francisco congressman who mapped out such districts for the whole state and then persuaded the Democratic legislature and governor to approve them. Burton liked Berman and took care of him, drawing in lots of Berman's Assembly district and including two registered Democrats for every registered Republican. Berman won the seat with 60 percent of the November vote.

In the same month, coincidentally, Lillian Garland went back to work —at Cal Fed. Reporters asked if she was not weakening her case by doing so. "I need an income," she shrugged, "and they're an okay company to work for." Meanwhile, the case that pitted her against her past and present employer was still pending before a federal judge in Los Angeles.

After arriving on Capitol Hill, Berman found that his energy and close ties to Burton could get him off to another fast start. He was installed on the Democratic Steering and Policy Committee, the executive board for the majority party (Democrats continued to dominate the House in the early 1980s, despite having lost the Senate and the White House). Steering and Policy assigned Democratic members to committees, often making or breaking careers in the process. Berman himself was given seats on Foreign Affairs and Judiciary (not especially glamorous but solidly middle-rank). He was interested in proposed revisions to the copyright law—a legislative briar patch with appeal for a lawyer whose district was home to the motion picture and recording industries.

Berman was three months into his second year in Washington when a ruling came down in the Cal Fed case. On March 21, 1984, Federal District Judge Manuel L. Real declared Cal Fed had been right: Berman's leave law violated federal statutes (including the Civil Rights Act of 1964) requiring equal treatment of men and women in the workplace because men could not avail themselves of maternity leave.

Many women activists were outraged. Not only had Real denied Garland's complaint and erased Berman's law, he had done it citing landmark laws that the movement regarded as its own. It bordered on blasphemy. Some even read the decision as part of a right-wing offensive, assuming Real to be a Reagan appointee (he had been named to the bench in 1966 by Lyndon B. Johnson).

Busy as Berman had been, Real's decision was about to make him busier. The clamor reaching him from the West Coast included the unmistakable voice of Maxine Waters, a state assemblywoman who had cosponsored his bill back in 1978. An aggressive advocate for African-Americans and for women as well, Waters told Berman she was on her way to Washington to get action. If the Pregnancy Discrimination Act was the problem, she said, it needed to be rewritten. If the Civil Rights Act was the problem, someone ought to rewrite that law, too.

Berman already knew what he wanted to do. He wanted to introduce a bill in Congress that would not only reverse Real but also secure the same rights for every woman in the country that he had tried to win for women in California. There had to be a way to require employers to grant leaves for new mothers—with job protection and benefits—without being impaled on any of the legal monuments to equality of civil rights.

But Berman also knew he needed help. It was the sort of delicate operation that demanded a specialist, someone who knew the intricacies of these particular laws and their legislative histories. He made some phone calls. One was to Donna Lenhoff at the Women's Legal Defense Fund. Lenhoff, then just thirty-three, had the title of associate director for legal policy and programs at the fund and the connections Berman was looking for.

She had come to Washington with her new law degree from Penn in

1976, put in two years of antitrust practice at the Justice Department and then become the first staff lawyer hired by the fund. Almost before her file boxes were unpacked, she had plunged into the battle over pregnancy benefits that led to the Pregnancy Discrimination Act of 1978. In a rush she met the full cast of activists and advocates: labor attorneys, law school teachers, feminist firebrands and members of Congress. And after the law was on the books, she became unofficial convener of what she called "the PDA alumnae association."

Lenhoff knew about Real's decision before Berman called. For years she had wanted a chance to revisit the legal questions arising from pregnancy, maternity and parenting. But the elections of 1978 and 1980, especially Ronald Reagan's ascension to the White House, had chilled the climate for feminist initiatives. It was a time for consolidating, defending laws passed earlier and applying them where possible. Lenhoff was just then working on a civil case against Ridgewell's, a catering service fashionable among Reagan administration hostesses (it was alleged to be paying women employees a dollar less per hour than men).

She told Berman she would meet with him. Then she started making calls. One of the first was to Wendy Williams, a law professor at Georgetown Law Center who had promoted the equal-treatment thinking central to the pregnancy discrimination law. Another call was to Susan Deller Ross, also at Georgetown Law, who had written a brief on behalf of equal treatment in a maternity leave case in Montana the previous year. In minutes, the core of a legislative drafting committee would be in place.

Berman's interest had brought these women lawyers together. But each of them was soon thinking the same thing: Berman did not need to be helped, he needed to be stopped. They saw the Californian rushing into an old and almost inevitable trap. Nearly a century earlier, states such as Wisconsin and Oregon had tried to outlaw exploitation of women workers. Some early feminists approved, others argued that limiting women's work hours merely codified the double standard and discouraged the hiring of women. Why not limit everyone's hours, instead?

In Williams's mind, laws that distinguished between the sexes were— eventually, perhaps inevitably—turned around and used against women. She believed that "protective" laws, even those written with the best of intentions on behalf of pregnant women and new mothers, were no different. This argument had deep roots. After suffrage had been won in 1920, the women's movement of that era split down the middle over the special-versus-equal conflict. Alice Paul, the National Woman's Party leader, managed to have a simple Equal Rights Amendment introduced in Congress in 1923. The next day it was denounced by the leaders of seven major women's rights organizations, including the League of Women Voters and the settlement-house movement of Jane Addams. They saw it as more important to seek special protection for the defenseless than to pursue utopian notions of gender neutrality. Congress looked at this schism, shrugged and went on to other subjects.

The same conflict had been the context for the Pregnancy Discrimination Act in 1978 and for the Montana case in 1983. Montana's legislature had called for "reasonable leaves" for new mothers. A state court found this discriminatory, and when the case went to the Montana Supreme Court some women's organizations defended special treatment. Others joined Georgetown's Ross in upholding equal treatment. The League of Women Voters' Montana chapter filed a brief on one side and its national board filed on the other (both were subsequently withdrawn).

Lenhoff was convinced that special treatment would prove a dead end for leave policies in the 1980s. But she did not want to be isolated as Paul had been, and she was resolved to cooperate with Berman and his West Coast colleagues. At the same time, however, she was just as resolved to talk them out of the special-treatment approach they seemed so determined to take.

Only a few days after Real's Cal Fed decision Lenhoff went to see Berman for the first time. His office suite was located in the Longworth Building, the dingy middle child of the three House office buildings. Waiting for Lenhoff were the congressman and three women: a staff member, Assemblywoman Maxine Waters and Berman's wife, Janis Schwartz. Lenhoff listened sympathetically while the Californians recalled how they had fought for their bill in Sacramento in 1978 (just as Lenhoff and her allies were fighting for the Pregnancy Discrimination Act in Washington). The California law had been enacted first, by a month. Waters, a woman of firm and insistent conviction, declared that someone in Congress simply had to "undo" Real's decision.

When it was Lenhoff's turn to talk, she said she understood how they all felt. Then she explained why she and her fellow feminist lawyers had chosen the route they had in 1978. Their principal target had been companies that offered benefits to employees who were injured or taken ill but denied those same benefits to women whose disability had to do with a pregnancy.

It had all begun, in a sense, with the Civil Rights Act of 1964. Although it is remembered primarily for banning racial discrimination, this milestone legislation also banned sex discrimination. It did so because a stratagem on the part of southern senators backfired. Hoping it would kill the bill, the Dixiecrats had added sex to the legislative language. As it turned out, their effort came too late in the debate to make a difference: The bill passed, and the sex discrimination language passed with it.

Thereafter, the Equal Employment Opportunity Commission was tasked with writing enforcement rules under Title VII of the act. The commission equivocated for years over pregnancy benefits, reversing field more than once. All the while the number of women in the work-force was increasing dramatically. In 1972 the commission finally decided that companies had to treat pregnancy much like other temporary conditions.

That rule was upheld by the federal courts until 1976, when the U.S. Supreme Court abruptly set a new course. The justices ruled that denying temporary disability benefits for pregnancy and childbirth did not violate the 1964 act, after all. That decision, in the case of *General Electric* v. *Gilbert*, led directly to the passage of the Pregnancy Discrimination Act in 1978.

Lenhoff readily agreed that the 1978 law had not gone far enough. Companies with fewer than fifteen employees were exempt (a concession to the highly effective lobbying of the small-business community). And the law's equal-treatment principle did nothing for those whose employers provided no employee benefits at all for either sex.

But how could those inadequacies best be remedied? Lenhoff argued that an attempt to amend the Pregnancy Discrimination Act would re-open the special-versus-equal debate and probably pry open the 1964 Civil Rights Act as well. Lenhoff reminded them how such legislative open-heart surgery could have unintended consequences. All kinds of changes might be made in the law, especially given the negotiations that would have to take place with the Republican majority in the Senate and the Reagan administration.

Moreover, Lenhoff argued, a law protecting maternity alone might not be the best policy. It might be protective, she said, but it would be the opposite of empowering. And in the long run, it could prove counterproductive for women.

As an alternative, Lenhoff said, Cal Fed should be fought through the appeals process (presumably to the U.S. Supreme Court), on the simple and obvious argument that Real had misread and misapplied Title VII. As the appeal progressed, publicity and interest generated by the case could be used to promote a new bill aimed not at maternity leaves alone but at a broad and ambitious array of employee rights all rooted in the principle of equal treatment.

Here Lenhoff reached the core of her argument. A leave bill had to be written so that all workers could benefit. Leaves would have to be justified on the basis of something more common than motherhood, or even parenthood. It had to be something anyone might face, such as a temporary disability or medical necessity within the family.

There would be no violation of the equal-treatment standards of 1964 and 1978 if all employees had the right to time off for temporary, non-work-related disabilities of their own and for family situations of a similar nature. Covered situations would include the care of sick children, as well as complications of pregnancy or childbirth.

Berman listened to the whole explanation as a lawyer, a legislator and a politician. And while he understood all the facets and nuances, he was struck by the practical challenge of legislating leaves—even unpaid ones —for such a wide range of temporary problems unrelated to work. He wondered how it could pass Congress and be signed by any president, let alone Ronald Reagan. Would it not be easier to do something federal for pregnancy only?

Easier, yes, for the short run, Lenhoff said. But it would be problematic in the long run because skimming off the motherhood component now would make it much harder to achieve a broadscale equal-treatment bill later on. Berman was impressed, but still skeptical. Show me something in writing, he said, and Lenhoff assured him she would.

Lenhoff returned to her office at the fund, which in those days was over the Second Story secondhand bookshop at 20th and P Streets near Dupont Circle. She sat down at her desk and began typing an outline for a rough draft.

REAL'S DECISION WAS NOT THE ONLY impetus to action on family issues that spring on Capitol Hill. Democratic Congressman George Miller, an aggressive liberal from California's Bay Area, had scheduled an April hearing on child care before the Select Committee on Children, Youth and Families, an ad hoc panel the Democratic leadership had created as an outlet for Miller's restless interest in social issues.

It had been years since concerns affecting children and young families had enjoyed much currency in Congress. In the late 1970s, Senator Alan Cranston of California had held Senate hearings on day care centers, but without legislative effect. Since 1980 the agenda had been so dominated by taxes, budget cuts, foreign policy and the defense buildup that a hearing devoted to talk about babies seemed unimaginable.

Nonetheless, at 9:38 on the morning of April 4, Miller swung his chair toward the audience in Room 2222 in the Rayburn Office Building. It was a smallish hearing room, more in keeping with the status of Miller's newborn select committee than with his aspirations for it. But if it lacked the grand dais and oil paintings of the big committee rooms, its size enabled the audience of a hundred or more to create a standing-room-only sense of popular demand. Several of Miller's colleagues had already joined him, but he scowled beneath his brush moustache at the empty seats to his left and right, each awaiting a missing member. Then he rapped his gavel, pulled his microphone close and opened a new front in his personal war against Ronald Reagan and the predominant politics of his time.

Broad-shouldered, blunt and impatient with disagreement, Miller was not one to understate his business. He immediately announced that the hearings to be held that day and around the country in future weeks would "raise the level of national debate" and "move public policy on child care from the 1950s to the 1980s." Earnestly he added: "The care of millions of children is at stake."

In an era of unabashed conservatism, Miller was an unreconstructed liberal. He believed government had not only a rightful role but a leading one. He made no apologies for the New Deal of the 1930s, the Great Society of the 1960s or the social reforms of the 1970s—some of which he had helped enact. Yet, having survived into the far different, free-market 1980s, the onetime high-school football star found himself almost constantly on defense.

Miller had come to public life naturally as the son of a longtime state legislator (for whom a Bay Area bridge was named) and as an undergraduate on the highly political campus of San Francisco State in the 1960s. He had run for the state Senate even before finishing law school at Berkeley, and he had been elected to Congress before he was thirty. As a freshman member in the "Watergate baby" class of 1974, he had helped depose senior committee chairmen and repeal antiquated caucus rules. But less than a decade later, still not forty, he had found his career and his causes becalmed. He persuaded Steering and Policy to give him a seat on the Budget Committee, where he could be part of the fiscal and philosophic fray. But he found the budget fight too often a rearguard action; and to be George Miller was to yearn for the vanguard.

Miller employed his powers of insistence to persuade the Democratic leadership to authorize an entirely new select committee on the problems of young people and families. Like the other, older select committees, this one would have no authority to generate legislation, amend it or bring it to the House floor for consideration. But it would have a half million dollars in budget and a mandate to delve into social problems from child care and nutrition to recreation and crime, making recommendations along the way. And it would fix the imprimatur of Congress on whatever probings and presentations might please its new chairman. The chairman, of course, would be Miller.

The committee, which some Hill staff called "Select Kids," soon loosed its staff of young female lawyers and graduate students to investigate the cost, quality and availability of day care in America. And, as all committee staff must, they planned a series of hearings. Given the wide horizon implied by the committee's name, they chose to concentrate on child care—a subject of interest to baby-boomer parents and a good bet to attract attention from the national media.

As the hearings got under way on that April morning, the staff and chairman had reason to smile. For the first time Miller was converting a personal agenda into a committee docket. And right here, on his own stage, Miller would have a supporting cast that provided not only political credibility but political cover as well. Under the benign penumbra of kids and families, Miller could enlist and involve members with widely divergent views, some of whom would otherwise avoid any association with him or his ideas. This was his chance to change the terms of debate, to cast the spending programs he supported in terms of children and families rather than welfare or bureaucracy.

His own opening statement was heavy on rhetorical questions. Could anyone have predicted that by 1984 more than 40 percent of the workforce would be female? And would anyone have believed that more than 40 percent of American women with children under the age of one would be in that workforce? "The need for child care today cuts across the entire spectrum of economic and social lines," declared the chairman. "And as a result child care is a less partisan issue than it has been in the past."

To prove his point, Miller was eager to introduce the man sitting to his left, Dan Marriott, an insurance underwriter from Salt Lake City and that city's representative in Congress, whom the Republicans had named the subcommittee's top-ranking minority member. A lifelong Utahn and a Mormon with four children, Marriott had an interest in family issues quite as passionate, in its own way, as Miller's. Conservative as his state, Marriott was nonetheless enthusiastic about the hearings at hand. When Miller handed off to him on this Wednesday morning, Marriott talked a lot about getting "the private sector" involved. But he also thanked Miller warmly "for making child care a major priority" and said he looked forward "to the solutions that come out of these hearings."

Next up was Pat Schroeder, a congresswoman who at forty-four had served nearly a dozen years representing Denver and become the senior Democratic woman in Congress. She was, for the moment, also the best known (a distinction she would lose in a few months to Geraldine Ferraro, a congresswoman from New York whom the Democrats would nominate for vice president).

On this particular dais, Schroeder had several reasons to chafe at her lesser status. Better known than Miller, she was also older, more senior in the House, more senior in committee standing and, as cochair of the Congressional Caucus for Women's Issues, more involved in women's causes. But select committees are special animals, and this one belonged to Miller. All the same, Schroeder immediately displayed her flair for the personal dimension.

"I want to say," she said, "that the child care issue has deep meaning for me. While we can cite statistics on the need, I remember the years when I had two very, very young children here in the Congress. People would ask me what my biggest fear was. I knew I was supposed to say something very serious—like, would peace be maintained?—but my greatest fear was that I would lose day care."

Schroeder had borne her own children under the old rules. Her first arrived in 1966, when she was just two years out of Harvard Law School and working as a field attorney in Denver for the National Labor Relations Board. Years later she recalled that she did not even inquire about a pregnancy leave policy at the time, presuming the policy was: "You get pregnant, you leave." Her husband was a successful attorney, so they could afford for her to stay home. Besides, as she remembered years later, she thought it better "if you could manage to be with a child the first few months after it was born."

Schroeder did not raise the issue of the "first few months" that morning. But as it turned out, the first witness to testify before the committee would do it for her. That witness was Sheila Kamerman, a professor in the School of Social Work at Columbia University and a fellow at the Center for Advanced Study in the Behavioral Sciences at Stanford. She was typical of the feature witnesses called to congressional hearings: a tenured academic whose publications and credentials gleamed with prestige. Such experts lend an air of scientific authority, and they are usually given the floor right after the last member present has finished talking (including guest colleagues who are not members of the committee but ask to speak).

Witnesses are rarely prepared for the severe abbreviation of their contribution. Some spend weeks preparing testimony, imagining themselves holding forth for hours before rapt members of Congress. In practice, much of every hearing is consumed by the committee members, who are sometimes hard to cut off. A witness importuned and flattered by staff into crossing the continent often confronts an impatient chairman asking for a five-minute summary (with the obligatory assurance that the full written testimony will be included "in the record").

But Kamerman used her allotted minutes efficiently, touching nearly every argument that would be heard supporting child care and parental leaves over the next several years of debate. And she surprised some of the members and some of the audience when she reached her recommendations. Her first one did not deal with day care or facilitating mothers' participation in the workforce at all. It spoke of keeping mothers home to care for their children.

Alluding to the high percentage of working mothers with infant children, she urged that "any policy consideration given to infant care pay attention to the importance of . . . parenting leaves from work, both unpaid and paid leaves."

Seated beside Kamerman at the witness table, facing the committee, was the equally distinguished Edward Zigler, a psychology professor who was also director of Yale University's Bush Center in Child Development and Social Policy. Shortly after the microphone was passed to him, he returned to the subject of infant care in the home. Zigler said he saw no problem with "supplemental child care" outside the home for toddlers and older children, but that "rather heated" debate surrounded the issue of day care for infants. "Even if high-quality infant care were affordable," he said, many parents and professionals would still be concerned about the potential effects of separating parents and infants in the first few weeks and months of life.

Some of the members looked at one another. Had he really said parents? Not just mothers? But in the next moment Zigler used the same word in seconding Kamerman's remedy: He liked the idea of parental leaves so that at least one parent "could be at home to care for a newborn." He spoke very much as if either parent would do.

"I would also like to suggest that the federal government begin to investigate the feasibility of a policy of paid infant-care leaves, commonplace in Europe and Canada." In that sentence Zigler was not only raising the economic ante enormously, he was also introducing a second discomfiting idea that would be heard often in the years to come: the idea that workplace customs and conditions in other countries might actually be superior to those in the United States. The members on the dais seemed to be listening intently.

When the first panel of witnesses had finished, Miller pronounced the material at hand "overwhelming" and noted with pleasure that members had been arriving on the dais in time to hear it.

But Miller's tone suggested he had not expected home care for infants to be this salient in the testimony. When he thought about child care, he thought about mothers at work and children in day care. His concern was for overcrowded day-care centers and working-class families unable to find or afford care. The direction taken by the leadoff witnesses might prompt the committee Republicans to take off on a tangent.

The first to do so was Dan Coats, an earnest second-term Republican from Indiana who had succeeded Dan Quayle in the House when Quayle became a senator. Coats had worked for Quayle and had an even more conservative reputation on social issues. Among the most intense opponents of abortion in Congress, Coats had been highly attentive that morning, especially at the mention of newborns. "That period when the mother and child needed most to be together," he asked Zigler, "was that six months or a full year?"

Zigler said the consensus would favor a full year, but that "if you're going to start somewhere, the first six months is where to start." Coats bore down, asking whether research had found adverse effects when children started day care at six months rather than a year. Zigler said he thought there might be some. Coats wanted to know whether Zigler would recommend the full year at home where "economically feasible." Zigler said he would.

Coats then began to question the notion of economic necessity. He wondered aloud how many women were really working to put bread on the table and how many to put "a new VCR under the Christmas tree."

The hearing moved on to the funding of Head Start and the ways the tax code might be used to encourage parents to stay home. But the news had been made at the outset. Zigler and Kamerman had brought to congressional consciousness an issue that had yet to appear there. Academic research in their field had been going on for years, but on the Hill it was as fresh as the April air outdoors.

It was the naturally insistent way that Kamerman offered her first recommendation that made it sound so acceptable. Suddenly, the idea of requiring employers to grant leave—perhaps even paid leave someday —was more than an academic hypothesis. While still far from being a bill, it was for the moment at least a proposal before Congress.

Miller's hearing had opened a window on Capitol Hill to a field of promise. Here was a new direction for social activism that even the most outspoken conservatives might hesitate to denounce. The idea of keeping parents with their children had scientific underpinnings, a research base and a wealth of anecdotal supporting evidence. Here was a chance for liberals to talk not about individual rights but about family needs, not about abortion rights but about parenthood, not about comparable worth but about keeping one's job. Here was a strategy for social legislation in the 1980s.

And, thanks to the decision of a federal judge in California just two weeks earlier, it had a built-in sense of urgency.

WHILE MILLER WAS ABSORBING WHAT he had heard in April and planning field trips to hear more over the summer, Lenhoff and her boss at the Women's Legal Defense Fund, Judith Lichtman, began a series of meetings of their own. Partly to help Berman and partly to prepare for a possible confrontation with him, Lenhoff and Lichtman enlisted like-minded lawyers and activists in a working group that met at their offices near Dupont Circle.

Among the first to join were Georgetown law professors Wendy Williams and Susan Deller Ross and Sherry Cassedy, a recent Georgetown Law graduate who was counsel for the Congressional Caucus for Women's Issues. Beyond that, Lenhoff and Lichtman wanted diversity of background, and they found it. They brought women from the Association of Junior Leagues, the Coal Employment Project (an arm of the United Mine Workers), the Children's Defense Fund and even the U.S. Catholic Conference.

In part because they were preselected, the women in the group arrived quickly at a shared understanding of the bill they wanted to see. Cassedy and Anne Radigan, executive director of Schroeder's caucus, were soon circulating a draft outline for a bill based on the group's discussions. It required all employers in interstate commerce to offer leave to any employee temporarily unable to work due to physical disability. The leave could be as long as twenty-six weeks—half a year—but it did not provide any compensation other than a continuation of seniority and benefits.

The leave benefit would be explicitly extended to parents of newborn or newly adopted children. There was also a new minimum of paid sick leave (ten days per year) for an employee's own illnesses (other than work-related injury) or for those of an employee's dependents. The outline did not exempt small businesses.

The one issue on which consensus did not readily develop was the issue of pay. Who could afford to take six months off with no money coming in? Certainly not single mothers or two-wage families below the median income. The European models all offered at least partial compensation, whether the money came from the employer or from government insurance.

But the women in the drafting group had been through the legislative mill on Capitol Hill before. They knew a new federal entitlement would have been a hard sell even in better times, let alone when Congress was becoming obsessed with budget deficits. Neither would Congress readily accede to stick private business with the bill in an era of anxiety over "economic competitiveness."

So while the intention had been to write a model bill rather than a modest one, the drafting group reluctantly chose not to press for paid leave. With that decision taken, the coterie was beginning to become a coalition. They agreed for the moment to call their work in progress the Family Employment Security Act, and Lenhoff began addressing her memos to the FESA Group.

LENHOFF HAD BEEN OPERATING UNDER the hopeful presumption that her March meeting with Berman had bought her some time, but he was still moving on his own. Berman had looked at Lenhoff's draft of an equal-treatment bill based on universal rights to disability leave, but he had remained unconverted and gone looking for more help. He had found Fred Feinstein, a lean, unprepossessing lawyer in his mid-thirties, who had once worked for Congressman Phil Burton, the powerful mentor to Berman, Miller and other House liberals (Burton had died suddenly in 1983). Feinstein had become the chief counsel and staff director for the Subcommittee on Labor-Management Relations of the House Committee on Education and Labor. Berman knew any bill mandating employee leaves would go straight to Ed and Labor, and to Labor-Management Relations, where Feinstein would have much to do with whatever happened next.

Berman told Feinstein he wanted to see some action. He said he understood why some of the national women's groups were hesitant to tinker with existing laws, but he also thought their broader bill was reaching too far. Maybe someday, he thought, but not in the mid-1980s. As for right now, Berman said, if we had a leave bill that just covered birth and adoption we could pass it tomorrow; we could make the case because all these people claimed to be pro-family and pro-life. If we wrote it right and pitched it right we could get it passed and signed into law. All the family-oriented social conservatives Miller had on his select committee would have to vote for anything so family friendly. And if they did, the White House might just be brought along.

The next step was to get a formal draft from the Office of the Legislative Counsel. Even the simplest bill must be rendered into legislative language to be officially introduced. This includes references to previous laws and citations of legal authority and empowerment. A simple change in the tariff applied to foreign oil, for example, can mean multiple amendments to the trade-governing Smoot-Hawley Act of 1930 and line-by-line alterations in the accompanying tariff schedules.

So, although members of Congress are often lawyers themselves, they delegate the legal research and drafting of their bills to the Office of Legislative Counsel, whose dozens of lawyers occupy a warren of offices in the Cannon Office Building (thoughtfully remote from the bustle of busier hallways and just a short jaunt through a tunnel from the Library of Congress).

Berman sent his ideas to Legislative Counsel in May. Meanwhile, Radigan and Cassedy were circulating a "time-line for action," which spelled out the immediate objectives, to others in the drafting group. They needed to get Schroeder and her caucus cochair, the Republican Olympia Snowe of Maine, to sign off on FESA. Then they needed to get Schroeder to press their case with Berman. They also wanted to get Congressman Don Edwards, the dean of the California delegation and a champion of civil liberties, to buttonhole Berman as well. They also hoped to find a prominent California feminist "to provide Berman some cover" if he dropped his own approach and supported the coalition's. Their "dream candidate" would be a state legislator or a celebrity, or perhaps a significant contributor to Berman's campaigns.

But all this would take time. And it would mean getting members together to talk over their differing aims and notions of how to proceed. By the end of May, Berman had his second working draft back from Legislative Counsel and seemed increasingly eager to act. He did agree, however, to see Lenhoff and her FESA colleagues on June 11.

There were too many people to squeeze into Berman's office in Long-worth, and Berman lacked the seniority or committee standing to command meeting rooms on short notice. So they found themselves crowded into one of the nameless, windowless rooms in the bomb-shelter basement of the Rayburn Office Building. Berman and his staff were joined by staff from several other Hill offices. Feinstein was there, as were

Cassedy and Radigan. Berman had also brought along Alan Reuther of the United Auto Workers and a woman from the California Attorney General's Office.

But Lenhoff had brought an impressive contingent as well: lawyers from the National Women's Law Center and the League of Women Voters, not to mention the original Williams-Ross combination and representatives from the National Organization for Women, the National Women's Political Caucus, the American Civil Liberties Union and others.

The meeting began in midafternoon. Berman made his case for doing what could be done in the here and now. "We can make a case to all the people who claim to be pro-family and pro-life," he said. On that basis, the bill might be passed and even signed by Reagan. The group discussed the option of two bills, one to do what Berman wanted and one to do everything else that the national women's groups wanted. But no one seemed to think the latter bill would have much of a future once the first bill had been passed.

It soon became apparent that some of the congressional staff, including the caucus women, liked the broad approach as much as Lenhoff's group of activists. If so ambitious a bill could not be passed in the foreseeable future, it might at least have political value as a defining issue in some future campaign. And if that left the short-term situation in California unresolved, so be it. The Cal Fed case was being appealed. As the meeting wore on, there did not seem to be so many Californians in the conversation.

In the end, Berman agreed to back off on his own bill. He even agreed to endorse whatever came out of Lenhoff's group, a coalition he sensed was firming up before his eyes. But at the same time, he said, if the bill was not going to be modeled on his California law, perhaps the coalition would want someone else to carry it in the House. Talk turned to George Miller, among other likely candidates, before the meeting broke up.

TWO DAYS AFTER LABOR DAY 1984, Miller was rapping his gavel again to reconvene Select Children. It was five months exactly since his first hearing. He had spent his summer witnessing history (the Democrats had come to San Francisco to nominate the first man-and-woman national ticket in major-party history) and holding a series of field hearings on child care in California, Texas and Connecticut. These hearings, Miller intoned, would conclude "the most in-depth congressional look at child care in a decade."

As if to reprove any who doubted the importance of that topic, Miller cited three articles on child care that had appeared in *The New York Times* the previous weekend and a cover story on the subject in the current issue of *Newsweek*. Parents working outside the home had "changed family life dramatically," Miller said. Economic and social changes abroad in the workforce were nothing short of "profound."

For the renewal of his hearings, Miller had secured the more honorific setting of the House Armed Services Committee's main hearing room in the Rayburn. But Miller was disappointed at the attendance of his colleagues at the hearing. Although the official record would later show ten members in attendance (out of the appointed twenty-five), the session opened with just Miller and two other members on the dais.

After plowing through his opening statement, Miller turned to Republican Dan Coats, whom he introduced as the "senior minority member currently present." Coats offered a wry correction: He was "the only minority member currently present."

Miller's staff had lined up scores of witnesses for that Wednesday and Thursday, covering every aspect of child care from psychology to tax policy. The question of work leaves would not be as prominent in these sessions as in April, but it would reappear in Miller's final recommendations, which would call for "personnel policies . . . which do not penalize parents for giving birth or spending an acceptable period at home with their infants."

Carefully worded to be gender-neutral and open-ended, the recommendation would also be respectful of business and supportive of family —enough so that Coats, Marriott and other Republicans on Select Children would feel comfortable signing off on it, just as Berman had predicted.

That achievement might have established Miller as the clear choice to introduce the bill providing for family and medical leave. Lenhoff, Lichtman and their working group were delighted with his attention to the issue, particularly the strongly worded recommendation from his report and the suggestion that he might hold hearings specifically on parental leave in the next session. But they were far from convinced that they had found their legislative champion.

The first problem was that Miller still preferred putting in a bill along the quick-and-narrow lines that Berman had proposed. The two were allies. They had a natural bridge between them in Congressman Henry Waxman of Los Angeles. Waxman had been politically associated with Berman since their days together at UCLA and with Miller since their days together as freshmen members in the renowned "Watergate babies" class of 1974.

Miller was also distracted by other legislative interests. He had been appealing because of his seat on the Education and Labor Committee, the House panel where parental leave (or any bill telling employers how to manage employee benefits) would surely be referred. He was even the chairman of the Subcommittee on Labor Standards, giving him the opportunity to schedule hearings on the bill on his own authority. But now, as the 1984 session was waning, Miller had decided to give up his subcommittee chairmanship and his seat on Education and Labor so as to be in line for a different subcommittee chairmanship on a different committee: Interior and Insular Affairs.

In this new job Miller would have vastly increased influence over water in the West, including California, an issue in which his interest approached obsession. He had been planning and positioning himself for a shot at this subcommittee chair for two years, and had devised his select committee largely to enable him to deal in children's issues even if he chose to leave Education and Labor. What was all well and good for Miller, however, was not so satisfactory for Lenhoff, Lichtman and their working group.

Before the 1984 session drew to a close in October, Berman and Miller had talked, and Miller and Schroeder had talked. Members of Congress often do business in impromptu fashion, in hallways and on elevators. They confer while milling in the aisles of the House chamber or congregating at the railing in the rear. And while nothing was decided in a formal way, the Californians seemed to be backing off, ceding the field to the Congressional Caucus for Women's Issues and, therefore, to Schroeder.

It was far too late to do a bill that year. Adjournment usually comes early in election years so that members seeking reelection can go home and campaign. It was enough that the general outline of the proposal had been glimpsed and the field of potential sponsors narrowed. Now, it seemed, a timely effort could begin with the new Congress, the 99th Congress, in January 1985.

2.

To the Hill

JANUARY 21, 1985, WAS A MIDWINTER Monday at the midpoint of a decade. Arctic air had settled over much of the nation, but it seemed especially cold in the capital, with a subzero temperature at dawn and a windchill of thirty below. Washington is accustomed to indignities of heat, enduring its summer with sodden, southern resolve. But it collapses in the cold. Plumes of white steam rise from its buildings to hang in the thin blue air like so many flags of surrender.

The record-shattering weather came at a conspicuous time. It disrupted the second inauguration of Ronald Wilson Reagan, a ceremony to be performed outdoors on the West Front of the Capitol before an expected 140,000 spectators. The swearing-in was held instead in the Rotunda, an immense interior space that for all its exceptional grandeur had never been used for this purpose before. While the expectant throng would be turned away, there was room enough for the families, the cabinet, the Supreme Court and all 100 senators and 435 members of the House of Representatives—a gathering as weighty, in its way, as the nine-million-pound dome that stood overhead.

Members of Congress attend inaugurations with varying degrees of enthusiasm. On this occasion, many were loath to cross the street from their office buildings on Independence or Constitution Avenue. They simply went underground, winding through the tunnels that connect the major structures of Capitol Hill to the Capitol itself. As they walked, or rattled along on their subterranean trolleys, thoughts naturally turned to Reagan's first oath-taking four years earlier.

Reagan had ridden into town in 1981 as the mythic western hero, a legend of the camera lens made flesh. But he was more than that, a genuine political phenomenon and a charismatic conservative invested with the full powers of the state. In what seemed but a few months—and by what seemed almost to be fiat—he rearranged the priorities that had dominated American government for half a century. He did it with style and flair, and with appeal to the average American. He even stood up to an assassin's bullet, full in the chest at close range.

But even as Reagan's presidency achieved rapid enactment of tax cuts and spending shifts, his mandate seemed to lose some of its urgency. The economy faltered through most of his first two years in office, and Republicans suffered accordingly in the congressional elections of 1982. Their net loss of twenty-six seats that November all but neutralized their net gain of thirty-four in the Reagan landslide of 1980. Democrats could once again be heard speaking of Reaganism as an interlude, a midcourse adjustment. Some suggested the old man might retire in 1984 rather than face a wised-up electorate.

All that was hard to remember on that frigid Monday morning in 1985. Reagan had not retired. He had run again and won again, bigger than the first time, sweeping every state but one. The scale of his triumph had dashed the special hopes of those who believed the nomination of a woman for vice president would make a difference. The Republicans also had resumed their march in Congress, protecting their majority in the Senate and gaining ground in the House. Southern Democrats, stunned by lopsided returns in Dixie, weighed their party allegiance. There was talk of wholesale party switching that might enable Republicans actually to control the House for the first time in thirty years.

Even if they retained control, House Democrats could forget about advancing their own issues and causes. Feminists, in particular, could scarcely expect to revive the Equal Rights Amendment or federal funding for abortion. The time for new laws and expansion of old laws had passed, and it would not be back for several years.

In the month following his inauguration, Reagan would give a tour-de-force State of the Union address, forcing Democrats as well as Republicans to stand, to applaud and even to cheer. In the TV minutes allotted afterward for a Democratic response, the nation saw the thirty-eight-

year-old governor of Arkansas. Boyish, half sitting on a high stool, Bill
Clinton talked about how Democrats had "learned a lesson" in 1984 and
would "learn to listen." He allowed that he personally heard the voters
saying they wanted something other than what his party had offered in
the past.

The conciliatory, even defeatist tone of the response rankled some
party loyalists, but it should not have surprised them. Clinton was a
charter member of a new group called the Democratic Leadership Council. Composed of governors, members of Congress and other elected
officials—nearly all of them white males from Sun Belt states—the DLC
was obsessed with what it considered the political mainstream. Its found-
ers worried that the GOP had established itself as the party of "work,
family and neighborhood," casting Democrats by contrast as the party of
feminists, gays, racial minorities and industrial labor unions. The DLC
vowed to prove the party was not captive to these groups.

In one sense, the Democrats in 1984 lost only what they had lost four
years before: the Senate and the White House. They still clung to their
majority in the House. But the Democrats of 1985 were dispirited by their
disappointment. When Miller had begun his hearings into child care in
the spring of 1984, he had entertained the hope that the issue might soon
be in the hands of a Democratic administration. Now, one heard talk of
a "Republican lock" on the electoral college. The 1984 election seemed
to have cost the Democrats far more than just four more years. It seemed
to have cost the party its hope.

As this climate settled over the capital that winter, the small group of
feminist attorneys who had conceived the Family Employment Security
Act in the more hopeful days of 1984 were distressed and divided. The
prospect of passing a new labor standard requiring employers to grant
leave for medical and parental circumstances had never been more than
marginal. It now seemed quixotic.

Pat Schroeder had been in the House long enough to have seen dis-
couragement before. She had first been elected to Congress in 1972, the
year Richard M. Nixon won a forty-nine-state landslide of his own. As
invincible as he had seemed that winter, Nixon would within a matter of
months be politically paralyzed by Watergate, which would drive him
from office.

Schroeder also recalled arriving on the Hill at a time when the Democratic House was still dominated by elderly committee chairmen, most of
them Dixiecrats as conservative as any Republican. Assigned to the
Armed Services Committee, she had arrived at her first committee ses-

sion to find that the ancient, hawkish chairman, F. Edward Hébert of Louisiana, had not set a chair for her (or for Ron Dellums of California, the black congressman from Berkeley who would, two decades later, chair the committee himself).

So in the winter of 1985, Schroeder was willing to smile and talk about a party comeback when few others would. An eager participant in floor debate, she was known for her quips and turns of phrase—including her description of Reagan as "the Teflon president."

At the same time, she had not served six terms without learning something about what worked and what did not. And when she looked at the memos and the drafts of bills emanating from Lenhoff and Lichtman's working group, she had misgivings. Her pragmatic side told her that, for the next few years, women's issues would be just that: topics for women to talk about in campaigns. The time for actually changing the laws would come later.

ALSO REVIEWING THE SITUATION THAT winter were Berman and the other California members interested in parental leave. Despite Reagan's easy victory in their home state, all these liberal members of the California House delegation had been reelected in 1984 by wide margins. But if these members felt secure politically, they were far from immune from the new pessimism.

Berman had agreed to withhold his own parental leave bill and support the broadscale family-and-medical approach. But now he began to think the timing was wrong for so ambitious a proposal. Given the Mondale-Ferraro debacle, it seemed to make more sense to scale back and secure what could be achieved. He saw some of the working drafts and feared the whole endeavor would fail for reaching too far. Berman understood the desire to put forward a bill that truly did the job. And he had his own misgivings about leaves that would be unpaid: Such a leave might help dual-career professionals, but not the Lillian Garlands of the world.

But while Berman sensed the dilemma, he also sensed a chance was being missed. At his occasional lunches with some of Schroeder's staff, he would always want to know what was happening with Lenhoff's group, and the staff women would always assure him they were nearing a final draft for formal introduction. Berman would be asked who he thought should sponsor the bill. He would say he did not think he should be the one, and that Miller was now devoted to the Interior Committee. Talk would turn to Barbara Boxer, the second-term member who represented parts of San Francisco and its more Democratic suburbs. Native to the Bronx, she had moved to California with her husband and worked as a journalist and stockbroker while raising two children. Her intense energy, still more East Coast than West, was all the more riveting in a woman not quite five feet tall. Boxer was among the House's most liberal members and most ardent feminists, and she was a member of Miller's Select Committee on Children, Youth and Families. But she was not on either of the standing House committees to which a parental leave bill would be referred, so she could do little to guarantee the bill a hearing. Moreover, she was closely associated both politically and personally with the very California feminists who wanted Berman to introduce his state statute verbatim at the federal level. She herself still favored that course of action, at least as strongly as Berman or Miller did. Why not get a piece of policy in place, she would ask, and come back later for the rest of it?

But when Berman and Boxer passed the word about their preferred provisions—which amounted to four months of leave to prepare or care for newborns or newly adopted children—the reaction from Lenhoff and Lichtman's group was not good. The working group of feminist attorneys, union officials and other activists did not simply prefer the broader principle of equal treatment; they were flatly opposed to anything less. The right to a leave had to be for fathers as well as mothers, and it had to relate to medical as well as parental situations.

The medical element was the key because it established a basis for benefits regardless of gender. Without it, the working group believed the concept would be so narrow as to be politically counterproductive and subject to legal challenge. So any bill providing special treatment for women would not only go without their support but would face their active opposition—even in the absence of a preferable alternative. Berman was taken aback by this stubbornness but impressed by it. He let several weeks go by without forcing the issue.

Through the winter months the working group had continued to meet regularly, growing to include representatives from more women's organizations and more labor unions. There was still a solid consensus on both the equal-treatment model and the inclusion of medical leaves, but the group was unresolved on the issue of pay. The newer members of the group were even less comfortable with the unpaid nature of the leaves than the original members had been. As one labor lobbyist who joined the group put it, "The idea of an unpaid leave tends to leave working people with an eyebrow cocked." At the same time, these labor representatives were keenly aware of how swing votes in Congress would react to a mandated paid leave. And some already knew how violently employers had recoiled from the concept when it arose in collective bargaining.

In the midst of this uncertainty, March 1985, parental leave was the subject of a conference in New York organized by the American Association of Junior Leagues. Despite the faintly fusty image of the quintessentially establishment sponsor, the conference featured the viewpoint being urged by the working group. Lenhoff and Lichtman were among the speakers, as were Williams and Cassedy.

Also on hand were some of the social scientists who had testified for Miller in 1984—including Kamerman of Columbia and Stanford, and T. Berry Brazelton, a pediatrics professor at Harvard Medical School who enthralled audiences with his accounts and videotapes of new mothers "bonding" with their infant children. *The New York Times* covered the conference, picturing Cassedy at one session with her two-month-old daughter, Cassedy Sullivan.

The conference's forty-five participants endorsed an "agenda for action" that almost perfectly matched the formulation already offered by Lenhoff's group: "Employees should have the right," it read, "to paid job-protected leaves with continuation of existing health benefits for temporary, non-occupational disabilities including those that are pregnancy-related or childbirth-related."

While endorsing paid leaves, the participants called for immediate legislation only to establish a national leave policy but added a mechanism to explore the financing of such leaves. By this means the critical question of pay would be finessed, not just by this conference, but by successive waves of legislative authors and advocates over the course of eight sessions of Congress.

WHILE CONSENSUS WAS EMERGING, some women in the working group saw no reason to rush: Better to get it right than to be hasty, after all. Virtually no one expected the bill to go anywhere in the 99th Congress anyway, so why not proceed deliberately and get it right?

This question of timing was not entirely rhetorical for the professional staff at the Congressional Caucus for Women's Issues. Both Cassedy and Radigan were keenly aware of the impatience of the California members. They had been holding off repeated inquiries from Berman and Boxer, who seemed less and less willing to wait for a comprehensive bill from the working group. Real's decision was now a full year old, and there was still no bill before Congress to reverse it.

Several days after the Junior League conference, Cassedy and Radigan were summoned to Berman's office, where they found themselves confronting both Berman and Boxer. The two Californians announced that they had decided to offer a specific bill with a limited leave for maternity or complications from childbirth. It applied to either parent, but it was clearly tailored to play as a motherhood bill. They had a draft back from Legislative Counsel and were ready to go, and they thought the caucus staff (and Schroeder) would like to know, as a courtesy, before they went ahead.

Berman and Boxer had been addressing themselves primarily to Cassedy, who felt increasingly uncomfortable. As staff for the women's caucus she worked not only for Schroeder but for the caucus's Republican cochair as well. When she hesitated to respond to what she took as an ultimatum, the less reticent Radigan broke in.

Radigan said she understood the California members' eagerness and sense of urgency, but she also begged them to give the working group a chance to carry its work to term. Then Cassedy spoke up, taking a softer line but stressing that the proposed broadscale bill would take the political heat off the Californians once it was finally introduced.

Both women reminded the two members of how implacably opposed to a narrow bill the working group women were. They ticked off some of the organizations involved in that group, including the National Organization for Women, and they hinted that this coalition would actively resist the sort of bill Berman and Boxer wanted.

The Californians again evinced dismay at the thought that their bill would be opposed by its natural allies. They knew the popular press would make much of such a fight within the feminist community. They knew there might be debilitating arguments over the best being the enemy of the good, and over the application of equal-treatment theories to the reality of working women's daily lives. If either camp tried to move a bill without the support and complicity of the other, the results would likely be disastrous.

But if Berman and Boxer did not do something, who would? Was anyone ready to go ahead and introduce an alternative? Yes, Radigan said firmly, Schroeder was ready. Radigan heard herself saying it could be done that week. Boxer and Berman thought it over for a moment. All right, they said, but only if the bill was going to be introduced right away.

Cassedy and Radigan returned to their office, their emotions a mix of excitement and dread. They had taken a chance, committing their boss before checking with her. But Radigan had feared that any delay, any hint of uncertainty, would mean the immediate introduction of a Berman-Boxer bill, a small-scale fix that would preempt any chance for a broader one in this Congress. So she and Cassedy had done what Hill staffers not infrequently do. They spoke for their boss with an air of confidence, counting on her to make their word good.

To their relief, Schroeder was as game as they had hoped and understood the need to proceed. The drafts had been accumulating for months, and the various drafting parties had begun to coalesce around a text at about the time of the Junior League conference in New York. Schroeder needed only to retrieve the latest of these efforts from Legislative Counsel, notify the various outside advocates of her plans and proceed.

The new bill would retain some of the "family economic security" language from earlier drafts but take a more direct approach in its title: Parental and Disability Leave Act of 1985.

The bill would require all businesses to provide up to eighteen weeks of unpaid leave for mothers or fathers of newborn or newly adopted children. It would mandate up to twenty-six weeks of unpaid leave for those with temporary disabilities that were not work-related (those that are work-related are handled under separate laws) and for employees with sick children.

In either instance, the employer would be required to continue health insurance and other benefits and to welcome the leave-taking employee back to the same (or a comparable) job. But the bill would neither require the employer to provide pay nor establish a governmental program of temporary disability insurance. Instead, it would create a commission to study means of providing income replacement and make recommendations within two years.

Schroeder's bill was at once a modest imitation of the policies in place in other countries and a tremendous leap into the unknown in terms of workplace customs and culture in the United States.

THE PHYSICAL PROCESS BY WHICH A member introduces a bill in the House of Representatives remains remarkably old-fashioned. Once the draft is ready, the member carries it down the aisle of the House Chamber to the well beneath the Speaker's rostrum. There, the member hands the bill, be it a thick sheaf or a single sheet, to a clerk at the horseshoe desk. Alternatively, and more typically, members drop the bill into a mahogany box near the clerk's desk that is called the hopper. Conversation on Capitol Hill regularly alludes to bills being "dropped" or "in the hopper."

Numbers are assigned as bills arrive at the desk or as they are taken from the hopper. Some sponsors take special care in timing a bill so as to get a certain number. Schroeder checked with the clerk to see what numbers were going to be coming up on April 4 and timed her submissions (she had two new bills to drop at once) to assure herself of a memorable one: HR 2020. For months thereafter, editorialists and headline writers would find 20-20 an irresistible metaphor.

The introduction was accomplished on April 4, and the bill made its debut in the *Congressional Record* with just a dozen lines of eyestrain type. The capsule description followed almost verbatim the policy statement produced the previous month at the Association of Junior Leagues conference, including the mechanism for exploring paid or insured leave. The *Record* listed no cosponsors, in part because the haste with which Schroeder had had to go to the floor left no time to solicit them, either personally or through the usual "Dear Colleague" letter circulated to all members' offices. All this sort of politicking and linking of arms would come later. At the moment parental leave legislation was born, Schroeder was its single parent.

The beginning was inauspicious, the climate forbidding, but the launch had been achieved, the idea was afloat. And the voyage of parental leave through Congress officially had begun.

ONCE TAKEN FROM THE HOPPER a fresh bill embarks upon a succession of trials and tests prescribed by centuries of parliamentary tradition. Some are applied with punctilio, others honored in the breach. For example, the requirement that a new bill be read in full to the assembled body is no longer followed. No modern legislature could afford to hear each text read, not with dozens of new bills being offered daily and thousands in a given year. Not even the few hundred measures that may be passed, or the few score that are extensively debated, will be read aloud in full. The first, second and third readings (all required for enactment) are generally dispensed with under the rules or—with unanimous consent of the members—disposed of via the small print of the day's *Congressional Record* (which notes that texts are reprinted as if read).

The next step, formal referral to committee, has been rendered routine in the contemporary House. Historically, the right of referral has belonged to the Speaker of the House, the individual elected by the majority party to preside over the body as a whole. At the turn of the century, autocratic Speakers used this power to smother bills they did not like by referring them to unfriendly committees. In reaction, Progressive Era reforms restrained the Speaker and distributed some of his powers in the years just before the First World War. For generations thereafter, senior committee chairmen dominated the institution. In the 1970s another wave of reforms restrained the chairmen and placed more authority in the majority caucus (to which all members of the majority party automatically belong). This led to the contemporary system in which bills are routinely assigned by matching their subject matter to predetermined committee jurisdictions. The Speaker, too, gained the power in 1975 to refer measures to more than one standing committee (concurrently or sequentially).

On landmark legislation the rule of thumb is to refer the bill to as many of the standing committees as might plausibly claim jurisdiction. Generally the House believes it better to err on the side of inclusion. A complex bill may be referred, in whole or in part, to as many as a dozen different committees, which, in turn, may assign it to a panoply of sub-committees. (In 1985 the House had twenty-two standing committees and more than 140 subcommittees.)

Nothing so intricate was necessary for HR 2020, however. The bill was referred to two standing committees, each of which referred it to two subcommittees. This multiple referral was made joint rather than se-quential, meaning that both committees were free to work on the bill at once and for as long as they pleased. But it was understood that the legislation would have its main trial in the Education and Labor Com-mittee, a frequent wrestling mat for ideologues of the left and right. Less strenuous sessions could be expected in the other committee to which HR 2020 was referred, Post Office and Civil Service, which was dominated by urban liberals and presumed to be friendlier to the bill.

Numbering, reading and referral are generally the end of the line for House bills. While the principal sponsor's office may issue press releases touting the bill's prospects, that sponsor usually knows from the start whether or not a bill will move. A bill is said to move if it progresses through the stages of active consideration: hearings and amending ses-sions in subcommittees or full committees, negotiations with the party leaders who act as gatekeepers to the House floor, deliberations in the Rules Committee that sets parameters for floor debate and, ultimately, consideration by the whole House.

But the House is under no obligation to consider bills, other than "must pass" fiscal measures to keep the government running or respond to crises. Continued operation of the government requires the passage of appropriations bills. And the 1974 Budget Act requires a budget resolu-tion and a "reconciliation bill" that harmonizes that resolution with other spending decisions and sets the result in law. The limit on governmental borrowing authority also needs to be raised from time to time, and certain popular programs must be reauthorized lest they expire.

Other than that, the House is free to take up or ignore the thousands of other bills introduced in each Congress. And the presumption favors inaction over action. Most committees never hold hearings on most of the bills referred to them, let alone the serious business sessions, known as markups, where amendments are debated and votes taken. It may be that the committee's docket is simply too full to accommodate all referrals. But chairmen enjoy some latitude in priority and selection. A bill arising late in a Congress may move quickly, even as other bills continue to languish in the queue. Some bills are offered by members who know that a certain committee chairman, constrained by time or inspired by hostility, will pay scant attention. Indeed, members may offer bills against their own best judgment, counting on that certain chairman to save them (and provide a convenient scapegoat in the bargain).

HR 2020 could count on a warm reception from at least one of the four subcommittees to which it was referred, the Post Office Subcommittee on Civil Service, where the gavel belonged to Pat Schroeder. The subcommittee was a legislative backwater normally of note only to federal bureaucrats and government employees' unions, but it had a claim on HR 2020 because the bill was written explicitly to cover federal workers. But it remained to be seen how many of the other three subcommittees to which the bill had been referred would take it as seriously.

LESS THAN TWO WEEKS AFTER THE fledgling parental leave bill had been introduced, news came from the judicial front. The Real decision that had brought the issue to the attention of Congress in March 1984 was reversed in April 1985 by a ruling of the U.S. Ninth Circuit Court of Appeals in San Francisco. The appellate court decided that Berman's 1978 California statute did not violate the equal protection provisions of the 1964 Civil Rights Act, as Judge Real had ruled.

Cal Fed and its allied business groups immediately announced they would seek review by the U.S. Supreme Court. But in the meantime Berman was free to declare victory in his home state, and the coalition of parental leave advocates was more than glad to do the same at the national level. They had the boost they had needed to get moving, and reason to feel more certain than ever about their strategic direction.

The Ninth Circuit opinion was a best-of-both-worlds document for the parental leave coalition. The court had not disagreed with Real about the primacy of equal treatment, it had disagreed with his application of the equality principle to pregnancy. In a sense, it was as if Real's decision had been revised by feminist advocate Wendy Williams herself, writing for the appeals court, granting Garland's claim while affirming the legal principle of equal treatment.

Far from obviating the legislative activity in Congress, however, the appeals court decision seemed to add fresh impetus. Schroeder gleefully told reporters that the ruling proved HR 2020 was the right approach to parental leave. A more narrow bill, designed to reverse Real and protect mothers only, was probably not necessary. What was called for, Schroeder could now contend, was a broad-based principle assuring workers of all kinds the right to job-protected leave when family duties demanded. So with zest renewed, Schroeder and her office and caucus staffs went to work planning a subcommittee hearing, the first step of the legislative march.

NOT LONG AFTER SCHROEDER dropped HR 2020 into the hopper in early April, the text came under scrutiny by congressional staff members and members of the outside support coalition. Quietly, and without wanting to disturb Schroeder or other members, Fred Feinstein of the Education and Labor staff and Donna Lenhoff began soliciting suggested revisions in the bill. Some advocates objected to the use of "disability" in the title of the bill. Union representatives wondered how the bill would fit into the Fair Labor Standards Act. Other potential supporters raised other questions. An informal redrafting team was formed, and lengthy sessions were held to thrash out the issues left unresolved in the April draft.

But if the hastily introduced HR 2020 was less than the ideal bill, it was for the moment the only bill. And Schroeder's staff could at least organize a hearing on the subject—if not the precise substance—of the bill. That summer they contacted potential witnesses and weighed the potential testimony. They had no trouble finding experts willing to testify, borrowing liberally from the witness lists of Miller's 1984 hearings and the March 1985 conference sponsored by the Junior League (including Brazelton, who was fast becoming to the 1980s what Dr. Spock had been to the baby boom).

The academics would be joined by an executive from General Foods (to be lionized as an enlightened employer) and an official of the United Mine Workers (the perfect heavy industrial complement to the testimony of feminist legal theorists). A greater problem lay in locating parents who could testify about their personal situations. There may be thousands of people with compelling stories to tell, but congressional committee staff often struggle to find individuals who can come to Washington and tell these stories to a panel of potentially hostile legislators.

Committee staff are not only called upon to cast a hearing but to script it as well, paying particular attention to the lines to be read by the star— the member who chairs the hearing. A strong chair will not merely preside at the hearing, he or she will conduct it like a chamber ensemble. The chair will amplify and sharpen testimony by asking the probing follow-up question.

But even the best preparation cannot guarantee that a hearing will come off as planned, particularly at the subcommittee level. Members are always overscheduled, having committed themselves to multiple subcommittees on each of their multiple committees. In the mid-1980s the typical House member was assigned to two or three committees and seven or eight subcommittees. Each of these assignments was competing for the member's time during the three days of the week it made sense to schedule subcommittee hearings: Tuesday through Thursday. Too many members are back in their districts or in transit on Monday and Friday. The middle three days of the week are when Congress convenes, and when roll call votes are taken on the floor.

Schroeder had hoped to streamline the process by holding a joint hearing under the auspices of all four subcommittees. Her own Civil Service Subcommittee and its sister Subcommittee on Compensation and Employee Benefits were both relevant because HR 2020 would be applicable to federal workers.

Two subcommittees would also be included from Education and Labor: the Subcommittee on Labor-Management Relations (chaired by William L. Clay of Missouri) and the Subcommittee on Labor Standards (chaired by Austin J. Murphy of Pennsylvania). All told, seventeen Democrats and eleven Republicans sat on one or more of these subcommittees in 1985.

The big cast made it seem likely the event would attract enough members to be worthwhile—even newsworthy. But the weeks of preparation and calendar-checking dragged on. It was too late to have the hearing before the long August recess and September was crowded with markups. Schroeder finally landed on the third Thursday of October. She arranged a good-sized hearing room near the Education and Labor Committee offices on the first floor of the Rayburn Building and hoped for the best.

But on October 17, 1985, the appointed day, Schroeder sat on a nearly deserted dais and watched anxiously as the clock ticked toward ten o'clock. The House Democratic leadership was holding a caucus (a general meeting open to all Democratic members) to discuss the afternoon's votes on military construction projects and the extension of daylight saving time. Schroeder could see her quorum disappearing down the tunnels that lead away from the House office buildings toward the Capitol.

At five minutes past the hour, Schroeder decided the hearing was better off with a ragged beginning than a late one. She gaveled for order and read her prepared statement, a rhetorical broadside combining box-car numbers ("96 percent of fathers work . . . more than 60 percent of American mothers also work") with gut-level appeals ("coal miners have been denied unpaid leave to care for their children dying of cancer"). Then she turned to the lean, prim man at her left, John T. Myers of Indiana, the senior Republican present. Myers promptly announced he had an important matter on the House floor at eleven o'clock and said, "I hope we can expedite this morning."

Looking around for the other three subcommittee chairs, Schroeder could find none. She could find no Democrat in the hearing room more senior than Charles A. Hayes of Chicago, the fifth-ranking member of Congressman Clay's Subcommittee on Labor-Management Relations. Hayes had with him a prepared statement from Clay, who was "as you know, unable to be here today."

Schroeder seemed tense at this announcement. "We are not sure," she said into her microphone, "whether the chairman is celebrating the winning of the pennant by his city or what." Clay was at home because his hometown St. Louis Cardinals had clinched the National League pennant the night before.

Hayes proceeded to read the brief statement from Clay, written by his subcommittee's staff director, Fred Feinstein. It essentially reiterated the points Schroeder herself had made ("half of all mothers of children under five work"), with some heightened emphasis on the single-parent household. Feinstein was sitting in the row of staff chairs just behind Schroeder, alongside Schroeder's staff. When Hayes had finished reading, Schroeder seemed more conciliatory. She thanked Hayes warmly and also thanked and praised "Chairman Clay, for his having been very, very helpful in bringing this hearing to fruition."

No one had arrived to read the opening statements of the other two chairs, Austin J. Murphy and Ohioan Mary Rose Oakar. Murphy had prepared no statement. Oakar would arrive later and submit one for the record (where it would be printed as if read at the beginning). At the time, however, Schroeder was free to summon her first panel of witnesses. First up was Lorraine Poole, a city employee from Philadelphia, and Councilwoman Joan Specter, a member of the Philadelphia City Council who had amended the city charter to permit parental leaves and who was also the wife of Republican Senator Arlen Specter.

As members arrived and took their places, they started questioning witnesses. Republican Harris Fawell listened to law professor Wendy Williams explain the legal history of the leave concept and then wanted to know how the bill would affect small operations such as his law firm back in Illinois.

Austin Murphy arrived and took up the small-shop cudgels as well. When assured that small firms could cope with a parental leave much as they coped with other disruptions, he gave Schroeder a mock warning: "Be careful," he said. "You know some of us guys really don't want this protection. We might have to stay home and take care of the kids." The room filled with laughter.

"There," said Schroeder, "is an honest man."

The committee then heard from Liberia Johnson, a checkout clerk from Charleston, South Carolina. She recounted how her pregnancy had been complicated by thyroid problems that had kept her from her job in a discount store. When she returned after giving birth, the store had a new manager who refused to take her back. When she applied for unemployment insurance, the state told her she did not qualify because she had quit her job. Johnson's had become one of two test cases that led to a successful lawsuit and a change in South Carolina's unemployment compensation law.

This testimony prompted a question from Tom Petri, a Republican from Wisconsin, who wanted to know whether the leave in HR 2020 would cover a problem pregnancy or would begin with the birth of a child. Law professor Williams saw here an opportunity to address the fundamental misperception about the bill, the notion that it addressed only the right of new parents—presumed in most cases to be mothers—to take time off.

"This bill," she said carefully, "provides for leaves and the right to return for workers who are disabled for medical reasons and, in addition, a parental leave." The sequence in which she placed these two provisions was not lost on the members, some of whom seemed to be appreciating the latter half of the "parental and medical" title for the first time. The parental leave was strictly for newborns and new adoptions, Williams explained, while the medical leave covered a much broader range of circumstances, "including, of course, pregnancy-related matters such as childbirth."

"So that would be in addition to the leave by reason of birth?" asked Petri. "Yes," Williams replied. "The leave by reason of birth would be available to parents of either sex and is not related to the medical leave provision."

Petri also wanted to know what would prevent someone from abusing the leave, "where people would leave the baby with Grandma and go off on a four-month vacation and be entitled to their jobs back."

Williams said the job protection was intended strictly to facilitate child rearing. Councilwoman Specter spoke up to say the city of Philadelphia had required parents to sign affidavits affirming that they were the child's primary caretaker.

That got Indiana's Myers into the game. What if a father decided to take the full twenty-six weeks allowed for parenting and used them to look for another job? "Gee," said Myers, "I will take this opportunity to try another job. If I like it I will quit [my old job] at the end of twenty-six weeks. If I don't, well, I will go back. I am protected."

Williams cited disability insurance programs in the states that had provided for various kinds of abuse over the years, and she suggested that similar regulations for parental and medical leaves might be written by the U.S. Department of Labor.

"I thank you," said Myers brusquely. "But we in Congress like to write the rules."

Shortly thereafter Schroeder introduced her panel of academic experts, which included Kamerman of Columbia and Brazelton of Harvard. Brazelton rambled a bit in his remarks, seeming less rigorous in his reasoning and less pointed in his argument. But he had brought along a film of a young mother bonding with her two-month-old infant. The baby would beam, then become agitated, as the mother alternately lavished and withheld her affection. Brazelton, too, seemed to come alive when the two subjects made contact.

"And look at those lighted eyes in the baby and the lighted eyes in the mother," he said, his own eyes alight and his voice urgent.

The members of the committee seemed to have forgotten the clock for the moment as they watched the screen with rapt attention. They let out long "ahhh" sounds along with the rest of the audience. One staff member would later say it was the only time she had heard members of Congress coo.

ONCE SCHROEDER ADJOURNED THAT hearing, her options were limited. She could always hold her own markup in her own subcommittee, but doing so would accomplish little. The bill would still need to be marked up by the full Post Office Committee, and it would still have to start over with the subcommittees of Education and Labor. Schroeder could seek a reprise of her hearing for one of the two full committees, or she could try for a markup in Post Office or perhaps in Clay's subcommittee. But she could not make any of these things transpire on her own; she could only ask. The decision to proceed would rest with one of these other chairmen.

Schroeder had never been particularly close to any of these men, but she thought she had what members call a good working relationship with each. Clay, for example, was a colleague on Post Office and had been an early cosponsor of HR 2020. He might be a bridge to the chairman of the full Education and Labor Committee, the venerable Augustus F. Hawkins of California (with whom he had cofounded the Congressional Black Caucus). Schroeder had also worked for years with William D. Ford of Michigan, whose twenty years of seniority had made him not only the chairman of the Post Office Committee but also the number-two Democrat behind Hawkins at Ed and Labor.

Hawkins had been representing Watts and other poor neighborhoods of central Los Angeles as a state and federal lawmaker since 1935. Ford was an unreconstructed New Deal Democrat, born in Detroit and raised on the gritty labor politics of Motor City. Neither had cosponsored HR 2020. They did not know many of the women in the support coalition, and as one labor lobbyist put it, they did not "cotton to" some of the others. The word was that the old bulls of the committee thought of parental leave as "that yuppie bill," a boon for two-income professional households but not for traditional working-class families.

Hawkins and Ford had other things on their minds. They were more interested in outlawing scabs ("striker replacements"), and they wanted a law requiring employers to notify workers well in advance of mass layoffs or plant closings. The latter issue was especially warm in the autumn of 1985, and Ford was its lead sponsor. He had been trying to pass plant-closing legislation for more than a decade, and the fight had become especially bitter in the 1980s. Spoiling for a fight they could win, labor and its champions on the Hill wanted to prove that the crushing defeat of Walter Mondale, their own favored presidential candidate, had not extinguished labor's political clout.

Earlier that year Schroeder had agreed to cosponsor Ford's plant-closing bill (HR 1616) as a matter of course and as a courtesy. In the meantime, however, she had heard from Denver area businesses about the onerous restrictions of the proposed law. She had asked a lot of questions about the actual benefits of advance notice. Did it save anyone's job? Did it help anyone get rehired, retrained or relocated? Might it actually eliminate jobs? She gradually came to consider the entire idea little more than a symbol, if not a counterproductive sham.

Plant closing came to the House floor for its climactic vote on November 21, 1985. The version being voted on was a compromise worked out between Ford and James M. Jeffords of Vermont, who was then the senior Republican on Education and Labor. It narrowed the scope of the notice requirement and the remedies available to workers in an attempt to secure the last few votes needed for passage.

On the floor, an amendment was offered that would have weakened the bill further. It failed, and Schroeder was among those voting against it. She still seemed to be on board; Ford and the other senior members of Ed and Labor who were managing the bill on the floor—including Hawkins and Clay—had no notion of a problem in the Colorado delegation. But when the vote came on final passage, Schroeder's light on the big scoreboard high on the House chamber's east wall went red instead of green. She had voted no. And the Ford-Jeffords compromise had fallen short of passage by just five votes, 208–203.

At the moment when Schroeder needed her connections to the Ed and Labor inner circle most, she had strained them severely. There were no stormy denunciations, no confrontations in the rear of the chamber or angry phone calls. But members talk to their staffs, and their staffs talk to one another. And in the waning days of that session, word got around. The men who had managed the plant-closing bill felt betrayed by Schroeder's vote. They would not be in the mood to do her any favors in the foreseeable future.

3.

Testing the Track

THE FIRST SESSION OF THE 99TH CONGRESS dragged on well into December 1985, as House and Senate leaders wrangled over an across-the-board cut in federal spending known as the Gramm-Rudman-Hollings bill. A popular, if Procrustean idea, GRH had Senate majority leader Bob Dole of Kansas threatening to stay in session as long as necessary and to sing carols Christmas Eve on the Senate floor. Rank-and-file legislators, held captive in the Capitol, tried to make the best of the time on behalf of their own pet bills.

But that long, talky December did not do much good for HR 2020. Its supporters were not sure whether to be encouraged or disheartened by their progress to date. They now had an actual House bill to point to, but no Senate companion. The coalition of outside supporting organizations had grown, but some potential allies were aloof because of problems with the bill's details. There had been a friendly hearing on the topic before four formal subcommittees of the House, but the hearing had not addressed the substance of HR 2020 directly. Forty members had become cosponsors, but many of those who might be considered natural allies (including most of the women in Congress) had yet to sign on. Just as discouraging, the key committee chairmen had yet to do so. The press had begun to notice the issue, but not the bill, which had yet to attract as much attention as the Garland case, then pending before the Supreme Court on appeal.

The picture was muddled further by the uncertainty over Schroeder's role as lead sponsor. Schroeder had been the woman of the hour in April 1985, seizing the initiative and introducing the broadscale bill. But the intrusion of the plant-closing issue had cost her the good will of the senior committee leaders and rendered her, on balance, a liability.

No one had ever expected success in the same year a bill was first introduced, nor even within the two-year life of one Congress. The idea was rather to acquaint Capitol Hill with the basic concept, provide a first draft and initiate the process of amendment and accommodation. But to achieve even this much, the bill had to show some sign of life. The vehicle needed to move.

Schroeder herself saw the problem clearly enough. If she clung to the pride of authorship, there would be no further proceedings. The least awkward way to go forward would be to sidetrack HR 2020 and introduce a new bill with a new number, a new title and a new sponsor. A new bill could correct the flaws in the first effort's drafting and present itself afresh to potential cosponsors. All in all, parental leave might emerge more marketable and battleworthy than ever.

FRED FEINSTEIN HAD BEEN PART OF the family leave story virtually from the beginning. Howard Berman had called him about the issue in the spring of 1984. When Berman held his first meeting that summer with Lenhoff's working group and other interested parties, Feinstein had been there. When Berman had contemplated a bill of his own, he had consulted with Feinstein. After HR 2020 was born, Feinstein met with the outside support coalition to talk through the drafting problems. And when the bill had its hearing in October, Feinstein was front and center in the row of seats for staff.

The bill was Feinstein's business as chief counsel for Clay's Labor-Management Subcommittee. It was of personal interest to him as the father of two small children. But when he returned to his office in the Cannon Office Building early in January 1986, he knew it was going to become something more. Because he knew the person best suited to take over for Schroeder as the champion of parental leave was his boss, Bill Clay.

When Clay's name came up, some of the women in the coalition recoiled. Was this not one of the senior Ed and Labor men whose animus against Schroeder had blocked HR 2020? But on further reflection, Clay made sense. He had been among the earliest cosponsors of HR 2020 and had cooperated in setting up the four-way subcommittee hearing in October. He had ceded the lead role to Schroeder even though his own subcommittee was arguably the most important of the four. And whatever his current resentments toward Schroeder, he seemed to have nothing against her bill.

Clay would not have the same affinity with the feminists that Schroeder had. But he could open doors on the Hill where Schroeder could only knock. And he could convene a hearing or even a markup in his own subcommittee, the unofficial guardian of the Fair Labor Standards Act.

An eight-term veteran, secure in his district, Clay was fourth in seniority on Ed and Labor and second on the House Post Office Committee. In all probability he would be chairman of one or the other in the near future, and that made him more important in the present. He could all but assure a markup in the full committee before the 99th Congress had ended.

Moreover, as a tough-minded African-American with a background in civil rights and big-city labor disputes, Clay confounded preconceptions of who family leave supporters were—feminists, social planners and suburban yuppie couples. He had begun his activist career while in the Army in the early 1950s, organizing protests of segregated facilities at his base in Alabama. He later served 110 days in jail for contempt of court after leading the picketing at a St. Louis bank he accused of discriminatory practices.

Clay came with an added dividend in the person of Feinstein, who had established himself as an invaluable resource and friend of the outside support coalition. Feinstein brought both savvy and vision. He was thinking past the next level, moves ahead, worrying about getting to enactment. And in that regard he was weighing the long-term cost of Clay's involvement.

Every bill that moves through Congress has multiple identities, each of which can affect its acceptance or rejection. The first identity is usually based in a bill's substance or effect, be it the building of a dam or the prohibition of racial discrimination in housing. In this dimension, members can react simply to the relative importance and desirability of the project or policy at issue.

But a bill is also an extension of its principal sponsor or sponsors. Members' names are often attached to their bills. Perhaps the best famous law of the 99th Congress (PL 99-177) was nearly always referred to as either Gramm-Rudman-Hollings or just Gramm-Rudman, for the names of its principal Senate sponsors: Phil Gramm of Texas, Warren B. Rudman of New Hampshire and Ernest F. Hollings of South Carolina. This tends to complicate members' feelings about a given bill, suggesting a variety of personal or political reasons for voting either way.

A bill may also be identified with its advocates outside Congress. The president's agenda, for example, comes to Congress in the form of various bills introduced by members of the president's party on his behalf. Each component of that agenda will then, in committee, be referred to as the president's bill (members of the opposing party may call each item "the administration's proposal" or "this administration's proposal"). A member's reaction to the substance of the legislation is then colored by his or her personal or political relationship to the president.

Similarly, when a bill is associated with a particular industry or interest it is often explicitly referred to as such: the milk producers' bill, the environmentalists' bill or the foreign car dealers' bill. Such labels are often affixed with malice, implying that a bill would serve only a privileged class of beneficiaries. The news media find it hard to resist the shorthand. That is why members who issue press releases showcasing their vote for, say, the "Quality Medicine Act" will still be asked why they voted for the "drug companies' " bill.

Later on, if a bill is among the few reported to the floor of the House or Senate by a committee in a given Congress, it may become the committee's bill for purposes of debate and for other purposes as well. Whether that helps or hurts depends on the power and popularity of the committee and, almost inevitably, of the committee's chairman. Bills emanating from a particular committee often trigger a certain pattern of floor voting, and individuals may cast their floor votes to settle scores or curry favor with a particular chairman.

Any of these identities—substance, sponsorship, outside support or committee connection—may predominate at a given point in a bill's progress. By the end, all may be in play at once.

Knowing this, Feinstein understood that Clay's lead sponsorship would make enemies for the bill in the House, as would its association with the Education and Labor Committee or the AFL-CIO. There would be no more bipartisan cooing over baby bonding. But some kind of risk comes with virtually any lead sponsor or powerful ally. And for that moment, what mattered was the Education and Labor Committee, where Clay and the unions could make all the difference. If their help carried a price, so be it.

The coalition, grateful not to be choosing between a sidetracked HR 2020 and no bill at all, lined up to follow the new leader. Schroeder, too, showed considerable grace in offering to support and work for the successor bill so long as the general principles of HR 2020 survived intact. Technically, she remained Clay's cosponsor in the introduction of the new bill. And with that, the ground was prepared for a new beginning.

A NEW BILL NEEDED TO BE WRITTEN. Feinstein and others had identified textual problems in HR 2020. One of these, the "super seniority" issue, stood between the bill and the AFL-CIO endorsement that was a prerequisite for success with the older Ed and Labor Democrats. The existing language had not established whether employees on leave would be rehired if, while they were gone, other employees who were more senior had been laid off. This question mark had discouraged prospective cosponsors in 1985 and was regarded as extremely serious. But it was resolved with one straightforward paragraph stating that employees on leave could not be called back before senior workers were reinstated.

More complex maneuvering was necessary to avoid a confrontation over abortion. Would women who needed time off for an abortion be covered by the leave policy? Most of the women in the working group were inclined to say yes. But the effort to build a coalition had succeeded in winning tentative support from the U.S. Catholic Conference, a strategic ally. That connection would be broken if the bill was seen to facilitate or subsidize abortion. A critical paragraph needed to be written to soothe both sides of the abortion debate.

On this one, Feinstein proposed sidestepping the land mine in classic congressional fashion. The issue would be blithely ignored in the bill itself but taken up in the committee report, the document that accompanies bills a committee approves for floor consideration. The committee report is the sidecar that accompanies bills to the floor. It recounts the bill's history and includes detailed statements from members who oppose the bill. It also elaborates on the often arcane wording of the statute itself, attempting to clarify what members intended in drafting it. This "report language" often contains explanations that are critical to the substance of the law. And in this instance the report would define the all-important phrase "serious health condition" to exclude "non-recurring conditions for which treatment and recovery last no more than a few days."

Initially, Feinstein suggested cataloging examples: the common cold or flu virus, routine removal of benign growths, abortions, miscarriages and other routine procedures with short recovery periods. But in the end, the committee report would rely on the language and omit the examples.

Another source of irritation in the original draft had been the title: the Parental and Disability Leave Act. Some advocates of the handicapped objected to the term "disability" enough to keep them from supporting the bill. So the Parental and Disability Leave Act became the Parental and Medical Leave Act, or PMLA.

The revisions not only strengthened the bill itself, they also strengthened the outside support coalition by permitting its expansion. Successful bills, unlike successful buildings, often undergo constant redesign by competing architects.

WHILE THE NEW BILL WAS BEING PREPARED and the coalition of supporting organizations was growing, it was equally important to improve the bill's credentials by fortifying the list of House cosponsors and making sure there would be a companion bill in the Senate.

Getting a bill up in "the other body" proved easy. Senator Christopher J. Dodd, a Democrat from Connecticut, had been interested in child care issues for years and had been in touch with the outside support coalition. He was on the Labor and Human Resources Committee, to which the bill presumably would be referred. And while still in his first term, he held the ranking Democratic seat on the Subcommittee on Children, Family, Drugs and Alcoholism. Dodd was glad to introduce a companion (in essence identical) bill in the Senate once Clay and Schroeder had presented theirs in the House.

Clay and Schroeder were ready as March began. Dodd was not quite prepared and wanted to line up more cosponsors. So he issued a press statement praising the House bill and promising to match it soon. Clay and Schroeder dropped their bill in the hopper on March 4 and saw it christened HR 4300. Dodd followed suit on April 6, introducing S 2278. Dodd's original cosponsors included some of the best-known Senate Democrats: Ted Kennedy, who was ranking Democrat on Labor and Human Resources; the colorful Daniel Patrick Moynihan of New York; and Gary Hart, a leading contender for the Democratic presidential nomination and a Colorado colleague of Schroeder's. Also on board from the start were Arlen Specter, the Pennsylvania Republican whose wife had testified at Schroeder's 1985 hearing; and Dennis DeConcini, an Arizona Democrat whose wife was also active in coalition activities in support of parental leave.

But in the Senate of 1986, Republicans held the majority and Democrats could not schedule hearings without their leave. And the chairman of Labor and Human Resources, Orrin Hatch of Utah, a Mormon who considered himself close to small business, had yet to decide his feelings about parental leave.

Back in the House, cosponsors of HR 4300 were finding the cosponsor problem to be challenging. HR 2020 had begun life as a one-woman bill and climbed slowly to forty cosponsors. That number was disappointing in a chamber of 435, three-fifths of them Democrats. Some of the logical candidates had come readily into the fold: The California contingent of Berman, Boxer and Miller signed on as promised, bringing several home state colleagues along with them. The Congressional Black Caucus was well represented, with fourteen of its twenty members becoming cosponsors.

But support was highly localized. Three-fourths of the cosponsors represented districts within one of the ten most populous metropolitan areas. These included four of the most outspoken voices of the urban left ever to serve in the House: Ted Weiss of New York, George Crockett of Detroit, Henry B. Gonzalez of San Antonio and Ron Dellums of Berkeley. That gave the initial group of cosponsors a distinctive tilt and discouraged moderates who might have enlisted.

Only two House Republicans had signed on, both of them from New York. Just as disturbing, cosponsors included just six of the more than two dozen women in Congress and fewer than one-third of the 120 members of the Congressional Caucus for Women's Issues (an informal group open to members of either party and either gender). Even Schroeder's CCWI cochair, Maine Republican Olympia Snowe, had not yet embraced the bill. Characteristically cautious, Snowe wanted time to study the effects on business and on preexisting benefit packages, and to hear more from her constituency groups. She had not been part of the drafting effort, nor had she been associated with the activists, feminists and unionists to be found in the support coalition. Following Snowe's cue, the other Republican women in the women's issues caucus withheld their support as well. By and large, the male Republicans who belonged to the CCWI did the same.

But after Clay circulated a "Dear Colleague" letter advertising the redrafted bill he and Schroeder were soon to introduce, new names began to appear on the cosponsor list. To the first two Republicans who had signed on to HR 2020 (Hamilton Fish Jr. and Bill Green of New York) were added two liberals (Silvio Conte of Massachusetts, the enormously popular ranking Republican on Appropriations; and Stewart B. McKinney of Connecticut, an advocate of the homeless) and two conservatives (John J. Duncan of Tennessee, a ten-term veteran soon to be ranking member on Ways and Means; and Christopher H. Smith of New Jersey, who had ridden into office in 1980 at the age twenty-seven). Smith, one of the House's most passionate opponents of abortion, reasoned that parental leave might enable more pregnant workers to carry their babies to term.

The increase in sponsorship among Democrats was less dramatic, at least numerically. But Clay's ties to Gus Hawkins were good enough to bring the chairman of Ed and Labor aboard. And adding that one name alone virtually guaranteed movement for the new bill in the 99th Congress.

JOHN MOTLEY FIRST BECAME AWARE of the parental leave idea in 1985 about the time of Schroeder's autumn hearing on HR 2020. He was then planning the next summer's White House Conference on Small Business, a facet of his duties as vice president for federal government relations at the National Federation of Independent Business. The NFIB, with its headquarters a few blocks down Maryland Avenue from the Capitol, was fast making itself known as an innovative and persistent pressure group. One big reason was Motley, a square-built man of forceful, direct personality who seemed to have walked every hallway on the Hill and darkened every doorway.

Prior to the White House conference, the NFIB held meetings in New York, Chicago, Atlanta and San Francisco. Motley heard the issue of parental leaves raised "again and again." Most of the people he heard from had been spooked by proposals in their state legislatures. But Motley was fully confident that any business regulation contemplated at the state level would soon be on his doorstep in Washington as well.

Motley was not immediately alarmed about parental leave, either as a concept or as a precedent, because he thought its prospects too remote. His information was that Schroeder was operating more or less alone, and that despite her status as a senior member and a subcommittee chair, she could scarcely propel major legislation on her own. The unions seemed no more than lukewarm, and Motley felt Schroeder could be counted on to alienate some of the people she would need. He did not mind that no business organization was invited to address Schroeder's hearing in 1985. That hearing was about the problem, after all, not the solution. And it was hard to be frightened of HR 2020.

But then disquieting things began to happen. A spate of press attention followed the Supreme Court decision to hear the Cal Fed appeal in the Garland case late in 1985. And word got around that HR 2020 was to be replaced by a new bill.

At about that time Motley decided to do what he always liked to do when approaching a new challenge. He took a poll. By sending an extensive questionnaire to some of the NFIB's 600,000 members, Motley could accomplish several goals at once. He could notify his troops of a potential new battle on the horizon. He could find out how they felt about the issue and at the same time emphasize his concern about their feelings. And he could compile the kind of polling data most useful in his communications with Congress. In fact, the poll results would be arranged by region of the country and delivered to every congressional office as soon as available. And from the first NFIB poll in 1986 until the last in 1992, nearly 85 percent of those responding would oppose parental leave.

Motley found arguments came readily to mind. Parental leave smacked of a new effort to transfer the cost and responsibility of social welfare from the public sector to the private. It was a throwback to the New Deal, except that in an era of big deficits the government would not provide services itself but force someone else to do it. "We had to raise the standard of revolt," said Motley. "Here we stand, we will not go back on it."

It was also in the early months of 1986 that the lights seemed to go on at the 16th and H Street headquarters of the U.S. Chamber of Commerce, the venerable organization that considered itself, and behaved as, the paterfamilias of the business lobby in Washington. Almost everyone connected with that lobby got a letter from the Chamber early in 1986 announcing the formation of a business coalition against the parental leave bill.

A meeting was held at Chamber headquarters to discuss the matter. The event was not quite momentous enough to merit the building's main room, the Hall of Flags, but it was held in a ground-floor conference room large enough to accommodate more than one hundred business representatives and association executives.

The gathering was introduced to Virginia Lamp, the labor relations attorney for the Chamber and its designated director for the new, one-issue coalition taking shape that day in that room. Lamp gave the invitees a briefing on the bill as drafted in 1985 and as it was to be amended by Clay and reintroduced that spring. She also had a list of the members of the House, as it was important to establish responsibility for each of the swing voting members. Who could speak to Sherry Boehlert, the liberal Republican from central upstate New York? Who would call on Jim Cooper, the independent-minded young Democrat from middle Tennessee? There needed to be at least one designated hitter for each. And where a team approach would be helpful, teams would be dispatched.

From the beginning most of the seasoned lobbyists in the room knew that the main event for parental leave in the House would be the floor vote. But it would be important to do as much as possible to slow and soften the bill in committee. That meant digging trenches across the one committee battleground on the Hill least altered by the Reagan era, the House Committee on Education and Labor. But the opposition coalition was up to it. When HR 4300 had its first markup before an Ed and Labor subcommittee on June 12, members throughout the House would receive letters of alarm and disapproval from the Chamber and forty-two other business groups that had joined its united front.

IN THE 1980S, "ED AND LABOR" WAS the House's best-known home for unreconstructed laborites and liberals, a refuge for Democrats who never really acknowledged Reagan's ascendancy and sulked through most of the decade in disbelief. In the early 1980s, Ed and Labor functioned as a last bastion against the priorities and program-cutting fervor of Reagan and his budget director, David Stockman. In 1981, when about $50 billion was targeted to be cut from all House spending plans put together, nearly one dollar in four was to be cut from programs under the control of Education and Labor. Initially, parental leave struck some senior Ed and Labor Democrats as something so new and unfamiliar as to arouse suspicion. But in 1986 the committee's old guard was ready for nearly anything if it meant a fight they could win.

If the Democrats on Ed and Labor brought wounded pride and grievances to their meetings, some of the committee's Republicans did too. The committee had once been known for its moderate "Main Street" Republicans. But in the 1980s it was being restocked with younger conservative hard-liners. In this camp were two Texans from Dallas and its suburbs, Steve Bartlett and Dick Armey, each of them aligned with the Young Turk faction of House Republicans.

This new generation, spearheaded on the House floor by Newt Gingrich of Georgia, rejected the old bipartisan buddy system. They were tired of going along with the Democrats in exchange for minor favors and slim shares of the legislative action. They were ready to obstruct the process, even to hamstring the institution, if that would cast harsh light on its failings and overthrow its majority party. For this group, a fresh federal mandate such as parental leave was a hopeless anachronism, an insult to business proposed only to appease special interests.

THUS FAR IN 1986, THE PARENTAL LEAVE idea had taken several meaningful strides toward success. It had been refined to eliminate drafting flaws and broaden its support. It had shed some of its image as an item of avant-garde social liberalism. These moves had allowed Clay to persuade Hawkins to cosponsor, which made possible the taking of several additional steps in rapid succession.

Clay knew he needed to hold formal hearings, not on the subject of leaves but on the specifics of HR 4300 itself. New hearings would make certain additions to the record (and the political impression) left by Miller and Schroeder's hearings in previous years. Clay began that process in Post Office and Civil Service, the bill's other committee of referral. As the number-two Post Office Democrat, Clay was careful not to slight it and careful to solicit the cooperation of its chairman, Bill Ford. The two relevant subcommittees held a joint subcommittee hearing on April 9, taking testimony primarily from government agencies and public employee unions.

Clay then switched his attention back to Ed and Labor, scheduling a hearing for April 22 before his own Labor-Management Relations Subcommittee and the Labor Standards Subcommittee chaired by Austin Murphy. This time it would be Clay who presided and read the opening statement about the changing workplace and the increase in the number of working mothers. This time the venue would be the main Ed and Labor room in the Rayburn Building, a cavernous space where the walls were hung with large oil portraits of past chairmen.

The greater grandeur of the setting did not do much for turnout. Clay and Murphy were joined by Charles A. Hayes and by Republicans Marge Roukema, Harris Fawell and Steve Bartlett. Two-thirds of the subcommittees' membership did not attend. Nonetheless, the hearing represented a significant transition in the life of the bill. Not only was Clay now the man in charge, but the impetus for the bill also had been broadened. To be sure, the Ivy League pediatricians and psychologists were heard from again, but so was Tom Donahue, secretary-treasurer of the AFL-CIO. The committee record would be fat with supporting statements from the likes of Moe Biller of the postal workers and Vince Sombrotto of the letter carriers. The academic and social activists pressing for the bill had been joined by Big Labor.

Clay's witness list that day was heavy with aggrieved parents, union officials, social scientists and agency personnel, but it also included the first adversarial witness to appear at a Hill hearing on parental leave. She was Susan Hager, president of a small public relations firm in Washington and a board member for a women's business group and several small-business groups. While she spoke for herself, she also carried the banner of the Chamber of Commerce: Virginia Lamp accompanied her and sometimes enlarged on her answers.

"Last year my company lost a significant amount of money," said Hager. "If I had two people, two professional people, pregnant that year, and I would have had to abide by this law, I would have gone under."

Hager offered the argument that would soon be familiar to all who followed the issue: Maternal leave or paternal leave or any other kind of leave was a marvelous idea and a perfectly legitimate benefit for an employer to offer. But the important thing was to keep the benefit an option within a flexible package of benefits freely offered by businesses and not mandated by government.

Hager, who said she had twenty-two employees, also wanted a rationale for the level of the small-business exemption: "If there is reason to exempt four or ten, why not twenty-five or a hundred?" she asked.

Hager had a ready listener in Roukema, the ranking Republican on the panel. Roukema had already announced that she thought the new bill "obviously too far reaching" and likely to "wreak havoc" on small business. She was exercised enough to question Dr. Brazelton's notions of baby bonding, saying she understood there was "conflicting testimony" on the subject. In later years, when this former high school teacher and housewife from suburban New Jersey had become one of family leave's principal advocates, it would be hard to remember how perturbed she had seemed about it in April 1986.

CONGRESSIONAL HEARINGS ARE LIKE practice games in which both sides hold something back. The true measure of support and resistance comes when the committee sits down to mark up a bill. To build momentum for this phase, Clay again decided to start the process in the Post Office Committee, where success was something of a foregone conclusion. The Republican members of Post Office seemed content to play the matador for the moment and allow the bill to charge past them.

The Post Office markup was held on June 11, and the handful of members present discussed the bill's potential impact on the federal workforce and moved swiftly to a vote. Had necessity arisen, Ford would have had the missing Democrats' proxies (written or oral commitments allowing him to vote for them as if they were present). But ranking committee Republican Gene Taylor of Missouri was not inclined to dispute the outcome, waving the bill through without a nay vote. Approval was therefore recorded by a vote of 18–0.

With the Post Office formalities accomplished, Clay was ready for his first true test, the markup in his own Labor-Management Relations Subcommittee. Here Clay had clear allies in Ford and at least five of the other six Democrats. The sixth, Mario Biaggi of New York, was a former police officer who had complained about the bill as a feminist excuse to meddle in family matters. To impress the senior members at Ed and Labor, however, Clay would need more than a party-line vote out of subcommittee. And as it stood, he had no friends among the panel's Republicans. Roukema, as ranking minority member, remained actively opposed. And she could count on all four of her subcommittee colleagues: Steve Bartlett and Harris Fawell, who had been at the April hearing, and Rod Chandler of Washington and Dick Armey of Texas.

The subcommittee got to work on June 12, the day after Post Office had waved the bill through without dissent. Roukema arrived with a significant set of revisions to the bill. In essence, her ideas extended the compromise that had been reached in redrafting the bill over the previous winter. But then committees fight less often over questions of kind than over questions of degree. And Roukema's changes of degree were relatively severe. She wanted to cut the twenty-six-week disability leave in half and chop the eighteen-week parental leave to just eight weeks. She also wanted to set "minimum service requirements" so that only employees who had proven some loyalty to the company would be covered. Most significantly of all, she wanted the small-business exemption extended to companies with as many as fifty employees.

Roukema had all six Republican votes in hand, including a proxy for Jeffords, who served on all the subcommittees ex officio as ranking member of the full committee. But Clay had corralled his Democrats, including Biaggi and Hawkins (who had an ex officio seat just like Jeffords), so he was able to rebuff Roukema's proposal 9–6.

Clay would obviously be able to deliver the same vote to report the bill to full committee. But he first made a point of speaking graciously to Roukema, thanking her for her interest in the bill and her effort to find a version of it she could support. He offered to "work with" her to fashion a more mutually satisfactory compromise before the full committee meeting. Roukema thanked the chairman and said she too wanted to "work with" the sponsors.

This pas de deux is often performed at the close of a markup, signaling in public a willingness to cut a deal in private. The olive branch is offered by whichever side has carried the day. If the other side agrees to talk, it should be prepared to support whatever settlement might be reached "out of court" before the next phase of the process begins.

The two sides in this instance did not have much time. Hawkins had scheduled the full committee markup for June 24, less than two weeks away. Any delay in that timetable would probably mean the bill would reach the floor too late for action in 1986. So, once again, with time being short, the task was passed to staff and to the members of the support coalition. Fred Feinstein convened a select group, including staff for Roukema and lawyers who worked for Jeffords on the full Ed and Labor staff. To this group he added Lenhoff from the Women's Legal Defense Fund, Jane O'Grady from the AFL-CIO and representatives from the National Council of Jewish Women and the Junior Leagues.

Working quickly, and leaving aside the contentious items such as compensation that had preoccupied the larger drafting groups, this ad hoc team concentrated on the items at which Roukema had taken aim on June 12. They extended the small-business exemption to companies of up to fifteen employees. They required employees to work 500 hours or three months before becoming eligible and capped the total time to be taken by one employee for both medical and parental reasons at thirty-six weeks in a two-year period.

But the negotiators' most important agreement was to extend the right to leave to workers caring for a seriously ill member of the family including an elderly parent, a spouse or a child. Lenhoff and others had favored this feature from the beginning, but it had not been incorporated into either of the bills as formally introduced. To highlight this move, the negotiators decided to suggest a name change, dropping the word "parental" and making the bill the Family and Medical Leave Act of 1986.

This change would have a significant impact. While it would clearly expand the bill's coverage, adding to its cost and controversy, it would eventually broaden the bill's base as well, bringing aboard the politically potent American Association of Retired Persons. The bill would take on a new dimension for Roukema, who had lost one of her own children to leukemia.

HAWKINS CONVENED THE FULL committee as scheduled on June 24 in the main Ed and Labor chamber. Turnout was excellent, as it usually is when a committee sits down not to listen to testimony but to exercise its power. Clay had prepared well for the showdown. He had taken the compromise worked out by Feinstein's negotiating group and made sure he had a strong majority prepared to support it. Roukema, despite her staff's participation in revising the bill, still wanted to offer the substitute she had offered in subcommittee. Jeffords, however, had agreed to go along with the amended version, assuring Clay of at least one Republican vote.

Getting to the final vote, however, was far from automatic. Tom Tauke, an Iowa Republican who was not a member of either subcommittee, felt the bill had not been adequately aired. He called it "a new precedent for federal involvement in employer-employee relations" and bemoaned the "rather slipshod manner" in which it was being hustled through the process.

Unable to stop the proceedings, he chose the one weapon available to slow them down. He insisted on his right to have both Roukema's substitute and the Clay-Jeffords compromise read aloud from start to finish. Reading both thirty-page versions of the bill took about an hour, and some committee members wandered off, endangering the quorum. But Clay shepherded them back in time and the formal consideration of amendments began.

The central test was the vote on the Roukema substitute, which differed from Clay-Jeffords most tellingly in the size of the small-business exemption. The original parental leave bill in 1985 had exempted no one, the original HR 4300 had set the threshold at more than five employees. The compromise had set the arbitrary level at fifteen, but Roukema was still insisting on fifty.

Committee members had been shown Census Bureau figures estimating that only 7 percent of the national workforce was employed by companies with fewer than five employees. Raising the cutoff to fifteen would leave 22 percent of the workforce unprotected, while raising it to fifty would exempt about 60 percent. Clay argued for fifteen as the obvious middle ground. Nonetheless, the vote on Roukema's substitute became that day's test of partisan loyalty (even Jeffords voted for it). But while all thirteen Republicans stood together for Roukema, all nineteen Democrats did the same against her.

With the Clay-Jeffords draft language left alone on the table and assured of adoption, the markup moved to lesser issues—items that, while relatively minor, can sometimes derail an otherwise done deal. In one ironic exchange Tauke was rebuked by Roukema for referring to "the yuppie bill." Roukema insisted that the "job security and humaneness" envisioned by the bill were "primarily designed to help those families in need."

Bartlett, meanwhile, continued an effort begun in subcommittee to make the bill's provisions apply to congressional staff, who had long been denied labor protections enacted for other federal workers or private employees.

Clay personally had no problem with this, but Hawkins ruled the amendment out of order because the section of the bill governing federal employees had been marked up by Post Office and Civil Service. Bartlett appealed the ruling of the chair but could get only three of his Republican colleagues to back him up.

The committee moved toward the climactic vote on the Clay-Jeffords compromise as an amendment "in the nature of a substitute" for the whole text of HR 4300. The Democrats were solid once again, and they pulled over not only Jeffords but also E. Thomas Coleman of Missouri, a soft-spoken member of the committee from the outer suburbs of Kansas City. Roukema, not satisfied with the shot she had been given at her own substitute, refused to vote for the compromise she had helped devise following the June 12 markup in subcommittee. "Philosophically, I am resistant to mandating standards," she said.

If Roukema's vote disappointed Clay and the other sponsors, it was canceled a moment later when Tauke cast an equally surprising vote in favor of the compromise. Tauke said he objected to HR 4300 and to the procedure, but that given the committee's determination to report a bill to the floor it was preferable to report the Clay-Jeffords substitute. The final vote to adopt the Clay-Jeffords compromise was 22–10. Thereafter, the bill as amended was approved by voice vote.

Weeks later, when the official committee report of HR 4300 was printed, it would include two separate dissenting views from committee Republicans. The first would support the guarantee of job security but protest the trampled rights of "that other important party, the employer." It would be signed by Jeffords, Roukema and two other committee Republicans, Steve Gunderson of Wisconsin and John R. McKernan Jr. of Maine. The other dissent would go lighter on praise for the impulse behind family leave and heavier on the critique of its "numerous flaws" and devotion to bureaucracy. It would be signed by Bartlett, Tauke, Armey, Fawell and Paul Henry of Michigan.

The four other committee Republicans, keeping their options open, signed neither dissent.

•   •   •

WHEN THE JUNE MARKUP HAD ENDED, the support coalition members watching from the sideline felt bruised but elated. The vote of approval in committee had been something of a near-death experience. The sight of the committee's Republicans arrayed en bloc in favor of Roukema's substitute had been sobering. Just as daunting was the appearance of outside opposition, fully engaged and increasingly organized. And with all this, some supporters of parental leave still found it depressing to see how much compromise it had taken to escape the markup alive.

At the same time, the glass had to be said to be half full. HR 4300 had been in play for less than four months and it now had the imprimatur of both committees to which it had been referred. By at least the most obvious criteria, it was now a legitimate contender for floor consideration before the end of the 99th Congress.

The criteria for promotion to the floor, however, are many. Committee chairmen generally want to see their handiwork go to the floor as soon as possible. They drive their staffs to produce the committee report, scrounge for additional cosponsors and lobby the party leaders for priority on the waiting list.

All this activity intensifies as the end of a Congress nears and more bills are reported by more committees. At the same time, the approaching end of a Congress means all House members' terms are ending, so most are eager to adjourn, go home and campaign for reelection. Because any bill not passed by the full body by the end of a Congress automatically dies with adjournment, the competition for attention becomes increasingly frantic.

Two gatekeepers control the flow of bills to the floor. One is relatively well known, the other obscure. The former is the Rules Committee. Through the long era in which committee barons dominated the House, the Rules chairman was among the most redoubtable of the autocrats. One such chairman, Howard W. Smith of Virginia, was born in 1883 and lived to stonewall the consideration of civil rights bills on the House floor until the early 1960s. Largely because of him, the House adopted new rules to restrain Rules. The Speaker now appoints the majority party members of the Rules Committee, and they tend to remember who put them there.

The other, less visible gatekeeper is the leadership committee of the majority party, which meets in private and functions as the majority's board of directors. In 1986 this was the Democratic Steering and Policy Committee, a gathering of about thirty members including the Speaker, the majority leader and majority whip, major committee chairs, appointees of the Speaker and about a dozen members chosen by regional caucuses. In addition to making committee assignments, Steering and Policy would discuss legislative strategy and the prospects for passing various bills. When Steering and Policy felt it was time to bring a bill to the floor, that bill would soon find itself under consideration by the Rules Committee.

The Speaker and other leaders are loath to block bills supported by the majority of their party. But neither are they eager to bring legislation to the floor if its chances of passage are uncertain. In broad terms, floor time spent on one bill is floor time denied another. And quality time on the floor, with the members in attendance, ready to debate and vote, is at an ever-greater premium as summer turns to fall in an election year.

So the leaders ask some practical questions. How long has a particular measure been waiting in the queue? When was its committee report done? How many members have cosponsored it? Does it have a respectable number of votes in the opposition party? And, not least important, what is the bill's status in the Senate? House leaders feel far less compulsion to take up bills that are not nearing passage in the Senate because any bill passed only by one chamber will die with adjournment.

Education and Labor staff, principally Feinstein and his aides at Labor-Management Relations, spent much of their summer grinding out the committee report for HR 4300 with all the necessary supplementary statements of cost estimate, inflation impact and the like. The document (Report 99-699) was submitted on August 8 to the House as a whole.

But time was unrealistically short. Congress would soon adjourn for the standard August recess. Returning after Labor Day, the House would be preoccupied with the annual appropriations bills and the brinkmanship often provoked between the chambers and between the executive and legislative branches. Beyond that lay the final paroxysms of struggle over the Tax Reform Act of 1986, a contentious drug bill, a major overhaul of the immigration laws, the final votes on reauthorizing the Superfund for cleaning up toxic waste sites and so on down the docket of first-tier necessities.

As a first-time bill, reported late in the session, family leave was well back in the queue. And the leadership knew that active resistance to HR 4300 had only increased after the Ed and Labor markup. Members were hearing from small-business people in their districts, lobbyists in Washington and other members who opposed mandated family leave.

In one interesting reversal of the usual lobbying pressure, some members of Congress wrote to supporters of HR 4300 urging them to reconsider. Congressman Tom DeLay of Texas, a true Reagan Republican and a supporter of right-to-work laws, signed a chummy-sounding letter to union leaders calling labor support for the bill "an obvious mistake." The letter reasoned that the bill undermined collective bargaining, "the cornerstone of labor activities." With a federal mandate on the employer, the letter argued, "you, the labor representative, are preempted from the start." And because machines did not need family leave, DeLay noted, bills such as HR 4300 would lead to faster replacement of workers by machines.

Had it been noncontroversial, HR 4300 might have been considered under a suspension of the rules. A separate "suspension calendar" is maintained for just such matters, saving time for all concerned. Had the bill been cosponsored by a majority of the House (or at least of the majority party), the leadership might have squeezed it into a crack in the schedule. But parental leave was new to most of the members, whose staffs were still receiving their copies of 99-699 and laying them aside to be read later (perhaps much later).

The leadership was willing, however, to have the Rules Committee consider HR 4300 and grant a rule for floor action as a show of interest and a precaution in case the issue suddenly came to life in the Senate as a rider on another bill. The Rules session was unremarkable. Chairman Claude D. Pepper, who had just observed his eighty-sixth birthday, welcomed the bill and warmly commended its provision allowing workers leave to care for elderly parents.

Pepper was failing in health, and the committee in those years was largely run by its number-two Democrat, Joe Moakley of Massachusetts, a close associate of Speaker Thomas P. "Tip" O'Neill Jr. Moakley's views were often watched for what they revealed about his mentor's views. And Moakley seemed to have no problem with the bill.

So Rules sent HR 4300 on its way on September 17, clearing its path to the House calendar. But it did so under an "open rule." That meant amendments would generally be in order from either party, as well as from the sponsors themselves and the majority leadership. Open rules not only permit amendments, they invite them. And floor amendments may range from rifle shots at specific provisions to broadside amendments in the nature of a substitute. The latter, if passed, may rewrite the pending bill from start to finish.

By permitting such a free-form floor session, the Rules Committee (and the party leadership behind it) risks seeing a bill fail or be dismembered. But ordering a "closed rule" or a modified closed rule, which would preclude or restrict the offering of amendments, can lead to angry opposition from the rank and file and the minority party. So the implicit message being sent on September 17 was that the leadership did not plan to expend its own political capital to protect this bill at this time. The corollary message was that the sponsors might wish to hold off until the next Congress.

All the same, the sponsors and outside supporters of family leave could pride themselves on having brought the latest iteration of their cause to the brink of floor action in the House within seven months of its introduction. In the next Congress, they fervently believed, the bill could be taken seriously in both chambers and by both parties—right from the beginning.

Part Two

REVISION:
THE 100TH CONGRESS
(1987–1988)

4.

Back Up on the Horse

DEMOCRATIC SENATOR CHRISTOPHER Dodd found the last two months of 1986 rather gratifying. Early in November he was reelected with 65 percent of the vote, the largest percentage ever for a senator from Connecticut. Having achieved this distinction at the age of forty-two, Dodd could look out on a political landscape much altered in just two years. He could look forward to a second term in a Senate far different from that of his first term—a Senate with a new attitude toward issues of interest to him.

Although divorced and childless, Dodd had been a champion of children's programs since his earliest days on the Hill, an active supporter of the Save the Children Federation and a cofounder and cochairman of the Senate Children's Caucus. He had been the first senator to show strong interest in parental leave and, in April 1986, the first to offer a bill. But in those days the Senate Labor and Human Resources Committee was chaired by Orrin G. Hatch of Utah, while the subcommittee relevant to Dodd's bill (Children, Family, Drugs and Alcoholism—informally known as Children and Families) was chaired by Strom Thurmond of South Carolina. Neither of these conservative Republicans would schedule a hearing on Dodd's bill, so the bill had not budged.

But when the new Senate convened in January 1987, the Democrats' senior members would be supplanting the Republicans' in the chairs of all the committees. The new boss at Labor and Human Resources, for example, would be Edward M. Kennedy of Massachusetts, Dodd's legislative ally and social running mate. And moving into the chair of Children, Family, Drugs and Alcoholism would be Dodd himself.

The Democratic recapture changed more than just a few offices and internal power relationships in the Senate. It tipped the balance of power in the federal government. For six years Reagan had been able to count on one chamber of Congress to support him, sustain his vetoes and offset the Democrats in the House. Now, Congress and its leaders would be united against him, just as the worst crisis of his presidency broke. The last weeks of 1986 had also brought a rash of revelations about clandestine arms deals with Iran intended to free American hostages in Lebanon and finance arms for anticommunist guerrillas in Nicaragua. The White House was on the defensive, legally and politically. The appointment of a special investigating committee invited comparisons with Watergate. Reagan would be president for two more years, but the Reagan era on Capitol Hill had come to an end.

Against this backdrop the Senate convened for the first session of the 100th Congress on Tuesday, January 6, 1987. Following tradition, the Democrats elected their most senior member, the wheelchair-bound John Stennis of Mississippi, as the Senate president pro tempore (the job largely consists of calling on the chaplain to pray each morning and then turning matters over to the majority leader). Robert C. Byrd of West Virginia, the Senate Democrats' elected leader for a decade, became the majority leader once again, while Bob Dole of Kansas became the minority leader. The Senate also voted that day to create a joint committee with the House to investigate the Iran-Contra arms deals.

It was a long day and a busy one, producing more than 600 pages in the *Congressional Record* for the Senate alone. Most of those pages were devoted to detailing the more than 280 bills introduced that day, including, at No. 249, Dodd's Parental and Medical Leave Act of 1987.

ON THE OTHER SIDE OF CAPITOL HILL that January, Pat Schroeder was feeling a resurgence of confidence. The November 1986 elections had seen the Democrats on the march again, widening their advantage in the House to 258–177. Tip O'Neill had retired, taking with him the careful approach to leadership he had inherited from his two immediate predecessors ("You don't take chances," O'Neill had liked to say. "You want winners"). His successor as Speaker would be the more aggressive Jim Wright of Fort Worth, Texas, a politician who gladly gambled when he thought he could gain.

Schroeder suddenly remembered how she had felt as a second-termer back in the Watergate years. Surely this was the beginning of a comparable Democratic comeback. Opinion polls that winter showed Schroeder's Colorado colleague Gary Hart running ahead of all other 1988 presidential contenders in both parties. Schroeder was national cochair of his campaign. And Hart was an original cosponsor of family leave in the Senate.

For many in the support coalition, at least for a moment, it was tempting to tote up the encouraging signs and press for a purer, uncompromised version of family leave. Why not try to return to the five-employee threshold and the half-year leave period? Better yet, why not start over with a bill that included some form of paid leave?

But Schroeder hesitated. The bill she had sponsored with Clay had gotten much further in 1986 than her solo effort in 1985, but it still had not reached the floor. No one really knew how many votes the bill would muster in the whole House, and it was going to take some time to know.

With the final gavel of the 99th Congress, the old bill, HR 4300, had died—along with all the other bills introduced in the two-year life of that Congress but not passed before adjournment. Now, with the January swearing-in of all the members elected in November 1986, it would be necessary to introduce a new bill with a new number. And the new bill would be referred once again to the relevant committees and subcommittees to commence its swim upstream. Another round of hearings would follow, and then, in all likelihood, another bruising markup.

Schroeder knew that if the new bill was essentially identical to the one previously approved by committee, the burden of proof would be on its opponents, who would have to persuade the committee to reverse its previous judgment. On the other hand, if the sponsors came in with a fresh wish list or a radical rewrite of the bill, committee support might well erode. Settled issues, like sleeping dogs, are usually better left alone.

Bill Clay agreed it was better to stick with the language his staff had worked out with Republican Jim Jeffords the previous June. That meant again the eighteen-week period for family leave and the twenty-six-week (half-year) period for an employee's own medical leave. The small-business exemption would again apply to all companies with fewer than fifteen employees. Also retained from the Clay-Jeffords compromise was the extension of the leave benefit to employees taking time off to care not only for a sick child but also for a sick parent.

On the Senate side, this extension was not immediately embraced by Dodd and his staff. They thought it might distract from the desired focus on parents caring for children. So, while Dodd willingly tailored his bill

(S 249) to match the Clay-Schroeder bill in all other particulars, he omitted the parent care provision. The difference was highlighted by the short titles: The House bill was now called the Family and Medical Leave Act, but Dodd stuck with Parental and Medical Leave Act (a source of some confusion because the bill with "parental" in its title was not the one that covered the care of parents).

The difference between the two bills reflected a division within the support coalition as well. Some of the earliest backers of the legislation, such as the Children's Defense Fund and the Junior Leagues, worried that going beyond child care might be stretching the bill's appeal too far, sacrificing the bill's "motherhood" aura even while raising the potential cost to employers. But others, including the American Association of Retired Persons and the U.S. Catholic Catholic Conference, liked the more inclusive notion of extended family and the concept of a multigenerational circle of care. The AARP, in particular, was already talking about leaves for people to care not only for their sick parents but for sick spouses as well. No vote was ever taken among the support groups to determine the predominant view on elder care, as it was sometimes called. The plain political fact was that the issue seemed to bolster the bill for purposes of approval in Ed and Labor. And that, more or less, was that. But the shift had consequences for the coalition, with the Junior Leagues curtailing their involvement and the AARP beginning to assume a more prominent role.

Clay and Schroeder introduced their new bill on February 3, after Congress had returned from the quickie winter recess it was then customary to take shortly after convening for a new session. The number they received, HR 925, was a special delight to one of the newer additions to the support coalition, the office workers' advocacy group Nine to Five.

At the press conference following the introduction of HR 925, Clay referred to family leave not as a benefit but as a labor standard, a distinction by which supporters hoped to recast the debate over what opponents called mandated benefits. "If the family is straining because nobody is left at home to care for the newborn or seriously ill child or parent, then a labor standard that can substantially relieve that stress is good and necessary public policy," said Clay.

Using the phrase "fast track," Clay said he hoped to see the bill through its several subcommittees and two full committees and out onto the floor by April. In retrospect, it would be noted that he had failed to specify which April.

• • •

ON OPENING DAY WHEN DODD HAD watched hundreds of new bills swamp the Senate clerk, he had thought about how hard it would be to gain serious consideration for even a fraction of them. He knew his Democrats, and he knew how six years in the minority had dammed up their urge to legislate. He was determined not to let parental leave be lost amidst the crush. Yet he also knew how hard it could be to distinguish one legislative idea among so many and drive it all the way home.

The Democrats might hold the majority in terms of titular party loyalty, but the division on almost any issue would be more complicated than that. The Republicans might have lost much of their strength, but their old ad hoc alliance with southern Democrats—a fact of congressional life since the end of Reconstruction—had by no means been dissolved. That old coalition was especially likely to rear up when challenged by a significant social change such as family leave.

Dodd could not even presume to have the active backing of the subcommittee he was about to chair. The Senate apportioned committee seats according to each party's strength in the chamber as a whole (the House committees had disproportionate numbers of seats for Democrats from the late 1970s until 1995). With the full Senate split 55–45, a sixteen-member committee such as Labor and Human Resources would have nine Democrats and seven Republicans. By the same rule, Dodd's own seven-member subcommittee would be split four and three. So on strictly partisan lines, the loss of one Democrat in subcommittee would stifle the bill. And in full committee, the loss of one Democrat might produce a tie, making it impossible to report the bill favorably to the floor.

Even if the committee process could be navigated successfully, as it had been once already in the House, floor consideration would again be the higher hurdle. Romancing the leadership was as necessary as in the House but not as sufficient, because the Senate leadership does not exercise the same authority over floor scheduling. Nor is there a functional equivalent of the House Rules Committee for regulating floor amendments. (The Senate Rules Committee deals with internal, institutional matters.)

With or without the leadership's blessing, any bill must weather floor debate under rules so liberal that virtually any amendment is allowed. And even if these direct assaults on the merits are repulsed, the Senate condones a bewildering array of procedural techniques designed to delay final passage ad nauseam. In the House, only blocs of votes usually matter and the dominant party can all but exclude the outnumbered minority from meaningful participation. But in the Senate, the minority matters a great deal—indeed, each individual senator may matter a great deal. A single senator can interrupt the flow of floor action almost at will, and a few together can paralyze the proceedings almost indefinitely with a filibuster (or even the threat of one).

Even knowing all this, Dodd felt good about family leave. He could see how well placed and suited he was for the challenge. He had his own subcommittee in which to initiate proceedings, and he had the ear of Ted Kennedy, the full Labor and Human Resources chairman, as well. Working with Kennedy, Dodd could virtually pick his targets and go after them. And once Kennedy had decided he would rather concentrate on the full committee's health agenda (preparing for what he and his staff expected to be a debate over national health insurance), Dodd had a clear field to dominate on his personal favorites: child care and parental leave.

Dodd would also profit from good timing. The first fortuitous turn of events was a favorable ruling handed down by the Supreme Court shortly after Dodd had introduced S 249 in January 1987. The High Court had been asked to reconsider the Cal Fed case from California in which District Court Judge Manuel Real had disallowed the claim of Lillian Garland and struck down the state's maternal leave law in 1984. Real had been reversed by the U.S. Court of Appeals, which found for Garland and against Cal Fed in 1985.

The Supreme Court affirmed the reversal, giving final validation to Lillian Garland's claim, now nearly five years old, and to Howard Berman's California statute, now nearly a decade old. But rather than obviating the parental leave legislation, this Supreme Court ruling, like the appeals court decision before it, heightened interest in the issue and energized the bill's supporters.

And if the timing seemed right, so did the lead actor. Among his assets Dodd could count his knowledge of the House and his long-standing relationship with its key players. He had been a member of the historic House class elected in the wake of Watergate in 1974. He had been among its most active and liberal members, often making common cause with the likes of George Miller and Henry Waxman. Like them, he had gravitated toward social issues affecting the family, both because they interested him and because they seemed a kind of Achilles' heel for the Reagan coalition. With Miller, he had sensed the chance to divide the social conservatives from the strictly economic conservatives by framing policy ideas in terms of family needs. For a time in the early 1980s, the two had discussed forming a joint House-Senate committee along the lines of Miller's Select Committee on Children, Youth and Families.

Dodd was also in good standing with his party's core groups. He was well thought of by liberals and labor activists, even if his once-perfect 100 ratings from the Americans for Democratic Action and the AFL-CIO had slid to 85 and 73, respectively, in 1986 (a typical happenstance in an election year).

In the Senate itself, Dodd was not yet a member of the inner circle of chairmen and senior statesmen, but he had become a candidate for inclusion; and the expectation of influence can confer some of its benefits before the fact. Dodd mixed freely within the institution's several cliques and networks. While associated with Kennedy first, he also had ties to the idiosyncratic Daniel Patrick Moynihan of New York and the upstart presidential hopeful Gary Hart (whose 1984 campaign he had supported early and loyally). Yet he enjoyed better-than-average rapport with Republicans, affecting the bipartisan camaraderie on which the institution prides itself. Dodd also seemed to have a sense of the Senate's tradition, the legacy of his father.

Senators often have famous fathers. Senator Nancy Landon Kassebaum of Kansas was the daughter of Alfred Landon, the GOP presidential nominee in 1936. The Senate's ceremonial presiding officer was Vice President George Bush, the son of a senator, and the majority leader in the early 1980s had been Howard H. Baker Jr., whose parents had both served in Congress and whose father-in-law was Senate Republican leader Everett McKinley Dirksen.

Christopher Dodd's father, Thomas Joseph Dodd, had served two terms in the Senate of the 1950s and 1960s, elected as a pro-labor liberal in 1958 but remembered mostly for his fierce anticommunism. When the younger Dodd was at Providence College in the mid-1960s, his classmates were singing the sardonic line "I believe in God and Senator Dodd" from the protest ditty "Draft Dodger Rag." Chris Dodd opposed the Vietnam War as a student and sidestepped the service by enlisting in the Peace Corps when he graduated in 1966. But generational differences in the Dodd family were subsumed when the father was caught converting campaign funds to personal use and censured by the full Senate in 1967. In 1970 he defiantly sought reelection but was denied the Democratic nomination. He ran as an independent, finished third and died seven months later at the age of sixty-four.

In the midst of his father's ordeal, Chris Dodd left the Peace Corps and enrolled in law school and the Army Reserve. He got his law degree in 1972, and two years later won a seat in the House at the age of thirty. Just six years later he would claim his father's old place in the Senate, defying the Reagan landslide of 1980 and defeating Republican James L.

Buckley (who had previously been a senator from New York). As he moved his belongings from the House side to the Senate, Dodd's siblings made him a present of their father's pocket watch and chain.

But Chris Dodd's times were not his father's times. The elder Dodd had served most of his Senate years under Presidents Kennedy and Johnson, supporting their prosecution of the cold war abroad but often opposing their pursuit of social causes at home. Conversely, the younger Dodd would serve two full terms under Presidents Reagan and Bush, resisting their anticommunist crusade in Latin America and protesting their passive response to domestic social problems. Of course, all this had meant the younger Dodd spent much of his first term on the liberal fringe of a Republican-dominated Senate. But as 1987 began, he was suddenly a rising star among the newly restored majority Democrats and an exponent of his party's left-center consensus on social issues. His hour had arrived.

MARY TAVENNER, A LOBBYIST FOR THE National Association of Wholesaler-Distributors, watched with resignation as Congress returned to Washington in January 1987. She had a fair idea of what to expect from the ascendant Democrats in the Senate and from the likes of Jim Wright in the House, and she was afraid her allies in the business community were not prepared to deal with it.

Tavenner had joined the NAW in April 1985, the month Schroeder introduced the first parental leave bill in Congress. She had come from a career as a Hill staffer, and she epitomized a Washington archetype: the fast-talking, wise-cracking woman who had breathed life into countless meetings and receptions, always in the service of some famous man's career and never with time for a life of her own. She had worked for a variety of Republicans, for conservative westerners and moderate easterners, for the middle-aged and fully aged, and after years of impossible hours for too little pay and less recognition, she "went Downtown," as Hill people say, to be "a lobster." Tavenner had served most of her years on the Hill under Republican presidents and Democratic congressional leaders. She knew it would not be enough to watch while the Democrats cranked out legislation that the president would veto. Family leave was far from being Tavenner's only concern that January. Hatch's tenure at Labor and Human Resources had kept plenty of other bills bottled up as well. With Kennedy now occupying that chair, the bottle would soon be uncorked.

In the same spirit the Democrats were likely to press ahead on multiple fronts in the House as well, knowing that they could now count on some consideration in the other chamber. Even if Reagan were to veto everything they did, he could no longer be sure his veto would be sustained (Congress can override with a two-thirds vote in both chambers). And even if the votes could be found to sustain a veto, the Democrats could dominate the news by passing still more bills, denouncing minority rule and making every veto into an issue for the 1988 campaign.

Family leave, in particular, would be likely to move. Tavenner saw it listed with a Senate bill number in the *Congressional Record* for the very first day of the 100th Congress. Dodd had wasted no time, she said to herself, as she started making phone calls. Dodd and Kennedy would shepherd family leave out of committee and make sure it got plenty of media attention in the process.

There did not seem to be a true companion bill in the House yet, Tavenner noted, but there was a family leave bill, HR 284, in the list for the first day bills were introduced. It had come solo not from Clay or Schroeder or any of the other Democrats but from Republican Marge Roukema. Tavenner thought it just a matter of time before Schroeder and Clay would get together with Jeffords again and find a way to bring Roukema on board. And once that deal had been reported out of Ed and Labor, they would have months—not just weeks this time—to string together cosponsors and build momentum for the floor.

Tavenner could see it all unfolding as she punched numbers on her Touch-Tone. She could picture a cozy session before the Rules Committee, with the Speaker's appointees all lined up for the bill and ancient Claude Pepper sitting slumped at the microphone, maybe asking a question about elder care. She could see the bill parked on the House calendar, which she would then be compelled to watch anxiously until the day the bill was suddenly called up on the floor.

In short, Tavenner saw family leave needing lots more minding in 1987 than it had the year before. Surely Reagan would threaten a veto, but he would be nearing retirement and, mindful of his legacy, he might be tempted not to veto something that sounded so cuddly and inoffensive as "family and medical leave." There would, of course, also be another national campaign in 1988, with some Republicans wanting Reagan to sign popular bills—or let them become law without his signature, a constitutional option—rather than hand the Democrats winning issues.

Clearly, the opponents of mandated family leave would have to be organized earlier and more effectively in this Congress than in any since the late 1970s. The first order of business would be to convince the business community that family leave was for real. In the 99th Congress, Tavenner had followed what she called her "typical drill": letters, newsletters and conference calls about Shroeder's HR 2020 and the subsequent substitutes. She found business owners did not take it all too seriously ("They wouldn't pass something like that, would they?"). Even those who could see the politics of the thing could scarcely imagine a signing ceremony in the Reagan Rose Garden. But Tavenner would shake her head and repeat her stock caveat: "Outrageous things become much less outrageous over time."

On the Hill, the opponents needed to be getting their arguments on the table and letting members know how strongly they stood behind those arguments. They needed to prepare questions for members to ask at the hearings and amendments for them to offer at the markup. They needed to find cogent messengers—real people from back home in the district who would come to Washington and talk directly to members. They needed to devise alternatives and specific changes in the bill that fence-sitters might support in committee (even if they eventually voted for the bill itself). A few good amendments might rearrange the bill enough to set the supporters to squabbling among themselves and weaken their resolve.

Tavenner was soon talking with the people she knew she would need the most. There was Virginia Lamp at the Chamber of Commerce, Dianne Generous at the National Association of Manufacturers, John Motley at the National Federation of Independent Business. Yes, they would do all they could to slow the works at the House Ed and Labor and at the Senate Labor and Human Resources Committee. But a quick review of the members of each committee suggested approval was likely in both. So the real focus would need to be on keeping the bill off the floor in one chamber or the other, and preferably in both.

In the House, that would mean holding virtually every Republican in line and picking off just enough Democrats to instill doubts in the Democratic leadership. Wright might be more willing to take on the White House than O'Neill, but he would not chance humiliation at the hands of his own party if he could avoid it. Once in a while he might permit an issue to come to the floor when the outcome was in doubt—if the issue was the budget or aid to the Contras in Nicaragua. But family leave would never be that imperative, so all Tavenner and her allies had to do was make it look like a potential loser.

In the Senate, the opposition could count on a seasoned corps of conservatives. Bob Dole, eager to be seen in Reagan's service as he conducted his own campaign to succeed him, would certainly use every parliamentary maneuver against it.

The strategy seemed sound, and it was reinforced by the reactions of other business lobbyists Tavenner talked to within the coalition of forty-three groups assembled the previous year by the Chamber of Commerce. But there was a problem, and it had to do with the Chamber itself. Sometimes when Tavenner and others tried to schedule meetings with members of Congress, they got feedback about the Chamber. Some members seemed to think the Chamber pushed too hard on too many issues at once. Some thought the Chamber had been inflexible, refusing to compromise and pressing to kill bills outright rather than negotiate and amend them. When one woman, lobbying for the National Federation of Independent Business, sat down to talk family leave with a staffer for Tennessee Democrat Jim Cooper, the staffer said, "You're not part of that Chamber group, are you?"

Tavenner reacted to this particular report with distress. Cooper was just the kind of Democrat she expected to see determine the fate of family leave on the floor. Although he had served just two terms, Cooper was already a member whose vote influenced those of others (more than would admit it). Still in his early thirties and already in his third term, Cooper had prepped at Groton en route to a Rhodes scholarship and Harvard Law School. Elected to Congress at twenty-eight, he had compiled a record of studied moderation. The Chamber's own rating of his floor votes averaged an even 50 on a scale of 100.

Cooper had just moved from Banking to a seat on the increasingly influential Energy and Commerce Committee, but he also sat on Small Business. He belonged to the Democratic Leadership Council and was part of its drive for a less liberal party profile. Just as important, Cooper was personally business-friendly. Tavenner knew that the people she would bring to the Hill would feel comfortable with his blend of courtliness and horse sense. Cooper fit Tavenner's purposes perfectly. She did not want him alienated by anyone on her side.

Tavenner went to her board members and proposed a new coalition, specifically to oppose passage of the family leave legislation. It would be a creature unto itself, leaving each of the component organizations to do its own lobbying and claim its own credit. There would be dues ($500 per organization) and a new name of Tavenner's devising: the Concerned Alliance of Responsible Employers (CARE). She met with representatives from the National Retail Federation, the National Restaurant Association and the National Retail Merchants Association. She met with builders and contractors and with NFIB's John Motley, who, like Taven-ner, had been warning people about the seriousness of family leave for many months. Motley had back the results of his polling among NFIB's 600,000 members nationwide. They were, as it turned out, overwhelm-ingly opposed to mandated family leave or mandated benefits of any kind.

Tavenner and her cohorts met with Lamp to discuss their plans. Lamp was taken aback. She did not see what the group needed that the Cham-ber was not providing, and she thought their efforts to organize sepa-rately would be a distraction. For a time the Chamber ignored CARE. But after a few months, and before either the House or the Senate had reached the markup phase on the new family leave bills, the Chamber and CARE were cooperating. The new coalition was already placing ads in Washington print media, finding witnesses for hearings and producing printed material to be distributed to members and opinion makers. CARE, with the Chamber as a partner, became the unofficial antagonist for the informal group of outside supporters that had evolved from Donna Lenhoff and Judith Lichtman's meetings and that was now usu-ally referred to as the "family leave coalition." But members of the latter coalition, along with much of the press, continued to refer to their adver-saries as "the Chamber," a name far more familiar and likely to provoke a negative reaction.

The Chamber also retained prominence in the lobby wars by virtue of its cost estimates for mandated family leave. Various members of the Chamber tossed out various estimates of the cost early in 1986 and 1987. But before long the official Chamber estimate had settled at $16.2 billion. Most of that cost was based on the presumption that every worker taking leave would be replaced full-time, for the entire length of the leave, by a temporary employee. The Chamber study also assumed that the temp would be paid substantially more than the employee on leave (a premium supposedly required to attract the temp) and be at least somewhat less productive.

After the first rounds of compromise had trimmed the number of businesses and employees to be affected (raising the exemption threshold from five employees to fifteen to twenty to fifty), the Chamber revised its numbers downward and calculated that the bill would have an annual cost to business of no less than $2.6 billion.

FAMILY LEAVE HAD MADE ITS DEBUT early in the 100th Congress, with Dodd introducing his bill on the Senate's first day and Bill Clay and Pat Schroeder doing the same in the House a few weeks later. For a while thereafter the House and Senate bills seemed to be racing, each on the fast track in its own chamber. Dodd would have his first hearing in his Subcommittee on Children, Family, Drugs and Alcoholism on February 19. Clay was not far behind, holding hearings in his Subcommittee on Labor-Management Relations on February 25 and March 5, both times with members of the Labor Standards Subcommittee invited as well.

It was mostly a pro forma matter for Clay, as the arguments had all been aired in the previous year (on HR 4300) and the Republicans had resolved to make their stand at the full committee level rather than in subcommittee. Similarly, both Clay and Schroeder were senior members of the Post Office and Civil Service Committee, where they could steer HR 925 smoothly through their respective subcommittees once again. The full Post Office panel held a hearing on HR 925 as it pertained to federal workers on April 2 and received favorable reports from Clay and Schroeder's subcommittees in May.

If all this was somewhat pro forma in the House, the power to convene hearings and invite long lists of witnesses was a new and delicious pleasure for Dodd in the Senate. In the previous Congress, as a member of the minority party, Dodd had to ask permission from Strom Thurmond, then the chairman of the Subcommittee on Children and Families, before he could invite Yale psychologist Ed Zigler to a hearing on a separate issue and ask him some questions about family leave. Now Dodd would be setting the topics and calling as many witnesses as he wished.

Putting together that first hearing on the issue had been a cherished objective, not only for the senator but for Marsha Renwanz, his staff person on children's issues. Renwanz was a doctoral candidate in anthropology at Stanford when she came to Washington on a nine-month fellowship in 1981, and she had been working for Dodd ever since. She staffed the Senate Children's Caucus, then moved to the Subcommittee on Children and Families when Dodd became its chairman. A single woman in her mid-thirties, Renwanz devoted long, intense hours to her work. And in the weeks leading up to that first Dodd hearing on family leave, she would be hailing cabs in the wee hours outside the Dirksen Office Building.

The day for the first hearing neared and Renwanz had compiled a list featuring names both familiar and new, including Zigler from Yale and Joan Specter, the city councilwoman from Philadelphia who had testified for Schroeder in 1985 and who was married to Senator Arlen Specter, cofounder of the Senate Children's Caucus and Dodd's first cosponsor on S 249. There were spokespersons from social service groups, unions, businesses and consulting firms. Dodd had told Thurmond (now the subcommittee's ranking minority member) he could have as many witnesses as he liked, and Thurmond had invited three. Speaking for the Chamber of Commerce would be a woman from Massachusetts who owned her own business. The president of a Baltimore canning company was coming to speak for the National Association of Manufacturers. The opposition would also bring in Mary Del Brady, president of the National Association of Women Business Owners.

Renwanz felt all right about allowing Thurmond three witnesses until February 17, two days before the scheduled hearing, when she started getting calls about a "family leave briefing" being held in the Dirksen Auditorium. She discreetly dispatched a junior staff member, who looked in on the proceedings and discovered a team of lobbyists from the Chamber of Commerce lecturing on aspects of Dodd's bill. A quick check of the sign-in list showed the briefing had drawn staff from Democratic as well as Republican senators.

Renwanz had thought of Dodd's upcoming hearing as a kind of introduction to the issue and a "consciousness-raising" session. Now she realized it needed to function as a kind of counteroffensive as well. She began making phone calls and riffling through her notes and files. She needed to contact the support groups. She needed to talk to Dodd before the hearing began and brief him on the new developments. And she had to prepare a point-for-point rebuttal of the case the Chamber had been making even as her side prepared to make its own.

The main issue to counter was the alleged cost family leave would impose on private business. The latest Chamber literature was using the figure of $2.6 billion, scaled down from previous Chamber estimates but still featuring the chilling sound of "billion." Renwanz did not have a cost estimate of her own to counter it. So the next day she drafted a letter for Dodd and Specter to send to the General Accounting Office, requesting an immediate, formal cost estimate for their bill.

She then sat down to read the Chamber literature. She found that, among other things, the study had assumed leave takers would be replaced hour-for-hour by temporary employees being paid at least as much as the worker on leave. She then surveyed newspaper want ads for temps and noted the wages being offered to temps. This would enable Dodd to challenge the Chamber representatives at the hearing. Waving a folded copy of *The Washington Post* in the air, Dodd would demand to know where the Chamber got its notion of temporary employee wages.

The Chamber was also contending that family leaves could be covered in flexible employee-benefit packages called cafeteria plans, and that such plans would lose other valuable benefits if forced to include family leave as a mandate. But after checking with business consultants specializing in benefits, Renwanz told Dodd to ask the businesspeople at the hearing one simple question.

"How many companies that now cover family leave in cafeteria plans dropped another benefit to make room for family leave?" Dodd would ask the businesspeople at the February hearing (and later at others). "Can you name me one company that has done that?" When none could do so, Dodd would sit back with evident satisfaction.

On the whole, the February 19 hearing went better than Renwanz had expected. The witnesses had delivered the science, psychology, clinical data and analysis. Mothers and fathers had provided the anecdotal examples and the emotional context. Most important, from the staff perspective, Dodd had been pleased. More than ever, the senator thought he had a winner.

But Dodd also thought he had his light under a bushel. The subject of family leave needed wider recognition, by the public and the media, before it would be compelling enough as an election issue to matter to lawmakers. And so Dodd told Renwanz he wanted to stage the hearing again, not just once, but half a dozen times or more—and not just in Washington, but in Boston, Chicago, Atlanta and Los Angeles. Renwanz could see many long evenings and late-night cab rides before her. But from the Senate perspective, Dodd's hearings would put the issue into play, contributing not only to political support but to the favorable media response the sponsors would enjoy throughout the life of the legislation. As Dodd toured in 1987, in each city the media proved attentive and affirmative. In Chicago, the hearing brought out both major newspapers and extensive local TV and radio coverage. In Boston, the media were lured by Dr. Berry Brazelton and by Ted Kennedy, who heard testimony from, among others, his own disabled son, Patrick. The senator proceeded to praise Dodd's bill and publicly declare his intention to cosponsor it.

In Los Angeles, the cameras came for actor Richard Dreyfuss and his wife, Jeremie (billed simply as parents), as well as for a bevy of politicians led by the mayor and Congressman Howard Berman, a founding father of the family leave movement. In Atlanta, the bill was endorsed by Martin Luther King 3rd and by a procession of individual parents from the metropolitan area who told their stories one by one.

In the final hearing, held back in Washington on October 29, Dodd was able to produce a two-day-old report from the General Accounting Office in response to Renwanz's request back in February. The GAO had studied eighty firms in Detroit and Charleston, South Carolina, to ascertain the likely use of the family leave benefit. They reported that only one in three workers on family leave would be replaced, and at costs somewhat below that of the regular employee. So GAO estimated that, given the exemption of small employers and the most recently hired employees, only about one worker in 300 would be absent at any given time and the cost (primarily for continuation of health insurance benefits) would be no more than $500 million a year nationwide.

This, then, was the final piece of the puzzle for which Dodd had been waiting. Back in Washington, he would buttonhole the other members of his subcommittee, and then the other members of the full Senate Labor Committee. He would have Kennedy's blessing, but Kennedy had set for himself a full array of health and labor issues and had little time for S 249. It was Dodd's baby. Specter was on board as needed, but his committee assignments were of little use and personal persuasion skills were not his forte. Dodd needed a partner, and he knew the best kind to have would be a Republican—the more conservative by reputation, the better.

He talked to Orrin Hatch, who was his first choice. The two-term veteran from Utah was the ranking member of the full committee and was still treated as its unofficial chairman by many in the lobbying community. He had moved toward the center in his years in Washington, saying he had never really deserved the ultraconservative label he earned fighting labor legislation in the 1970s. He was also receptive to Dodd personally, serving on his subcommittee (Children, Family, Drugs and Alcoholism) and showing real interest in some kind of joint bill on child care. Were he to cosponsor family leave, or merely step aside for it, Hatch might offer perfect cover for other Republicans who might want to vote for the bill.

Hatch was a Mormon and a great believer in making sacrifices for the family. Family leave also offered a chance to moderate his rather austere image just in time for his 1988 reelection campaign (in which he might be facing his state's popular former governor). Hatch had even talked about the bill to John Motley, who remembered the senator saying he "needed" something like family leave for leverage when dealing with his committee colleagues on other issues.

But that conversation had brought a scorching letter of response, not from Motley but from Motley's boss, John Sloan Jr., the president and chief executive officer of the NFIB. "This is an extremely difficult letter for me to write," Sloan began, adding that he was "incredulous to hear from my staff that you are contemplating a compromise on parental leave legislation pending before the Senate Labor Committee." Sloan explained that parental leave and mandated health benefits were "the greatest threats to small business in America," and that defeating parental leave was the NFIB's foremost concern in the 100th Congress. "Unfortunately," Sloan concluded, "we need this one too, Senator."

The letter was written in December 1987, one month after the long, bitter Ed and Labor markup in the House. It arrived in the senator's office on a tidal wave of protest letters from NFIB members in Utah, who had been alerted by an emergency message from Motley. Hatch never did enter serious discussions on the bill with Dodd, and may never have considered doing so. But years later Motley still referred to other members whom he importuned to maintain their opposition to family leave as having been "Hatched."

Dodd also worked on Dan Quayle, a member of the committee who had been willing to cooperate with Kennedy on job-training programs. Dodd thought Quayle had more going for him than conventional wisdom acknowledged. The two men were just three years apart in age and had known each other in the House before they were elected to the Senate (both in 1980). They talked. But their discussions of family leave late in 1987 usually came to the same inconclusive conclusion. Quayle was interested in a bill that took care of new moms but put minimal burdens on business. Talking about mandates or broader benefits turned him off.

So Dodd kept looking.

5

A Breakthrough in Committee

LIKE OTHER WOMEN IN HER GENERATION, Marge Roukema came to politics only as a second or even third career. She had first raised a family and taught high school (history and government). She served a stint on the school board, which led to involvement in the suburban Republican politics of Bergen County, New Jersey. Even after several terms in the House, Roukema still liked to describe herself simply as a mother—someone who wanted to be thought of as "a good, solid dependable person."

Roukema rode the Reagan tide of 1980 into Washington, but she was no Reaganaut, belonging rather to her party's northern liberal wing (known as gypsy moths, the mirror opposites of the Democrats' southern conservative "boll weevils"). She opposed abortion restrictions and high defense spending, yet she shrank from being called a feminist and declined membership in the Congressional Caucus for Women's Issues.

Roukema also brought conflicted feelings to family leave. From the start she was skeptical, even questioning the claims of child psychologists about the relationship of parents and infants. When expressing these doubts, she would usually cite her husband, a psychiatrist. Roukema had also been sensitive to the anxieties of businesspeople, especially small employers. On the windowsill of her Rayburn office stood a squad of miniature Minutemen statues, the "Sentinel of Small Business" awards given by the National Federation of Independent Business to members who vote as the NFIB urges.

But Roukema was also uncomfortable with being against family leave, and she tried to reconcile her impulses by exempting as many small businesses as possible. Then, when the bill's coverage was expanded to comprise not only new babies but also sick children and parents, Roukema's sympathies were engaged on the other side. The central trauma of her adult life had been the loss of her seventeen-year-old son to leukemia in 1976. Roukema did not discuss that aspect of her feelings when the bill first came before the Ed and Labor Committee in 1986. At the time she had simply offered an amendment to raise the threshold of small-business exemption from fifteen employees to fifty. The bill's backers had dismissed that number as far too high, but Roukema had refused to bargain. Even after the original HR 4300 was softened by the Clay-Jeffords compromise in committee, Roukema still voted no.

Yet she was unhappy having no version of the bill to be for, so Roukema brought in her own bill (HR 284) at the outset of the 100th Congress. She introduced hers on the first day, a full four weeks before Clay and Schroeder's. Roukema's approach not only tracked closely with what she had proposed in committee in 1986, it also foreshadowed the eventual family leave law. Yet at the time her efforts attracted virtually no support from either party. Democrats were waiting for the Clay-Schroeder bill, and Republicans were not looking for a family leave bill in the first place.

Roukema had also found no friends when the Labor-Management Relations Subcommittee held its hearings in February and March 1987 or when it met for a markup on May 13. At that markup Clay's bill was the one under discussion. Roukema, the ranking Republican on the subcommittee, offered the essence of her own bill as a substitute. Clay promptly dismissed it as exempting far too many businesses and employees. The Republicans on the subcommittee were equally disapproving. Dick Armey of Texas, seated next to Roukema that day, pronounced himself "unalterably opposed" to any family leave mandate.

"I hope," said Roukema, "I am not going to be bludgeoned from both the left and the right." But that was precisely what happened: She paid the price often paid by Ed and Labor members who dared to seize the middle ground. When Clay called for a voice vote (a shorthand alternative to a roll call), Roukema's was the lone voice raised in support of her proposal. Shortly thereafter, the subcommittee approved HR 925, the

Clay-Schroeder bill, essentially as drafted and sent it on to the full committee.

At that moment in May, HR 925 seemed to have all the ground speed it would need to take off—perhaps even before the first year's session of the 100th Congress had ended. But almost as soon as all the subcommittees of both Post Office and Ed and Labor had reported the bill—the last of them chiming in on May 19—the bill stopped moving. Neither of the full committees' chairmen seemed overly interested, and neither Clay nor Schroeder seemed to be pressing them to schedule a markup. It was as if all concerned had agreed to call time out; and, in a sense, they had.

Despite the early appearance of the bill in the 100th Congress, the political facts of life had changed little from the previous year. There would be enough votes on Ed and Labor to report the bill, but not enough to build confidence in its potential floor strength. And if the Democratic sponsors had managed to find one or two friendly Republicans, the opponents were lining up more than a few votes among southern and midwestern Democrats.

Looking to the other chamber, Clay and Schroeder could see that Dodd, by conducting hearings from coast to coast, was pointing toward a markup in the second session (1988), so they backed off their own notion of a fast-track strategy and focused on recruiting cosponsors. At midsummer they had about a hundred signed up, which was fifty shy of the target set by the House Democratic leadership.

Meeting that 150 figure was crucial because the House was under new management in 1987, with Wright as Speaker and the hard-charging Tony Coelho of California as the majority whip. Neither could be called timid, but they had set an ambitious agenda of their own on the budget, welfare, trade and foreign policy. They were not eager to divert time and effort for the sake of bills that could not demonstrate some momentum of their own. Moreover, they already had a standing queue of bills that some of their own Democratic members were begging them not to bring to the floor. Many southern or western Democrats were willing to "walk the plank" once or twice in a session for bills of preeminent party priority. But was it really worth risking the hornet's nest of business antipathy for family leave?

So large a group of adverse Democrats had formed that Schroeder and Clay concluded their bill had no future as drafted. "That's not a feeling," Schroeder would argue later. "We did the whip counts, and the reality is the votes weren't there."

At this point the House sponsors knew they needed the same thing Dodd did, a new partner who could command fresh support for the bill.

To this end they had been engaged in quiet negotiations through the summer and fall with staff for Jeffords (who had supported the bill in 1986) and Roukema, as well as with representatives from the family leave coalition. Gathering in the office of Fred Feinstein, the chief counsel and staff director of Clay's Subcommittee on Labor-Management Relations, or in one of several subcommittee conference rooms, the intermediaries met not so much in secrecy as obscurity. Carefully they brought together the differing concepts of family leave held by Democrats, Republicans and the various coalition elements. Slowly, they distilled what mattered most to all and identified the items that could be compromised.

The essential particulars, all seemed to agree, were that the bill establish a new minimum labor standard (such as child labor laws and the minimum wage), that it apply regardless of gender, that it include not only new babies but also sick children and parents, that it require post-leave reinstatement (in the same job or its equivalent) and that it require the employer to maintain other benefits such as health insurance during the leave period.

Beyond these basics the congressional staff expected to haggle over the numbers in the bill, including the size of businesses to be exempted and the length of the leaves. Staff typically negotiated over such things, much as attorneys dicker over the details of a settlement. But they found some of the coalition partners more attached to the existing values than they had expected. The leave lengths were meaningful, not only because they represented sensible blocks of time in months (three and six) but also because they were rooted in existing state laws. Similarly, the fifteen-employee threshold for small-business exemption was a standard feature of several labor laws already on the books. In the end, however, these defenses gave way to the negotiating process, to the need for a deal, and to Jeffords's and Roukema's insistence on concessions that would mean something to their constituencies and their colleagues.

Surprisingly, the unofficial negotiators found less resistance to exempting more medium-sized businesses and more resistance to shortening the period of leave. The predominant view in the family leave coalition was that the length of the leave was essential to its quality, a matter close to the principle of the thing. The threshold of small-business exemption was seen as a less critical detail, a number easily changed in later years. Better to guarantee a meaningful leave for some, they reasoned, than to guarantee a leave too brief to matter for a greater number.

As a result, Roukema was forced to yield on her initial demand for shorter leave periods. She had proposed two months for family care, three for an employee's own medical leaves (the coalition wanted to hold

firm at three months and six months). In the end pressure for an
agreement led the two sides to split the difference on family care at ten
weeks (within a two-year period) and grant just fifteen weeks for employee
leave (within a calendar year).

Roukema also moved the bar on the question of employee eligibility.
Instead of qualifying for the leave benefit after just three months of work,
workers would need a full year of at least twenty hours per week to be
eligible. Roukema also worked in a wrinkle by which employers could
exempt the top 10 percent of their payroll from the leave mandate (so
long as they could show the employee's absence would "constitute a
hardship" for the business).

The linchpin, however, was still the small-business exclusion. The bill
Pat Schroeder originated in 1985 had applied to all businesses with five
employees or more. That excluded only the smallest mom-and-pop shops
and pleased virtually all the support groups. But by exempting any businesses at all, it also opened a window for future negotiations. If the
sponsors conceded from the outset that some businesses were too small
to bear the burden of family leave, the question became: How small is
too small? And once that was the question, the sponsors almost inevitably
had to give ground.

Early on, Roukema had seized on the exemption of small business as
the fulcrum for the entire family leave debate. It enabled her to associate
herself at once with the aspirations of the sponsors and the concerns of
the adversaries. And as early as the first markup in Ed and Labor in 1986,
she had pegged fifty employees as the political point of tolerance. When
the full committee had refused to consider her number, she had voted
against the bill. When Clay's subcommittee had balked at the same number in May 1987, Roukema had again voted against the bill. So fifty
remained Roukema's line in the sand as negotiations dragged into the
autumn.

But fifty seemed much too high for many of the support coalition. The
General Accounting Office figured such a cutoff would exempt all but
the largest 5 percent of the nation's companies. The groups appealed to
Schroeder and Feinstein not to accept such a sacrifice, and the talks
bogged own. In such moments in a legislative negotiation, the initiative
sometimes passes to the staffers who are doing the dealing. Feinstein was
the sort of staff lawyer who always seemed to have one more idea, one
more alternative means of reworking the problem. If fifty was all
Roukema would sign off on, and if that left Schroeder feeling the bill had
been gutted before her eyes, then there had to be a way to make both
sides give ground without feeling they had given in. Feinstein suggested

that the bill be amended to fifty at the outset but also include an automatic lowering of the threshold after a stated period.

After vetting that notion with their respective members, the staff people returned to say okay. And after discussing the idea with their respective organizations, most of the members of the support coalition were willing to go along. After all, they reasoned, the relatively few companies still affected were by far the largest employers, accounting for, by the GAO count, 42 million workers, or 39 percent of the workforce. Phasing in family leave would give the in-between businesses a chance to prepare and benefit from the experience of bigger ones. When a lower threshold of thirty-five employees was in place, the GAO estimated, the bill would apply to 43 percent of the workforce. And after all, as Schroeder stated the argument, "some coverage for some people is better than none for anyone."

After the last negotiating session, the product in several key aspects resembled HR 284, the bill Roukema had quietly introduced on the first day of the 100th Congress. Roukema's original bill had featured a threshold of fifty, shorter leave lengths and higher minimum service requirements. Like the ugly duckling, HR 284 was initially pleasing to none. But after a season of being rejected out of hand, it seemed to have been quietly adopted as the answer.

Having paid so dearly to bring Roukema on board, the sponsors of HR 925 felt they had a purchase on her. They expected her to help move the bill through Ed and Labor and recruit Republican support in the chamber as a whole. They especially counted on her to enlist other Republican women, several of whom had held back as if waiting for a cue. Almost immediately, Claudine Schneider and Nancy Johnson, moderate-to-liberal Republicans from Rhode Island and Connecticut, respectively, announced their support of Roukema's substitute. Even Olympia Snowe, the cochair of the women's issue caucus whose reluctance to commit had been a source of dismay since family leave was first an issue, declared herself ready to back the bill.

Suddenly, after months of rain delay, it was time to play ball. And just to make sure everyone knew it, Clay and Schroeder held a news conference on November 10 to announce that they had Roukema on their team. Each of the three read statements to a packed room, and the three new Republican women cosponsors appeared as well. Roukema called the new compromise "workable . . . one that business can live with." Clay was equally pragmatic: It was a deal, he said, "we think can pass the House."

Also featured at the event was the latest report from the General

Accounting Office. Building on the analysis done for Dodd's Senate bill, the GAO had projected a cost for family leave, assuming the specifications of the latest HR 925 compromise bill. If Dodd's bill was to cost $500 million, the fifty-employee threshold made the House deal look far cheaper: $188 million a year nationwide at the outset, and $212 million (13 percent more) when the cutoff was lowered to thirty-five employees.

For all of the enthusiasm sounded at the news conference, some of the questions from reporters were highly skeptical. Had any of the business groups opposing HR 925 endorsed this compromise? Were the supporting groups happy with a bill that left out roughly three workers in five? Schroeder and Roukema tried to accent the positive in their answers, but beneath the verbiage the answer to both questions was no.

All the same the sponsors saw themselves on the verge of victory. They could go to markup with the ranking Republicans of the full committee (Jeffords) and key subcommittee (Roukema) actively backing the bill. They now had near-unanimous, bipartisan support from the women members of the House. And, as if overnight, the sponsors found they had amassed the 150 cosponsors the leadership had required.

With the tide running at last, Gus Hawkins scheduled family leave for markup in Ed and Labor on November 17, one week after the news conference. He and Jeffords sounded out the committee's Democrats and Republicans. The Roukema substitute would have a bipartisan majority on the committee. Some even dared hope the opposition might collapse and allow the panel to grant its blessing peacefully, perhaps even by voice vote.

But it was not to be.

THE FALL OF 1987 WAS A FRUSTRATING season for Republicans, particularly those who had come to Congress earlier in the decade to be part of a conservative takeover. They saw Ronald Reagan skidding through his second term in comparative weakness. His would-be successors in the GOP were engaged in fratricide in the early snows of Iowa and New Hampshire. And back on the Hill, almost nothing seemed to be going right.

The Iran-Contra mess lingered on, distracting the media and sapping the administration's energy. Reagan could no longer veto bills and rely on his stalwarts to block the two-thirds vote needed to override a veto in both chambers. Not long after the Democrats took control in 1987, thirteen Republican senators defied a personal plea from the president and voted to override his veto of a highway spending bill. And that October, with the whole political world watching, the Senate spiked what Reagan had called his top domestic priority: the Supreme Court nomination of Robert H. Bork.

In this atmosphere some of the soldiers who had marched on Washington under Reagan's banner felt themselves betrayed and abandoned. While unshaken in their conservative faith, they were spoiling for a counterattack. And for a few, in a small way, the chance came just before Thanksgiving in the House Committee on Education and Labor.

Ed and Labor was once known for harboring the kind of Republicans who preferred a small piece of the Democrats' legislative action to no part of the action at all. Some of these minority party members could mesh fairly smoothly with the majority, at least on the education agenda. Jeffords was one of these, a congenital independent from Vermont, a product of Yale and Harvard mindful of the leftward shift in the politics of his home state. Another was Bill Goodling, the committee's second most senior Republican, a small-town politician from western Pennsylvania. He was usually more concerned about the economic decline of his Rust Bowl constituency than about the ascendance of unfettered free-market philosophy.

The committee had always tended to be more partisan when it turned from education to labor-management issues, an arena in which the differences between Democrats and Republicans were long-standing and clearly marked. Most of the Democrats on the committee represented big cities or heavily unionized constituencies or both, while most of the Republicans hailed from districts dominated by farms, suburbs or smaller cities.

In the late 1980s another kind of Republican had arisen on Ed and Labor, identified with a newer, more aggressive Republicanism—avatars of Reaganism and the "movement conservatism" that had dominated the party since the defeat of President Gerald R. Ford in 1976. Most visible among them were Steve Bartlett and Dick Armey, both from the Dallas–Fort Worth area. Armey and Bartlett delighted in bearding the old Ed and Labor liberals on fundamentals as well as details. It was rare for the duo to succeed; the committee ratio, after all, was stacked 3 to 2 in favor of the Democrats. But the long odds did not keep them from vigorously contesting the issues, as if one day their arguments alone might prevail.

Both Armey and Bartlett had come to Ed and Labor willingly. Bartlett, elected in 1982, had concealed his interest on the advice of a senior colleague who said that taking the assignment "reluctantly" could earn a favor from leadership later. Armey, elected two years later, had written Ed and Labor at the top of his list of preferences when queried by the

House Republicans' Committee on Committees. Both loved to argue, and both had made their careers arguing with liberals. Armey was a professional economist and former college professor whose ready phrases included "market forces" and "voluntary transactions." In his office he hung a poster of galloping horses with the words: "If you're not making dust you're eating dust." Bartlett, heir to a family business, had served on the Dallas City Council before coming to Washington and compiling the single most consistently pro-Reagan voting record in the House.

Armey and Bartlett detested the family leave bill even before they had heard from their first constituent or business group. It smacked of everything they found outrageous about the federal government and the social advocacy groups they saw setting its priorities. "This is a totally Inside-the-Beltway phenomenon," Armey would say, using the standard derisive description of Washington as a planet unto itself, defined by a freeway loop. Armey liked to tell the story of a group of firefighters from Arlington, Texas, who lobbied him on the bill but admitted they had never thought of having such a benefit until their union's national organization put it on the list.

From the beginning Armey and Bartlett realized the bill would win approval in committee, and they knew the Rules Committee would bar them from amending it much on the floor. Their best opportunity to make a difference would come at the markup, and they wanted to be sure they had plenty of amendments to detail their objections, needle the sponsors and exploit what would be their one day in court.

The November 17 markup in the main Ed and Labor hearing room drew a wall-to-wall crowd. Besides dozens of representatives from supporting groups, the audience included many from opposing groups— Virginia Lamp of the Chamber of Commerce, Mary Tavenner of the Concerned Alliance of Responsible Employers (CARE) and John Motley of the National Federation of Independent Business. Committee Chairman Gus Hawkins opened the proceedings by praising the bill and its cosponsors and thanking them for all their work. He spoke as though he hoped the whole matter could be disposed of quickly. Jeffords and Clay also spoke briefly, thanking everyone again and praising the compromise hammered out over the preceding months.

Soon the time came for Roukema to offer her amendment "in the nature of a substitute," an extensive rewrite that replaces the text at hand in its entirety. Roukema and Clay spoke in favor of the compromise, which then became the operative text for discussion and further amendment.

At that point the fireworks began. "The young men and women of this country deserve opportunity and fairness," said Armey. "Not repression and intrusion." Armey's objections to the bill had nothing to do with the details and everything to do with the principles of public and private prerogative. So he was no more interested in Roukema's package deal than he had been in Jeffords's the year before. But the best vehicle for discussing any part of a bill in markup is an amendment to change or delete that part, so Armey, Bartlett and their cohorts had brought amendments by the armful.

Armey wanted to amend Roukema's substitute to allow businesses to reduce other benefits to pay for family leave. The sponsors responded with the General Accounting Office numbers, first released the previous month at Dodd's Senate hearing, which showed the cost to business as minimal. But Armey noted that even the GAO had seen the potential for much higher costs (perhaps half again as high or more), depending on the definition of "serious illness." He cited other studies that pointed to costs other than health insurance, including recruitment and training costs and productivity losses difficult to quantify.

Bartlett offered a less direct challenge to the bill by attempting to extend it to workers employed by Congress. The House and Senate had regularly exempted themselves from labor laws they passed since the New Deal, claiming that enforcement of such laws would violate the separation of powers between the legislative and executive branches. Republicans had become increasingly hostile to this exemption in the 1980s, viewing it as another example of arrogance on the part of the Democratic majority (and another useful campaign theme). Hawkins declared Bartlett's amendment out of order, saying it was outside the committee's jurisdiction. He did agree, however, to seek a letter of permission from the Committee on House Administration so as to allow debate on the subject if HR 925 ever came to the floor.

(A letter was subsequently received from the Administration chairman, who said he would be happy to review House leave policies once the act was passed but that it was inappropriate to force such policies on the House by law. This was, of course, exactly what Hawkins had expected. It was also what the Republicans had anticipated, and in a later compilation of their arguments they noted that the House was reserving for itself exactly what every business should have, the freedom to review its own policies and not have anything forced on it by law.)

Armey, Bartlett and their allies continued sending amendments to the committee clerk as the afternoon wore on, and members looked anxiously at the wall clock. Some could be seen checking the index card on which members typically carry their daily schedule, tucked in a breast pocket or purse. No sooner had one amendment been voted down or ruled out of order than another took its place.

Some of the ideas, including one that would have exempted all elementary and secondary school teachers, were touching nerves among the committee members. Among the lobbyists in the committee room that day was Mike Resnick, the seasoned spokesman for the National School Boards Association. Resnick's organization was ready to mount a major offensive against the bill if teachers and other school personnel were to be covered. He carefully noted the votes as this exemption amendment, too, went down.

In the end, the Republicans in rebellion were able to force roll call votes on seven of their amendments. They lost on all seven, with the tally dividing more or less along party lines. Their one consistent convert on the other side of the dais was Timothy J. Penny, the youthful but gloomy Democrat from southeastern Minnesota. He had joined the committee in the previous Congress as a favor to the leadership and was more focused on his work on Agriculture and Veterans' Affairs. He had little in common with the urban, labor-oriented Democrats on Hawkins's committee and was increasingly at odds with them.

But while Penny cost the Democrats their unanimity, Jeffords and Roukema more than countered his impact on the total vote. And the margins by which the panel was stiff-arming Republican amendments clearly showed the Roukema substitute was on its way to approval. Markups may be brief or protracted. Complex money bills sometimes require many hours of markup, even lasting into the next morning or necessitating more than one meeting. On as simple and straightforward a matter as this one, once the pattern of votes has been established the members usually proceed to the foreseeable conclusion. But on this late fall afternoon, the spirit of noncooperation held sway. Three hours rolled by while Hawkins permitted the process to run its rancorous course. When a Democrat pleaded that the bill had been much watered down, a Republican observed that "even diluted poison can kill." And when Clay became impatient with what seemed to him obviously dilatory tactics, Republican Steve Gunderson of Wisconsin accused him of "creating a hostile attitude." Clay shot back that he had no objection to amendments as long as they were sincerely intended to improve the bill. But these amendment authors had made it clear "they don't want a compromise," Clay said, and "even if all their amendments are adopted they still wouldn't vote for it."

On the final votes, nineteen of the twenty Democrats favored adopting the Roukema substitute and reporting it favorably to the floor. They were joined by Jeffords and Roukema. Goodling, the committee's other swing voter, voted "present." Penny once again joined the Republicans in opposition, fixing the final tally at 21–11.

The inner circle of supporters went straight from the markup to a news conference with leaders of the supporting groups. Although they had carried only two Republican votes, they proudly declared a bipartisan triumph and spoke of floor action as if it were imminent. Motley of the National Federation of Independent Business, meanwhile, walked out of the Ed and Labor committee room with a smile on his face. By any immediate, objective measure, he had just been licked. But Motley knew the battle of perception had just begun, and he was prepared to sound upbeat. When approached by the first of several reporters in the Rayburn hallway, he predicted confidently that the bill would go no further than this markup. Family leave, he said, "has reached its high-water mark."

Motley may have been speaking for effect, but he also knew how to count votes; and, by his reckoning, floor consideration was still a long way away. On that November afternoon, Motley was not concerned about what the committees might do. He felt sure the bill was no candidate for quick consideration by the whole House. As far as he could tell, members were hearing next to nothing about family leave from their constituents. And at the same time Motley knew his own message was getting relayed to House and Senate offices by hundreds of small-scale business owners from coast to coast. He wished he could be inside the meeting of the House Democratic whip organization when family leave was first brought up that winter. He wished he could see the look on the sponsors' faces when they saw what a little NFIB homework could do.

THE PRESIDENTIAL ELECTION YEAR OF 1988 began with both hope and bewilderment for Dodd and the other sponsors of family leave. Dodd's seven hearings in 1987 had left him more convinced than ever that his bill was addressing a real need. Years later he recalled, with a certain satisfaction, that testimony from a group of mine workers who were forced to choose between their jobs and a chance to be with their children during leukemia treatments at a distant hospital had reduced even some at the press table to tears.

But as the 1988 session opened, Dodd looked out on a legislative situation that offered little real encouragement. Clay's companion bill in the House had been approved by Ed and Labor in November and would be approved by Post Office in February. But now, waiting its turn for floor consideration, it seemed to have gotten stuck. In the Senate, Dodd could create a sense of movement by holding a markup in his own subcommittee anytime he wanted. But doing so would prove little and advance the bill not at all. What Dodd really wanted was a markup by the full Labor and Human Resources Committee. Kennedy, as full committee chairman, was willing to schedule the bill, but neither he nor Dodd wanted to make that move until they were sure the committee action would be not only favorable but strongly so. It would not be enough to limp out of committee with a bare, partisan majority. They needed momentum.

But even after seven hearings in five cities, it was not clear that what Dodd called his "education process" was having the desired effect on the committee itself. None of the committee's GOP members attended the road show hearings, and Dodd was still hunting for his Republican partner. And while the seven Republicans on Senate Labor included two New Englanders, both moderate-to-liberal on social issues, he had yet to make headway with either (one was Lowell P. Weicker Jr., his colleague from Connecticut and the man who had taken the senior Dodd's seat in the Senate).

Dodd also assayed the committee's more conservative Republican members once again. But Hatch was still not interested, and Quayle, while willing to talk, was far from willing to commit.

Without at least one GOP backer, Dodd would need every one of the nine Democratic votes on Senate Labor or his bill would fail on a tie. And at the moment even some of the Democrats were not entirely on board. Howard Metzenbaum of Ohio liked the bill but thought it ought to apply to people who needed time off to care for a sick parent or a sick spouse. The House bill, unlike Dodd's, already applied to parents; but neither the House nor Senate sponsors had been willing to add the spousal provision yet. Dodd was not opposed to expanding the leave benefit to cover the illnesses of parents and spouses, but he feared doing so would make the bill look less like a protection for children. For the moment at least, he would keep his own version simpler and see how the broader approach fared in the House. He was content to address any differences between the House and Senate versions after both had been passed. At that point there would have to be a conference committee with members from both chambers.

This special panel, often referred to as the conference, would resolve differences between the bills and report back a single unified version to both chambers. This conference report would have to be approved by both chambers before it could be sent on for the president's signature.

Deliberations in conference sometimes matter as much as those in the House and Senate. Bills that differ significantly may require many weeks and extensive revision in conference. And although conferences are not supposed to initiate changes in the pending bills, in practice they often do. The landmark overhaul of the tax code in 1986 was largely written in conference by just two committee chairmen, Bob Packwood and Dan Rostenkowski, and their staffs.

While Dodd tried to drum up new support in the Senate, HR 925 had been slowed in the House. Committee action had been completed since February 1988 (when Post Office and Civil Service had once again approved the section dealing with federal employees). Now the baton had been passed to Tony Coelho, an ultra-ambitious Californian who had been elected the majority whip at the beginning of the 100th Congress. As the liaison between committees and the Democratic Caucus leaders, Coelho served as a kind of legislative midwife: organizing the Democratic floor votes, cajoling members to vote with the caucus and delivering accurate vote counts to the majority leader and the Speaker. Coelho also had excellent ties to almost every segment of the Democratic Party, including the feminist community. He declared himself a supporter of family leave but was cagey about a commitment to bring it to the floor.

Coelho appointed a "whip task force" headed by another Californian, Norman Mineta, a hint that floor consideration might be near. Such task forces count votes and apprise the leadership of a given bill's chances. Sometimes they find out what kinds of amendments might help or hurt the bill on the floor. Then, if the bill looks ready, the leadership can send it to Rules, set a time for floor action and activate the overall whip organization to firm up the vote.

That May the National Organization for Women managed to have 25,000 Mother's Day cards directed to members of Congress from around the nation, each urging action on family leave. But Mineta and his task force had been hearing from members who had yet to receive any mail or other contact on the bill that was not generated by an organization such as NOW. Quite a few of them saw family leave less as a progressive piece of legislation than as one more thankless labor issue that might cost them votes or contributions in what was, after all, an election year. House members expect tough votes now and then, but the leadership should not ask too often. Besides, what was the point, unless the Senate was going to act, too? Having surveyed the caucus, Mineta concluded that his colleagues "want to support the bill but don't want to vote on it."

So as summer neared, bringing long calendar interruptions for the two national political conventions, the House leadership had neither set a floor date nor slated an appearance for the bill before Rules (a stage that family leave had actually reached once before, despite the rush hour crush at the close of the last Congress). Dodd suspected the House leaders were taking one step forward and two back.

For his own part, Dodd was increasingly distracted by his work on Central America and on child care legislation. In the spring Dodd's staff director for Children and Families, Marsha Renwanz, had decamped for an anthropology research project in the Shetland Islands. After two years and two bills and seven hearings, family leave was not really moving in the Senate.

At this point in the spring of 1988 Dodd decided to promote a junior legislative aide he had recently hired away from a job in the House. His name was Rich Tarplin, and he was still in his late twenties when Dodd made him the new staff director for Children and Families. Among his first assignments on the job, Tarplin was to report back on how to move S 249 through committee before that year's session ended.

Tarplin embarked on several weeks of intense briefings on the bill, its particulars and its problems. He listened to Lenhoff and Feinstein, and to staff from the AFL-CIO, the National Council of Jewish Women and the Junior League. He listened to everyone he could find and read all the bills. And he concluded that family leave was going nowhere.

The problems posed by the various Democrats on Senate Labor were fixable. Dodd could, for example, give Metzenbaum every reason to think that elder and spousal care would be added to the package later on. But without at least one Republican, the bill was going to leave committee on a partisan 9–7 vote and command no special notice or respect in the queue of bills waiting for floor action in the final weeks of the session.

Tarplin went back to Dodd with a simple recommendation. The bill needed to be modified. There had to be one or two Republican votes for the bill in the markup, and if that meant making major renovations, so be it. There would be no family leave bill at all if S 249 remained in its current form with four months of parental leave and six months of medical leave, applying to all businesses with fifteen employees or more. Dodd listened and agreed. Within a few weeks, in consultation with House staff working on HR 925, Tarplin had delivered new specifications to the Senate Legislative Counsel and gotten back a new bill. On June 8, Dodd introduced the new bill, got a new number (S 2488) and held a news conference to announce what he called "a breakthrough."

The new Dodd bill was, not coincidentally, close to the compromise approved in Ed and Labor the previous fall. It allowed an identical ten weeks for family care and a slightly less generous thirteen weeks for employees' own medical leaves. But it applied to all businesses with twenty or more employees—giving it broader coverage than the amended HR 925.

The real news, though, was the emergence of two supporters on the Republican side of Senate Labor. One was Connecticut's Weicker, a natural target from the start, and the other was Robert Stafford of Vermont, a quiet and courteous Yankee serving his last months before retirement. Stafford's seat would soon belong to Jim Jeffords, who had been a confirmed friend of family leave in the House and who had been instrumental in winning Stafford over.

With Weicker and Stafford aboard, Dodd could go to a full committee markup the following month with eleven votes in the bag. But if he could lure one or two more, then so much the better. He kept trying to do that right up to the night before the committee met on July 14. Tarplin got an early call from Quayle on that morning. Dialing in from his car phone to reply to Dodd's late-night entreaty, Quayle said he would like to be "on the bill" but he had decided it just was not right for him. Dodd would think back to the call a month later, when Quayle was named as George Bush's running mate for the White House. Was Quayle aware he was on the short list in July? Had it been the wrong moment to ask him to cross the aisle on a high-profile issue?

The markup itself on July 14 was anticlimactic, as Dodd had already lined up the votes. But it was the first formal meeting of any kind that brought the issue out of the House and Senate office buildings and into the Capitol itself. The markup was held in a small Senate meeting room off the old Senate chamber (a smaller, domed space used by the full Senate until 1859). There, the members of the committee could escape the adversarial arrangement of the regular committee hearing room and face each other across a polished hardwood table. The Capitol meeting room was also a symbol of seriousness and movement toward the floor. And in terms of a bill's progress, such symbolism is anything but unimportant.

Although Dodd was in his eighth year as a senator and his fourteenth in Congress, he had never before gone to a Senate markup as the principal sponsor of the bill at issue. Tarplin, of course, was equally inexperienced at staffing a senator in such a position. The hallway outside the committee room was filled with milling lobbyists. Tarplin recognized faces of women he had met in recent months while learning the issue, women who were not pleased to see the weeks of leave being pared and pared again. He also saw faces he knew from the business lobby, faces unhappy that this markup was happening at all. As he entered the hallway with Dodd, he heard people calling to the senator. He also heard his own name called out. It may have been a reporter or a lobbyist trying to get his attention, but it was the urgency he found strange.

Then the senator and his young aide had slipped through the tall doors behind the uniformed Capitol guard and begun spreading their papers on the table. Kennedy arrived and sat at one end of the committee table, prepared to preside. Hatch sat to one side, with Thurmond beside him. Although technically only fourth ranking on Senate Labor, Thurmond was the most senior member in the Senate and sat where he pleased. Stafford was next, easing himself into a chair with some effort, and then Quayle, looking practically collegiate next to his two senior colleagues. Weicker, a large man whose manner of dress fell somewhere between preppy and unkempt, occupied the next chair on the Republican side. After him were the committee's most recently appointed GOP members: Thad Cochran of Mississippi, the first true wizard of Republican hegemony in that state; and Gordon Humphrey, a former airline pilot who had found a forum for his particularly astringent strain of conservatism in New Hampshire.

On the Democratic side, Kennedy and Dodd were joined by the spectral Claiborne Pell, a Newport blueblood who had won five Senate terms talking to the ethnic blue-collar workers of Rhode Island in the languages of their European roots. Then came the combative Metzenbaum, a parking lot magnate from Cleveland; and Spark Matsunaga, one of Hawaii's first statehood politicians. The table was filled out by Paul Simon, recently returned from his fling in the presidential primaries; Tom Harkin of Iowa, who would have his go at it in 1992; Brock Adams of Washington and Barbara Mikulski of Maryland.

In the moment when a Senate committee actually convenes, no senator or staff aide can ever feel entirely sure that he "has the votes." Things happen. Tarplin knew how restive some in the support coalition were, how perturbed at the seemingly endless rounds of compromise and retrenchment. Had any of the supporters bailed out and taken a senator with them? Would commitments be retracted in midmarkup?

Thurmond spoke up to say that a mandated benefit would "have a discriminatory impact on those it tries to help." He said employers faced with otherwise equal applicants would hire "the one that doesn't need the benefits." Some of the Republicans also raised a distinction between this new minimum labor standard and some of its famous precedents. Child labor laws and the Fair Labor Standards Act of the 1930s had been designed to help entire classes of workers. This new benefit, the unpaid leave with guaranteed reinstatement, would seem to aid primarily those who could afford time off without pay. As Quayle put the question to Dodd at the markup: "Is this for the yuppies? Are poor people going to take unpaid leave?"

Quayle was prepared to go further. He had brought along an amendment that essentially rewrote S 2488 to respond to his previously stated objections. It granted pregnant women or new mothers up to four months off, pointedly saying nothing about any of the other employee situations Dodd wanted to cover. In a sense, Quayle's substitute was reminiscent of the simple maternity leave bill Howard Berman had advocated back in 1985, which had always had a certain appeal.

Its appeal, however, was not enough to break Dodd's grip on this markup. Quayle got votes from only half the other Republicans (Hatch, Cochran and Humphrey) and was rebuffed 10–4. Tarplin was actually pleased to see the amendment offered. Quayle was, he noted later, "crossing a philosophical threshold" by suggesting any kind of mandated leave benefit at all. Years later Dodd would say, "I think Dan got it."

The committee did accept one amendment to the compromise bill. Weicker proposed that the definition of a son or daughter for purposes of the bill be expanded to include those older than eighteen who were incapable of self-care because of mental or physical disability. With little additional fuss, the committee was prepared to vote. To the great relief of both Dodd and Tarplin, the votes they had been promised came through. Only Hatch, Quayle, Thurmond and Humphrey voted against a favorable report, while Stafford and Weicker joined all nine Democrats in voting for the bill.

HAVING SURMOUNTED THE COMMITTEE hurdle that had once loomed so high, Dodd still had no guarantee of floor action. The House bill, after all, had been stalled since the winter with no prospect of a floor date. And for legislative purposes, the 100th Congress in July 1988 was already into its waning weeks. Recess would swallow nearly all the remainder of the summer, and the fall session would be abbreviated so members could go home to get reelected.

But if political considerations were quickly consuming the calendar, the looming election might also be used to the opposite effect—as a goad to make the Senate act with uncharacteristic speed.

6.

Hitting the Wall

CONGRESS OFTEN ACTS AS THE CENTER of its own universe, regarding the other branches, agencies and levels of government as a grand system of satellites. But every four years, in the weeks that follow the national nominating conventions, the presidential campaigns exert a special gravitational pull of their own. Congress feels the tug as these glamorous campaigns are conducted nightly on the network news. Some issues benefit from the heightened exposure, others suffer. For family leave, the dynamics of the 1988 presidential race were a boost in the Senate and a millstone in the House.

In the Senate, campaign considerations powered family leave all the way to the floor in the early autumn of 1988 and forced Republicans into a filibuster to stop it. But in the House, the reelection fears of moderate and conservative Democrats, many of them uncomfortable with Democratic presidential nominee Michael S. Dukakis, helped shelve family leave for yet another year.

Just four days after Dodd's bill (S 2488) was marked up in Senate Labor in July 1988, the Democratic Party convened in Atlanta to nominate Governor Dukakis of Massachusetts for president. Dodd had been an early Dukakis supporter, finding it easy to endorse another liberal from a neighboring state. Dukakis was also an enthusiastic supporter of Dodd's causes in the Senate, including Central America, child care and family leave. Dukakis had even shown up for the hearing when Dodd brought his family leave road show to Boston in 1987.

Dodd had made contact with the Dukakis campaign weeks earlier, not long after introducing his June compromise. Tarplin had been dispatched to Boston to meet with Dukakis's issues director and other staff, pressing the case for featuring family leave in the fall campaign. The 1988 Democratic Party platform, drafted under the tutelage of party officials and Dukakis aides, was a relatively brief and thematic document. Yet it found room to mention family leave in its early paragraphs (asserting that "worker productivity is enhanced by . . . family leave policies that no longer force employees to choose between their jobs and their children or ailing parents"). In Atlanta, Tarplin met again with Dukakis staff and talked about having Dodd campaign with the nominee to highlight the family issues—both family leave and the child care bill Dodd had also introduced in the 100th Congress. But what the Dukakis staff wanted most was to have Dodd and the Democratic leaders in the Senate open a "second front" in the Senate itself in September.

They hoped to see majority leader Robert C. Byrd and the committee chairmen bring several hot-button bills to the floor for debate, even if they were far from ripe for passage or sure to be vetoed if passed. They had in mind not only child care and family leave but also a 36 percent increase in the minimum wage and a bill to require notice of toxic risks in the workplace. That way the news from Washington would resonate with the themes Dukakis would be thumping on the stump. Bush could be pressured to choose sides. If he were president, would he veto higher wages? Safer workplaces? Day care? Time off for new moms?

As it happened, Byrd was going to have plenty of floor time on his hands that September, a circumstance that was also partly attributable to presidential politics. Since the Democrats had taken over the Senate, Reagan had escalated his complaints about the congressional spending process, so that year leaders in both chambers were determined to handle the annual appropriations bills strictly according to Hoyle: They would consider and pass each of the thirteen categorical spending bills separately and on time, which meant finishing by October 1. By doing so, they would abandon the recent practice of bundling several different appropriations bills into a single, massive "continuing resolution" and daring the president to veto it—a maneuver that meant Reagan could not spike any specific expenditure without shutting down wide sectors of the government.

Rolling everything into the "CR" was an obvious abuse and an invitation to Republican attack. But the good government approach took a good deal of time. Every appropriations bill passed by the Senate had to be reconciled with its counterpart from the House. When House-Senate conference committees sat down to work out the conflicts, they sometimes sat for weeks; subgroups of negotiators, some as small as two members, would haggle for hours in secluded basement rooms of the Capitol and its surrounding office buildings, carefully avoiding the interested inquiries of lobbyists and journalists. Even without such distractions, the process was taking so long that the Senate would reconvene after Labor Day with little to do but wait for the conference committees to report. So, to fill the time as profitably as possible, Byrd was glad to accommodate Dukakis and to bedevil the Republicans with a series of bills the Democrats saw as ballot-box winners.

Meanwhile, Bush had told his August nominating convention in New Orleans that he wanted to be a "kinder, gentler" president. The broad theme was sharpened somewhat when Bush subsequently told a meeting of women in Rockford, Illinois, that he saw no reason a woman who had a baby should have to lose her job. In this remark, supporters of family leave perceived—or wanted to perceive—a subtle break from Reagan, who had opposed the bill upon its first introduction and largely ignored it ever since. By bringing family leave to the floor for an extended debate that would capture media attention, the Democrats hoped to corner the vice president. Would he sign a family leave measure or not? Would he stick to Reagan's hard line or be "kinder, gentler" after all?

There was nothing unusual about this strategy in an election year. With Reagan retiring, the majority party in Congress sensed it had a shot at winning back the White House. In the 100th Congress, Senate Democrats in particular had felt themselves uncomfortably wedged between the House, with its aggressive new Speaker, and the White House, where Reagan's declining force had created a kind of vacuum. Throughout the year the Iran-Contra scandal had droned on through hearings and court proceedings that degraded the investigated but produced no heroes among the investigators.

And if Byrd's September strategy was baldly partisan, it was also much in keeping with the mood of the Senate in that era. Some of the Senate's inclement weather could be blamed on the Bobs—Byrd and Dole—and the deterioration in their relations over the four years they had been the chamber's rival chieftains. In the first two years, Dole had the votes and the upper hand. Sometimes he pushed harder than Byrd, the traditionalist, could countenance, allowing, in one case, some dubious confusion over the whereabouts of a bill's official copy to impede consideration of the bill. When Byrd denounced him for such tactics, Dole fired back that he "did not become majority leader in order to lose." Byrd, in high dudgeon on another occasion, warned Dole that "the worm will turn."

It turned, of course, in January 1987, when the Democrats became the majority. But when the two Bobs reversed their roles of majority and minority leader, their relationship changed little. If Dole's dogged and lawyerly insistence nettled Byrd at times, the Democrat's sanctimony and pedantry were often too much for Dole. Yet when they clashed, it was less a conflict of personalities than of institutional roles being played to the hilt. Each was less a creature of ideology than of partisanship, defined and delimited by his party's history and geography. And each clung to his own credentials as an underdog and an overachiever, a poor boy risen above adversity by dint of hard work and determination.

Byrd had been an orphan, raised by relatives in the coal patch of West Virginia. Although he graduated first in his high school class, it took a decade before he could attend college. The only degree he ever earned was a 1963 law degree for which he studied at night during his first term in the Senate. Byrd was still studying at night in his seventies, plowing through the Bible, Shakespeare and the unabridged dictionary—each one over and over.

The young Byrd had once belonged to the Ku Klux Klan and the middle-aged Byrd had delivered one of the longest speeches of the 1964 Senate filibuster against the Civil Rights Act. But when the majority of the Senate moved toward more liberal attitudes, Byrd moved with it. He had been a hawk on Vietnam, but by the 1980s he had become a major opponent of foreign intervention and military adventurism. Throughout, Byrd earned his repeated reelection as leader by staying out of the policy spotlight and performing countless favors for colleagues behind the scenes, catering to their amendment needs, scheduling wants and even occasional whims. He was a source of discomfort for some of the younger Democrats, who tended to be more liberal or more media-conscious. But in a chamber where members cherish their standing as official equals, Byrd offered just the right blend of deference, service and parliamentary guile to suit most of his colleagues.

Dole, too, was steeped in his humble origins. His family had been so hard-pressed in Depression-era Kansas that they once lived in their own basement while renting out the rest of their home to oilfield roughnecks. Gifted as an athlete, Dole had gone to the University of Kansas on scholarship in 1941 and excelled in track. But World War II took him to Italy, and in the final days of fighting he was severely wounded. He spent the next several years in a succession of Veterans Administration hospitals, undergoing more than two dozen reconstructive operations that left him without the use of his right arm. He habitually carried a pen clutched in his right fist to deflect proffered handshakes.

Dole and Byrd both entered politics in the early 1950s, each in a part of the world where one party routinely won all the elections. Each joined the dominant party and got elected to the state legislature before going to the House and on to the Senate (each on his first try). Neither had a serious reelection challenge thereafter. Dole sought national office unsuccessfully three times (in 1976, 1980 and 1988). The most painful setback came in 1988, when he won the Iowa caucuses and briefly seemed bound for glory. But he had stumbled as the front-runner in New Hampshire, then scotched any hope of recovery by angrily denouncing George Bush as a liar the same night on national TV.

Six months later the Republican Party would toast Bush as its nominee in New Orleans, nominate Quayle for vice president and send Dole back to Washington to be in charge of Bush's political rear guard. If it seemed a bitter task at the time, Dole would prove more than equal to it.

THE DEMOCRATS' FALL OFFENSIVE IN the Senate began on September 15, with Byrd calling up the minimum wage bill. In the Senate, the majority leader does not order a calendar item into play by fiat, as the majority leadership does in the House. Instead, the leader proposes it, making a motion that the Senate proceed to its consideration. The motion to proceed is fully debatable and often contested. In recent years outnumbered opponents of a bill who want to stop it by filibustering have typically chosen to do so on this "motion to proceed." This tactic, when successful, technically prevents the bill from coming up at all. Senators may discuss the merits of an issue for days as the filibuster continues; but if the motion to proceed ultimately fails the subject has never formally been considered.

With the minimum wage bill, however, the Republicans chose a less direct means of resistance. Bush was fully aware of the Democratic strategy, and he and his campaign staff decided to give ground in the first round. Bush indicated he could accept some kind of increase in the base wage if it was balanced by a new, temporary "training wage." Two days before Byrd called up the bill, the White House announced that President Reagan might also consider such a compromise. No deal had yet been reached, nor did any seem probable. But the Reagan-Bush posture allowed Dole and his GOP troops to vote for the motion to proceed and present themselves as prepared to do business. The motion passed 87–7.

Soon enough, however, the Democrats balked at the training wage deal, as Dole had known they would: Organized labor was unalterably opposed to the concept. So days passed while senators gave speeches for and against the bill. Byrd and Kennedy, the floor manager for the bill, tried to get Dole to negotiate a time agreement limiting further speeches and amendments to the bill. This is the standard procedure by which the Senate leaders haggle out a daily schedule. But on this matter Dole remained aloof, alluding to issues still to be elucidated and amendments yet to be offered. So the debate went on. From time to time the Senate would, by unanimous consent, shelve the wage bill temporarily so as to consider a nomination or an appropriations conference report. But the bill always remained the underlying, pending business. And behind the scenes, in the hallways and in the leaders' offices, negotiations between floor leaders, senior committee members and other senators rambled on into a second week. No one needed to use the word "filibuster," as anyone could see what was happening.

Few words bespeak the special culture of the Senate so well as "filibuster." In Spanish, a *filibustero* (derived from the Dutch word V*rijbuiter*, "freebooter") was once a free-ranging mercenary who traveled places to foment rebellion. The word appeared in the Congress of the 1850s as a metaphor likening one particular prolonged debate to an insurrection. Although first used in the House, the word found a permanent home in the Senate, where the rules permitted unlimited debate.

The first limits on Senate debate did not arrive until 1917, when a filibuster prevented the arming of ships crossing the U-boat–infested Atlantic. That moved the Senate to adopt Rule XXII, which provided for a two-thirds vote of the whole Senate to cut off debate. This new limitation, known as cloture, required all subsequent amendments to be germane (the Senate usually does not demand that amendments be relevant to the bill at hand) and restricted ensuing debate on the bill and all amendments to one hour for each senator.

It took another forty-two years, until 1959, before the Senate was able to amend Rule XXII so that cloture could be invoked by two-thirds of those present and voting. Then in 1975 the Senate lowered the threshold of cloture to three-fifths of the whole Senate (or sixty votes). In 1986, the year the Senate opened its doors to TV coverage via C-SPAN, Rule XXII was further amended to allow only thirty hours of postcloture debate (with each senator to be recognized for up to one hour on a first-come-first-served basis).

The idea behind these reforms was to diminish the filibuster as a feature of Senate life. But reforms tend to have unintended consequences. And when the filibuster lost some of its portent and potency, senators became less reluctant to use it. No longer a kind of nuclear weapon, to be used only *in extremis*, the filibuster gradually became a conventional tactic—part of any senator's standard arsenal. Once it would have been unthinkable for Republicans to filibuster a minimum wage bill, but by 1988 it could be done almost casually. And Byrd, with a correspondingly routine air, filed a cloture petition almost immediately after consideration of the bill began.

A cloture petition requires the signature of sixteen senators and a cloture vote must be taken one hour after the Senate convenes on the second day after the petition is filed. Thus, a prudent leader may wish to file multiple cloture petitions so as to be able to hold cloture votes day after day if need be. (Some senators will never vote for cloture until a bill has been on the floor for at least a week or two.)

As debate on the minimum wage bill entered its second week in September 1988, Byrd filed several petitions for cloture. The closest Byrd came to cloture was fifty-six votes, so he withdrew the bill from consideration. The Republicans had managed to block the bill even while positioning their presidential nominee as reasonable and accommodating. Round One of the confrontation had gone to the GOP.

Next up would be family leave.

ON THE SAME MONDAY AFTERNOON when Byrd "took down" the minimum wage bill, he offered a motion to proceed to Dodd's S 2488. Dodd was ready. Byrd had called him the previous week to ask whether Dodd was prepared to take family leave to the floor.

Dodd had then phoned Tarplin to tell him the news. Family leave was not only going to be included in the party's autumn blitz, it was going to be in the vanguard. Get ready, Dodd had said, we are going to the floor Monday or Tuesday. Tarplin had never gone to the floor to staff a senator who was managing a major bill in debate before. For that matter, Dodd, having served nearly all his years in the minority, had never been the floor manager for a major Senate bill before. Tarplin went to Byrd's floor staff for advice. They were helpful, but they were preoccupied with finding votes for cloture on the minimum wage. It seemed that the rookies would be largely on their own.

With the help of the Senate majority whip, Alan Cranston of California, Dodd put together his first vote count on family leave. The whip, the number-two person in the party hierarchy, maintains near-constant contact with his colleagues, sounding them out on all issues likely to reach the floor, including bills and major amendments. Senators can be evasive, if not downright deceptive, and the accuracy of Cranston's counts depended on hearing what his colleagues meant—not just what they said. After two decades in the Senate, Cranston could read most of his colleagues and their intentions before speaking to them.

Starting with the nine Democrats and two Republicans who had voted for S 2488 in committee, Dodd slowly made his way down the two party lists. When he got to the bottom, he had counted just over forty votes for his bill. He did not even have a plurality for passage, let alone anything like the sixty votes he would need for cloture. He was losing a handful of Democrats—including both senators from Alabama and one each from Louisiana, Oklahoma and Montana. Against these likely defections, Dodd could counter only a few Republicans who were willing to buck the business lobby—not to mention the White House and Dole—on the issue.

Once again, Dodd became convinced he needed to make a move to build momentum. An emergency meeting of the family leave coalition's strategy committee was called over the weekend of September 24–25. Tarplin communicated the situation to the assembled representatives. The bill was going to come to the floor. It was the first time it had come so far in either chamber. Clearly, this was a signal moment for family leave. But bringing the bill to the floor would probably not mean passage that year because there would not be enough votes for cloture. Of course, even a defeat might be useful, if the bill at least got enough votes to look like a future winner. Besides, Tarplin added, the debate in the Senate would help Dukakis make a national issue of family leave and perhaps contribute to his election. There was great enthusiasm for this prospect among the coalition representatives, nearly all of whom were Dukakis supporters. The presidential campaign was young and hopes ran high.

But then Tarplin told them the bad news. To make a political success of this trip to the floor, it would be necessary to amend the bill and render it more acceptable to business. Otherwise, there would be a chance of a bad defeat—a cloture vote so weak that the bill itself looked like a loser. The spirit of the meeting changed. The women in the room wanted to know how much the bill would be changed. They wanted to know who was going to decide how and when to change it. Tarplin listened and tried to assure them that Dodd would not go too far. But he also let them know it had to be Dodd's call.

The bill reported by Senate Labor had provided for ten weeks for child care and thirteen weeks for an employee's own illness, and had applied to businesses with twenty or more employees. Tarplin could plausibly argue that this was a stronger bill than House Ed and Labor had approved in 1987 because it applied to more businesses. But in discussing the point with the coalition, he could see that the women's groups, the originators of the campaign for family leave, felt the bill's integrity was threatened by the continuing reduction in the leave length. There seemed to be less anxiety about the precise size of the businesses to be exempted. After considerable debate and amidst great apprehension, Tarplin went back to his office for another redrafting session.

On Monday, September 26, Dodd and Tarplin were finalizing the details of the amendment they would offer to their own bill on the following day. The length of the leave for an employee's own illness would be trimmed from thirteen weeks to ten (the period allowed for child care). But the big move would come in the small-business exemption. Dodd proposed that his threshold of twenty employees be raised all the way to fifty employees, matching the House bill (but not adopting that bill's subsequent reduction to thirty-five). This meant that instead of covering 47 percent (or nearly half) of all the workers in the country, the family leave benefit would be extended to just 39 percent. But it did enable Dodd to claim that the overall cost of the bill to American business would be lowered to less than $150 million. This was intended to melt the resistance from moderate Republicans and Democrats who wanted something to tell small-business lobbyists such as Motley and Tavenner.

Dodd had also been considering removing the parental care provision he had recently agreed to add to S 2488, a provision he had always thought risky. But when this idea reached the American Association of Retired Persons, a relatively recent addition to the list of supporting organizations, it produced a sudden and sharp reaction. Michelle Pollak, the AARP lawyer-lobbyist on the bill, told Tarplin the AARP would immediately leave the coalition and vocally oppose the bill if elder care were removed. Elder care stayed.

Even so, the compromise Dodd brought to the floor on September 27 was enough to strain the coalition's cohesion. The length of the leave, a key element for the women's groups from the beginning, had now been slashed to less than half of the twenty-six weeks initially proposed. The leave period had even dropped below the twelve-week minimum prescribed by the American Academy of Pediatrics. Moreover, the decision to exempt more than 90 percent of all businesses seemed to marginalize the entire endeavor. These objections on substance were compounded by supporters' painful sense that they had lost whatever control—or even influence—they once had over the process. And it seemed especially frustrating because the concessions Dodd made on just the second day of floor consideration had brought no concessions from the other side— and few if any new friends. "We were negotiating with ourselves," said Pollak. "We were compromising with no one but ourselves."

Despite the concessions Dodd still found the status of his bill on the floor ambiguous at best. He counted now nearly fifty votes for passage and perhaps a few more for cloture. But while this represented progress, he had hoped for a more dramatic altering of allegiances. It did not help that the same day Dodd had offered this amendment on the floor, the Reagan White House had issued a formal, written threat to veto the bill if passed. Again, as with minimum wage, the White House allowed a glimmer of willingness to negotiate. If the bill would grant a business certain incentives to make leave benefits available—with no mandate— then the president would be interested.

Dodd and his staff looked over the president's letter in a hallway out-side the Senate chamber that Tuesday and read it carefully again back in the office that night. It did not really propose a compromise. The essence of the bill was the setting of a new minimum labor standard, patterned on child labor restrictions in the Fair Labor Standards Act of the 1930s. To set that standard was to impose a mandate. Surely the White House had realized this before saying it could consider a compromise, so per-haps some sort of terms might be reached. Was there a glimpse of day-light? In the end, Tarplin could not see one, and neither could Dodd. No other feelers were received from the Republican side.

It was time for a new strategy, and once again Dodd conjured up a bold one. On Wednesday, only the third day of consideration, Dodd agreed to combine S 2488 with another piece of pending legislation that would increase the penalties for producing or selling child pornography. The family leave coalition was aghast. The coalition members may have had mixed feelings about the "kiddie porn" bill itself, but virtually all regarded it as an item in the agenda of conservative Republicans (espe-cially those they viewed as "the religious right"). Its principal sponsor was Strom Thurmond, the senior senator from South Carolina who had led the fight against the family leave bill in committee just two months ear-lier. But Dodd saw a chance to win over a few more Republicans who might have liked a convenient excuse to vote for family leave. And if the mission seemed far-fetched, it apparently made sense to the Senate: Thurmond's motion attaching his bill to Dodd's was agreed to by a vote of 97–0.

But before the political value of that odd coupling could be truly tested, it was overtaken by a successor strategy. Byrd moved on Thursday to send S 2488 back to committee with instructions to combine it with yet another separate piece of legislation: Dodd's own child care bill, which had been marked up following the Democratic convention in July. Formally titled the Act for Better Child Care and informally known as the ABC bill, it was to provide $2.5 billion to subsidize day care centers directly or give day care vouchers to poor families with preschool children.

But the voice vote by which Kennedy and Hatch reported the ABC bill out of Senate Labor had concealed real divisions between the parties over the amount of money to be spent, the standards to be set and the use of federal funds for centers located in churches. Many Republicans were not happy with the ABC bill, and many Democrats were not satisfied with it yet either. Moreover, Bush himself had come out with a tax-credit plan just weeks before to help poor families pay for child care. With all these loose ends hanging, the ABC bill was far from ripe for the floor. But it was also plain that Byrd's and Dodd's real objective was not to focus on child care so much as it was to force a vote on family leave. Otherwise, the Republicans would continue debating the issue until the Senate adjourned or turned to other bills—just as they had talked the minimum wage bill into oblivion the previous week.

The GOP leadership, meanwhile, had become exasperated with the Democrats' parade of sweet-sounding legislation, all of it coming to the floor without sufficient support to pass. "This is solely a ploy to play games, to embarrass George Bush," said GOP Senate whip Alan Simpson of Wyoming, a personal as well as political friend of the party's nominee. "If they are good bills, you do them normally. You don't trot them up with just hours to go and pretend the nation's future is at stake." Simpson said the Democrats wanted only to see the Republicans "painted as slavering poops who do not like child care or parental leave."

The Connecticut senator had huddled three demonstrably popular ideas under one umbrella, but with the GOP leadership holding firm the Senate seemed prepared to turn its back on all three. Dodd was having his moments on the floor and impressing his colleagues with his commitment to family leave. But his efforts to reshape the bill itself, as well as his willingness to see the bill wedded to unrelated legislation, seemed to be buying him more grief than gain. The embrace of Thurmond had given pause to some of the liberals who were Dodd's support base. The addition of child care had brought with it all the rivalries and conflicts inherent in that related issue. Just as bad, the grafting on of child care had revived the issue of cost: $2.5 billion that would have to be paid by the taxpayer.

Dodd had spent many hours wrangling with business people and colleagues who still had the Chamber of Commerce's various billion-dollar estimates in their minds with respect to family leave. Now, after arguing that his bill would cost only $500 million—and then, following all the downsizing revisions, less than $150 million—Dodd found himself talking about billions again. The opponents of both bills could not have been more delighted, and the family leave support coalition could not have been more distressed.

It was now Friday, September 30. Senators were coming by the floor occasionally, voting now and then on other legislation when necessary and listening for a minute or two to their colleagues' comments on family leave, kiddie porn and child care. Only five weeks and three days remained before Election Day, and many senators would be on the November ballot. But even those who were not desperate to get back home and campaign at that moment were tired of the tactics on both sides. With canny timing, Dole tried on that Friday to push parental leave off the stage: He moved for a postponement of its further consideration until October 6. Although less than a week, the delay sounded fatal. Byrd immediately moved to table Dole's motion and was supported by a vote of 52–42, divided predictably along partisan lines. The issue at hand was still Byrd's motion to recommit the bill to Senate Labor (with instructions that child care be added). Debate on that motion continued until the Senate quit for the weekend.

On the following Monday, October 3, Dole switched his tack and allowed that he might just bend to Byrd's breeze. He told his colleagues to vote for Byrd's motion to recommit rather than let the political trap be sprung on them. "I do not want tomorrow's headlines, written by the liberal media that cover this place, to report that Republicans are frustrating . . . child care legislation or . . . parental leave," he said. So, suddenly, all but a half dozen Republicans joined the Democrats in voting for cloture on Byrd's earlier motion to recommit family leave to committee.

With cloture invoked, thirty additional hours were available for those who wanted to debate the matter further before the actual vote on re-commital of the bill. Not all thirty were spoken for, and the leaders were able to expedite the next vote on Wednesday the fifth. As the outcome was now not in doubt, the vote was taken by voice. Only one senator was clearly audible when the presiding officer called for nay votes. Ironically, it was Dole. Having given the green light for the bill to return to committee, he also took the opportunity to signal his continuing opposition to the entire procedure.

On Friday the seventh, the committee sent S 2488 back with the ABC bill attached as instructed. But because the bill had been off the floor, Byrd needed to make a fresh motion to proceed. Knowing this, and knowing that the Republicans could filibuster that motion, Byrd had already filed a cloture petition on Wednesday that would ripen on Friday. The Republicans had, by that time, already filed several amendments with which they might delay S 2488 when it returned.

Dodd was desperately seeking votes for cloture and Republicans were filing amendments by the stack. Don Nickles of Oklahoma produced eight germane amendments and one on limiting the size of campaign contributions from political action committees. John Danforth of Missouri produced three amendments all intended to exempt schools from S 2488. Steve Symms of Idaho weighed in with nine amendments. On Friday, October 7, the amendment cataract kept flowing. Thad Cochran of Mississippi, who had battled family leave in committee earlier that summer and filed two amendments earlier that week, presented the Senate clerk with no fewer than thirty-five separate amendments to S 2488.

But in the end, all this ammunition would prove unnecessary. On that Friday morning Dodd arrived on the floor knowing he was well short of the sixty votes for cloture. He was not even as close as Kennedy had been when the minimum wage war had reached the same point. The Senate was debating a technical tax corrections bill until the moment of the vote. Dodd made his way around the floor and in and out of the cloakroom, talking to other senators in both parties. He had five Republicans: his original cosponsor Specter, Stafford and Weicker from the committee, and two other northern moderates: John Chafee of Rhode Island and David Durenberger of Minnesota. But there were eight Democrats outside the fold. And after a final pass at several of them, Dodd knew he was done.

The cloture motion got just fifty votes, fewer even than Dodd had thought he could get a week earlier. They were ten votes short, and falling that far from the mark seemed to cost Byrd his stomach for the fight. The Democratic leader "took the bill down," foreclosing further consideration on the floor. It was dead. Dole took the floor for a brief postmortem, suppressing the urge to gloat and carefully stressing his party's interest in the human needs in question. "We've said, 'Slow down,'" said Dole. "These are not urgent measures that have to be passed in the 100th Congress." In the end, all that would survive of Byrd's legislative onslaught would be Thurmond's antiporn bill. After going down with family leave, the porn provisions were revived and passed with another unrelated bill the following week—just before the 100th Congress adjourned for good.

"I had always thought a lot of Bob Dole," said Tavenner after the filibuster fight ended. "But in those two weeks I learned how smart he really was."

Dodd and Tarplin were exhausted following the two weeks of floor confrontation, but they could not help feeling they had done pretty well. They had brought the issue to national attention as never before. And they felt they had built a base on which a filibuster-proof and veto-proof majority might be erected. After all, the votes for cloture may never have been available under any compromise. Nearly all the Republican senators were fixed in opposition to family leave that fall, if only to spare Reagan (and Bush) from an ill-timed and unpopular veto. But the financial cost of the legislation helped Republicans explain their position in more palatable terms to constituents inclined to favor family leave. And if that relieved some of the pressure Dodd had hoped he was bringing to bear, his efforts were backfiring. The Republicans were also doing well in communicating their view of the month's events through the media.

In the end, however, the Democratic strategy of using family leave as poisoned veto bait faltered for another reason. To force the White House into a veto decision, Congress would have to do more than raise the issue. It had to "get a bill," which is Hill jargon for pushing a piece of legislation all the way through both chambers, through the House-Senate conference and onto the president's desk. Even if Byrd and Dodd had succeeded in stifling Senate debate, the bill had no visible prospects of a floor vote in the House. And that fact, in turn, made the Senate all the tougher for Byrd and Dodd.

THE HOUSE COMMITTEES HAD, OF COURSE, long since finished their work on HR 925. Ed and Labor had done its part when it marked up the Roukema-flavored compromise in the previous November, and Post Office had followed suit in February. The full report from both committees had been available since early March. But after the whip task force headed by Norman Mineta of California had brought in its dour assessment of the bill's chances for passage, the House Democratic leaders had moved on to other matters.

Even after Senate Labor had approved the bill in July, Wright and Coelho continued to look the other way in the House. Mineta's conversations with members had found too many of them unconvinced of the political value of family leave and, at the same time, anxious over the antibusiness feel of the bill. These middle-of-the-road Democrats knew that one of their own, Tim Penny of Minnesota, had stubbornly resisted the bill in Ed and Labor. Beyond casting the one Democratic vote against HR 925 in committee, Penny had campaigned against the bill in 1988. When the office workers' group Nine to Five circulated a cost study based on states with family leave statutes of their own, Penny joined with several Ed and Labor Republicans in a "Dear Colleague" letter rebutting the claims.

The presidential election dynamic was alive in the House, but it worked against the bill as much as for it. If Dodd was comfortable with Dukakis, many House Democrats were not. Southern and midwestern members, many of them affiliated with the Democratic Leadership Council, had preferred another candidate in the primaries and feared Dukakis was positioning the party too far to the left, especially on social and cultural questions. When Dukakis made forays into the Deep South, he had trouble finding House members or congressional candidates willing to appear with him. In Mississippi, Democratic House candidate Mike Parker actually bought TV time to declare that he had never endorsed Dukakis for president. So the more family leave seemed a Dukakis issue, the less allure it had for the forty or fifty House members who made the difference between a toss-up vote and a healthy (even vetoproof) majority on the floor.

Wright and Coelho would compile a remarkable record of success on the floor of the 100th Congress. By their own count, they never lost a contested roll-call vote on which they had whipped their rank and file. But to win that often, any leadership team must be selective in picking its fights. And while Coelho had more personal enthusiasm for family leave than others in leadership, he recommended that supporters wait until the next Congress. Wait until we have both chambers and the White House, he said. Then we'll need only 51 in the Senate and 218 in the House (a majority of the 435 voting members) to get a bill.

But even as House Democrats were deciding to put off family leave in the late summer of 1988, the NFIB was mobilizing to make doubly sure the bill would die with the 100th Congress. Tens of thousands of NFIB members got letters from Motley urging them to write their congressman immediately and block consideration of HR 925.

The letters were customized for each congressional district. So small-business owners in the 15th District of California, for example, were informed that their congressman, Tony Coelho, was "the driving force behind efforts to enact mandatory leave." Motley warned that business owners should not be fooled by the small-business exemption in HR 925. "That's only temporary," he assured them, adding that the sponsors' "stated aim" was "paid leave for all employees" and that Coelho himself was "pushing hard to schedule HR 925 and pass it."

In Mineta's district, business owners received nearly identical letters fingering Mineta as "the driving force" who was "pushing hard to schedule HR 925"—a special irony given that Mineta's discouraging words had been largely responsible for shelving HR 925. Copies of the letter deluged scores of other districts, each identifying the local congressman as the "driving force."

On September 15, when it was clear the bill would not even go to Rules, Motley wrote to thirty-two House members (including Penny and a dozen other Democrats) warmly thanking them for the letter they had collectively sent to Speaker Jim Wright, asking him not to schedule family leave for the floor that year. "With your help," wrote Motley, "we will achieve that goal."

Some of those who worked the family leave issue through four or even five separate Congresses would remember the fall of 1988 as their lowest point. Fred Feinstein recalled watching Congress go home that fall having failed to get a straight floor vote on the merits of the bill for the second time. He thought back to the first meetings in 1985 and wondered how long members could continue to push the issue and how long the coalition could sustain itself. Some in the news media seemed to have lost interest in the issue after the committee process and floor amendments. They saw it as a hollow bill, compromised so often that it had lost its core.

What hope the backers of family leave could muster in that October rested on one of two equally slender reeds. One was that Dukakis would win the White House. The other was that George Bush would prove far friendlier to the concept of family leave as president than he had been as Reagan's vice president.

Part Three

"So Near, and Yet":
The 101st Congress
(1989–1990)

7.

New Beginnings

GEORGE BUSH WAS SWORN IN AS THE forty-first president on January 20, 1989, a day of intermittent clouds and middling temperatures. The inaugural ceremony was held outdoors on the Capitol's historic West Front, which had recently shed the scaffolding from a two-year restoration project on the original exterior walls.

Arrayed between the presidential podium and the fresh walls of the Capitol itself were ranks of chairs for the members of Congress and other grandees. Seated at the front were the Supreme Court and the senior heads of the legislative branch, including Speaker of the House Jim Wright and Senate majority leader George J. Mitchell. Wright was about to begin his second Congress as Speaker. Mitchell had been elected a month earlier by his party colleagues to succeed Robert C. Byrd, who had voluntarily stepped aside at the end of the 100th Congress. Bush, in his inaugural address, made a prominent point of offering to work with Congress. He even turned to that first row and gestured with his right hand. Wright beamed back with his wide Texas grin, Mitchell offered the more measured smile of a Mainer.

A few feet back in a row reserved for senators, Dodd found some encouragement in the tenor of Bush's speech. Dodd wanted to move quickly on several fronts in 1989, and he would need White House cooperation if he was to succeed. He hoped the first post-Reagan administration would be willing to negotiate with Hill Democrats on Central America, federal aid to child care and family leave. And he hoped to be among the major actors on all three fronts.

A few rows farther back, among the House Republicans, Marge Roukema watched the proceedings with a sense of impending fulfillment. She believed that once Bush occupied the Oval Office in his own right, he would find it in his interest to make deals with the Hill on a variety of issues, family leave among them. And surely this would be accomplished through sympathetic and well-placed congressional Republicans such as herself.

In the new Congress, the 101st, Roukema would be a full-fledged cosponsor of family leave from the outset, receiving equal billing with Bill Clay and Pat Schroeder. And, having added the care of sick children and parents to the bill in the 100th Congress, she would press now for the addition of spouses. By generalizing the coverage, Roukema hoped to build an even broader coalition of support for the bill. If she could not sell her fellow Republicans on family leave as policy, she would make it irresistible to them politically. In time, she believed, there would be sixty to seventy Republican votes for family leave. And when that happened, Bush would know he had no choice but to sign the bill.

A similarly sanguine attitude prevailed among family leave advocates in general, despite the disappointments of 1988. The bill would once again be in the hopper early, and this time it would have 136 cosponsors in the House, including more than a dozen Republicans. In committee, its prospects looked more promising than ever. Clay was fully engaged as chairman of the Labor-Management Relations Subcommittee of the Ed and Labor Committee, and Bill Ford was increasingly interested as chairman of Post Office and Civil Service. On the Senate side, Dodd was prepared to reintroduce family leave with nineteen cosponsors, and together with Kennedy he had the Senate Labor and Human Resources Committee under control.

The House and Senate bills were both introduced on February 2, 1989, with the House and Senate cosponsors holding a joint press conference. Both the House bill (HR 770) and the Senate companion (S 345) provided ten weeks of "family leave" for new parents and for those needing to care for sick children or parents. For employees' own illnesses, the House bill was slightly more generous in granting fifteen weeks of unpaid, job-protected leave; the Senate bill provided just thirteen weeks.

On the other hand, the House bill did not cover as many businesses.

The House bill once again relied on the fifty/thirty-five compromise: Businesses with fewer than fifty employees would be exempt for three years and businesses with fewer than thirty-five would remain exempt thereafter. Dodd's bill applied to all businesses with twenty employees or more. That had been the level of coverage contemplated in the bill as reported by Senate Labor the previous July (and before the peregrinations it had gone through on the floor that September). Dodd did not want to give ground again on this issue, a point of contention within the support coalition. Even with the threshold at twenty, he argued, two out of five workers were going to be excluded from coverage. Raising the threshold any further would exclude a majority of the workforce.

In fact, both S 345 and HR 770 were tailored to resemble the committee products of the previous Congress. Some of the sponsors, and many in the outside support coalitions, would have preferred a return to the original, stronger language. But to reintroduce the bill as first written would have meant fighting all the old battles again in committee. By using the last committee report as a base, the sponsors hoped to minimize, if not obviate, further haggling at the committee level and expedite the journey to formal floor consideration. The sponsors in both chambers believed it critical to move quickly so as to demonstrate the vitality of the issue and avoid the legislative logjams they had experienced in the closing days of the previous Congresses.

There would be no need for cross-country hearings or long months of negotiation this time. The substance of the bill had been defined over the previous four years, and the politics had come to focus on a relative handful of swing votes in each chamber. The goal was to get floor votes in both House and Senate by the end of the first session of the new Congress, which corresponded with the calendar year 1989. That timetable required the bill to clear committee in both chambers before the summer recess. Because it would take several weeks to produce committee reports, the markups would have to be held in the spring. And that meant getting the hearings out of the way in the late winter weeks.

To this end, Tarplin now had another full-time staffer at Dodd's Subcommittee on Children and Families. She was Jackie Ruff, a Harvard-trained lawyer who had spent the past several years working for the Service Employees International Union. Ruff's specialty was writing child care and family leave policies into workplace contracts. Working for Dodd, she wrote them into federal law for workplaces nationwide.

Preparing once again for a hearing and markup would be a time-consuming chore; but the committee was also a known challenge, a hurdle that had been measured and cleared before. The real problem was the path from committee to the floor. To that end, Dodd had been busily lobbying his colleagues in the weeks that followed the November election.

Dodd began with momentum that winter because Byrd had forced family leave onto the floor the previous fall. For better or worse, no member of the Senate was unaware of the issue. But he also began with a handicap because Byrd's tactics (preelection grandstanding, the yoking of child care and family leave) had left some of the Republicans feeling bruised. Even without the residual rancor, getting family leave out on the floor again in 1989 would require a far different scenario. This would not be a campaign-season exercise orchestrated for political impact more than legislative success. This time it had to be for keeps. It would not serve the bill's interests to force consideration again without having the fifty-one votes in hand for passage. Indeed, it might be futile to debate the bill on the floor at all unless the sponsors could count on sixty votes —the number needed for a cloture motion that would limit debate.

Casting a cold eye on his vote count over the winter, Dodd found it less than reassuring. He resolved to add another layer of support before reaching the floor again. And he wanted as many Republicans as possible. Sitting down with Tarplin and Ruff, Dodd quickly drew up a list of roughly forty-five senators he thought he could count on and another list of fewer than forty he knew would be hard to reach. That left a target group of about fifteen, and Dodd went to work on them.

He knew it would take something beyond the usual "Dear Colleague" letters and the casual conversations he might have with a colleague on an elevator or off the floor. So he went beyond these conventional means of senatorial communication and asked to meet with these targeted colleagues in their offices. He showed up for his appointments with Ruff or Tarplin in tow, burdened with a sheaf of charts. After the usual pleasantries Dodd launched a nonstop stream of salesman patter. Such door-to-door drumming is not unknown in the Senate, but neither is it typical. Senators may beg votes rhetorically, imploring their colleagues on the floor in the midst of a speech, but to seriously importune a peer face-to-face is to risk rebuke. It may even strain one's senatorial dignity. Yet Dodd did it, partly because he thought it the only way to amass the majority he would need for family leave and for another initiative he hoped to move with dispatch in 1989—the child care bill.

The child care bill that had appeared on the floor the previous autumn had been as much Dodd's property as family leave and considerably more popular. Dodd had managed to recruit the support of Senate Labor's senior Republican, Orrin Hatch of Utah, whose objections to the $2.5 billion spending program were outweighed by his interest in children and day care centers. Hatch liked having an issue on which he seemed to confound partisan expectations, and child care lent him some political leverage on the committee and back home in family-oriented Utah as well. As the 101st Congress began, the judgment of the Senate leaders was that child care had a chance to move quickly. That blessing was signified when it received S 5 as its bill number. The majority leadership generally reserves the first five bill numbers for its own favored priorities and then lets the Senate minority leaders designate the next five (thereafter numbers are assigned first-come, first-served).

To some in the family leave coalition, Dodd's commitment to child care smacked of infidelity. While sympathetic with its aims, the Women's Legal Defense Fund and the AARP, for example, had no special interest in the child care bill. Yet there were others within the coalition, such as the Children's Defense Fund, for whom child care was of equal or greater importance. Marian Wright Edelman, the founder and president of the CDF, had made no secret of her distress when family leave appeared to be taking precedence over child care for floor consideration in the summer and fall of 1988. CDF is committed primarily to poor children, and Edelman saw more urgency in child care for the needy than in unpaid leaves for the relatively affluent.

From his perspective Dodd did not see his loyalty as being divided. He preferred to think of it as being shared. He saw the two bills as symbiotic, and he saw the effort he invested in each as an investment in the other. And it seemed utterly natural to him to talk to his colleagues about family leave and child care in the same breath. They were, he felt, facets of the same concern for families.

Dodd wanted to move both bills again in the new Congress, either as a package or one at a time. And with just a few more votes, he believed it could be done. When he sat down with each of the colleagues he had targeted he would let his natural exuberance spill out with his words. Each of his targets had voted against cloture for the family leave and child care package the previous October. But when Dodd went knee-to-knee with them, making his pitch so personally and earnestly, some seemed willing to take another look.

One vote Dodd wanted badly was that of Pete Domenici, a no-nonsense Republican from New Mexico who was his party's gimlet-eyed leader on budget issues. A firm advocate of small business, he might have seemed a remote objective, but he had eight children, one of whom had serious health problems, and he knew something about family sacrifices. Domenici heard Dodd out, showing interest in his charts and graphs.

"I think you've got a good idea and I think it's the right thing to do, but . . . ," he said. His expression became stern and he pointed the pen he was holding at Dodd. "You can't put it on business like that."

Dodd kept on plugging. He worked hard at converting Republican Nancy Landon Kassebaum of Kansas, who had just been assigned for the first time to the Senate Labor Committee. Although her voting record was thoroughly conservative, Kassebaum had a personal dimension of empathy that Dodd thought he could speak to. She had managed her own career in politics while raising four children. But Kassebaum, like Domenici, balked when it came to the mandate on business.

Still, Dodd refused to be deterred. And sometimes he sensed subtle encouragement from unexpected sources. He thought, for example, that he was getting more than just a polite hearing from Republican Christopher S. Bond, the junior senator from Missouri. Bond was generally viewed as a Chamber of Commerce conservative, well suited to his seat on the Small Business Committee. His family fortune had come from making bricks, and through two decades of political life he had been principally associated with business. But Bond was also attuned to attitudinal shifts. He had known his share of close races, winning his Senate seat in 1986 with just 53 percent of the vote against an ardent feminist. And while Bond had neither a committee connection nor a previously stated interest in the issue, his attentiveness seemed more than merely respectful.

Some of Dodd's targets told him, directly or indirectly, he was wasting his breath. A few others said they would rethink their position. And then there were those who had ideas for improving the bill. One, Dave Durenberger of Minnesota, promised to have his staff send Tarplin a memo on his suggestions. When it arrived, the memo ran to more than thirty pages.

DODD KICKED OFF THE NEW SEASON FOR family leave with a hearing in the Subcommittee on Children, Family, Drugs and Alcoholism on February 2, the morning of the day his family leave bill (S 345) was introduced. Joining Dodd on the big dais in the Senate Labor hearing room (Dirksen 430) were two Democrats (Claiborne Pell of Rhode Island and Brock Adams of Washington) and two Republicans (Orrin Hatch of Utah and Dan Coats of Indiana). Dodd reached for a bipartisan effect by calling on one of the bill's Republican cosponsors, Bob Packwood of Oregon, before Hatch, the ranking member and former chairman of Senate Labor. Packwood praised Dodd's bill and then his own state for having similar legislation already on the books. He referred to the country's "democratic revolution," then corrected himself: He said he had meant to say "demographic."

"We will accept 'democratic,' " said Dodd amiably.

"We will accept the word 'revolution,' too," Hatch interjected. That gave both parties something to find amusing, and the room filled with the sudden, liberating laughter peculiar to solemn settings.

Thanks to Tarplin and Ruff, Dodd was not calling on the usual stock list of experts and advocates but a fresh panel, including a man from an adoption organization in St. Paul and a woman who represented cancer survivors. There were experts from New York and Washington once again, but this time there were also witnesses from Ohio, Indiana, New Mexico, Oregon and California.

Still, the advocates of family leave had found it hard to produce live testimony from families that had needed a leave in dire circumstances and been denied. The most poignant story entered into the record that February morning came from an anonymous letter by a rural southern woman whose son had died after a five-year battle with lymphoblastic leukemia. The letter, which had been sent in by a social worker at St. Jude Children's Research Hospital in Memphis, was moving, but it would have done more to move the bill had that mother been available to testify in person, with cameras rolling.

Anchoring the antimandate side, once again, was the gruff and glib John Motley from the National Federal of Independent Business. Although always a fierce adversary, he joshed with Dodd both inside and outside the hearing room. The two had been classmates at Providence College.

Motley was always careful, as were all the opponents of the bill, to emphasize approval of family leave as an idea. They fully supported it wherever employees wanted it and employers could afford it. But where those criteria were not met, Motley stressed, the mandate was onerous and unnecessary. And he had affidavits from eighteen small-business owners who said so.

Dodd's main riposte for Motley's standard argument was the testimony of small-business operators who said they could live with a leave policy. Determined to shrug off the "yuppie bill" label, Tarplin and Ruff made sure their witnesses included the likes of Martha Ditto Hamilton, owner-operator of Martha McCool's Restaurant at the Holiday Inn in Tucumcari, New Mexico.

And Dodd did not let Motley get away without asking him the question he had become fond of asking at hearings around the country in 1987: "Can you name one business that you know of that has a parental leave policy in place that has reduced its benefit package?" Motley said he could not. And on that basis alone Dodd would always remember that day's proceedings as a smashing success.

Having held his hearing so quickly, Dodd could hand the bill off to Kennedy almost immediately for the scheduling of a markup in Senate Labor and Human Resources. Remarkably, given the time it had taken in the previous Congress, family leave was ready for markup in full committee before the new Congress was four months old.

ON THE HOUSE SIDE, COMMITTEE staff was under the same pressure to stage quick hearings and rush the latest version of family leave to markup. Here the onus fell on Fred Feinstein, as staff director of the Ed and Labor subcommittee (Labor-Management Relations) most responsible for the bill. He had been involved in the family leave saga since Howard Berman called to ask for his advice back in 1985. And he had been the lead staffer in the House since his boss, Bill Clay, chairman of Labor-Management Relations, became the chief sponsor of family leave in 1986.

Feinstein and other staff organized a hearing nearly as quickly as Dodd's troops had done in the Senate, bringing together the members of Clay's subcommittee on February 7—just five days after HR 770 hit the hopper. Here again, an effort was made to bring in fresh voices and viewpoints. But the hearing's most dramatic moment was an inadvertent one. It began when Clay lost his patience with a witness opposed to the bill and began to berate him. The chairman was revisiting a vein he had worked before, at full committee markups of the earlier bills. Characteristically irascible and blunt, Clay had denounced Republicans for trying to amend a bill they planned to vote against in any event. At the February 7 hearing Clay wanted to know why groups like the Chamber and the NFIB bothered to participate. "Why are you even here?" he asked. The room fell silent, waiting for an answer. When none was forthcoming from the witness at hand, another lobbyist waiting his turn at the witness table reached for the microphone.

"I'll tell you why I'm here," volunteered Mike Resnick, representing the National School Boards Association.

"I know why you're here," Clay interrupted, leaning into his micro-phone. "And we're going to take care of it."

Resnick was taken aback, as were the other opponents of the bill pres-ent—although not for the same reason. For most of those crowding into the Ed and Labor hearing room that day, Clay's remark broke the news that Resnick was negotiating a separate peace. For Resnick himself, and a handful of staff, the surprise had to do with Clay's timing.

Resnick's organization had long been opposed to family leave—it had been a charter member of Tavenner's CARE coalition, the Concerned Alliance of Responsible Employers. Tavenner had been especially pleased to have a nonprofit, public service association with her. It added a dimension to all the retailers, manufacturers, restaurateurs and building contractors. Just as important, having the NSBA meant having Resnick, one of the most accomplished of all the association lobbyists who worked the Ed and Labor beat.

Resnick had sat down with a copy of the first family leave proposals in the mid-1980s and reacted with what he called "a subtle wow." As a lawyer thoroughly familiar with the daily and yearly operations of a school system, he could see problems for school administrators sprout-ing from nearly every page. And when the momentum behind the bill led to the formation of CARE in 1987, Resnick became part of its inner circle—one of the fifteen or so who came to Tavenner's office at 13th and K Streets on Fridays to talk strategy and tactics. His national organization released a statement saying the federal government should not be "im-posing priorities among employee benefits or determining the details of how those benefits will be provided by the nation's 16,000 school dis-tricts."

But any organization of such size and diversity is likely to harbor dissent. And beginning in mid-1988, when the Senate bill was making its way toward the floor, Resnick became aware of ambivalence within his constituency. When family leave had been on the Senate floor in Sep-tember, Resnick had persuaded Republican John Danforth of Missouri to carry an amendment exempting schools. But it had run afoul of another amendment being pressed by another Senate Republican, Alfonse M. D'Amato of New York. In the end, that snafu did not matter. But over the winter, before the new Congress had convened, the New York School Boards Association had voted to support a federal family leave law.

Resnick saw immediately how dissension within his own organization would weaken his hand, ending his chance of an outright exemption.

Moreover, he saw the House and Senate preparing to exclude businesses with fewer than fifty employees. If that happened, how intense would the small-business opposition continue to be? As the bill got smaller, it would be easier to swallow. And Resnick had no way of knowing what the White House might do when faced with a scaled-down bill. Bush might just sign it. So if this bill was on its way into law, the time for getting the most important, school-sensitive amendments incorporated was now, not later. Resnick put in a call to Tarplin, who called Feinstein.

The result was a series of seven meetings, beginning in January 1989. Resnick wanted to tick off his worries about the bill and haggle out a deal on each with Feinstein and a few other staff. Tarplin attended about half the meetings, which were usually held in Feinstein's out-of-the-way office in a far corner of the Cannon Building. Despite the awkwardness of having their talks exposed at the February 7 hearing, the negotiators continued meeting once a week throughout that month and into March. Resnick would bring the NSBA general counsel with him to meet with Feinstein and other staff lawyers for Ed and Labor. And, as agreement neared, Feinstein brought in still more lawyers—two from the National Education Association and two from the American Federation of Teachers—to massage the compromise that would eventually constitute about eighty lines of the family leave statute and five paragraphs of equally important language in the final committee report.

Feinstein had been intensely interested in turning the school boards around. He knew just how much Resnick meant to the opponents of the bill and how much the schools' opposition tended to change the tenor of the debate. Resnick was an artist at casting the administrative concerns of the school boards in terms of their effect on students. With phrases such as "class disruption" and "educational mission," he could conjure up an ill-served child as quickly and as vividly as anyone in the family leave coalition. "After all," Resnick said, "these are not widgets we're producing."

But if Feinstein was eager to accommodate this wavering opponent, he wanted to be sure the victory would not prove Pyrrhic. He did not want to appear to gut the bill for one set of employers, setting off a full-scale rebellion among the bill's labor backers, specifically the teachers—powerful supporters of the family leave concept.

When Resnick, Feinstein and the others were close to a deal, Resnick was told there would be one further delay. Whatever terms the teachers' representatives accepted would have to be approved by the other elements of the family leave coalition as well. Resnick "moderately flipped," in his words, but Feinstein assured the school board advocate that he could sell the agreement as long as he had the support of the teachers' unions. While those negotiations continued, Feinstein gave Clay the high sign and the chairman called for an early markup at the subcommittee level. It was still February, the same month in which HR 770 had been introduced, when Labor-Management Relations met and approved the bill without amendment on a vote of 11–5. Roukema cast the one Republican vote for the bill.

Resnick, meanwhile, did not feel it immediately necessary to withdraw from CARE. He continued to attend the Friday sessions at Tavenner's, even after Clay's outburst at the February hearing. He wanted to explain to the others that NSBA was not switching sides. It was not joining the support coalition or endorsing family leave. Rather, he said, the school boards were "just sort of going to go away." Reaction to his news among the other opponents was generally matter-of-fact. The school boards were getting what they wanted and getting out. Tavenner would recall thinking Resnick had done "what any good lobbyist would." Resnick was not so much surprised as he was "relieved they were so gracious about it."

ON MARCH 8, JUST EIGHT DAYS AFTER Clay's subcommittee markup, HR 770 went before the full Ed and Labor Committee. Gus Hawkins, then eighty-one and starting his fourteenth term in the House, was in the chair. But he deferred to Clay as the sponsor and relevant subcommittee chairman, and Clay opened the proceedings by making the simple case: "It's not fair to ask a man or woman to choose between their job and caring for a newborn baby." Again, the principal appeal was to new motherhood, even though the bill itself went far beyond that single circumstance to cover sick children and parents and an employee's own illness.

After the opening statements, the committee got down to business. Hawkins had promised back in 1987 to study the idea of applying family leave requirements to Congress. In the intervening months he had received the results of that study, and on this occasion he offered an amendment to include House staff under the bill. The committee agreed to that by voice vote, and the relevant portions of the bill were referred to the House Administration Committee for further action.

Committee Republicans had raised the issue of family leave for congressional staff in the previous Congress, only to be rebuffed by the chairmen of Ed and Labor and House Administration. But if the Democrats seemed to have undergone a conversion on the question in 1988, it was not quite the reversal it appeared to be. Exempting Congress from labor laws had become increasingly controversial. So the more politic solution now would be to apply new laws to Capitol Hill employees but set up a separate enforcement mechanism for them. The idea was to avoid charges of hypocrisy while preserving the separation of powers and keeping the Justice Department and federal court system out of members' own office matters.

Roukema, in her capacity as ranking Republican on Labor-Management Relations, offered the package of amendments prepared by her staff and by the team that had been negotiating with Resnick. Aside from Roukema, the other committee Republicans had not been part of the school board negotiations. But Resnick had a long-standing relationship with Bill Goodling, the Pennsylvanian who had succeeded Jim Jeffords in 1989 as the full committee's ranking Republican. Before the markup Resnick laid out the deal's details over lunch with Goodling's committee aide at the Capitol Hill Club (a restaurant inside the Republican National Committee Building). Goodling, as it turned out, would have some reservations. If family leave was onerous for public employees such as teachers, why was it acceptable for the private sector?

Those committee members displeased with the NSBA deal eventually swallowed their objections: Roukema's "education amendments" were adopted by voice vote.

In all, there were twenty-seven amendments offered, debated and voted upon at the Ed and Labor markup that March. Leading the opposition once again was Dick Armey of Texas, who called the bill "yuppie welfare" and "a perverse redistribution of income." He maintained that firms would have to penalize lower-status workers by cutting their benefits to compensate for the costs of family leaves taken by the more affluent. Armey offered one amendment after another, all of them handily defeated. In the end, the committee approved HR 770, with the education amendments and the extension to cover House employees, on a vote of 23–12. All twenty-two Democrats voted aye, as Tim Penny had moved to another committee assignment over the winter. Roukema cast the lone Republican vote in favor.

But as Resnick stood happily in the Rayburn hallway that afternoon, accepting congratulations, he was already thinking ahead. Two more House committees still had to approve HR 770 (Post Office and House Administration), but for his purposes the next real test was on the Senate side, where the full Senate Labor Committee would hold its markup the following month. Resnick felt sure that Tarplin understood what had been negotiated in the early weeks of the year, but he could not be as sure about Dodd. Days and then weeks went by. Finally a call came from Tarplin. There would be a problem putting in the special language for the schools at the committee level, he said. Other groups were going to want special clauses of their own, too. Resnick was getting nervous. "We'll take care of you on the floor," said Tarplin. "Show me something in writing," said Resnick, and Tarplin soon produced a letter with Dodd's signature.

THE SENATE LABOR PANEL THAT took up S 345 on April 19, 1989, was unchanged on the majority side: Kennedy and Dodd had been rejoined by all seven of their Democratic colleagues from the previous Congress. But most of the faces on the minority side were new. One Republican, Stafford of Vermont, had retired, and another, Quayle of Indiana, was now vice president. Weicker, Dodd's cordial if not-quite-chummy Connecticut colleague, had been defeated for reelection, and Gordon Humphrey of New Hampshire had swapped his seat on Senate Labor for one on Environment and Public Works.

Stafford, a backer of family leave, had been replaced in the Senate and on the committee by Jim Jeffords, the Vermonter who had befriended family leave when he was ranking member of the House Ed and Labor Committee. Another new member was Durenberger, a Minnesota moderate who had backed family leave in the previous Congress (even voting for cloture on October 7) and been eager to talk about amendments to improve it. The other two replacements, Coats and Kassebaum, were more problematic. Coats had been appointed to Quayle's Senate seat after a career in the House, where he was known as a militant conservative on social issues. Kassebaum, although widely liked by Democrats, had a solidly Republican voting record and rarely crossed her senior Kansas colleague, Bob Dole.

It was Coats who would put forward the GOP's main alternative to S 345 in markup that April. Rather than offering the usual battery of amendments, the minority put its muscle behind Coats's motion to substitute a "sense of the Senate" resolution endorsing incentives to encourage employers to provide family leave. The sense of the Senate resolution has no force of law (one Senate parliamentarian has described it as the equivalent of "a pious hope"). But it is often used, or at least proposed, as an alternative to doing something real and risky on matters of controversy. By voting for such a resolution, members may show their hearts are in the right place without incurring further exposure.

On this occasion Coats's motion allowed committee Republicans to vote in favor of family leave in the abstract but against S 345 as a law. It also functioned as the party's unity vote on the matter: All seven Republicans voted for it, even Jeffords and Durenberger. But with all nine Democrats voting against it (Kennedy and Dodd had made sure they had the proxies for members who might miss the meeting), the sense of the Senate alternative was laid to rest. The committee then voted to report favorably on Dodd's new bill, with Jeffords joining the Democrats to make the tally 10–6.

WHILE THE HEARING-TO-MARKUP process had proceeded apace in both House and Senate, there was not yet any House-side equivalent to Dodd's door-to-door salesmanship. Neither Clay nor Schroeder had the disposition for it, and it probably would not have done them much good had they tried. Roukema was willing to work the phone and importune fellow Republicans. But in the end, in the House, family leave needed to make new friends in bunches—not just here and there. It needed enough new friends to impress the leadership, which remained skeptical after four years and two full Congresses.

This aloofness on the part of leadership had begun to wear on the family leave sponsors and the committee chairs. They saw it as the responsibility of the Democratic whip operation to firm up support for the bill within the Democratic Caucus. In the previous Congress, the House Democratic leaders had set 150 cosponsors as an informal prerequisite for floor consideration. Now the three principal authors and their allies had signed up more than 150. More than one-third of the House was now officially on board. So when would the leadership apparatus be engaged?

On the Senate side, the markup had been held on April 19; and, as the Senate does not normally refer a bill to more than one committee, this amounted to the final step in the committee process. In the House, after the rapid-fire approval of HR 770 in Ed and Labor, the Post Office Committee had handled its relevant section on April 12. Six days later, House Administration's relevant subcommittee (Personnel and Police) endorsed the inclusion of House employees under the same terms as other federal employees (at the markup, Bill Dickinson, an Alabama Republican, called the measure "ludicrous in the extreme," adding, "I don't need eighteen weeks off if my wife has a baby"). The full House Administration Committee added its imprimatur on April 26 by voice vote.

The time had come for the party leadership to show some respect. In the previous Congress, the task of devising a leadership response to family leave had fallen to majority whip Tony Coelho, the number-three figure in the House hierarchy after the Speaker and the majority leader. The whip job had been around since the late 1800s, taking its name from the steward who kept the hounds in line at an English fox hunt. At one time, the House whip's task had consisted primarily of rounding up his colleagues and hauling them back to the Capitol for a party-line vote. In the contemporary Congress, most members are loath to miss a roll call, but they are also far more independent in their voting. The modern whip conveys the will of the caucus leaders to the rank and file, but he also reports back all the dissent and dissatisfaction he hears from the rank and file. The operation has become less of a disciplinary exercise and more of a two-way communication.

Under Coelho, the phrase "whip operation" had taken on new meaning. He had at his command a chief deputy whip, ten deputy whips, nineteen zone whips (each with a geographic focus) and nearly sixty other assistant whips who were assigned to cover their colleagues by state or year of first election. The group was so large that its regular Thursday morning meetings, to which Democrats who were not whips were also admitted, came to resemble meetings of the Democratic Caucus. And with all these assets to mobilize, Coelho would sometimes reach outside to recruit others ad hoc. In so doing he would create task forces, expanding on an idea that had evolved during the speakership of Thomas P. "Tip" O'Neill Jr., the Massachusetts Democrat who led the House from 1977 until 1987.

The idea was to "whip the bill" in the traditional sense, having each assistant report back to zone whips with a vote count; but also to organize a compromise based on the feedback from the members, piecing together the amendments that could not get enough votes to put the legislation over the top. The amendments could then be packaged together and brought to the Rules Committee for approval. The Rules Committee in the late 1980s was the province of the majority Democrats, who stacked the committee nine to four against the minority Republicans. The nine Democrats had been appointed by Democratic Speakers (some by Tip O'Neill, some by Jim Wright), and they could usually be counted on to vote as the party leadership expected. That included favorable treatment for whatever amendments the whip operation and the relevant committee chairman put together to get a particular bill passed on the floor.

The problem in 1988 had been that leadership was not ready to use all these tools on behalf of family leave. Too many other bills were competing for attention, and too many of them—such as plant closings and the minimum wage—had the potential to strain the Democratic coalition along the same seam. Many rural and suburban Democrats, especially in the South and West, preferred to balance their voting records and qualify for middle-of-the-road ratings from business lobbies. One divisive labor bill too many could produce a sudden and embarrassing loss on the floor. Wright and Coelho did not like to lose, and they saw family leave as too great a risk. No formal "whip count" had been taken in 1988, as the bill was never scheduled and such counts are only taken pending floor consideration. Coelho had convened a whip task force on the issue under fellow Californian Norm Mineta, whose downbeat report all but scotched the prospects of the bill for the year.

But if the NFIB and its allies on the Hill had kept HR 925 on ice in 1988, there were signs that 1989 would be different. As a rule, members are more receptive to new ideas that arise in the first session (the odd-numbered calendar year) of a given Congress. The rapid movement of family leave through the committees in 1989 bespoke a new momentum, and Dodd's bill now seemed assured of another shot at the Senate floor in its own right. None of this had escaped the antennae of Coelho, who could sense the members warming to the concept and resigning themselves to the inevitability of a vote.

The logjam of labor legislation also had eased a bit. The plant-closing bill had been enacted late in the previous year, having metamorphosed from its ugly duckling stage in the mid-1980s to political darling status. The bill that once had caused Pat Schroeder to fall from grace with her colleagues had not only been passed by Congress but also signed into law by Ronald Reagan (acting on the anxious advice of George Bush and Bush's campaign manager, James A. Baker 3rd). If Bush had backed that bill, reasoned family leave supporters, he might well adapt himself to some of the other labor bills on the docket, including a minimum wage increase, a child care bill and perhaps even family and medical leave.

Or so it seemed in the soft spring days of 1989. As May began, all the markups had been completed and the staffs of all the relevant committees were busy writing their reports. It seemed reasonable to expect Coelho to do a formal whip count in the weeks ahead and for Rules to schedule a hearing. It appeared that family leave's luck had finally changed.

But timing is the critical component in legislative luck, and the best strategies are often overtaken by events. May 1989 would bring unprecedented upheaval to the Democratic leadership. By month's end, both Coelho and Wright had resigned, partisanship had reached new heights of intensity and family leave was on the back burner once more.

8.

A Year of Living Dangerously

CONGRESS WAS CONCEIVED AS THE branch of government closest to the people, but it has rarely been popular. Americans have felt affection for presidents, some presidential aspirants and a handful of influential senators and representatives. But the Congress as a whole has often been an object of scorn. Mark Twain called it the nation's only "native criminal class," Will Rogers labeled its workings "a joke." Generations later, David Letterman could get a laugh on national television by reporting an accident on the Capitol Hill subway and adding: "Tragically, no one was injured." Like other parliamentary bodies, Congress has scores of vivid personalities but no one unifying, symbolic face. The result is an institution that can be at once intensely human and oddly impersonal. It has always been easy to believe the worst about Congress.

Even so, the first session of the 101st Congress stands out as a model of unease, rancor and bad reviews. Within weeks of Bush's conciliatory inaugural address, the Senate had rejected the nomination of former Senator John Tower as secretary of defense—a rare and stunning rebuff for a new president. When Bush offered to compromise on the minimum wage, Congress ignored him and swiftly passed an increase the administration had specifically vowed to veto. And when Bush said his top domestic priority was a reduction in the tax rate on capital gains, Senate leaders used a procedural rule to deny the president a vote on the merits. For the year as a whole, Bush's stated positions would prevail on just 63 percent of the roll call votes in Congress—the lowest percentage for any first-year president in the postwar era. Bush responded by spiking ten bills with vetoes, mustering enough of a minority in every instance to fend off an override, which requires a two-thirds vote in each chamber.

The Senate not only stiffed the president on a cabinet appointment but also humiliated a recent alumnus in the process (Tower had retired just four years earlier as chairman of Senate Armed Services). Tower was roughed up for his reported drinking habits and behavior toward women, and to some degree he paid for having made few friends in the Senate. But it was also unmistakably a gauntlet tossed toward the new president. Not a few Senate Democrats regarded Bush's presence in the White House as a fluke, a product of Reagan's residual aura and Dukakis's failed campaign. Now, Bush was being placed on notice by a Senate majority intent on its own status and power.

The Tower rejection was the Senate's doing, but it had a significant and totally unforeseen consequence in the House. Bush's second choice for the Pentagon was Dick Cheney, the exceptionally able Wyoming congressman who was also the GOP House whip. The early favorite to succeed Cheney was Ed Madigan, an old-style Farm Bureau conservative from central Illinois. But the Young Turks, most of them from Sun Belt districts, wanted someone different—someone to shake up the place. So, in fact, did many of the House's older, more mainstream Republicans who had wearied of long years in the minority. In a close-fought contest decided by just two votes, the change faction carried the day. The new GOP whip was Newt Gingrich of Georgia, one of the most controversial firebrands ever to reach a position of formal leadership in either party.

Gingrich had come to Congress in 1978 after teaching history at a small Georgia college and earning a reputation as a gadfly candidate. In the House, he aligned himself with Jack Kemp of New York and a handful of other "movement conservatives" who founded the Conservative Opportunity Society at the outset of the Reagan era. Gingrich became famous for his "special orders," floor speeches made at the end of the day to a deserted House chamber and a nationwide cable TV audience. Sometimes, Gingrich would act as though he were addressing other members who were present—even challenging them to respond. Speaker Tip O'Neill detested this and ordered the House cameras to pull back and show the rows of empty seats. This enraged the House minority, and when O'Neill was forced to defend himself later in a live session of the

House, he said Gingrich's behavior was "the lowest thing I have ever seen." This violated the House rule against personal remarks and the Republicans immediately moved that it be "taken down" (stricken from the *Congressional Record*). The Democrat who was at that moment wielding the gavel in O'Neill's stead had no choice but to comply with the motion and reprimand the Speaker.

Gingrich had gone much further in bearding the Democratic leadership after O'Neill was succeeded by Jim Wright of Texas. Buttressed by editorials in *The Wall Street Journal*, Gingrich railed against Wright for aiding insolvent savings and loans in Texas. Later, the critique shifted to various forms of outside income received by Wright and his wife. Gingrich's call for an ethics investigation was eventually taken up by a larger chorus of editorialists and by such citizen groups as Common Cause and the National Taxpayers Union. Wright had reaped profits from a vanity-press book deal and enjoyed other favors from businessmen who might benefit from his friendship. He had allowed his political and personal funds to mingle in dubious ways. But the seriousness of the charges against him was a matter of interpretation and partisan debate. And after the Senate's rejection of the Tower nomination, some saw the pursuit of Wright as little more than the GOP's retaliatory witch hunt.

Simultaneously, Wright had to handle a political hot potato: a congressional (and federal judicial) pay raise. Although defensible—a presidential commission had recommended it—it was very unpopular with voters.

The question of whether or not to vote on the raise bedeviled the House throughout the month of January. (The pay raise was to take effect automatically unless voted down.) The Speaker knew his unstated task was to endorse the recommendations of the commission and stand firm against efforts to force a vote. But, as it turned out, he was not well disposed at that moment to serve as a heat shield for the institution.

Wright had begun to think the Congress would be better off with a 30 percent increase, rather than the 51 percent recommended by the presidential commission. The lower raise could be portrayed as a trade-off for the banning of speaking fees and honoraria. But Wright decided to let the raise take effect, then hold a rescinding vote on February 9, at which time he would offer the 30 percent raise yoked with a ban on honoraria. But he and his leadership team could not hold control of the floor on February 6, when Republican insurgents staged a rebellion. The leaders tried to adjourn, but the Republicans were able to characterize the vote on adjournment as a test vote on the pay raise. Knowing he was licked, Wright went to the floor to concede defeat. He announced he would schedule an up-or-down roll call on the issue the following day. The raise was rejected by a vote of 380–48. Members who had been counting on the money for months, if not years, were stunned and bitter —and not a few of them blamed Wright.

Worse was still to come for Wright. On April 17 the House Ethics Committee issued a damning report on his behavior. It was clear that he was in serious jeopardy, and his travails dominated discussion on the Hill. Yet the backers of family leave had to soldier on, meeting their schedule. On April 18 the House Administration Committee became the last House panel to approve HR 770. And on the following day the Senate Labor Committee held its markup of S 345.

Theoretically, the bill could move to the floor in the House just as soon as reports could be written and the Rules Committee could meet to write a rule for its consideration. But as a practical matter, there was no reason to rush. Leadership had to allocate its resources and husband its capital, particularly in the House. Even in the best of political health, Wright would not have set himself up for a labor-management donny-brook any more often than necessary. The only unavoidable business pending in the labor queue was the minimum wage increase, a bill with enough momentum and importance to have been designated HR 2 at the session's outset.

As THE DARKNESS GATHERED FOR Wright, speculation mounted concern-ing his successor. Next in line was Thomas S. Foley of Washington, sixty, a twelve-term veteran who had been appointed the House Democratic whip in 1981 and elected majority leader six years later (when Wright moved up to Speaker). Foley had many friends and few personal ene-mies, but some saw him as too moderate in politics and mild in manner to lead the caucus against a Republican president. Rumors had Coelho, the number-three man, plotting a coup of his own. That speculation continued until one Friday late in May when Coelho suddenly an-nounced he would resign—not just as whip but as a member. Newspaper stories reported that he had profited from his relationship with junk bond dealers, including the firm that had all but invented the junk bond mar-ket. Although maintaining his innocence (he was never charged with a violation of the law or House rules), Coelho said he did not wish to go through what Wright had.

Five days later, on May 31, Wright too called it quits. Standing alone in the well of a packed House chamber, the Speaker offered up an emo-tional one-hour defense of himself and his wife. Then he announced he was resigning as of the end of June, offering up his job as "propitiation for all the bad will" that had plagued the institution. "All of us, in both political parties," he said, "must resolve to bring this period of mindless cannibalism to an end."

Within a single week the House Democrats had lost three of their best-known leaders: Coelho, Wright and Claude Pepper, the venerable chairman of the Rules Committee, who died May 30 at the age of eighty-eight. Pepper, who had come to the Hill as a senator in the 1930s, seemed to belong to an age of greater civility. His passing served as the coda for a month of dissonance.

The top slots in the leadership were soon filled, but not without a few moments of anxiety. In the final days before the caucus met on June 6 to select a new Speaker, a flurry of rumors—fanned by a sly memo issued by the communications office of the Republican National Committee—implied Foley was a homosexual. For a period of roughly two days, his fate seemed to hang in the balance. During that time President Bush denounced the RNC memo as "disgusting" and the communications aide responsible for it resigned. Foley was elected Speaker at the June 6 caucus meeting by acclamation.

There was more competition for the next two jobs, but not much. Richard A. Gephardt of Missouri, whose 1988 presidential candidacy had ended soon enough for him to reclaim his House seat, was elected majority leader. The number-three job of majority whip was won on the first ballot by William H. Gray 3rd, a minister from Philadelphia, who became the highest-ranking African-American in House history.

THE NEW LEADERSHIP TEAM'S FIRST legislative task was to clear HR 2, the minimum wage increase, for delivery to the president. Their performance on this test would be read as a sign of their power to move other troublesome bills then pending at various stages of the process, including family leave. Both chambers had passed the minimum wage bill in April and sent their respective versions to be harmonized in a House-Senate conference committee. Conferees are appointed by the party leaders of each chamber, but they are nearly always the senior members of the committees involved. The conferences are usually held in open session, but the public meetings mostly ratify agreements that have been thrashed out privately, in smaller confabs of members and committee staff. The conference committee produces a "conference report," a unified document wherein all differences between the House and Senate bills have been expunged or compromised. If both chambers vote to adopt the report, the bill is said to have been "cleared for the president's signature." It is then "enrolled," reprinted on parchment and delivered to the White House, where the president has ten days (not counting Sundays) in which to sign it, veto it or let it become law without his signature.

The conference report on HR 2 was cleared May 17. Given the tumult in the House in late May, however, few noticed that the parchment (which must be signed by the Speaker and the Senate president pro tempore) was not actually delivered to Bush until June 13. The House and Senate leaders scheduled a 2 P.M. news conference to announce the delivery of the bill to the White House and to implore the president to sign it. The White House, however, had already issued the president's prepared veto message at 1:30 P.M. Less than one week into their new regime, Foley & Company had their first crisis: the first veto of George Bush's presidency.

Eager to show themselves equal to the challenge, they brought the veto to the floor for an override vote the very next day. They got 247 votes—a clear majority, to be sure, but 37 shy of the 284 needed. Twenty-eight Democrats deserted the new leaders and sided with the president. Minnesotan Tim Penny, the old nemesis of the majority in his years on Ed and Labor, was one of only three non-southern Democrats defecting.

When either chamber fails to muster the two-thirds majority (of members present and voting) prescribed in the Constitution, the veto is sustained and there is no need for the other chamber to bother. So Bush's first veto was a smashing success, and the implications for family leave could not have been more ominous. If a president is willing to veto popular legislation, and if he can hold a core of support in either chamber, he becomes the final arbiter of federal lawmaking—even if his party is badly outnumbered in both House and Senate.

For family leave, that meant the only route to enactment would be through a compromise with a White House that remained uninterested in negotiating. Two weeks before the veto of HR 2, White House lobbyist Fred McClure had said the minimum wage bill would have to be vetoed to prove Bush's resolve in resisting labor's agenda. As an example of other objectionable items on that agenda, McClure had cited family leave.

Through the remainder of the year, the Foley-Gephardt-Gray team would struggle against disarray in the majority caucus. In September sixty-four Democrats would defy the leadership to vote for Bush's tax cut on capital gains. The "boll weevils," as the southerners and other conservatives of the caucus were known, powered the tax cut to an easy victory in concert with the chamber's Republicans. The scenario was reprised when the House took up the issues of catastrophic health insurance for the elderly (as enacted in 1988) and new rules for distributing pension funds more equitably among employees (as enacted in 1986). Both measures had been hailed as progressive when passed, but both had run afoul of angry constituents who either had to pay an extra tax or fulfill complex administrative requirements. The new Congress, under heavy lobbying pressure, repealed both laws.

Here again, the combined influence of the Chamber of Commerce, the National Association of Manufacturers and the National Federation of Independent Business was such that scores of centrist Democrats felt they had to vote for repeal. These lobbies were highly effective largely because they mobilized individuals within the districts to contact their members on their own and push hard and demand commitments—much as the NFIB had done in opposing family leave in 1988.

Having taken a beating from roughly the same coalition of lobbies on all three of these issues, House Democrats were less than eager to take them on again soon. And, of course, these groups had made no secret of their position on family leave.

While the new House leaders had difficulty keeping their rank and file in line, they had their hands full with some of their committee chieftains. They could not resolve, for example, the contretemps that had held up the child care bill for a second consecutive Congress. Gus Hawkins, still the chairman of Ed and Labor, wanted direct appropriations to finance subsidies for child care. Tom Downey of New York, an acting subcommittee chairman on Ways and Means, favored the use of tax credits, refundable even for those with no tax owed. He argued that credits, not being subject to the whim of the appropriations committees, were a more reliable financing mechanism. But the debate over policy was darkened by conflicts both jurisdictional and generational. Hawkins was eighty-two that summer and serving his final term as chairman of a committee increasingly conscious of its declining status. Downey, less than half Hawkins's age, was gunning to succeed Rostenkowski someday as chairman of Ways and Means, the queen bee of congressional committees.

The preponderance of pressure was brought to bear on Hawkins. But he held firm, and at year's end the House-Senate conference committee resolving budget disputes stripped all child care provisions from their conference report and shelved child care. Hawkins had prevailed in a sense, but the struggle had hurt his committee's other bills, including family leave.

.   .   .

AS THE MONTHS OF 1989 ROLLED BY, the advocates of HR 770 saw their
spring momentum dissipate. They were thrown back once again on their
own resources—the constituent parts of the support coalition. Feinstein
never tired of telling anyone who would listen that the family leave coalition had to be bigger, more assertive and more diverse. Family leave was
in need of a bigger family.

Five years had passed since the first group of Washington lawyers and
activists had met to talk about parental leave in the wake of the Cal Fed
decision in 1984. At first, they had been able to gather within the confines
of Judith Lichtman's office at the Women's Legal Defense Fund. The
founding group had begun with the legal theorists from Georgetown Law
Center and other feminists, but it had also included women from the
Association of Junior Leagues, the National Council of Jewish Women,
the Children's Defense Fund, several unions and even the U.S. Catholic
Conference.

In the early sessions they had thrashed out the themes of the bill,
including the emphasis on general medical and family circumstances
rather than on maternity alone. They had formed a bond that helped
them weather years of exposure and disappointment on the Hill. And
from that core, the group had grown to comprise literally scores of organizations in a coalition that would eventually exceed 250 members. The
ranks swelled with additional labor unions, religious groups and other
entities not often identified with feminism.

When Congress was in session, lawyer Donna Lenhoff of the Women's
Legal Defense Fund would convene meetings of the family leave coalition in various locations on the Hill and elsewhere to discuss strategy and
circumstances—and to keep everyone's spirits up. Usually the meetings
were monthly, but when the bills were in motion the meetings would be
held weekly or even more often. Lichtman and Lenhoff were the main-
stays—in effect, the chairman of the board and the chief executive officer, respectively. But if the group had resembled at first a cadre of
committed idealists, it soon took on the cast of a mainstream political
party. When members asked, "Who's for this bill?" they would hear a list
of the most meaningful and prominent names, usually beginning with a
few women's organizations and the AFL-CIO and then moving on to the
odder bedfellows—such as the Junior Leagues, the Catholic Conference
and the American Association of Retired Persons (AARP).

As far back as the 99th Congress, when the base-broadening process
began, the first phase was to enlist organized labor. Her Ivy League
credentials notwithstanding, Lenhoff was a labor-oriented liberal: Her

wall art included a framed poster commemorating the 1912 textile workers "Bread and Roses" strike in Massachusetts. From the outset of the family leave crusade she had proclaimed it a labor issue and therefore "obviously unattainable without active support from labor." Such support, however, was not automatic.

An auxiliary of the United Mine Workers took part in the earliest organizing meetings, and the Service Employees International Union became part of the group soon thereafter. The mine workers provided some of the most affecting testimony at hearings. Many mining families had children suffering from various environmental cancers, and the parents were giving up their jobs to be with their kids at treatment centers in cities far from coal country. The SEIU was a natural rebuttal to the "yuppie welfare" argument because so many of its employees worked in relatively low wage jobs with minimal benefits.

But the larger labor movement was less swift to embrace the cause of family leave. Not until Pat Schroeder's original HR 2020 was supplanted by HR 4300 early in 1986, with Bill Clay on board as cosponsor, did the unions pile onto the bandwagon—and then only after the bill's language had been carefully scrubbed by labor lawyers as well as staff for the Ed and Labor Committee. And even then, although organized labor came to regard family leave as part of its official agenda, it did not immediately regard the bill as a high priority—nor did it recognize the political potential of the issue.

For the truly passionate advocates of family leave, the attitude of organized labor was often exasperating. It was clear the leaders' appreciation for the cause was constrained, and it had the effect of bottling the bill up year after year, waiting its turn in the queue behind legislation the labor leadership considered more important, such as minimum wage. At the same time, the resistance that arose from Republicans every two years in Ed and Labor and again in Senate Labor reminded all concerned that without the votes of the labor Democrats on those panels, the bill would never have moved.

One labor official who did take the bill and the issue seriously was Jane O'Grady, a lobbyist working the Hill for the AFL-CIO. But she had to deal with a mind-set among her senior, male colleagues that regarded family leave as a perk for affluent female professionals. It was scarcely surprising to hear such skepticism within the AFL-CIO's concrete citadel on 16th Street (midway between the White House and the Washington Post Building). After all, one could also hear the "yuppie bill" label from some veteran Democrats and their staffs on the Ed and Labor Committee. Even some of the key advocates for the bill—such as Clay and Bill Ford at Ed and Labor—were uncomfortable initially with some elements of the support coalition, dominated as it was by women, some of whom could be highly assertive.

Whether she was pushing for the bill on 16th Street or on the Hill, O'Grady was offended by the yuppie label. She would argue that yuppies, such as lawyers and other professionals, were likely to have generous leave policies already. It was the hourly wage earner who rarely received such treatment, even though such workers were more vulnerable to job losses and benefit cutoffs. Under certain circumstances virtually anyone could be forced to stay home; and O'Grady saw the bill as a bailout for just such cases, where people had to leave work and had minimal individual bargaining power. Would they be better off with paid leave? Surely. But what if they had no choice? Would they not prefer a job guarantee and interim benefits as opposed to walking away with nothing at all?

The union leaders began to relate to the bill differently with each successive Congress. In some cases their own contract negotiators had started to come back with contract benefits beyond minimal maternity leave. The atmosphere on the Hill warmed as well. "Later on, we started to get a new kind of member of Congress," O'Grady said. "They were younger professional men who had younger professional women for wives. They knew right away what was going on with this bill. But with older members it took a lot of selling."

The enthusiasm ran higher at certain union headquarters than at others. Besides the Mine Workers and the Service Employees International Union, the strongest support came from the American Federation of State, County and Municipal Employees (AFSCME) and its national leader, Jerry Klepner. Over the years the coalition would scale back its steering committee from twenty-five to fewer than ten members, but Klepner would always be one of them. By 1989, the coalition had added a relatively young union of office workers known as Nine to Five, the National Association of Working Women. Nine to Five's Ellen Bravo would become a spokeswoman for the issue on TV and newspaper op-ed pages around the country. She was often the perfect antidote for the "yuppie bill" criticism, presenting case after case of wage-earning women who lost their office jobs when they had babies or needed time for sick family members. And after Bravo nurtured and lobbied a family leave bill into state law in Wisconsin in 1988, she acquired a certain folk hero status within the movement.

"Thinking about this issue changed as we went along," Bravo said years later. "People were shocked to learn that other countries do better than we do on this. People got activated, the ones who would say they had never called their congressman before. It got to the point where we did not need to tell them to call, they asked when to do it."

Nine to Five did not confine its missionary work to the readily converted. Bravo worked for years on Steve Gunderson, a Wisconsin Republican who had been among the staunch opponents of the bill on Ed and Labor. And the Atlanta chapter of Nine to Five made a special project of Sam Nunn, Georgia's senior Democrat in the Senate.

Labor support was an essential factor in the family leave strategy from the 99th Congress forward, but it was also a complicating factor. While labor counteracted the stereotype of feminist activists, it laid a trap of its own. Any given set of friends in Congress implies a complement of enemies. To be wed to labor was to curry automatic disfavor not only with Republicans but also with moderate-to-conservative Democrats, especially those representing districts in the South and the West.

That made it all the more important to billboard the backing of other organizations with entirely different political valences, such as church groups and lobbies for children, the elderly and the disabled. The presence of the Catholic Conference in the front ranks of the coalition tended to surprise members and news media alike. Lobbying bishops were usually associated with the issue of abortion and imagined to be at loggerheads with feminists. But the conference had separate policy committees for abortion-related issues and for family-related issues. And the latter committee had been foursquare in favor of family leave since the introduction of the earliest legislation (HR 2020 in 1985). Sharon Dailey, a staff lobbyist for the Catholic Conference's headquarters in Washington, had attended the earliest meetings in Lichtman's office.

Dailey was glad to see the base broadening year after year, in part because it relieved her of the burden of being the coalition's main bridge to conservatives. In the early going, she recalled, it seemed the answer to every political image problem was, "Get somebody with a collar in there." When lobbying targets were being assigned to coalition members and a particularly tough-sell Republican name came up, someone was sure to say, "Catholics, that's you." Dailey was also surprised and energized by the personal involvement of Roukema.

"I picked up the phone one day and this voice said, 'Sharon, hello. This is Congresswoman Roukema and I want to talk to you about family leave,'" said Dailey, looking surprised even years later. "That is the only time in my career a member ever called me directly."

In the Senate, the conference established an easy relationship with Dodd, a Catholic with whom the family-issues policy committee had often worked before. But the greater challenge was finding a churchman in each archdiocese to contact other senators individually, by letter or by phone. Thus Joseph Cardinal Bernardin of Chicago would be asked to call on Democratic Senators Alan Dixon and Paul Simon, or John Cardinal Carberry of St. Louis would be asked to call on Republican Senators John Danforth and Kit Bond. Others, such as Bernard Cardinal Law of Boston, contacted the conference on their own and volunteered to lobby legislators.

From the beginning the coalition had enjoyed some support from pro-life members, including Christopher H. Smith, a boyish-faced New Jersey Republican who believed family leave would encourage working women to carry their pregnancies to term. But if Smith was outspoken in his views, he was not especially influential with his colleagues. It would take a bigger symbolic figure to effect a breakthrough, and the Catholic Conference had its sights on the biggest: Henry Hyde, the snowy-maned majordomo of the pro-life movement in Congress. Hyde was a Catholic and a father of four, a lawyer from the suburbs west of Chicago who had been a leader in the Illinois state legislature before coming to Congress in 1975 (one of a tiny handful of Republicans in the post-Watergate class). Now in his mid-sixties, he was still known primarily for an amendment he had authored as a freshman, barring federal funding of abortion. The Hyde amendment had since become a standard feature of the appropriations process, prompting annual attempts to repeal or weaken it. But when not holding forth on abortion, Hyde would sometimes ally himself with House liberals on social conscience issues—including health benefits for poor women with children.

Relying on that side of Hyde, the Catholic Conference dispatched its frontline lobbyist, Mark Gallagher, to sell him on family leave. Gallagher did not go in without substantial logistical support. He had a letter in hand from John Cardinal O'Connor of New York. Perhaps the church's leading antiabortion spokesman in America, O'Connor was also the chairman that year of the conference's policy committee on family issues. He had written to all the House members in the 101st Congress, urging their support for family leave. But Gallagher had another letter just for Hyde, invoking the cardinal's strong rapport with the congressman. Despite this heavy armament Hyde made no public statement of his position on the bill. And with Hyde uncommitted, as many as a score of other pro-life members in both parties seemed beyond the coalition's reach.

The conference's participation diverted the family leave debate from its left-right, labor-management rut and furnished moderate and conservative members with excellent cover if they chose to support the concept. But it was not yet enough. Feinstein continued to pester the coalition's officers for more help. The bill needs more friends, he would say, more people pushing. Family leave was already a "motherhood" issue, literally and figuratively. But the concept needed to expand its appeal into yet another dimension. And in the 101st Congress it got that boost from the increased participation of the American Association of Retired Persons.

The AARP was among the largest and most potent lobbying groups in Washington, in a class with the National Rifle Association, the American Medical Association and the mainline veterans' groups. All these wielded considerable power, but the myth of their power was greater still. Tip O'Neill liked to say that when people in Washington thought you had power, that was when you had power. And there were members in both parties who believed that to cross the AARP was to risk their political careers.

For a time the family leave coalition had courted AARP in vain. Lenhoff began calling on them as far back as the 99th Congress, making the case that family leave meant overburdened grandparents would be relieved of emergency child care. "The feeling was we might get involved sooner or later," said Michelle Pollak, the AARP attorney who would become responsible for family leave. An early concern of AARP was the loss of pensions and other retirement income by women who were forced to leave their jobs for family care. But it was not until Marge Roukema and others pushed to have the bill cover the care of family members, particularly elder family members, that the AARP threw in with the coalition. Long-term care for parents was an essential issue for AARP. And once the group had come into the coalition, it moved inexorably to the front rank.

The first thing Pollak and her organization wanted to do when they entered the fight was to broaden the terms of engagement still further. In addition to elder care, they wanted the bill to cover spousal care so that a husband or wife could have job-protected leave to care for a sick spouse. The advantages of this for older couples, in particular, were manifest. But even some of family leave's staunchest allies balked. It was not politically savvy to keep broadening the bill, they said. It was one thing to add elderly parents, but adding spouses would fling the gates too wide. Moderate members might be driven into the arms of the business lobby.

Nonsense, argued Pollak. What you wanted was as broad an application of the leave benefit as possible so as to multiply the beneficiaries and maximize support. Why should an employer grant twelve weeks of leave for a sick child but not for a sick husband? Yes, the idea might drive the bill's opponents crazy, but, after all, the opponents could scarcely become any more hostile and unyielding than they already were. So why not?

The coalition did lose members over the expansion of leave to spouses. The American Association of Junior Leagues eased away from the effort, fearing that the original focus on young children was being lost. The withdrawal was keenly felt by some of the original advocates of leave, who had greatly appreciated the mainstream image and earnest energy supplied by the Junior Leagues. But there was no corresponding diminution of support on the Hill, and the trade-off between the Leagues and the AARP clearly favored the latter. The AARP brought dozens of votes within reach that had been out of the question. "We were always able to talk to people who could not be talked to by anyone else in the coalition," Pollak said with a shrug. Lock in elder and spousal care, and "the level of the AARP commitment would increase in direct proportion."

The back-and-forth over elder and spousal care would continue every time the bill came to the floor now. Pollak always saw Dodd as being on the verge of deleting one or the other to secure a few more Senate votes. "We were always worried that we were seen as expendable, and we did not want to be thrown over the side as sops to the business lobby," she said. In negotiating with Tarplin, Dodd's legislative aide, whom she had known for years, Pollak always made it clear that AARP's departure from the coalition would not be a quiet retreat under cover of darkness. The press and the members would be put on notice. Besides keeping this defensive vigil, Pollak worked the chambers on offense. She made a special project of Republican Senator Kit Bond of Missouri, for example. And in the House she was glad to have one Republican colleague confide that he had become a convert when his mother retired from the company where she had worked her entire career and discovered her pension would be $150 a month.

On the House side, Pollak relied on Lenhoff to "put the kibosh" on any talk of cutting elder and spousal care provisions because "she was not willing to lose us." And in return, the AARP decided that "the only way to keep our stuff on the bill was to come in with both feet." Before the final battle for family leave was over, the AARP would be paying much of the coalition's tab for printing and other expenses.

By the later stages of the struggle, the initial Sturm und Drang of the opposition had become familiar and less effective. But just as important was the increasingly professional air of the support coalition—a direct result of the emergence of the AARP and the exertions of labor and the Catholic Conference. Gone were the amorphous meetings of two dozen steering committee members, arguing over ends as well as means. Gone were the early days of wondering who might have an entree to so-and-so, or who might put in a word with leadership. By the later stages, the family leave coalition was playing in the same organizational league as its antagonists.

WITH ALL THE PINPOINT LOBBYING provided by interested organizations, family leave survived a year in which business lobbies otherwise carried all before them. And before 1989 ended, there was cause for hope. Months of postveto negotiations—involving both parties in both chambers, organized labor, business lobbies and the White House—had produced a minimum wage bill Bush could sign. The new level would be the $4.25 hourly wage Bush had offered at the beginning of the year, taking effect in 1991. There would be, as Bush insisted, a separate "training wage" provision, but it would affect only teenagers in their first three months on the job. The willingness of labor to accept so much less than it had wanted, and to swallow the hated wage differential, was a testament to emerging realism. The agreement by Bush suggested future deal making on other issues.

There was also a gleam on the horizon for child care. The Senate, facilitated by bipartisan cooperation from Orrin Hatch and by the door-to-door salesmanship of Dodd, had moved its version of child care all the way to the floor in June (the month of the minimum wage veto). Dodd's bill was cut back some, from the $2.6 billion approved in committee to $1.75 billion. Dodd also gave ground on the requiring of federal health and safety standards. Thus trimmed, Dodd's S 5 passed the Senate on June 23 by voice vote. When the Senate takes a voice vote, the senators present merely say aye or nay and the ayes are deemed to "have it." No one's individual vote is recorded. The idea is to dispense with the pending business via anonymous approval, a useful device when there is no quorum or when the Senate wishes to dispose of a matter without further ado.

Tactically, a voice vote on an important matter implies that the opposition has decided not to force the issue further. This may be done to mask the strength or weakness of the opposition, to minimize media interest or simply to relieve senators of a vote against a bill with a sympathetic name (in this case, the Act for Better Child Care). It can also be useful for senators reluctant to contradict their earlier votes on an issue or to commit themselves to vote the same way on similar issues in the future. It was a maneuver of particular value to Dole when he was a minority leader wedged between the Senate majority on the one hand and a president of his own party on the other—and it would prove of particular value to family leave as well.

9.

A Vote in the House

CONGRESS GREETS A NEW YEAR BY opening a new session, an occasion for persistence and hope. As the 101st began its second year in 1990, some members hoped that Congress and the Bush administration could accommodate each other on budget-deficit reduction, on the Americans with Disabilities Act and pending civil rights legislation. There was hope that the House Democratic leadership might make peace among its committees and pass a child care bill. If all that could happen, and no new obstacles arose, then perhaps there could be an agreement on family leave.

The committee reports on HR 770 and S 345 had been completed the previous summer. The new Democratic leadership had been preoccupied, but family leave had never quite been forgotten. To the contrary, it had become a special interest for David Bonior, House whip Bill Gray's chief deputy. Bonior had held the same title under Coelho, having been appointed to the job by Wright. Yet his fortunes had not suffered appreciably with the fall of either his boss or his benefactor. Moreover, Gray and Bonior seemed to be working well together even though they had been rivals for the whip job Gray had won.

Bonior's special talent seemed to be reconciling differences and bringing together the disparate elements of the caucus. He represented a tradi-

162   Conflict and Compromise

tionally Democratic blue-collar constituency in Macomb County, just across the street from Detroit. He was a Catholic and a strong opponent of abortion (a position unique within the upper reaches of the Democratic leadership) who had become a strong proponent of family leave, an issue that allowed him to please both the economic liberal and the social conservative within his nature.

As the frustrating year of 1989 ended and the second session of the 101st began, Gray and Bonior looked for an opening for family leave. And when the compromise took shape on minimum wage, leaving open a lane for family leave to run in, they started to talk task force. This was the same device Coelho had initiated with Norman Mineta in the 100th Congress, but this time the nod went to Pat Williams of Montana. Williams was deputy whip for labor issues, a Catholic and a product of union politics in his home state. He was also a senior member of the Ed and Labor Committee, in line to chair its Labor-Management Relations Subcommittee in the next Congress (when Clay was expected to give it up to become chairman of the full Post Office Committee). And if all that did not make Williams the natural choice, his reputation as a scrapper in tough causes did. He had become the leadership's favorite defender of federal funding for the arts, among other often controversial interests.

Working closely with Fred Feinstein of the Labor-Management Subcommittee, Jane O'Grady of the AFL-CIO and others from committee staffs and organized labor, Williams and a coterie of other members began to tinker with HR 770 in the winter months in the midst of the 101st. They wanted to poll the caucus informally to get a sense of the bill's backing and its baggage. The central tenet of the task force mission is that members almost always become friendlier to a bill once they have had a chance to amend it. So who might still be won over, and what would it take?

Working closely with the members was Steve Champlin, an intense and fast-talking former divinity student at Yale. He had come to Washington as a staffer for a Vietnam veterans organization, later worked for Bonior, then became Tony Coelho's top floor aide in 1989 and stayed on to do the job for Gray. Champlin could glean information from the dozens of assistant whips and other listening posts in the chamber, load it all into his customized, computerized data base and project vote counts with remarkable accuracy. He could also manipulate the data further to show how many votes might be added or subtracted by toughening or softening a single provision of the bill.

In his many conversations with members who did not support HR 770,

Williams sleuthed out not only their stated specific objections and political pressures but also their level of interest in the bill and in finding a compromise to save it. Now and then, this process was a source of new supporters; and this time around, the process turned up a pair.

One, Curt Weldon, was a Republican from the suburbs south of Philadelphia; the other was Bart Gordon, a Democrat representing the hills and towns of middle Tennessee. Weldon was a conventional Pennsylvania Republican, well to the right of most Democrats but far too concerned with the future of Rust Belt industry to march with his own party's New Right conservatives from the Sun Belt. Weldon courted his numerous working-class constituents and received vote ratings from the AFL-CIO that were relatively high for a Republican. Gordon, on the other hand, was a clean-cut lawyer from Murfreesboro who had been chairman of his state party and come to Congress in the teeth of Reagan's landslide in 1984. He had been a moderate's moderate on most issues, but with the influx of auto assembly jobs into his district in the late 1980s he had shown increasing interest in labor issues.

Neither Weldon nor Gordon had been a cosponsor of family leave in its previous versions, as both had been impressed with the objections raised by the business groups. Weldon was a regular winner of the "Sentinel of Small Business" statuette with which the NFIB rewards congressmen whose votes it approves. The opposition had counted on Weldon, and Tavenner had hoped for Gordon's vote as well. But as the task force process wore on and Weldon's involvement with the bill grew, his meetings with at least some of the business lobbyists deteriorated into nasty confrontations, leaving him more determined than ever to broker a compromise.

Neither Weldon nor Gordon had a seat on Ed and Labor or any of the other committees of jurisdiction. But Weldon was a father of five and sat on the Select Committee on Children, Youth and Families (the panel where George Miller had introduced the topic of family leave to Capitol Hill back in 1984). Gordon was single and not known for an interest in children's issues, but he had a seat on the Rules Committee—a point of entry into almost any legislation. And both seemed to appreciate what they could do for their own plans and career profiles by getting involved with family leave at this juncture.

Gordon, in particular, could use a new highlight in his legislative biography. He had been closely associated with Jim Wright, who had picked him out as a comer in the small class of 1984 and moved him onto Rules after just two years in the House. With Wright gone, Gordon still had his seat on that committee, but his main contact within the leadership now was Bonior, who also owed his job to Wright and who was now taking a special interest in moving family leave.

But it was Weldon whose enlistment meant the most, not only because he was a Republican with a good small-business record but also because he was willing to evangelize among his colleagues. Roukema, of course, had been talking up the bill in Republican circles. But her estimates of GOP support—she would typically predict sixty or even seventy votes from her side of the aisle—always proved optimistic. Weldon promised little but quickly brought in two Pennsylvania colleagues and helped with other unexpected votes as well. With the number of Republican commitments rising into the thirties, the Democratic leadership was warming to the notion of taking family leave to the floor.

BY THE SPRING OF 1990, FAMILY LEAVE had been moldering for nearly a year on the waiting list called the Calendar of the Committee of the Whole House on the State of the Union (the Union Calendar, for short). This might normally be enough to justify an obituary. But Williams and Bonior remained upbeat, and they had a simple strategy.

The first step would be to call the bill from the calendar for consideration on the floor. This is accomplished by the Speaker, who consults with other party leaders. During the era of Democratic control the Speaker had an executive committee called the Steering and Policy Committee that nominated all committee chairmen (subject to approval by the caucus) and made all committee assignments (a privilege of the Ways and Means Committee until 1974). Steering and Policy consisted of six caucus officers and the chairs of four committees—Appropriations, Budget, Rules, and Ways and Means—plus a dozen members elected by region and eight more appointed by the Speaker. The Speaker acted as chairman of the committee and chose most of the staff. So when Steering and Policy recommended a course of action, it was usually safe to assume the Speaker had something very much like it in mind himself.

Before a bill can actually be considered, however, it needs a rule—a method of procedure. And when a bill comes to the floor with less than strong support, its sponsors want a favorable rule for protection. Thus the next step for HR 770 would be to have the Rules Committee fashion a careful order of procedure that would allow an omnibus amendment to be offered as a substitute for the committee's bill. This substitute would incorporate all the amendments agreed to by the negotiating sponsors, leaders and other interested members. The amendment would be offered not by the bill's sponsors or the committee's leaders but by the unassuming and unthreatening Gordon and Weldon, who would be presented as sincere moderating influences.

The substance of the Gordon-Weldon substitute, under negotiation for more than a month, would incorporate several of the sensitivities mentioned most often in conversations with members. In essence, it would soften the committee-approved bill just enough to reassure the wavering and give everyone a chance to cast a positive vote (whether they liked the bill or just liked the idea of diluting it). This, in turn, would create a sense of momentum in advance of the final vote. It would also allow the sponsors and the leadership a chance to gauge their strength before voting on final passage (and to bail out, if necessary, to avoid an embarrassing defeat). If the bill could then be passed with plenty of votes to spare, the sponsors could press the Senate for a fast follow-up and, with a little luck, spook the White House into signing the bill into law.

To do any of this, however, would require the supporting coalition to buy off on yet another substantial curtailment of the bill. The Gordon-Weldon substitute would address several of the features most often cited as problematic in the bill, including the length of leaves and the discrepancy between leave periods for different purposes. It would telescope the previous fifteen/ten formula (fifteen weeks for personal medical leave, ten weeks for family leave) into a single-standard leave of twelve weeks per year for all causes. It would also fix the fifty-employee threshold as the permanent small-business exemption (deleting the later reduction to a threshold of thirty-five).

There were other, smaller changes as well. The committee bill allowed both parents to be on leave at once; the substitute would allow only one parent to be on leave at a time. The committee bill applied in cases where in-laws or stepparents required care; the substitute tightened this to apply only to biological parents. The committee bill allowed certification of an illness by any health care provider; the substitute insisted on certification by a doctor.

The one notable expansion of the bill in the substitute package was the inclusion of spousal care, along with the care of sick children and parents, as a cause for family leave. But that one item was critical to retaining the active support of the AARP, which objected to the new restrictions on elder care. If all these changes could be packaged and enacted together, Champlin's vote-calculating computer said the bill would be a winner on the floor of the House.

The details of the deal were still being reviewed and negotiated by the support coalition and cosponsors even at the beginning of May. There was a sense of haste, of opportunity that might evanesce if not seized. Mother's Day was May 13, and there was a thought that this might actually affect the mood of the House. Once again the otherwise monthly meetings of the family leave coalition intensified into daily rounds of telephone calls and gatherings. Feinstein laid out the case for the compromise to Lenhoff and to all the other principals. He had to warn them that, even with all the proposed changes, the bill might simply fail on the floor. If that were to happen, after all the compromises had been accepted, there would be no chance for any meaningful family leave bill for the foreseeable future.

Despite what was being sacrificed in the deal, and despite the risk of defeat, the coalition members proved willing to go for it.

MEMBERS WHO RIFFLED THROUGH THEIR mail on the first Monday in May 1990 found a "Dear Colleague" letter from Joe Moakley of Massachusetts, the chairman of the House Rules Committee. It informed them that on the following day, Tuesday, May 8, the committee would hold a hearing on a rule for floor consideration of HR 770. The letter advised members interested in offering amendments to this bill to deliver them to the Rules clerk no later than 6 P.M. on May 7—the day the letter arrived. Although couched in all the standard courtesies of the genre, this particular "Dear Colleague" struck more than a few of Moakley's colleagues like a slap.

The letter had apparently been issued only a few days before—on Friday, May 4, a day on which no votes were scheduled and relatively few members would be expected to be in their offices (or even in town). For that matter, no votes were scheduled on Monday, either, and many members were still back in the district—a typical long weekend routine for members, especially in an election year.

In the three House office buildings, staff members scrambled to reach their bosses on the phone and to get a reading on the situation from their respective cloakrooms (the Democratic and Republican areas off the House floor where members of each party congregate and aides to the leadership provide information and communications). Who had decided this bill was ready for the floor and when? Some proponents of the bill were taken by surprise, but the real panic took hold among those who were opposed. John Motley's telephone began to ring. So did Mary Tavenner's. Did the NFIB and CARE know the leadership was about to bring up family leave? Did the sponsors really think they had the votes?

Was the White House solid on its veto threat, or was there a deal in the offing?

Tavenner was in touch with Nick Calio, a former boss at the National Association of Wholesaler-Distributors, who had moved into the White House legislative lobbying office. No, said Calio, there had been no change in the White House posture. Family leave was still veto bait. To reinforce that vow, Bush's chief of staff, John Sununu, met with representatives from several business groups before that Monday was out. Tavenner emerged from the meeting looking confident. "I had John Sununu look me straight in the eye and say that the president would veto it," she said. But for those who preferred that the bill not reach the president's desk at all, the House leadership's sudden green light posed problems.

There were a few members, of course, who were not caught unprepared by Moakley's call for amendments. Principal among them were the whip task force, with its Gordon-Weldon substitute, and Bill Clay, the cosponsor of HR 770, who would serve as its floor manager. Clay's staff was already developing several amendments to counter unfriendly amendments they expected to face. Also ready to go on short notice was Tim Penny, who had already introduced his own miniversion of family leave as a separate, freestanding bill (HR 3445). All Penny needed to do was to send Rules the text of his bill, which provided ten weeks of unpaid leave only for parents of newborns or newly adopted children. Similarly, Steve Bartlett was all set for the floor, well stocked with amendments he and fellow Texas Republican Dick Armey had thrown at the bill in committee over the past several years.

Others had to hurry to put their ideas into bill language on short notice. Charles W. Stenholm, a Texan and the chairman of the House's Conservative Democratic Forum, wanted to address the question of an employee's requalification for work. Amo Houghton, a moderate Republican from the southwestern tier counties of New York, wanted to limit the bill to businesses with a hundred employees or more. Houghton, an heir to the Corning Glass Works fortune and one of the wealthiest men in Congress, was generally associated with the positions of business. But Democrat Bob Carr of Michigan, usually associated with his party's liberal wing, had an even more radical reduction in mind. He wanted merely to ask businesses to develop family leave policies and file disclosure statements about them with the federal government. That would provide a "data base" for further study. Mike Parker, a conservative Democrat from Mississippi, wanted to institute the provisions of the bill for

Congress only, using the institution as a family leave laboratory and applying the lessons later to the private economy.

Moakley gaveled Rules to order on the afternoon of Tuesday, May 8, and took the usual testimony from representatives of the three committees to which HR 770 had been referred, in whole or in part. He heard from the chairmen and from the ranking members. Bill Goodling, the Pennsylvania Republican who was senior on Ed and Labor, wanted to extend the typical one-hour allotment for debate and was granted two hours. The leaders of the Post Office Committee, where the bill had been noncontroversial, were satisfied with a thirty-minute allotment.

Moakley listened to the committee leaders explain why there would be a substitute offered by Weldon and Gordon, and why that substitute ought to allay the concerns of members pressing their own amendments. Then he called the other members who had amendments one by one, hearing each explain why his concerns were not met by the Gordon-Weldon substitute. Gordon, of course, was there to judge for himself— being one of the nine Democrats on the Rules Committee. Another Rules member was Bonior; and still another was Louise Slaughter, a New York congresswoman who had cosponsored family leave for years.

There was little suspense about the outcome. For two decades following the Watergate era, Democrats stacked Rules 9–4 in their favor and usually prevailed. Rules remained interesting mostly as a struggle for tactical advantage and a window on the thinking of the leadership. In 1990 none of the Democrats on Rules owed their seats directly to Speaker Foley. They had been appointed by his predecessors. But Foley was a rightful heir, and it is not illogical for ambitious members to transfer their loyalty to successive Speakers. For that matter, individuals inclined to resist authority rarely find themselves on Rules in the first place.

Moakley heard everyone out. Then he swiftly roughed out the features of what would be called a "modified open rule"—a euphemistic phrase in which the operative word is "modified." Under a truly open rule, any amendment consistent with the House rules on relevance (referred to as germaneness) would be allowed. What Moakley was proposing was, rather, a restrictive rule: a strict delineation of which amendments would be in order and when. The rule as crafted would allow for two and one-half hours of debate. It would allow the Gordon-Weldon substitute (referred to officially as the Gordon substitute) along with amendments by Stenholm, Penny and two Republicans from Ed and Labor: Bartlett and Fred Grandy of Iowa, a recent addition to the committee minority who was best known for his previous career as a TV actor (he had a

featured role on *The Love Boat*). The rule restricted Clay to one amendment, to be offered if Stenholm's amendments were presented. The
amendments proposed by Houghton, Carr and Parker, however, would
not be in order.

The rule Moakley outlined also allowed for one motion to recommit
the bill to committee. Motions to recommit are guaranteed as a privileged
right of the minority. So the more restrictive the rest of the rule, the
more important the motion to recommit becomes (in some instances, it
is the opposition's one shot at stopping a bill). The House has two kinds
of recommittal motions. The simple motion to recommit, the bare minimum required by the chamber's permanent rules, is understood to be a
killer amendment that ends consideration of the bill if approved. But
simple recommittal scarcely ever carries. The more interesting maneuver
is the motion to recommit with instructions. In essence, it is a last-ditch
alternative means of jamming a major amendment or substitute into the
bill at issue. When such a motion is successful, as happens from time to
time, the instructions become part of the bill. The wording of the motion
notwithstanding, the bill is not actually returned to the committee process. The motion to recommit on HR 770 was a motion to recommit with
instructions.

These provisions, then, became the essence of the rule, officially
House Resolution 388, which if adopted by Rules and by the House
would enable the Speaker to put HR 770 in play and, at the same time,
establish the rules of the game. Moakley put the question to his committee and the rule was approved on a party-line vote. Motions offered by
senior Rules Committee Republicans to allow the Houghton, Carr and
Parker amendments were defeated, also on party-line votes. And a motion by ranking Republican Jamie Quillen of Tennessee to bring the bill
to the floor under an open rule, permitting any amendment, met the
same fate.

That same afternoon, Dick Gephardt announced on the House floor
that on the following day, Wednesday, May 9, the House would proceed
to consideration of HR 770, the Family and Medical Leave Act, pursuant
to House Resolution 388.

THE NEXT DAY, AS SCHEDULED, FAMILY leave was brought up on the floor
of the House. Or, more precisely, the rule by which family leave was to
be brought up was brought up. Louise Slaughter, the lone Democratic
woman on Rules, was accorded the honor of presenting the rule and
allocating time in its defense. Quillen, the ranking Republican on Rules,

rose to object. He reviewed the Friday-to-Monday "Dear Colleague" and the stiffing of several members' proposed amendments. He then rehearsed the general litany of arguments to be heard against the bill itself and turned the floor over to a visibly unhappy Democrat named Bob Carr.

"The leadership of this Congress told us we would have an opportunity to vote on a variety of approaches," said Carr. "Perhaps I was a little foolish in believing that would actually be done." First elected with the Watergate class of 1974, Carr had never been a docile member. In one of his first floor speeches as a freshman, he had called for the resignation of Speaker Carl Albert, his own party's leader. On this occasion the still combustible Carr spoke of both parties being "straitjacketed" because "the Committee on Rules in its infinite wisdom decided we were not even to be allowed to debate the issue or raise a new idea."

Gerald Solomon, a New York Republican from the Hudson valley who was second-ranking on Rules, was at his blunt and abashed best. He held up a copy of the fax his office had received the previous Friday, dated 3:37 P.M.—"after I had gone home and 95 percent of the other members of this body had gone home." Solomon proceeded to absolve "Joe Moakley" and the rest of the Democrats on Rules from blame. Addressing Speaker Foley, who was not present, Solomon shouted: "Mr. Moakley did not have anything to do with this, Mr. Speaker, it was you and the Democratic Caucus." Why the rush? asked Solomon. The schedule for the rest of the week was "not exactly back-breaking," why not spend the week debating amendments to HR 770—taking all comers?

At length, Slaughter yielded time to Pat Schroeder to answer Solomon. Schroeder tried to introduce the body to her perspective on the bill: the five years, the hearings, the committee work, the waiting for "a window of opportunity" to bring the bill to the floor. She noted how her bill had been modified, and then remodified, and how it was about to be changed again in the Gordon substitute. "I have trouble supporting this compromise because it has been watered down so much," she said.

At that point Solomon asked the chair if he could interrupt Schroeder for a question, adding, "I respect her very much." When Schroeder agreed to yield, Solomon burbled: "The gentlewoman is making my point. The gentlewoman says the bill is watered down so much she has trouble supporting it. Why do we not have a rule that would allow us to debate this issue, and let the gentlewoman, for whom I have great respect in this House, offer the amendments to strengthen this bill?"

This brought appreciative nods and murmurs of amusement from Solomon's side of the aisle, where such rhetorical thrusts were often the central source of satisfaction in a legislative day.

"If I thought the gentleman from New York was going to join me in strengthening this bill, hallelujah, I would be with him," responded Schroeder. "I would vote against this rule. The gentleman cannot even say it with a straight face."

This brought applause from some of the Democrats on the floor.

"I have listened to the minority leader say he feels so bad because it is not paid leave," Schroeder continued. "Now, if your side really wants to offer paid leave, we would be more than happy to fix the rule up."

This remark brought chuckles from both sides, with Democrats relishing the sarcasm and Republicans enjoying the implicit admission that the rule could be "fixed up" at will.

"But let us be perfectly honest about this," said Schroeder, turning serious. "This is a compromise because we know nothing else will pass."

Schroeder's message was that there was no need for a week's deliberations on the floor when the idea had been around for years and had survived the committee process three times running. No one should complain about hurry-up procedures if he had waited this long to show interest in the bill. And second, she had said directly that the rules process was being manipulated by the leadership to maximize the chance of a vote on a favorable compromise before the bill could be eviscerated by amendment. This was no more than what everyone in the chamber already knew, but hearing it stated in candor had a certain bracing effect.

The opponents of the restrictive rule ended their assault with Grandy, who had an amendment that Rules had been willing to allow. "I appreciate being one of the lucky ones," he said. But he took to the floor in opposition to the rule anyway, objecting to the bill as co-opting the states' prerogatives and demonstrating that he himself had not been co-opted.

Shortly before seven o'clock, as the members milling in the aisles and lounging at the back rail were becoming restless, Pat Williams of Montana came to the floor to wrap up the case for the rule. Williams, who had run the task force on HR 770 for Gray, had heard the complaints of his colleagues whose amendments had been denied floor time. So he had done some checking with Rules and discovered that the only Republican so denied was Houghton, and that Rules had thought Houghton's amendment essentially identical to one Bartlett had already been cleared to propose. Williams said the Republicans objecting to the rule did not really care about procedure, only about defeating the bill at hand. Williams then went on to the substance of that bill, without mentioning the

172 Conflict and Compromise

two Democrats who had been turned away by Rules, or the Friday letter with the Monday deadline.

Williams noted that 72 percent of the mothers with children eighteen or younger were working outside the home. He called that an evolution in the workforce comparable to what had occurred in the early 1900s and the 1930s, eras when "Congress moved in to provide this new work force with adequate statutory protections." Williams cited the two-worker and single-parent families, people who were "in the work force because they are required to be in the work force." He admitted he did not know a lot about "bonding," but said he thought the real purpose of the bill was to put people by the bedsides of their sick children and sick elderly parents. "Will some people be able to bond better with their children? Absolutely. And that, too, will be good."

The House then voted, plugging the flat white cards each member carries into voting machines scattered around the House floor. As the bells rang to signal the vote, the wall panels above the press gallery revealed the members' names and voting lights. The tally began as members watched from below: green lights for yes votes, red for no and yellow for present. To no one's surprise, the rule got 251 yes votes and 151 no votes (31 members abstained). With a few exceptions, the vote followed the party line. Like votes for Speaker and other internal matters, votes to adopt restrictive rules are partisan affairs that determine the dominance of one party or the other. It is rare for a rule to be defeated, even in cases where the issue at hand is closely divided and the rule-making process itself has been strained.

There followed ten minutes of back-and-forth between Gingrich and Gray over which portions of the bill would be discussed that night and which the next day, with asides from the floor managers representing the Ed and Labor Committee and the Post Office Committee. Then, shortly after seven-thirty on the night of May 9, 1990, the House resolved itself into its Committee of the Whole mode for the purpose of considering family leave. This time-honored parliamentary device (technically called the Committee of the Whole House on the State of the Union) waives certain parliamentary restrictions on debate and allows business to be done with as few as 100 members present rather than a full quorum (218). Once an amendment or a bill has been considered by the Committee of the Whole, a vote can be taken by voice or by electronic device (the latter is mandatory if requested by twenty-five members). Thereafter, the committee votes to "rise" and report what it has done to the full House.

· · ·

AS CONSIDERATION OF THE BILL BEGAN that evening, Fred Feinstein was on the floor with Steve Champlin, Gray's top floor aide, and other leadership aides, half listening to the debate while comparing notes. Feinstein figured they had just over 220 votes for the bill, a bare majority (218) and perhaps a few to spare.

Bill Clay opened the floor debate with a speech designed to lay out the basic case for the bill and to shame its opponents. "Political rhetoric about the need to reestablish family values is abundant. It's too bad that some of those most vociferous on the subject are also the ones most opposed to improving the welfare of families."

Clay laid on the statistics. He said about a hundred other countries had family leave, and many of them, including Germany and Japan, supplied pay during that leave. He noted the General Accounting Office study that said the maintenance of employee benefits would cost business an average of $5.30 a year for each covered employee.

As for the objection to mandates, the essence of the case against the bill, Clay scorned it as a smoke screen. The term "mandate" was "a code word that is designed to stir businessmen, even those responsible, compassionate businessmen, to oppose all legislation intended to improve the quality of life for the workers of America. . . . This is precisely how labor standards have come about in the past," Clay said. "To back away from mandating benefits, Congress would have to repeal sixty years of labor law."

After Clay's biting introduction, the sponsors brought out Connie Morella, the Republican congresswoman from suburban Montgomery County, Maryland, to deliver the first speech on behalf of the Post Office Committee. She noted that the United States and South Africa were the only two "industrialized Western nations" without a family leave policy. She also alluded to a Gallup poll that found 81 percent of its respondents in favor of unpaid leave for workers with new babies or sick family members. Morella also noted that the federal government was biting the bullet too—all the harder—by granting its own employees leaves under the terms of the family leave bill from 1986 (eighteen weeks' parental leave and twenty-six weeks for an employee's own serious illness).

That got Grandy to his feet asking Morella to yield. He wanted to know if these leave periods were going to apply to congressional staff. Morella said that had been the case in the committee-approved bill and in the committee report, but that the Gordon-Weldon substitute was going to apply the less generous private-sector standards to congressional staff.

A short while later Morella yielded eight minutes of the time under her control to Gary Ackerman, a large and loquacious Democratic member from Queens, New York. He recounted how, as a teacher in New York City in 1970, he had applied for an unpaid leave to spend time with his infant daughter, Lauren. He found a gynecologist who was willing to make out the leave application citing "fatherhood" as the "infirmity." When he was turned down, nevertheless—by principal, superintendent and school board—Ackerman sued and won, and got his name in *The New York Times*.

After a small parade of members had held the floor, praising the bill and scolding Republicans for opposing it, Iowa's Grandy returned to state the case in opposition. He recited a litany of bills recently passed or soon to be passed that placed special responsibilities on employers. He mentioned the newly finalized minimum wage increase and plant-closing notification, and, among pending bills, the clean air legislation and the Americans with Disabilities Act (both of which would clear in the 101st Congress). Was this not just a bit too much to ask of American business in so short a time?

"Ironically," said Grandy, "this week is National Small Business Week, and it so happens that the national winner of that National Small Business Person of the Year award happens to come from my district. His name is Barney Roberts. He is from Storm Lake, Iowa, a community of about 10,000 people."

Grandy reported calling and finding out that Barney Roberts already had a family leave policy for his business that provided six weeks of unpaid leave—or more, when they had "a sustained problem." Grandy said this proved the "work force is changing, even in a state like Iowa," and that business was changing with it. "I believe this Congress ought to listen more to Barney Roberts and figure out what he knows rather than try to tell him what to do."

Marge Roukema was next up to bat for family leave, and she was as pointed in her own way as Clay had been earlier. "Members of both parties talk a good game and give lip service to family values," she said, "but turn their backs when a concrete proposal to give much needed support to working families comes forward."

But the climax of the Wednesday night debate came shortly before eight-thirty when Tim Penny rose to speak. His appearance at the podium at that hour amounted to a signal, because Gingrich and Gray had agreed that no amendments would be offered until Thursday. If Penny sought recognition now, it might mean he was going to spike the amendment Rules would let him present. Penny began by recounting his days on Ed and Labor and the markups he attended on previous family leave bills. He then segued into his trademark "plague on both your houses" critique of the chamber's modus operandi. "The debate over this legislation has become a political screaming match," he said. "Both proponents and opponents seem primarily interested in scoring political points for November."

The Minnesota Democrat faulted the Bush administration for opposing not only the bill at hand (HR 770), but also Penny's far milder alternative that applied only to new mothers (HR 3445) and all other alternatives from all quarters. He took a poke at his Democratic colleagues as well for pushing their bill when they had no assurance of Senate action and every assurance of a presidential veto. "Barely a majority, if that, will vote for this bill," Penny said, "far short of the two-thirds required to override a veto." The fact that Penny was right about the prospects of HR 770 made his assessment of the situation all the more galling to the sponsors of the bill, whose antipathy toward him had been a factor in his leaving Ed and Labor at the beginning of the 101st.

Penny thanked the Rules Committee for sanctioning his amendment, then announced he would withhold it. "The debate we will have today and tomorrow is about key votes by special interest groups and political gamesmanship by the political parties; it is not a serious attempt to address the issue and I will not be party to it."

The sponsors were relieved to hear they would not have to beat back Penny's "motherhood" amendment, especially given that they were counting on the proximity of Mother's Day (the following Sunday) for at least a psychological boost. But they still found Penny's solemn rectitude difficult to bear. "Someday we may approach this question with a bit more sincerity on both sides," said Penny as he concluded. "If so, I'll be ready with my amendments."

Through the remainder of the evening session the bill's opponents called on former businessmen from within their ranks (Houghton and Harris Fawell of Illinois and Clyde Holloway of Louisiana) while the bill's backers called up a procession of women members from both parties. The Republicans included Olympia Snowe of Maine (the once reluctant cosponsor) and Susan Molinari of New York (who had just been elected that March to succeed her father as the member from Staten Island).

The first round of debate concluded shortly after nine o'clock, after a verbal duel between Clay and Grandy concerning the power of organized labor in the 1990s. Roukema wrapped things up for the proponents by reading a list of key organizations supporting family leave that were not labor unions. It included nurses, psychiatrists, pediatricians, the American Association of University Women, the national PTA and the United Methodist Church. But the very first group she named was the Catholic Conference, and that may have served as a warning bell for some on the opposition side.

ON THE FOLLOWING DAY, MAY 10, the House was gaveled to order at 10 A.M., a typical time for a Thursday, when many members come to the floor with their airline tickets in their suitcoat pockets or their handbags. Outside the House chamber that morning, the lobbying activity approached the frenzy of a Friday-night high school football game. Inside the House chamber, a Methodist preacher from Virginia furnished that morning's prayer, referring to the men and women of the House as "a group of very human beings in a profession that takes its toll on our humanity."

Several members offered brief prescheduled remarks on general subjects—"one minutes," in the parlance of the House—with the dominant topic being the interminable negotiations between the White House and congressional leaders over the budget for the next federal fiscal year. After twenty minutes of these preliminaries the House turned again to the pending business of family leave.

The first speeches of the day broke no new ground, with proponents of the bill talking about minimum labor standards and families while opponents tried to wrestle the debate back onto their terms. The opponents who spoke were drawn primarily from the minority ranks of Ed and Labor, led by the ranking Republican Bill Goodling, Grandy and Bartlett —who seemed by far the most exercised participant. "It's the principle of the thing," said Goodling. That principle, as he saw it, was the right of private employers and employees to negotiate flexible benefits without federal mandates. Armey submitted a written statement but did not join the live debate. Neither did the remaining committee members, or, for that matter, the chamber's other reigning Republican rhetoricians. Grandy complained bitterly after the debate that he had been forced to the podium time and again to answer the Democrats because no other Republican was available to speak.

The Democrats, meanwhile, had members coming forward from a variety of committees, regions, races and other subcategories to support the bill. Richard Gephardt took the floor, briefly recounting the story of his son's lengthy bout with cancer. The majority leader said he had been lucky enough as a congressman to be able to take "large chunks of time off." Had he not been so fortunate, he said, "I would have quit my job." Vic Fazio of California spoke of his daughter's leukemia and the time they had been able to spend together when she was in pediatric cancer wards.

The Thursday debate included several male backers of the bill from the Republican side. Some were northeasterners such as Sherwood Boehlert and Raymond McGrath of New York. But there was also the occasional boost from Lamar Smith, a conservative from San Antonio. Smith did not linger in the well to speak, submitting his statement instead in written form for the record. But the next member up was John Rowland of Connecticut, a mustachioed Republican still two weeks shy of his thirty-third birthday. He was the youngest member of the House and had been so for five years. Rowland was also a Catholic, a father of three and an outspoken opponent of abortion. When he came out strongly for the committee bill, even before the introduction of the Gordon substitute, it was bad news for the opposition on two levels. Rowland contributed to the bipartisan case being made on the floor, and the timing of his speech suggested the proponents had an even bigger pro-life supporter in reserve.

That supporter was Henry Hyde, the grand prize captured by the Catholic Conference. Without being immodest, he could calculate what effect his decision might have on members who shared his views on abortion. And he decided he could maximize that impact with a bit of dramatic timing.

By the morning of the vote, the sponsors believed they would have Hyde's vote but not his voice, although they were encouraged to see him in the chamber both Wednesday night and Thursday morning, listening to his colleagues. Shortly before eleven-thirty that morning, the Republicans' excitable floor lieutenant Robert Walker wrapped up the general debate for his side by denouncing claims that HR 770 was in any sense "a family bill." A few minutes later, barely able to suppress a smug smile, Roukema quietly yielded her final minute of floor time to Henry Hyde. The chamber actually hushed. Tall, heavily built and reliably eloquent, Hyde always seemed to dominate the well of the House chamber when he stood to speak. In his evidently spontaneous remarks, he announced that he had "agonized over this bill considerably." He said he saw the seriousness of the objections and conceded that the bill was undeniably a mandate. "On the other hand, I am not appalled that this is a federal mandate. We mandate job security for jury duty. We mandate job security for ROTC service. It seems to me that for motherhood, for caring for a sick member of your family, that our economy and our society should be compassionate. . . ."

Weighing all the arguments, Hyde said, "we get down to the fact that society should have a policy of encouraging motherhood, not encouraging abortion. It seems to me if a working woman becomes pregnant she needs to have job security and have an incentive to have that child, not to exterminate that child so she does not lose her job."

Hyde needed just three more sentences to conclude his remarks: "There are very few bills that involve apple pie and motherhood. This one does not involve apple pie, but it does involve motherhood and it seems to me a social policy of encouraging motherhood is good. Therefore, for that reason, I will support this bill."

Hyde's speech was one of the shortest of the day, taking only about a minute. But it was the one most remembered by those who were there.

JUST AFTER HYDE FINISHED, GORDON was recognized under the rule for the purpose of offering his substitute. He did so, then began his defense of it by thanking Tim Penny for his "constructive role." Gordon said he hoped the hardware store on the square in Murfreesboro, Tennessee, or the beauty salon in Weldon's hometown of Aston, Pennsylvania, would give their employees the same benefits as larger businesses, but that it was necessary to exempt businesses with fewer than fifty employees. "America's small businesses really are special," he said. "They need special flexibility."

Gordon also noted that advocates of family leave were saying "we haven't done enough," while opponents were saying "we go too far. That tells me our bipartisan compromise amendment is just where it should be."

That seemed to make sense to another southern Democrat the sponsors were grateful to have on the team, Ed Jenkins of Georgia. Jenkins, a senior member of Budget and Ways and Means, was a business-oriented conservative from a primarily rural district. His Chamber of Commerce voting score was always higher than the one he got from the AFL-CIO. But he had remained to one side of the family leave debate and become something of a prize in the lobbying wars. It was unclear what he would do on the floor.

Unlike Hyde, Jenkins seemed to have little sense of the potential importance of his vote. He had been sitting in the chamber throughout the debate, listening to the speakers and chatting with colleagues from time to time. Late in the morning of the tenth he walked up to the large wooden table where the bill managers and staff were huddled over their vote counts and copies of amendments. Almost casually, he asked Gordon whether there might be time available for him to speak. At first,

Gordon did not even look up from his papers, saying only that all time had been allocated to other members. But when staff director Fred Feinstein looked up and saw the short, slight Georgian slipping away up the aisle, he nearly shouted out loud. Gesturing to him and to Gordon, Feinstein nodded as if to say yes, time could be found for him to speak. Jenkins graciously indicated he would not require much, and Feinstein began scrambling to find someone on his list of final speakers who could live with three minutes less.

Jenkins not only said he would support the bill, he also expressed some pride in having worked on the substitute. And he warned members who thought they should vote no that they would want to "retrieve" that vote later on. Jenkins said even unpaid leave would help the poor who had to leave jobs temporarily but wanted them back. And he expressed bewilderment at the "yuppie bill" argument that Bartlett had been banging a few minutes earlier. "Say it only helps middle-income people, the so-called yuppies," Jenkins hypothesized. "What is wrong in America today in occasionally helping a middle-income worker?"

Jenkins signed off by reiterating Hyde's argument about the pregnant working woman deciding between birth and abortion. In the galleries and in the hallways outside, feminist activists were experiencing that peculiar mix of emotions that accompanies political courtship between philosophical adversaries.

The debate thereafter returned to the familiar groove of the morning and the previous evening. Along the way, Howard Berman of California entered a written statement recalling how his state statute in California, enacted twelve years earlier, had led to the emergence of parental leave as an issue in Congress. While he had supported strictly maternal leave in the early going, he said, he had been convinced that the broader coverage of all workers' family and medical emergencies was the preferable path for legislation.

The penultimate speaker for the Gordon-Weldon substitute was Weldon, who advertised his credentials as a pro-business Republican. He reminded his colleagues of his late conversion to family leave, and counted off the tough votes he had cast out of loyalty to his party and its leader. He had stood by the president on the minimum wage, on workplace hazards and on unlimited liability in the oil pollution bill. "But business sometimes overreacts," said Weldon. "There is a responsible role for the government to play in setting parameters for the private sector."

The emotional center of Weldon's message seemed to be that he had been the youngest of nine children, that his wife had been one of seven and that he and she understood the exigencies of family life.

"It is not about management versus labor, it is not about employers versus employees and it is certainly not about the AFL-CIO versus the Chamber of Commerce," said Weldon, drawing smiles and some chuckles from the press gallery and from the House chamber's rear railing, where members congregate during a debate.

And then time allowed under the rule for debate on the amendment had expired. Shortly after noon the question was called on the pending Gordon-Weldon substitute. The standard voice vote seemed dominated by ayes except for the usual shouted noes. Weldon asked for a recorded vote, and the vote was taken using the electronic device. Before many minutes had passed, it was clear from the proliferation of green lights that the sponsors were going to get their momentum-building vote. The official tally was 259 votes for the substitute and 157 against. There were 17 members who did not vote.

The good news for the bill was that forty-seven Republicans had crossed the aisle to vote for the substitute, most of them women or northeasterners. The bad news was that thirty-four Democrats had gone the other way, and that at least some of the Republicans supporting the substitute apparently did so merely to weaken the bill prior to its passage.

But in general, the floor battle was proving surprisingly smooth. Not only had Penny decided not to offer his "Mother's Day" amendment reducing the bill to maternal leave, but Stenholm had decided to withhold his as well. While it was not as likely to peel away votes as Penny's, Stenholm's amendment had more than a little allure. He wanted to redefine the leave benefit as a kind of guaranteed rehiring mechanism, allowing employers to replace the worker on leave but requiring them to rehire the leave taker when a later opening allowed. The task force had prepared a Clay amendment to Stenholm's amendment that they hoped would enable them to defuse it. But Stenholm's capitulation obviated this tactic and expedited matters greatly.

Bartlett himself had pulled the plug on three other moderating amendments, insisting that there could be no meaningful compromise and calling the Gordon-Weldon substitute "a Clay compromise with Schroeder."

When all amendments had been disposed of under the rule, the Committee of the Whole "rose" and reported its handiwork to the full, formal House. Thus begins the endgame, the last formal phase of a bill's consideration. It consists of a report from the Committee of the Whole, a motion to recommit the bill to committee and, assuming the recommittal motion fails, an up or down vote on approving the bill itself. In this case, the motion to recommit included instructions to strike the bill's essential sections and substitute the gist of the disallowed Carr and Parker amendments—two years of data gathering and study while the Congress acted as the official laboratory for family leave. After a few minutes of debate, the vote was taken.

This time the result was even more one-sided, as the House rejected the motion to recommit 264–155. Fewer members were missing on this vote, and only twenty-six Democrats sided with the Republicans in voting to recommit. The chamber then moved immediately to a vote on passing HR 770 as amended.

The vote to pass the bill was 237 for, 187 against.

The sponsors, proponents and advocates of family leave felt a sudden rush of conflicting emotions. They had triumphed and passed the bill. Their strategy had worked. They had lined up the people they wanted and they had surpassed a majority of the full House by nearly a score of votes. Yet somehow, in the exhilaration of that moment, they were also feeling a twinge of disappointment.

No one should have been surprised that the final vote had been closer than the previous two, but the sponsors had to wonder why it was so much closer. The momentum had seemed to build from the beginning of the debate to the end and from the first vote to the second, and in contrast the final vote represented a falling back.

Feinstein and Champlin were checking their vote tallies. Nine Republicans who had voted for the Gordon-Weldon substitute had switched and opposed final passage. So had sixteen Democrats, most of them from the South. In a sense, the two votes were identical, "but you could explain it different at home," said Stenholm, who had voted against both.

Still, there had been thirty-nine Republicans on the bill at final passage. And of the twenty-eight women in the House, all but six had backed the bill. There were sweet spots throughout the roll call. Besides Hyde and the other conservatives who had spoken for the bill, the sponsors found Solomon, the angry protester against the rule that limited debate and the number of amendments that could be offered, crossing the aisle to vote for final passage. And the three House Republican women who were running for the Senate that fall—Lynn Martin of Illinois, Claudine Schneider of Rhode Island and Patricia Saiki of Hawaii—had all voted for the bill.

In the hallways, stairways and sidewalks outside there were hugs, kisses and tears. The next day *The New York Times* ran a picture of Schroeder

cheek to cheek with the Women's Legal Defense Fund's Judith Lichtman
(who was misidentified as Marge Roukema). Schroeder also tossed off
what became the quote of the day. Noting the nearness of Mother's Day,
she said: "We finally did something real besides chocolate and cards."

In the aftermath of the vote, with the proponents still aglow, a tight-
lipped Bartlett said he had spoken with the White House and that President Bush's veto message was all but in print. "The bill is dead," Bartlett
said. "Any modest improvement in the bill had some potential risk for
reviving it."

The remark was reminiscent of John Motley's pronouncing family
leave dead after its first success in an Ed and Labor markup in November
1987. And in the week following the vote on HR 770, Motley himself
would be back on the House side of the Hill working hard. The Senate
had yet to act on the bill; but Motley, anticipating a veto, was firming up
the House votes he was counting on to sustain it.

10.

The Veto

Dodd was delighted at family leave's success on the House floor in May 1990. The bill had not only passed but had done so with a modicum of bipartisanship. The strategy of the Gordon-Weldon substitute had worked, jostling the fixed points of reference and letting members take a fresh look. Those members most comfortable in the political median strip got a chance to have it both ways, voting to weaken the bill as well as to pass it. And while elements of the coalition supporting family leave found this same dynamic disconcerting, Dodd saw it as the one road home.

Dodd had taken to heart something Kennedy had said to him years earlier after a discouraging markup on another matter. Just as it takes more than one generation to change the way people think, Kennedy said, it takes more than one Congress to pass a meaningful bill. You have to offer ideas that get ignored and then go out and campaign on them as issues. You have to come back and offer those issues as bills again and again until they get considered. Then you have to push them to the brink again and again until they finally get over.

Dodd saw the family leave bills he had introduced in three consecutive Congresses not as finished products but as opening bids. The specifications would have to be modified to make enactment possible. Other senators who weighed in would want their ideas to be visible in the final version. Dodd knew he would not be entirely pleased with the result, but he also believed that the result would be better, both substantively and in some other, ineffable sense, for having endured the process. This was the way the Senate worked, and Dodd believed in the Senate.

The Senate, however, had yet to show much faith in S 345, the family leave bill approved by Senate Labor in April 1989. The legislation had been idling off the track for ten months since the committee report was printed that July. Like other senators, Dodd had been subject to myriad distractions from Central America to child care. The Senate had passed a patchwork of child care grants, credits and programs in 1989, as had the House. But jurisdictional and financing disputes had kept the bill from going to a conference committee until May 1990. The conference had begun, on the same day the House had approved the rule for consideration of family leave.

Negotiations over that issue continued to drain Dodd and his staff. They also colored every meeting he had with another senator or House member and every conversation he had with an administration official. The interplay and competition between the two issues was a constant complication. "Everything became a trade-off," his aide Rich Tarplin said later. "Do we see this guy on this issue or that one? Where do we need him more?"

And yet, with its May 10 vote on HR 770, the House had handed Dodd the family leave ball with very little time left on the clock. The 1990 session was nearly five months gone, and immediate floor consideration would be necessary so that a House-Senate conference committee could be appointed in time to finish its work before the August recess and put a conference report on both floors in September. Any slower pace would probably subject the bill to killer delays, as this was another election year and the session was sure to end by October.

So, to expedite both the floor debate in the Senate and the House-Senate conference committee to come, Dodd decided to set aside his own bill in favor of HR 770, the House bill in the amended form just passed. By so doing, he could not only circumvent some of the controversy in his own chamber but also minimize any problems in conference. And he could simplify the case he was making to his colleagues and the news media.

Dodd knew, of course, that he would be disappointing some of the advocates of family leave. Knowing the difficulties of the House, some in the coalition had been willing to sit still for the Gordon-Weldon compromise in hopes of improving upon it in the Senate. Dodd and Kennedy had, after all, already seen through committee a bill that had ten weeks for family leave and thirteen for medical and applied to every business with twenty or more employees. Their bill also had the benefit kicking in sooner, requiring just 900 hours of work for eligibility rather than the 1,000 hours in the House bill. At the same time, switching to HR 770 also meant covering spouses' illnesses, which had not become part of Dodd's bill at that point. Dodd had been getting heat on the spousal issue from Howard Metzenbaum, the number-three Democrat on Senate Labor, who had pressured him earlier on elder care.

In the end, Dodd was less interested in the details than he was in closing the deal. He wanted something that would sell in the Senate, and HR 770 had sold in the House. So, with a minimum of further fussing, Dodd persuaded Kennedy to sign off on his new approach. The next step would be to remove S 345 from the Calendar of General Orders and put it out on the floor, where the substance of HR 770 could be substituted for the original text. So Dodd and Kennedy went to the one man they needed to make the next step happen: Senate majority leader George J. Mitchell of Maine. Mitchell was then concluding his first eighteen months as the successor to Robert C. Byrd, the longtime Senate Democratic leader who had been in charge when family leave went to the floor in September 1988.

Byrd, after a dozen years as the Democratic leader, had voluntarily relinquished the job. That struck some laymen as odd, but Byrd was swapping his old title for two new ones: Senate president pro tempore and chairman of the Senate Appropriations Committee. The first of these posts is mentioned in the Constitution and stands third in the line of presidential succession, after the vice president and the Speaker of the House. Although largely ceremonial, it provides unparalleled dignity and some of the best office space in the Capitol. Moreover, as Appropriations chair, Byrd was able to enlarge the budget for the pro tem over the next few years, even as he was also directing more than $1 billion in new federal spending to his home state of West Virginia.

When Byrd had announced his intentions in April 1988, two other candidates for the leadership quickly installed themselves as the favorites, one by campaigning in the media and the other by asserting his seniority. Mitchell campaigned quietly, in conversations with colleagues well out of public view. In the closing days before the vote, Mitchell refused to claim any particular number of votes. He offered only his characteristic soft-spoken assurance that he would win. And he did, easily, on the first ballot.

The son of a janitor and a Lebanese immigrant woman, Mitchell had attended Bowdoin College on scholarship. As a guard on the basketball team, he was known for his ball handling and tenacity on defense. He brought some of the same qualities to his work as chairman of the Democratic Party in the once "rock-ribbed Republican" state of Maine in the 1970s. In 1978, Jimmy Carter appointed him to the federal bench on the advice of Maine's senior senator, Edmund S. Muskie, for whom Mitchell had once worked. When Muskie became Carter's secretary of state in 1980, Maine's Democratic governor appointed Mitchell to fill Muskie's term. Many thought Mitchell miscast in the Senate, with his bookish looks and his penchant for legalistic precision. But he won a full term in his own right in 1982 and a second elected term six years later with more than 80 percent of the vote. Three weeks after that, he was the Senate's leading man.

In that role, Mitchell would be largely responsible for denying George Bush the honeymoon he had expected in his first year. The fifty-five-year-old former federal judge had been elected by his party colleagues a few weeks after Bush was elected president. And he had shown a talent for using not only his party's majority but also the Senate's procedures to frustrate the new administration. While committee chairmen provided critical assists in both cases, it was Mitchell who led the floor fight against Tower and against the capital-gains tax cut.

Mitchell had been known as a liberal but never as an ideologue. His rare moments of passion were usually triggered by issues that mattered to Maine. He could become quite intense about acid rain, footwear imports or the price of home heating oil. But as a rule, the Mitchell style was lawyerly and low-key, self-assured but amenable to compromise. That was why his stiff resistance to the new president seemed surprising. Bush, after all, was notoriously a "people person," renowned for his handwritten notes. After both men were elected to their new jobs in 1988, Bush would head for his place at Kennebunkport and offer Mitchell a lift home courtesy of the Air Force. But if Mitchell was wooed, he was not won over. And by the end of Mitchell's first eighteen months at the head of the Senate, Bush had reason to feel he would have been better off with Byrd.

But with all his success in seizing the reins, Mitchell was under no illusions regarding his power. The Senate majority leader has been described as *primus inter pares*—"the first among equals." Apt as the phrase may be, the emphasis should be on the *pares* more than the *primus*. In the hierarchical House, the majority dictates the schedule and the rules without regard for the minority. But in the lone-wolf world of the Senate, the minority has considerable rights because every individual senator has rights. And each senator's privileges and prerogatives are observed to an almost religious degree.

The Senate has a majority whip, but he is not the equivalent of the House majority whip, with all his troops, task forces and computerized data bases. The Senate has a Rules Committee, but it deals primarily with internal administration and has no authority to order specific floor debates or exclude amendments. In the Senate, bills come to the floor only when the majority leader moves all the planets into the proper alignment. He must first enlist the support of his own party, but he then must go a long step further and solicit the cooperation of the minority party as well because any member can, by the rules and traditions of the Senate, exercise his or her right to unlimited debate. This imperative is captured in the key phrase of the Senate's daily life: unanimous consent.

Day by day, and sometimes hour by hour, the majority and minority leaders arrange the proceedings on the Senate floor with ad hoc plans they have cleared with literally every other senator. Frequently, these agreements include specific allotments of time for certain amendments to be offered and debated, which is why they are also called time agreements.

A unanimous consent agreement, often called a UC, is typically "propounded" on the floor toward the beginning of the day, and the leaders usually close each day's proceedings by announcing what has been agreed to for the following day. But the UC agreement may be altered throughout the day, depending on the circumstances. The two party leaders have open telephone lines to every senator's office at all times, so they can "shop a UC" among their colleagues without leaving their own offices or respective cloakrooms (the closely guarded clubhouses just off the chamber floor where everything is off the record and senators call one another by their first names). Then, when the leaders have contacted every office and secured every senator's cooperation, the plan for the next few hours of floor time can go into effect.

Considering the tedious and time-consuming demands of the leader's office, it was not surprising that some of the chamber's leading lights had shown scant interest in it. Bill Bradley of New Jersey had resisted all suggestions that he run for leader, as had Lloyd Bentsen of Texas, Sam Nunn of Georgia and Dale Bumpers of Arkansas. Kennedy had shown some ambition for the leadership in the 1960s, but he had been bumped from the ladder in 1971 (two years after Chappaquiddick radically altered his career trajectory).

In the spring of 1990, Dodd and Kennedy were both long-standing

Mitchell allies who had worked closely with him on child care. Dodd had also been coaxing him for years on family leave. The House vote obviously necessitated some kind of response in the Senate, but what kind? Mitchell was getting calendar conscious, and he remembered the cataract of amendments the Republicans had unleashed on the issue in the fall of 1988. How many days of floor time would it take to do family leave? Which other bills would not make it as a result? Dodd told Mitchell he was ready to strip his own bill and take up the House-passed version instead. Mitchell could appreciate that, but he also had a bigger question: How many votes would Dodd have for cloture?

Dodd had thought he had a majority of the Senate on the merits of family leave back in the fall of 1988, even before his door-to-door campaign and before the passage of the bill in the House. Now he thought he might be close to sixty, if the vote were on the merits of the bill itself. But getting to sixty for cloture is always a separate issue. Some senators refuse to vote aye on the first motion for cloture because they respect the principle of "extended debate." And extended debate seemed a high probability in this case. Republicans would be under pressure to kill the bill and spare their president the discomfort of a veto. If that meant a filibuster on a mom's apple pie bill, Mitchell expected the GOP would not shrink from its duty. So Mitchell told Dodd to have sixty votes if he wanted a date for the floor.

THAT SENT DODD AND KENNEDY back to their vote counters. It also raised the question of how they might leverage Mitchell. The Democratic Policy Committee of twenty Senate Democrats included half a dozen at least whose support for family leave was suspect. But, unlike the House, there seemed no active opposition to the bill on the part of any Democratic senators. Moreover, by means of a discreet inquiry here and there, Dodd and Kennedy had identified several allies in the Senate Republican Conference as well. Dodd, who had always considered Dole a friend— after a fashion—liked to think that the Republican leader would stand aside at some strategic moment rather than pursue a Pyrrhic victory on a family issue.

Besides, Dodd could argue, why should Senate Republicans expend the energy and incur the political costs of filibustering family leave when they knew their president was going to veto the bill anyway? Dole seemed to be worried about the House sustaining that veto, keeping it from returning to the Senate. But assurances to that effect were available on every hand. Motley of the NFIB was certain, and so were Tavenner of

CARE and the others who had been working the bill most closely. Nick Calio, Bush's legislative director for the House, was doing his own soundings and believed the sustaining minority would be solid.

That May ended with all sides still checking their ammunition. Tarplin, Dodd's aide, felt far more prepared this time than he had when, on three days' notice, Byrd brought the bill out on the floor in 1988. On that occasion, which was Tarplin's first floor battle, Byrd had entangled the bill in a thicket of procedural maneuvers and ancillary issues, and Dodd had been forced to hold the fort nearly alone against attack from all directions. Tarplin had been at his side, sitting in the simple chair that senators may request be set alongside their own for staff use. Tarplin had spent many long, sometimes harrowing hours in that chair, wondering at times what was going on. It had been a humbling experience.

Thereafter, Tarplin had immersed himself in Senate procedure, poring over manuals and watching hours of instructional videotapes produced by a former floor assistant (known in Hill offices as the Marty Gold tapes). He was ready when his next chance to get back on the horse arrived in March 1989. That was when he staffed Dodd in the debate on S5, the child care bill, which underwent extensive revision on the floor. Tarplin also had compiled a fat dark blue notebook of his own material on family leave. He had detailed talking points for each argument he had ever heard raised against it. He had case histories of families, statistics on costs and descriptions of family leave programs in other countries. He had dozens of sample amendments that might be offered and outlines of rebuttal arguments against each. He was ready to go.

But in the weeks that followed the House vote of May 10, the Senate players most concerned with family leave were all preoccupied with the conference committee on child care. Mitchell continued to check with Dodd for probable vote counts on HR 770. He also solicited what information he could from Alan Cranston, the four-term Californian who had been the Senate Democrats' best man with a tally sheet even before becoming their whip in 1977. Cranston supported family leave, but was increasingly distracted by the Senate Ethics Committee investigation into his ties to Charles H. Keating Jr., a kingpin in the savings and loan scandal. Even under the best of circumstances, however, the Senate whip system could do little more than guess which senators were truly committed to a bill. The Senate leadership had little to hold over anyone's head, and no power to alter legislation with task forces and creative rules for floor consideration—as in the House.

As best Mitchell could tell, to pass family leave would necessitate making it the main pending business on the floor for at least a week, even if the Republicans did not mount a filibuster. If opponents used the full bag of tactics, it would take two weeks. That would allow for initial debate prior to the filing of a first cloture petition, the ripening of the petition, the cloture vote itself and the debate that would follow (even if cloture were invoked). Assuming the votes were there for cloture, which Mitchell did not, it would take two weeks to plow through the amendments. During that time, under a helpful procedure devised by Mike Mansfield as majority leader in the 1970s, it would be possible for the Senate to consider some other bills temporarily. It might be possible to consider a child-care conference report, for example, should there be one. But family leave would bulk large on the calendar whether Mitchell attempted to do it prior to the July 4th recess or prior to the August recess. It would have helped to have some idea of what the Republicans were thinking; and, for a time, everyone seemed to be listening at everyone else's keyhole.

In the end, Dodd's instinct about Dole proved at least partially correct. The GOP leader came to Mitchell with a proposal. They could do family leave as a full-dress floor debate that summer and take two weeks at it, or they could expedite the matter on an anonymous voice vote and do it in a matter of hours. Dodd could have his bill and Mitchell could have his two weeks of calendar back in the bargain. It seemed too good to be true —and it seemed too generous to be Dole.

But the Republican leader was in earnest. He could draw a distinction between the interests of the bill's outside opponents and those of his Republican colleagues on the Hill. Unless he had the votes to defeat HR 770 straight up, Dole would have to lead his party in a filibuster that the news media were likely to view as families versus business. Not many Republicans seemed eager for that. Orrin Hatch, the ranking member of Senate Labor, had seemed more enthusiastic about helping Kennedy and Dodd on child care than about defeating them on family leave. Moreover, the 1988 filibuster had left some hard feelings in the Republican Conference. There had been some tough talk about killer amendments in the GOP cloakroom and at the regular Tuesday policy lunch, but few of those doing the talking had shown up to make good on it. Senator Thad Cochran of Mississippi had complained about it at the time, saying, "You can't get them down to the floor to offer the amendments."

Why undertake such a battle, Dole asked, if you were not sure of winning? Why not let the bill slide through with minimal fanfare, scuttle it in the White House and give the House GOP the satisfaction of sustaining another veto? In the meantime, the lack of a Senate floor fight would lower the profile of the issue, draining the conflict and suspense and deflating media interest.

Motley, Tavenner and the Chamber understood Dole's reasons and felt sure they could still prevail with the White House and the House. But they were disquieted by the sight of a bill they had opposed so vehemently for so long passing the Senate in a procedure one could miss while taking a bathroom break. A voice vote might be interpreted by the media as a stamp of unanimous approval, and it might weaken the resolve of some opponents in the House. Moreover, from a strictly parochial point of view, how could a given trade association, political action committee or business group know whom to scold and whom to praise—and whose campaign coffers to replenish—if no votes were recorded?

For Mitchell, the choice posed by Dole was not a difficult one. For Dodd, the matter was far more complicated. When aides Tarplin and Ruff sounded out the support coalition, the reaction was mixed. Some were distressed that Dodd had adopted HR 770 instead of pressing his own bill in the Senate and improving the House-passed bill in conference. Now they saw Dodd refusing to demand a vote that would put the Senate on record for family leave. Dole must know he was licked or he would not offer these terms of surrender, so why not go ahead and win? Surely Bush could not veto the bill after it had passed in both chambers by recorded votes.

Despite this feedback Dodd ultimately found the choice nearly as obvious as Mitchell did. Both men had their hands full with child care, an issue with a chance of being negotiated through to a settlement. Family leave, on the other hand, seemed to be veto bait. So why not take this opportunity to pass the bill in both chambers and force the president's feet to the fire? The veto might be fodder for a campaign speech or two in the fall, and they could start over in 1991 with a comeback bill that already had cleared both chambers.

On June 14, a warm Thursday in early summer, the Senate convened early for a lengthy program of debate on a proposed amendment to the Constitution banning flag desecration. Senators were also eager to proceed on a budget resolution for the next fiscal year, a housing bill and a crime bill (a hardy biennial that blooms in years that end in elections). Also in the air was talk of a deal on family leave, which otherwise threatened to sabotage the rest of the month.

As the afternoon waned, Mitchell and Dole came to the floor and Mitchell pulled his microphone from its holder. Staff members inhabiting the couches around the chamber's perimeter sat forward in anticipation. In the press balcony above the Senate floor, a reporter banged through the swinging door and into the gallery on the other side. "Mitchell's up," he said, signaling to his colleagues that the leader was about to set the program for the next day. But as reporters filed out of their workspace and slid into the rows of balcony seats, it soon became apparent that something more than just a schedule was in the works.

In his usual flat style, Mitchell said that he and Dole "and several of the committee chairmen and other interested senators have spent virtually the entire day discussing a unanimous consent agreement that would permit us to complete action promptly on two important pending matters. . . ." As Mitchell continued, some of the reporters began to leave the balcony to call their editors. Mitchell and Dole were about to pass two newsworthy bills—the budget resolution and family leave—and they were going to do it without a recorded vote on either one.

First, Mitchell said, he wanted to have a motion to proceed to consideration of HR 770, the family leave bill, which would be debatable for two hours, with the time equally divided between proponents and opponents. At the end of that time, Mitchell said, the motion to proceed would be adopted by voice vote. Then, according to the agreement, the bill would be "read for a third time" (a formality almost always dispensed with) and "passed without any intervening action, motion or debate."

The rest of the elaborate UC granted the same swift fate to the budget resolution and set out an order for further consideration of the flag amendment, the housing bill and the crime package as well. But for family leave, the bottom line was that final passage was just two hours away.

Several senators appeared on the floor to converse formally with the leaders, making sure that their individual interests had been protected in the overall deal. This jousting continued for some minutes, while Dodd and Kennedy were coming to the floor with their notebooks and their staffs. But when it was over, it was clear that no one would object to the UC. As the floor managers for HR 770 took their places on the floor, they knew they already had prevailed.

Dodd rose to speak with an air of mock regret. "I had come suited up, the armor was on," he said. "I had mounted my charger, my lance and broadsword in hand. I had entered the field to slay the dragon, and there are no dragons. We have a consensus on a bill that I thought was going to be debated for a number of days. . . ."

As if to prove he had been prepared, Dodd proceeded to enumerate the arguments for the bill and offer rebuttal to the usual critique. He also averred that he would have had the votes to invoke cloture, although it would have taken time. He saluted the minority leader for his wisdom and added: "I learned a long time ago that you do not argue about a victory when you are handed one." And for good measure, he entered in the *Record* the editorials from sixty-two newspapers and magazines that had endorsed the bill and urged Bush to sign it. They represented papers of all sizes and regions—from Duluth, Minnesota; to Hobbs, New Mexico; to Augusta, Maine—and they implied a mighty tide of public opinion.

Kennedy also took a turn on the floor, speaking in his most stentorian voice and thanking staff one by one, name by name. Kennedy twice admonished the president to read the speech Barbara Bush had given that spring at Wellesley College in Massachusetts, a plea for the claims of the family in competition with an ambitious career. Mitchell added a few remarks, quoting a full paragraph from Bush's own Rockford speech of 1988 assuring women they could get their jobs back after the birth or serious illness of a child.

To round out the program, Orrin Hatch came to the floor with an armload of charts and presented a full-dress assault on the bill. He had all the research from the NFIB files readily at hand. The bill would drive small employers out of business. It would stunt growth, kill jobs. And it was unnecessary to boot because businesses were already providing family leave when needed. Hatch was joined in his remarks by a few of his colleagues—Cochran of Mississippi, Thurmond of South Carolina and Conrad Burns of Montana. Toward the end of the time allotted, Dole rose to state his own opposition, reading into the record a veto-threat letter from the secretary of labor, his wife, Elizabeth.

The speeches having been given, under the previous order the Senate turned to the budget resolution without a backward glance. And with that, a family leave bill had been passed by both chambers of Congress.

BECAUSE THE SENATE HAD TAKEN UP the House bill and passed it without amendment, there was no need for family leave to go to a conference committee. All the bill needed was the standard packaging for its trip down Pennsylvania Avenue. Any House bill upon passage is officially reprinted ("engrossed") and signed by the clerk of the House. Any Senate bill upon passage is also engrossed and signed by the secretary of the Senate. After final approval by both chambers the bill is "enrolled," meaning that it is reproduced on parchment and certified as accurate by the clerk of the originating chamber. Then the Speaker signs it, the president pro tempore signs it and it is hand-delivered to the White House. The president then has ten days (not counting Sundays) to sign the bill into law or return it to Congress unsigned with his objections— that is, to veto it. If the allotted days pass without presidential action of either kind, the bill becomes law without his signature.

GEORGE BUSH'S RESPONSE TO FAMILY leave had been a subject of debate and uncertainty since before he was president. The 1988 campaign speech in Rockford, to which Kennedy and others had alluded gleefully in floor debate, had not been specific to any legislation. And it had not envisioned all the circumstances to be covered by the family leave bills introduced since.

But it was just enough of a scrap for the hopeful, and they seized upon it at the time and clung to it for years afterward. It was repeated more than once by proponents of family leave when HR 770 was debated on the House floor, and it became a touchstone in the presentations of many members and family leave supporters thereafter. The Bush campaign had clarified the Rockford remarks almost immediately, saying the candidate never meant the assurance should come from an intrusive governmental mandate. And Bush himself had been consistent on the point in subsequent public statements on the issue. Yet some continued to hope.

Prominent among these was Marge Roukema, the bill's Republican mainstay in the House. Roukema's view was that the president wanted to sign the bill but felt constrained by circumstances: "They just made a decision to throw one to the business groups," said Roukema, "because they had gone against them on so many others."

Letters were sent to Bush by many of the Republicans who voted for HR 770 on May 10, a group of thirty-nine dominated by the New York City region and the rest of the Northeast: nine GOP aye votes from New York, three each from New Jersey and Connecticut, five from the New England states and three each from Pennsylvania and Ohio. There were two votes for the bill from Illinois Republicans (Hyde and Martin) and one each from Republican women in Florida, Maryland, Nebraska and Hawaii. The other GOP votes were cast by men from widely scattered states: South Carolina, Texas, Michigan, California, Alaska and Washington (where there were two).

A popular theory among advocates of family leave, especially Republicans, was that Bush liked the idea and that only the intervention of John Sununu, the White House chief of staff, was preventing a Rose Garden signing ceremony for HR 770. Sununu seemed more than willing to foster this impression himself, just as he seemed prepared to take responsibility for every decision Bush made. The former governor of New Hampshire, who had helped Bush win that state's critical primary in 1988, played the role of the administration's conservative heavy to the hilt.

But in truth, the hopes for a Bush signature may always have been vain. While disposed to negotiate on child care and a variety of other social issues, the administration had frowned steadily on the family leave bill and had never sat down to discuss any compromise. Dodd called his former colleague Vice President Dan Quayle, wrote to Barbara Bush and promised to "open every window and door" at the White House. But a certain amount of this chest-thumping was an attempt to finagle the White House into negotiations. And the White House was not to be budged.

Roukema called everyone she knew in the administration repeatedly. She, too, wrote to Barbara Bush, asking for an appointment to discuss the issue. The first lady replied politely that she saw no reason to discuss it because she never got involved in legislation. "I can't imagine they never did have that conversation about it," Roukema said later, referring to George and Barbara.

But the response from the White House never varied. Prior to the House vote, Sununu had come to the Hill to reassure Republicans there would be no White House reversal, no sudden embracing of the bill that would leave them dangling from their no votes. Sununu had repeated this pledge to a hastily convened group of lobbyists in the White House's West Wing on May 7, the day the House found out the bill was coming to the floor. And on June 14, the showdown day in the Senate, the administration had delivered a letter to each senator's office: The veto decision on family leave had been made.

All the same, one could scarcely blame the bill's backers for trying to change the president's mind—or its opponents for doubting his resolve. This was the spring in which Bush agreed to a "budget summit" with House and Senate Democrats, a negotiation that would force him to abandon his "no new taxes" pledge. At the same time, deals were being negotiated that would lead to enactment of two other landmark laws directly affecting employers. One, the Americans with Disabilities Act, had been passed by the Senate in 1989 and would be passed by the House later in the same May as family leave. The ADA was a mandate on business, and it would require billions of dollars to be spent on new entryways, access ramps and other facilities. But it had enormous momentum, not only among Democrats and an array of activist interests, but also among many Republicans (led by Dole, who had lost the use of his right arm in World War II).

The Bush administration was also negotiating with Hill players on a civil rights bill that had been introduced in February 1990. The bill had been written to overturn six Supreme Court decisions that had narrowed previous laws barring job discrimination. Initially, Bush said the bill would force hiring by racial quota and vowed to veto it. But by May, Bush was saying he wanted to sign the civil rights bill if objectionable features could be removed. Here again, business groups were frantically lobbying the White House not to yield.

Steve Gunderson, a Republican from Wisconsin, served on Ed and Labor throughout the life of family leave on the Hill. He never saw a scenario by which it made sense to sign family leave. "If you were George Bush and you looked at those three bills [ADA, civil rights and family leave] and you felt you had to be hard-line on at least one of them, which would you pick?"

Even if there had been some ambivalence about the president's position at one time, there could not have been any after the actual House vote was taken on May 10. During the floor fight Steve Bartlett had decided not to offer several amendments even after Rules had declared them in order. Nothing could be further from the combative Bartlett's nature, but he made it clear he was folding his tent after consultation with the White House. He had been assured there would be a veto, and he saw no point in moderating the bill to increase its appeal.

The White House issued Bush's veto of HR 770 two weeks after the voice vote in the Senate. It was June 29, a quiet Friday on which much of the Hill seemed to have taken the day off in advance of the coming holiday week. In his veto message Bush reiterated his belief that "time off for a child's birth or adoption or for family illness is an important benefit for employers to offer employees." But he said those positive feelings were trumped by his profound distaste for "rigid, federally imposed requirements." Bush's veto message systematically restated each of the arguments raised against the bill by the opponents in the House and Senate and before that by the business lobbies. He said any new requirements on business might eliminate jobs or retard job creation. And he emphasized the flexibility that businesses might need and that employees might want, such as the freedom to substitute a brief paid leave for what Bush called the "lengthy" unpaid leave contemplated in HR 770.

· · ·

BUSH'S VETO OF HR 770 WAS HIS THIRD of the year and the thirteenth of his presidency. Congress had yet to muster the two-thirds majority in both chambers to override any of his vetoes, but it had been getting closer. The bid to override Bush's ninth veto (a bill resolving the Eastern Airlines strike) had reached 261 votes in the House. And on the tenth (an extension of special immigrant status for Chinese students), the House managed a staggering 390 votes to override (the Senate failed to follow suit the following day by four votes).

The House then mounted something of a streak, voting to override vetoes on an Amtrak bill (294 votes) and a bill loosening limits on the political activities of federal employees (327 votes). But in the last two cases the Senate failed to reach two-thirds by three and two votes, respectively. That streak, however short, gave House leaders some thought that they might do well on a family leave override. Dodd, meanwhile, was saying publicly that he thought the Senate would come as close as it had in its last three attempts.

Foley scheduled the override vote in the House on Wednesday, July 25. At the previous Thursday's whip meeting the best intelligence indicated little if any movement in the vote. The NFIB continued to make the bill a top priority in allocating its time and calibrating its rhetoric. Chamber of Commerce lobbyists in Washington were making sure their local Chambers were calling the Hill and insisting upon votes to sustain Bush's veto. The phone calls, letters, telegrams and fax transmissions from businesses in members' home districts had never been heavier.

On the day of the vote, Tavenner's organization made sure its red T-shirts (they had CARE emblazoned on them) and "No Mandates" buttons were everywhere in the halls. Summer interns recruited from the antitax think tank Citizens for a Sound Economy and other business and conservative organizations were brought in to act as human billboards as the hour of the vote approached. Harris Fawell, an Illinois Republican from Ed and Labor, saw all the young people in their regalia and said, "If we could get this every time we'd win a lot more often."

Democrats who might have voted to override just to stick it to Bush seemed to believe the Senate would come up short again and spoil the partisan party. And it was nearly impossible to add any new Republicans, as those disinclined to vote for the bill in the first place were hardly disposed to do so by their president's veto. The vote was without suspense. The final tally showed just 232 votes to override and 195 against. A lusty cheer went up from the Republican side as the vote was announced. They were the minority, but they had won on this one. The majority was 53 votes shy of the 285 needed to override, given that 427 members were present and voting. Even more discouraging for the bill sponsors was the decline in support compared to passage in May: The override vote featured five fewer green lights on the board and eight more red.

The drop of five aye votes was due to four Democrats failing to vote on July 25 and one Republican, Virginia Smith of Nebraska, changing her May vote to sustain the veto. The additional votes against the override came from four Republicans and three southern Democrats who had missed the vote in May but who turned out to oppose the override in July.

"We shall override, someday," said Pat Schroeder sadly.

With the veto sustained, the Senate would take no override vote of its own and the issue was dead for the year. It was no worse a fate than the advocates of the bill had anticipated, and yet it seemed deeply disappointing. The elation of passing the bill on a dramatic House vote in May had been tempered by the anticlimax in the Senate and the steadfast stonewalling by the White House. And it all seemed overshadowed by the futility of the effort to override.

After more than five years of trying, the advocates of family leave felt they had finally surmounted all the many obstacles, only to encounter a still higher and more immovable barrier in the power of the presidency. Yet Fred Feinstein would remember that summer as "the turning point" for family leave, not only because passage had been achieved in both chambers but also because the administration had taken the political monkey onto its back.

The White House had scarcely ended its celebration of the July 25 override vote when David Gergen, a former Reagan communications director, in a TV appearance, chastised Bush and the GOP in general for missing the boat on family leave. The issue was a winner for the Democrats, Gergen said, because the Republicans were making it one. The issue would keep returning, he warned, and it would be bigger every time it came back.

Part Four

FORCING THE ISSUE: THE 102ND CONGRESS (1991–1992)

11.

Testing the Mettle

BY THE TIME THE 102ND CONGRESS convened in January 1991, family
leave had lost some of its cachet with the press. Raising the subject with
a reporter often prompted a yawn or a rolling of the eyes. Reporters had
not lost their personal interest in the bill—an interest increased by the
growing prevalence of women in the congressional galleries—but they
had tired of trying to interest their editors in the bill. To some degree,
the lack of enthusiasm on the part of news editors and producers
stemmed from frustration. News managers like stories with beginnings
and endings, and stories about legislation rarely seemed to end. Because
the legislative track requires multiple station stops before arriving anywhere, reporters are constantly explaining why some intermediate milestone matters. The editors usually succumb to exasperation and say,
"Call me when they really do something."

Family leave arrived as major national news in May 1990, when House
passage of HR 770 brought it to the front page of *The Washington Post*
and the *Los Angeles Times* (and to extensive inside-page play in *The New
York Times*). Scores of large metropolitan papers rely on these three
national newspapers and the wire services (primarily the Associated
Press) to augment the work of their own bureaus in Washington. Thus
the news judgments of these three newsrooms resonate far beyond their

own publications. Also influential was the mention the bill received on the major broadcast TV networks, whose news programs were still the main source of public affairs information for most Americans and whose news judgment colored that of other journalists.

But soon thereafter, a combination of circumstances consigned family leave to media oblivion once again. Passage in the Senate in mid-June was little noticed. Dole's maneuver, allowing HR 770 to pass on a voice vote, effectively squelched its news value (a brief account clung to the bottom of an inside page in *The New York Times*). The veto made news, of course, as did the attempted override. But the override attempt came so much later (nearly a full month) and fell so far short that the story played mostly as the undefeated veto record of George Bush. But none of these machinations made much news in comparison with Bush's decision to drop his "no new taxes" pledge and include new revenues in the budget-deficit reduction deal he was hammering out with Democrats. By August, Iraq's invasion of Kuwait had moved the news focus once again to the Middle East, where it would stay for most of the next nine months.

But while the media moved on to other priorities in the winter of 1990–91, the sponsors of family leave did not. They were determined to make this the Congress in which their bill became law, and they got an immediate and substantial boost when, for the first time, the leadership in both the House and Senate decided to include the issue among their top five priorities in the new Congress. The latest renewal of the bill was christened HR 2 in the House as soon as it was in the hopper and S 5 in the Senate as of January 3, 1991, the day the 102nd Congress was sworn in.

The lineup of power players with an interest in moving the bill was more imposing than ever. In the Senate, the team was still composed of Dodd and Kennedy, with the support of George Mitchell and, as needed, Senate majority whip Wendell Ford of Kentucky. On the House side, Gus Hawkins had retired and left the chairmanship of the House Education and Labor Committee to Bill Ford of Michigan, who had become far more engaged in the family leave fight in the 101st Congress (especially on the floor). Eager to show he could move legislation, Ford was more than willing to make family leave one of his first priorities. Also moving up on the committee roster was George Miller, the Californian whose Select Committee on Children, Youth and Families had initiated congressional discussion of family leave policies in 1984. Miller had taken leave from Ed and Labor for several terms, but he had maintained his seniority in absentia, and in the 102nd Congress he was back.

Seated right next to Miller on the committee dais was Bill Clay, now in his fourth Congress as the lead sponsor of the family leave bill and as the third-ranking Democrat on Ed and Labor. Clay had given up the subcommittee chair at Labor-Management Relations because he was now the full committee chairman at the Post Office and Civil Service Committee (which would once again be family leave's second committee of referral). But Clay's successor at the subcommittee was Pat Williams, the Montanan who had run the task force on HR 770 in the 101st Congress and acquitted himself memorably in the floor debate as well. At the third committee of referral, House Administration, Chairman Charlie Rose of North Carolina had clambered aboard the bandwagon with enthusiasm in the previous Congress. Here, too, Clay was a senior member of the committee, well positioned should the bill need any help.

On the discouraging side, there had been no apparent change in the White House position. But some friends of family leave took heart from the appointment of Lynn Martin, the former House member from Illinois, as the new secretary of labor (replacing Elizabeth Dole). A new boss at Labor might provide a pretext for a new position, and there was talk of support for the concept within the department's policy apparatus. Beyond that, Martin herself had voted for the bill in the House the previous year. One of the ironies of the Rules Committee hearing in 1990 had been the lecture Republican Martin gave Democrat Tim Penny when he appeared with his amendments to HR 770. She now seemed a natural fulcrum on which to turn the administration's policy.

But legislative timetables often fall victim to distractions, and in early 1991 the distractions were more exotic than usual. President Bush had issued an ultimatum to Saddam Hussein to leave Kuwait by January 15 or face massive military reprisals. Even before the first bombs hit Baghdad on January 16, members of Congress were becoming accustomed to armed protection both on the Hill and at home.

The Persian Gulf conflict yielded a swift military victory, which Bush proclaimed to a joint session of Congress on March 6. His approval rating, which had been relatively high throughout the winter, soared to a stunning 89 percent in the Gallup poll that March (and even higher in some other polls). It was the highest rating for any American president since George Gallup Sr. had begun taking the public pulse for Franklin D. Roosevelt half a century earlier.

At first glance Bush's immense popularity that spring of 1991 might have been daunting for the family leave coalition. One man appeared to stand between them and success, and that one man now seemed on the verge of political deification. But the House sponsors were undeterred.

Clay and Schroeder had been around for the heady days that followed Republican presidential landslides in 1984, 1980 and 1972 (Clay had even been around for the first Nixon inauguration in 1969). And anyone could see that Bush's approval numbers were wildly inflated by the highly successful and brief war. Just a few months earlier, after the rejection of the budget summit agreement in October 1990, Bush's overall approval had been barely above 50 percent. As his poll numbers inevitably drifted back to earth, the trend would create an impression of waning popularity.

For their part, Dodd, Marge Roukema and a few other congenital optimists saw Bush's sudden popularity as an opportunity. Perhaps Bush would be too strong to be challenged, on family leave or any other issue. But if so, he might just be secure enough to change his mind and sign a bill he previously had vetoed. This line of reasoning had appeal for those who believed that Bush would have preferred to sign HR 770 all along. If Bush's second term was now assured—as it surely appeared to be—he could now set aside political fears and laugh at political pressures. All that was needed was to persuade this new, omnipotent president to look kindly upon family leave—perhaps by fashioning a bill just different enough to justify a fresh look.

To that end, Dodd had his staff team of Rich Tarplin and Jackie Ruff talking constantly to other Senate staff and keeping close contact with Donna Lenhoff, Michelle Pollak and other key people within the support coalition. Dodd had already renewed his door-to-door negotiations with Republicans he had talked to in the previous Congress when he was recruiting votes for cloture. One of them was Kit Bond, the first-term senator from Missouri who had voted against the bill in 1988 but had shown real interest since. When Dodd's staff sent over memos about possible amendments, Bond's staff hit them back over the net. Dodd passed the word to Marge Roukema, who called Bond and gave him a sales talk on family leave. Pollak, who had worked with the Missourian before, told him the issue would be good for him. She had regular lunches with his legislative director, Julie Dammann, and other staff, pitching them her "every Republican needs an issue on which he's not a Republican" line.

DESPITE THE WAR AND THE COMPETITION from other legislative matters, the House committees moved HR 2 with the dispatch befitting a bill number in single digits. Pat Williams held what would serve as the one full-dress hearing in the House in the 102nd Congress, in the Labor-Management Relations Subcommittee on February 28. The arguments aired were more than familiar for all but the newest members of the subcommittee. The most notable word spoken at the proceedings came from Secretary of Labor Martin, who sat down at the witness table and immediately said: "Veto." Despite her earlier support for the bill Martin was now on the Bush team, and she made it clear the White House was not wavering.

The following week, on March 7 (the day after the joint session heard Bush announce victory in the Gulf War), Williams engineered a largely pro forma markup in the subcommittee. Its fifteen Democrats were solid, and they were joined by ranking Republican Roukema, who had a nice line in the debate: "This is not about working families getting rich, it's about working families getting by."

The only amendment discussed was offered by Congressman Tom Petri, a Republican from Wisconsin who had been visible on the edges of the family leave debate for several years. Petri, like his in-state colleague Steve Gunderson, had spoken fondly of "giving people leave" but rejected sternly the federal mandate. If some form of government regulation was desirable, Petri said, why not let the states set their own standards? To that end, Petri offered a rough approximation of the law just enacted in his own state (with the signature of a conservative Republican governor). The Wisconsin statute required six weeks for birth or adoption but just two weeks for serious illness. The amendment did not provide for elder or spousal care leaves. Petri did not call for a recorded vote on his amendment, which died on a voice vote. But a marker of a kind had been laid down, and staff and members alike took notice. More than a few of those who had opposed family leave in 1990 had given thought to adjusting their position in the 102nd Congress. And among those who were casting about for something to be for, the Petri substitute offered a starting point.

Over in the Post Office Committee, now the bailiwick of full committee chair Bill Clay, the relevant subcommittee did its work on March 12 and the full committee added its imprimatur the following day. For federal workers, the leave periods in the bill would still be eighteen weeks (for family) and twenty-six weeks for employees' own medical leaves. The subcommittee had also approved an amendment restoring spousal care to the situations enumerated under the bill. Although it was an essential article of the bill to the American Association of Retired Persons, spousal care had been inexplicably missing in the version of HR 2 that emerged from the Legislative Counsel and found its way into the hopper on January 3.

On March 20, one week after the Post Office action, the handiwork of Williams's subcommittee was taken up by Chairman Ford at the full Ed and Labor Committee. Unlike in past years, when committee Republicans felt duty-bound to contest the markup, this round was relatively calm. Roukema warned her party colleagues not to oppose "a distinguished pro-family bill" and ranking Republican Bill Goodling of Pennsylvania delivered the veto threat that was now expected at all proceedings on the bill. But this time there was no flurry of amendments from Steve Bartlett, who had resigned from Congress earlier that month to run for mayor of Dallas. His former coagitator, Dick Armey, did not renew the old confrontation, and HR 2 was reported by the full committee on a voice vote.

Another reason for the Republicans to accede to a voice vote was that a recorded vote would have been 28 to 11 in favor of the bill, well beyond two-thirds. Roukema now had two Republican colleagues on the full committee who were willing to vote with her for family leave. One was Susan Molinari, a Republican who had succeeded her father in the Staten Island seat in time to vote for family leave in 1990, and the other was yet another Wisconsin Republican, Scott Klug, who had joined the committee as a freshman in the 102nd Congress.

It is unusual for any committee to have more than one Republican from a given state, and Klug was the third from Wisconsin on Ed and Labor. But it was not always easy for the Republicans' Committee on Committees to fill its fourteen seats on this particular panel, so anyone asking for the assignment usually got it. Klug, the first Republican elected in his liberal Madison-based district since 1956, wanted Ed and Labor as a showcase for his social views—the less conservative side of his political profile. So Goodling could see three of his troops, including both of the women, going against him. He did not want a momentum-building vote on the record, nor one that looked too bipartisan.

Bipartisanship was the theme Dodd was after on the Senate side as well. That was why he kept working with Bond, Dave Durenberger and others. He wanted to have so many Republicans on the bill that he could not only fend off a filibuster but even dictate terms, as it were, to Bob Dole. He wanted not only cloture, but enough strength to demand a roll call vote. If successful, this might help matters in the House. And Dodd was busy calling some of his former colleagues in that chamber, too. He had made scores of phone calls to the House before the failed override of the previous July. And if the House could be goaded into a big vote for the bill, Bush might finally see the light. Surely the president would rather make a deal for the sake of families than risk marring his perfect record on vetoes.

Dodd waived the subcommittee proceedings that spring and Kennedy scheduled a full committee markup for April 24. By this time, Dodd's negotiations with Bond had reached the point where the Republican was willing to support the bill with a few relatively minor changes. But Dodd decided to hold off on that transaction until after the committee markup. "If we did the Bond amendment in committee, we'd have to do five other amendments on the floor," staff aide Tarplin explained. "We wanted to do it once."

At the April 24 markup the amendments were relatively few. Kennedy himself offered one that applied the provisions of the bill to Senate staff. It was approved by voice vote. Durenberger, a potential source of multiple amendments, focused on trimming the leave length from twelve weeks to ten and tinkering with the medical leave provisions (which had consistently bothered him). But hearing no vocal support for his modest adjustments, he withdrew them.

Also noteworthy at the markup was a new study by the Small Business Administration which disputed the high cost estimates still being circulated by the Chamber of Commerce and other business lobbies. The SBA suggested that replacing workers permanently cost more than substituting for them temporarily. The study, less than a month old, was interesting primarily because it was based on a broader sample (1,730 businesses nationwide) than the GAO study that had been relied on in past debates. But its positive spin was also eye-catching for more subliminal reasons. The SBA was a bit player among federal agencies, a perennial target for budget cutters proposing its elimination. But it had the key words "small business" in its title, and it was being run in 1991 by Pat Saiki, the former congresswoman from Hawaii who had been a family leave supporter in the House.

But if the April 24 markup was short on amendments, it was long on speeches. Kennedy told of caring for his son, Patrick, who lost a leg to cancer in 1973. And Paul Wellstone, a freshman Democrat from Minnesota attending practically his first markup, told of time he had taken off for his parents, both of whom had Parkinson's disease. It was unusual to hear the parental care aspect of the legislation highlighted.

When Dodd had his moment, he went for the high-impact overstatement. "For the first time ever," he said, "we have a strong bipartisan consensus in this committee and the Congress at large." Orrin Hatch, the ranking Republican on the committee, immediately called Dodd's bluff. "Neither the legislation nor the political landscape has changed," Hatch said, challenging Dodd to prove him wrong. Dodd was not prepared to talk about his dealings with Bond that day, nor did he know that he had another unrevealed ally among Hatch's colleagues.

But before the final vote was taken, and without a word of advance notice to Dodd, Kennedy or their staffs, Senator Dan Coats, a Republican from Indiana, pulled his microphone to him and announced he would be voting for the bill. Coats had voted against previous family leave bills as a House member and in his first Congress as a senator. But he had thought the matter through again, he said, and its potential impact on families and on women who might otherwise consider abortion (so as not to lose their jobs) had come to weigh on him. He said he still believed it best to allow employers to set their own leave policies, but he was willing to see the government set a minimum standard as a starting point.

Dodd was delighted, Hatch was stunned. The business lobbyists were all but speechless. "He could have had the courtesy to warn us, to give us a chance to talk to him before he did that," Motley of NFIB said, shaking his head in disbelief and disgust. Coats was known to the political world mostly as the man who had succeeded Dan Quayle: first in the House, and then in the Senate. In 1977 he had been Quayle's home district representative back in Fort Wayne. When Quayle ran for the Senate in 1980, Coats ran to succeed him in the House; and both won. When Quayle became vice president, Coats had been appointed to fill the vacancy by Indiana's Republican governor (he was presumed to be Quayle's choice as well). After his appointment in 1989 he had faced the voters in 1990 and won election to the rest of Quayle's term.

A fiscal conservative, Coats was nonetheless known for his willingness to spend money on programs he saw as worthwhile for families. During his years in the House, Coats was known for his work as the ranking Republican on George Miller's Select Committee on Children, Youth and Families. He had been among those who sat listening respectfully at the seminal hearing on child care in April 1984, when family leave was first broached on Capitol Hill.

Hatch had already counted on the defection of Jim Jeffords, a long-standing supporter of family leave in the House and Senate, when it came time to vote. Now, with Coats gone too, Kennedy would surely insist on a roll call to emphasize the bipartisanship of the majority. When the committee clerk called the roll, all ten Democrats were for the bill, and Jeffords and Coats made it an even dozen. It did not matter for purposes of committee approval, but the majority exceeded two-thirds, just as it had in the House Ed and Labor markup. A signal was being sent.

Even before the markup George Mitchell had said he thought family leave might be on the Senate floor before the Memorial Day recess. On the House side, where the last committee vote had been taken in March, committee leaders had spoken of going to Rules before summer. The tide seemed to be running.

Still, Dodd did not want to go to the Senate floor until he was sure his strength would be overwhelming. And so, after the markup, Dodd went back to work behind the scenes. He already had the outline of a compromise worked out with Bond, but he wanted to bring still more Republicans and southern Democrats on board. The talks went on throughout the summer, and they began to involve Wendell Ford of Kentucky.

Ford was the new majority whip in the Senate, having succeeded Alan Cranston at the start of the 102nd Congress. The whip is technically the number-two man in the party hierarchy. As a practical matter, however, his power is limited. First elected to the Senate in 1974 after a stint as Kentucky's governor, Ford was well liked and conservative enough to weather the Reagan era in his home state. But having won a third term in 1986 without breaking a canter, he found himself stalled on both of his major committees behind chairmen and other senior members who were politically secure and disinclined to retire. He had the gavel on the Senate Rules and Administration Committee, but that panel deals primarily with institutional housekeeping and only occasionally with legislation. So Ford set his sights on the whip job. He argued that the leadership needed someone from the South and someone who was not an Americans for Democratic Action liberal. The first time Ford tried for the job, Cranston beat him easily. But late in 1990, Cranston gave up the job voluntarily, battling both cancer and an investigation of his ties to a savings and loan kingpin. Ford was elected to succeed him.

Ford was an old-fashioned legislator who still smoked in committee meetings and liked to talk about Kentucky's "fast horses, good whiskey and beautiful women." But he made it his business to make friends with Mitchell and the new breed of Democrats who increasingly ran the Senate, much as he had found ways to accommodate the Republican regime during the early 1980s. His forte was the negotiated understanding, and he practiced it as a craft. Ford had a good feel for Republicans such as Bond. They were both former governors from border states who had begun running for public office in the 1960s and had been through two decades in statewide office. Both knew well the necessity and dynamics of compromise, the importance of perception and good political marketing.

The summer weeks passed and Congress adjourned in August without further evident action on either HR 2 or S 5. But shortly after the Labor Day recess, Dodd and Bond were ready with a package. Once again there would be a press conference, with the usual reporters called in and the usual claims adduced for family leave. Once again the latest deal on the details would be hailed as a breakthrough. But this time the news was not so much the bill, or even the changes, but the presence of Bond and the carefully balanced rhetoric of compromise. "I think we still have the basic elements needed to protect the family unit, and we have done so in a way that really minimizes the burdens on business," said Bond.

To find the actual stuff of this compromise, however, even experienced observers had to search the small type. Businesses would still be required to grant leaves of up to twelve weeks, and the threshold for the small-business exemption would still be fifty employees (exempting 95 percent of all U.S. businesses and about 60 percent of all workers). What was new in the compromise was scarcely more than a wrinkle here and there: Employees would be required to have worked 1,250 hours, or twenty-five hours per week, in the previous year in order to be covered, instead of 1,000 hours, or nineteen hours per week. The compromise package also adopted the House's "key employees" provision, allowing businesses to exclude the top 10 percent of their payroll from the family leave benefit. The key employees' wrinkle had been a feature of every House version of the bill since Clay and Schroeder had first struck their bargain with Roukema, but it had not been in Dodd's bill. The Dodd-Bond compromise would require employees to give thirty days' notice in cases of foreseeable leave, and it would allow employers to recoup the money they had paid for health premiums during a leave if the employee in question never came back.

The most significant change brought on by the compromise reduced by half the penalties a court could impose on a business found to have wrongfully denied an employee leave. Treble damages had been the standard in earlier Congresses, but in the 102nd Congress the bill as reported from committee featured quadruple damages. The Bond compromise brought it back down to double damages (for lost wages, benefits and other remuneration).

"The compromise isn't much of a compromise," said Tom Scully, associate director of the Office of Management and Budget and a spokesman for the Bush administration on the issue. Tavenner of CARE tagged the changes "simply marginal" and said they would do nothing to move the White House or the business community. "You just can't fix it," she said.

But then the Dodd-Bond deal was never intended to "fix" the bill, at least not to the satisfaction of the business lobby. It was meant, rather, to bring aboard at least one notable Republican senator with impeccable small-business credentials who had not backed the bill before. Beyond that, it was to be traveling music for other senators who might be interested in switching their position. If this could be accomplished with minimal effect on the bill's substance, so much the better. The alterations made for Bond were manageable enough that Tarplin and Ruff found it easy to sell them to the members of the support coalition.

Bond's earnest performance at the news conference was all Dodd could have asked. The Missourian told the reporters he would not be alone in switching his vote. He did not name anyone, but he did not really need to (some of the reporters made a note to call Durenberger's office for comment). The idea was to reinforce the impression of a bipartisan effort that was building momentum. Any senator who might be considering a shift on the issue now had a rationale, and political cover, for doing so. He could be for the "Dodd-Bond bill" or "the Bond compromise."

That was why Bond's carefully planned turnaround in September was even more of a boost than Coats's had been in April. And, coming when it did, it also signaled the moment for Mitchell to bring S 5 to the Senate floor. Mitchell immediately made it clear he was ready to shop a unanimous consent agreement by which the Senate could proceed to the bill in the last week of September 1991.

THE LEADERS AND SPONSORS COULD move this quickly after the Dodd-Bond announcement in part because no senator had placed a "hold" on S 5. The hold is another of the traditional privileges by which any individual senator may assert at least a temporary right to interrupt the process. To place a hold, a senator merely informs the party leader, by letter or personal message, that he or she wants advance notice before a given bill is called up. The pretense of advance notice, however, is a fig leaf for what is really a threat to filibuster the motion to proceed.

Holds can be especially effective in blocking minor nominations, which are usually considered less essential business than bills and may have a hard time overcoming the encumbrance. But it is not uncommon for a bill sponsor or committee chairman to be hampered by holds on legislation, too. Holds can be especially vexing because they are not a matter of public record. The party leaders may accept requests for holds in confidence, and they are not required to identify the senator who requested them.

Holds, like filibusters, were traditionally reserved for special situations. When Dodd's father served in the Senate, there might be half a dozen filibusters in a year. By the 1990s, however, there were more likely to be fifty in a year, and it was not uncommon to have more than one cloture petition ripening at a time. Holds, too, have become everyday means of leverage in matters large and small. While the leaders try to discourage the practice and shorten the duration of holds, they must be careful not to push any senator too hard. The tyranny of rule by unanimous consent is such that the leaders must take pains to accommodate every colleague and every request, reasonable or not.

Family leave was not hamstrung by any substantive holds, but it was subject to the usual traffic delays. Dole was not about to allow unanimous consent to proceed on S 5 until he had worked out a few problems of his own, and tops on his list of priorities in late September 1991 was the nomination of Clarence Thomas to the Supreme Court. Earlier in the month the Senate Judiciary Committee had subjected Thomas to lengthy and awkward questioning during which he often seemed evasive about his views. The committee had then split 7–7 on the question of confirmation, sending the nomination to the floor without recommendation. The White House was pressing for a floor vote that week so that Thomas could begin the new Court term, which opens each year on the first Monday of October. It was Dole's job to get Mitchell to agree.

But Mitchell was reluctant to allow a vote. The early fall air on Capitol Hill was rife with rumors about another witness whose testimony the committee had not heard, a woman who had worked for Thomas when he was chairman of the Equal Employment Opportunity Commission in the 1980s. Her name was Anita Hill, and as her charges of sexual harassment were whispered in Senate offices in late September, some Senate Democrats began talking quietly about reopening the hearings.

Over the course of the next two weeks Hill's allegations would be made public and the hearings would be reopened. Hill would present hours of dramatic testimony detailing Thomas's alleged behavior, and the nominee would fight back with an impassioned defense that denied the charges categorically and likened the proceeding to a "high-tech lynching." Present throughout his testimony was his wife, Virginia Lamp, who had been the Chamber of Commerce lobbyist opposing family leave. The nation would watch in mordant fascination, and a new awareness of sexual harassment in the workplace would enter the mainstream of American life. Nevertheless, on October 15, the Senate would confirm Thomas by a vote of 52–48, and a potent element would be added to the forces already shaping the 1992 elections.

All of this lay immediately ahead as Mitchell and Dole debated the schedule for late September and early October. Hill's allegations were yet to become public, and while both Dole and Mitchell had known of Hill's charges for several days, they still presumed that Thomas would have at least sixty votes for confirmation (far more than the simple majority required). At the same time Mitchell was less than eager to rush the Thomas vote, needing time to decide how to deal with the potential problem of the uncalled witness and to allow for all the senators who wanted to ruminate about their Thomas vote in floor speeches.

Getting S 5 out on the floor was complicated further by the need for a comprehensive time agreement limiting the consideration of amendments. Kennedy and Dodd wanted to offer the Bond compromise as a substitute for S 5 as reported from committee. Beyond that, their highroad bipartisan strategy would force them to entertain at least a few Republican efforts to amend the bill as well. But flinging wide the floodgates might mean a torrent of amendments that had been prepared for various Republican senators—Cochran, Hatch and Durenberger among them. That sort of free-for-all would take hours and perhaps days of floor time.

Normally, the prospect of a time-consuming debate would be more distressing to the majority than to the minority, but in this instance it was Dole who wanted to clear the decks for an early vote on Thomas. Mitchell made it clear that a messy fight on family leave would push the Thomas vote well into October.

Mitchell and Dole were still negotiating when Mitchell made the motion to proceed to S 5 on Friday, September 27. Dodd and Kennedy were on the floor to manage the bill, and they had Bond and Ford on hand to help—much as the Democratic sponsors in the House had relied on Curt Weldon and Bart Gordon in 1990. The Republicans, led by Hatch and Cochran, came to the floor prepared to speak against the bill at length. Dole had several senators indicating an interest in amending the bill. Mitchell asked Dodd and Kennedy how many votes they had for cloture and was assured they had enough.

After a weekend adjournment the Senate returned to debating the motion to proceed on Monday, September 30, while the leaders continued their negotiations. As various senators took the floor to address the question at hand (or speak on other subjects), Mitchell conferred with Dodd and Kennedy (who was also involved in the Judiciary Committee fracas), while Dole spoke to Hatch and Cochran, each group meeting in its respective cloakroom. The senators, in turn, conferred with staff, who waited in the comfy leather couches lining the chamber's wall.

From time to time Tarplin would venture out into the Senate reception area at the east end of the chamber to brief the lobbyists waiting breathlessly for word. Donna Lenhoff and Judith Lichtman of the Women's Legal Defense Fund were there, as were Michelle Pollak from AARP, Joel Packer of the National Education Association and several other labor lobbyists. At one juncture Kennedy emerged to talk with the group personally. He was both animated and exasperated, describing the multidimensional chess game in progress. At one point, in mock despair, he banged his head theatrically against one of the ornately painted walls, not far from the marble bust of Richard Nixon (whose likeness adorns an alcove near the Senate chamber because as vice president he served as president of the Senate).

The negotiations reached a climax on the evening of Tuesday, October 1. Mitchell then came to the floor and was recognized to speak. He announced that there would be a vote on the Thomas nomination on Tuesday, October 8. He also said that S 5 would be the business before the Senate on Wednesday, October 2, and he detailed a time agreement for consideration of that bill. He did not say anything about a cloture petition (none had been filed) or any quid pro quo for the scheduling of the Thomas vote. But the next day, by unanimous consent, the Senate proceeded to consideration of S 5. And the Senate voted on the bill the same day.

In the course of the October 1 debate, Dole took the floor and conveyed his reasons for striking his tent on family leave. The Republican leader brandished a letter from the White House dated two days earlier saying the Dodd-Bond language did not address the administration's concerns and reservations. Dole had another letter, this one from the president himself, dated the previous day, that said: "Should S 5 or any other mandated leave legislation be presented to me, I will veto it." Dole had a way of reading documents with an air of finality, as if by doing so he had swept the field. Given the certainty of the veto, Dole said, there was little point in tying up the Senate any longer than absolutely necessary.

Dole's argument had a certain plausibility, but it still rang like a call to retreat. Had Dole had the votes to prevent cloture, he surely would have preferred to spare Bush the bother and political cost of another veto. His willingness to allow a vote signaled his acceptance of Dodd's claim to sixty votes.

Still, some of Dole's colleagues were going to have their inning before it was over. Durenberger gained the floor and offered an amendment to make the bill more palatable to business. It would strike the various enforcement proceedings under the bill, which involved the Labor Department and the federal courts, and substitute an arbitration process. On the floor, the bill sponsors dismissed this as a "gutting amendment," one that would weaken the legislation to the point of being meaningless. Offstage, Durenberger had been arguing strenuously that his amendment was a keeper, a potential key to a two-thirds vote in the Senate and perhaps in the House as well. Whether convinced of this or not, Dodd and Kennedy were loath to alienate Durenberger because they were counting on his vote as part of the two-thirds veto-proof majority.

In the reception area, the coalition lobbyists debated the importance of that one vote and the onerousness of the amendment. Pollak insisted they could have the one without the other. "I've had a lot of experience with Durenberger on this kind of thing," she said later. "He always says he won't vote for the bill unless he gets his amendment; he never gets it and he always caves."

The sponsors refused to accept the Durenberger amendment and it went to a vote. Durenberger got thirty-nine senators to join him on it (including three Democrats). But that uprising did not alarm the sponsors. A quick check assured them that their key Republican crossovers who had voted for Durenberger (including Arlen Specter of Pennsylvania, John Chafee of Rhode Island and Bill Cohen of Maine) would vote for S 5. The Durenberger vote was actually useful in this regard, giving the crossovers a chance to stand with their party colleagues and still leave the bill unscathed.

The main event was still the vote on Bond's substitute. This would not only transform S 5, it would also allow the bill's backers to demonstrate their strength. Once the voting began, the outcome was almost immediately apparent. Typically, when a Senate roll call vote is taken, the clerk reads the names alphabetically at a brisk clip and those already in the chamber may respond with an aye or a no. Some prefer to signal with a thumbs-up or thumbs-down sign. Some come to the clerk's table front and center to respond to the clerk. Others reply from their desks, from the aisles or even from the doorways that lead into the cloakrooms or the antechambers. But in order to vote they must be physically present in the chamber, and they must be acknowledged by the clerk.

Once the clerk has read through the roster once, he names the senators voting aye and no. He does not give a numerical tally (the Senate has no voting by electronic device, and there is no tote board for watching the vote). After this, the clerk begins to call out senators' names singly, as they indicate their readiness to vote.

At this point, a swarm of senators is usually milling in the well of the chamber, chatting and looking at the roll of votes already cast. Senators who have not been following the debate on a particular amendment may look for key names on the roll as cues for their own vote. In these moments in the well, the final politicking on a vote takes place, and it is not unusual for votes to be turned. Now and then, a senator who has voted will signal the clerk again and change his vote. In this case, the clerk corrects the record and announces the new vote without embarrassing the senator by calling attention to the switch.

As the senators voted that evening, Lenhoff and the other coalition leaders were once again gathered in the Senate reception area. They had crowded around the desk of the reception clerk, who has a small TV monitor tuned to the same Senate TV feed seen on C-SPAN. The monitor is usually muted, but the sound was turned up for the roll call. The knot of anxious lobbyists marked their tally sheets, listening eagerly for the Republicans in particular.

They had known they had Bond and Coats, of course, as well as longtime backers Jeffords, Specter, Chafee, Packwood and his colleague from Oregon, Mark Hatfield. But here, too, came Cohen of Maine, Alfonse M. D'Amato of New York, the uncertain Mr. Durenberger and Bond's Missouri colleague, John Danforth. The coalition people in the reception room cheered for each, feeling uninhibited in part because their counterparts from the opposition were not in evidence that afternoon. And they really got a chance to whoop when they pulled in four of the most conservative Republicans: Bill Roth of Delaware, John McCain of Arizona, and Ted Stevens and Frank Murkowski of Alaska. In all, fifteen Republicans bought into the Bond substitute and only four Democrats rejected it (two from Alabama, one each from Oklahoma and South Carolina).

The overall total was 65–32, two-thirds of those present and voting. Better yet, Dodd was satisfied that the three senators missing that afternoon, all Democrats, would be in his camp if he needed them (one was hospitalized, the other two, Tom Harkin of Iowa and Bob Kerrey of Nebraska, were on the hustings in early presidential primary states). That meant sixty-eight votes were now aligned against the president's stated position, despite the last-minute White House appeal.

Hatch, however, was not quite finished. He had an amendment of his own that, even more than the Durenberger amendment, struck at the mandate element of the bill. His alternative was to deny workers leave but grant them preference in rehiring, so they could take up to six years to bond with their children and still have a right to priority in rehiring (with restored seniority and benefits). Hatch's amendment allowed him to turn some of the sponsors' own rhetoric against them, arguing that leaves measured in weeks were far too short to confer the benefits desired.

Hatch's substitute was derived from legislation he had introduced in the early weeks of the 102nd. That bill (S 418) had a companion on the House side (HR 1270) presented by Charles W. Stenholm of Texas, who had originally intended to offer it as a floor amendment in 1990 but never did. The alternative had enough compromise value to attract the interest of the U.S. Chamber of Commerce, which gave a wink and a nudge by not opposing the Hatch-Stenholm bills.

Here was a relatively fresh angle on the debate, a chance to talk about helping parents and other responsible family members while maintaining management control. But the Senate did not seem eager to tackle a new concept when it was this close to a decision on a familiar one. The Senate seemed to view the vote on Hatch's substitute as no more than a repeat of the previous vote. Hatch did better by three votes among the Republicans but lost three votes among the Democrats, so his amendment failed by the inverse of the vote on Bond (32–65).

Having now lost two roll calls by ratios of 2 to 1, Dole seemed to have had enough. He made no further effort to amend the bill, and his colleagues signaled their resignation by drifting away. Hatch, too, let it be known he would not press the case further. Just as in 1990, there proved to be no one Republican sufficiently motivated in his opposition to mount an extended debate. After all, the White House was committed to a veto, which its operatives assured all concerned the House was certain to sustain. So what was the point? Mitchell moved the bill be passed by voice vote at 6 P.M. and, by previous agreement, there was no objection.

The sponsors once again congratulated one another on the floor and thanked their staffs. Outside, the lobbying members of the support coalition, weary from a long day on their feet, shook hands and hugged, and gave quotes to the reporters spilling down the stairs and out of the elevators from the press gallery above.

This, then, was how it felt—not just to have the votes to win, not just to have the votes to cut off debate, but to have the votes to override. Of course, the House still had to act on the Dodd-Bond language. But it was the Senate that had the filibusters and the unforeseen roadblocks. The Senate was supposed to be the more conservative chamber. Surely now, with this triumph, the tide would rise in the House as well. Surely now, at last, the administration would be compelled to negotiate.

12.

The Penny Affair

THE VOTES OF OCTOBER 1991 SIGNALED the collapse of organized resistance to family leave in the Senate. But on the House side, where the last committee vote had been taken in the previous March and where committee leaders had spoken hopefully of going to Rules before summer, the bill had bogged down. At the White House, the willingness to accept the consequences of a veto was intact. To buttress that will, a phalanx of Republicans and Democrats in the House stood ready to sustain the president. A two-thirds vote to override might be virtually a reality in one chamber, but it was no more than a chimera in the other.

Still, at least one House member who had been fighting the bill for years underwent a change over the winter of 1990–91. Tim Penny, the Democrat from Minnesota, had said time off for family or medical matters was a sensible benefit for an employer to offer but not a sensible thing for the federal government to oversee. He had been willing to buck his own party on the issue in the Ed and Labor Committee, in Rules and on the floor. Yet after opposing the bill in three separate Congresses, he had come to believe that some form of leave benefit was likely to happen one way or another, sooner or later. And to Penny, the manner in which it came to pass seemed important.

He foresaw that the bill would be fought through to the end along party lines, with each side playing to its own grandstand. But in his own idealization, the issue might be an occasion for bipartisan cooperation, a chance to show that Congress could concentrate on solutions rather than confrontations. Penny calculated that his previous objection to the bill, vociferous and well noted, might enable him to act as a go-between for the rival camps and an honest broker in the negotiation. And, as family leave once again seemed to languish, it was plain that someone needed to do something.

Despite its new priority status, family leave had been slowed partly by competition from other legislation. Negotiations toward a civil rights compromise (HR 1) occupied Ed and Labor Chairman Bill Ford and some of the other family leave players throughout the spring and summer. So did the talks on the striker replacement bill and the extension of unemployment benefits. Jawboning on all three of these matters continued into the fall.

Another distraction within the House Democratic leadership was the June announcement that Bill Gray, the House majority whip for two years, would resign in September to become president of the United Negro College Fund. His departure ignited a brief but intense struggle of succession in the caucus, which eventually decided to promote David Bonior, a good friend to family leave as chief deputy to Gray (and before that to Tony Coelho). On the night before his July 11 election, Bonior demonstrated his qualifications to be chief vote counter by telling reporters he was sure of 160 votes. The following day, the caucus met and elected Bonior by a vote of 160–109.

But there was yet another reason the House had gotten nowhere on family leave from March until autumn, and that was the leadership's reluctance to gamble on the bill as reported by the committees in March. The zone whips and the at-large whips, who talked daily with their colleagues, sensed that HR 2 was good for no more than 250 votes at best. With the president scaling pinnacles of popularity, the chances of an override seemed nil. So what was the point in pressing the bill?

Jane O'Grady of the AFL-CIO recalled hearing "groans and moans" from some members she visited whenever she got to the family leave item on her shopping list. "Why are you making us do this?" they would ask. Was it not enough that the House would pass the striker replacement bill and the civil rights bill that year? Was it not enough to be bending every effort to pass an extension of unemployment benefits? Did the AFL-CIO want to drive moderate Democrats to extinction? Being friendly to small business was one of the ways southern and western Democrats inoculated themselves against charges of leftism and liberality in their reelection campaigns. They cared about the ratings and score-cards issued each year by the business lobbies, and they tended to display the plaques and trophies awarded by such groups. Once, while she and others from the coalition were calling on Oklahoma Democrat Dave McCurdy, O'Grady let her gaze wander to the shelf with the congress-man's collection of statuettes from the NFIB. "Why are we here?" she asked herself.

Bonior and others from leadership were hearing similar tales at the regular Thursday whip meetings. There seemed to be a cadre of at least thirty Democrats whose votes were beyond reach. Either they were unal-terably opposed to the bill or they had irretrievably committed themselves to the Chamber of Commerce, the CARE coalition or the NFIB (which seemed to have the tightest grip). But there were perhaps twenty other Democrats who were still listening, still trying to make up their minds. Some said they wanted a chance to vote on Stenholm's bill (the preferen-tial rehiring bill, sponsored on the Senate side by Hatch) and others wanted a different meliorative substitute.

With so many players taking a dim view of the bill's prospects at that moment, it seemed fitting that the next move should be made by Penny, the House's preternaturally gloomy Norwegian. Others might have been more vituperative in criticizing family leave, but he always got noticed for the dourness of his disapproval—which seemed to extend to much of the congressional enterprise. His political roots could not have been more remote from the urban machinery that produced so many of his caucus colleagues. Born in tiny Kiester, Minnesota, in 1952, he had attended nearby Winona State University on the Mississippi River. He became an aide to a Democrat in the state legislature while still in school and ran for a seat of his own when he was twenty-five. The territory was deeply Republican, but the relentless young man with the flop of brown hair and the toothy smile visited every household in the legislative district no fewer than three times en route to election with 52 percent of the vote.

Six years later, with the national economy scraping the bottom of its worst downturn since the Depression, Penny ran for Congress. South-eastern Minnesota had last been represented by a Democrat in the House in the 1890s, but Penny once again campaigned door-to-door, shaking hands on street corners in 150 different towns. When the GOP suffered a divisive primary, he exploited it by appealing directly to backers of the eliminated candidate. In November he won with 51 percent of the vote.

Once in Washington, Penny busied himself building a bipartisan rec-ord. He continued to court the conservatives in his district, partly by becoming chairman of the Freshman Budget Task Force and accumulating other parsimonious-sounding titles (he was a cofounder of the "Porkbusters" caucus). After two terms he was winning reelection regularly with more than 70 percent of the vote.

But he paid a price for seeking a space of his own between the parties. It was not always easy to win cooperation from colleagues on Agriculture, his lifeblood committee. And his years on Ed and Labor were so rocky that his departure from it had elements of both a resignation and a dismissal. Penny had found it easy to cooperate on the panel's education agenda, which often occasioned bipartisan agreement. But the committee had a split personality, and when the subject was labor the liberals and conservatives reverted to open ideological war. In this atmosphere Penny's congenital yearning for the middle ground angered some of his senior colleagues. And when he questioned and opposed such labor-backed legislation as family leave and the minimum wage, the committee leaders were livid. As far as a politician such as Bill Ford was concerned, one either voted like a Democrat or looked for another party. And when Ford took over as Ed and Labor's chairman in 1991, it was clear he would not mourn Penny's departure.

Penny kept a sign at the front of his office desk that read "I AM a Democrat," but through much of the 1980s he opposed his party in floor fights more than one-third of the time. While his ratings from the AFL-CIO ranged around the 50s, his scorecard from the Chamber of Commerce was just as good or better. Yet it was mostly Penny's manner, the high seriousness verging on sanctimony, that left colleagues cold. More than a few Democrats found it hard to pronounce his name without an expletive.

Family leave was well outside the spheres of fiscal and farm policy where Penny had made his mark, but it was the sort of bill that intrigued him. It had to do with people's real problems, but it dealt with them in what he saw as a flawed and awkward fashion that might well have unforeseen consequences.

So Penny decided to involve himself in the effort to bring HR 2 to the floor, checking in with Bonior, who encouraged him to do what he could, and with the sponsors and committee chairmen, who were less enthusiastic. He told them he was willing to rethink his opposition if they would rethink their approach to passing HR 2 and cooperate on a compromise as a path to a two-thirds vote. Clay and Ford wanted to know how many votes Penny could bring to the table, with Clay invoking his state's famous motto: "Show me." Give me a compromise with two-thirds of the

House on board and I will consider it, said Clay, who was not going to shelve the bill he had introduced and shepherded until he saw the names. For his part, Ford wanted those who were switching over from voting to sustain the last veto on family leave to commit to do so publicly.

It was one thing to find roughly twenty new votes in each party for an override. It was another to nail them down months before the bill had even been passed (let alone vetoed). But the hardest thing of all was to find Republicans who would pledge in public to override their war hero president in the summer of 1991. "It was clear then," Penny would say, "that all the committee leaders wanted was an issue to hit the president with." Nonetheless, he stoically accepted their challenge.

Penny sought feedback from a few receptive colleagues. He went to Jim Cooper, the Tennessee Democrat whom Tavenner had wanted to recruit for her side when the teams were first forming. He went to Butler Derrick, a Rules Committee insider from South Carolina, well connected among southern Democrats, who had voted against previous family leave bills. And he went to John LaFalce, the intelligent and underrated Democrat from Buffalo who had come with the Watergate class of 1974 but set a more conservative course than most of his classmates. LaFalce was now chairman of the Small Business Committee, a largely thankless job because the heavy-duty issues affecting his jurisdiction were usually skimmed by the prestige committees: Energy and Commerce, and Ways and Means. Now LaFalce saw his committee losing ground to Education and Labor and thought he had seen enough. He had asked the leadership to add Small Business to the list of committees handling family leave, and he had been rebuffed. So when Penny came to him with ideas about revising the bill, LaFalce wanted to play.

Penny also visited with more than a dozen Republicans he thought he might be able to influence, and he tried to reach out to the business groups for help. He found the lobbyists unhappy with him for playing at compromise in the first place. Tavenner, for one, had thought she could count on Penny, one of her favorite Democrats, to oppose the bill to the end. And when he begged the business lobbies to recognize that something was going to pass, like it or not, they replied that a small mandate was as bad as a big one. Penny found a few listeners at the National Retail Federation and some of the other second-team players in the opposition. But the core groups—the Chamber, the NFIB and the National Association of Wholesaler-Distributors—were still implacably opposed.

Penny persisted throughout the summer and into the fall of 1991. On the Senate side, Dodd was picking up the votes he needed for cloture and for an override via the deal he had swung with Bond. But on the House side, where Penny was proposing far greater changes in the substance, the trick was not being turned. He appealed to the leadership and got a sympathetic hearing from Bonior, who was willing to put some of his organization to work "whipping" the Penny substitute to assess its strength. Every time Penny thought he had buttonholed a colleague and gotten a commitment he would pass the name on to Bonior, but the names accumulated slowly.

Where Penny seemed to make his greatest headway was with the outside support coalition. The Minnesotan always seemed to show the coalition members the respect they had not felt in the years since Schroeder's first, fledgling bill was set aside. Penny seemed to understand their sensitivities, but he warned them that the men controlling their issue's legislative fate—especially the sponsors and committee chairmen on the House side—would balk at any changes he suggested. These men would resist any loss of control over the substance of the bill or over the political strategy for enacting it.

This analysis, coupled with Penny's "let's get it done" attitude, captivated some of the family leave advocates who had wearied of the endless process and frustration. After all, what the coalition wanted most was to establish a broad but simple principle: a new minimum labor standard. The exact details, definitions and penalties were of secondary importance. Once the principle had been set in law, it could be built upon and expanded in the future.

But while the advocates were willing to parley with Penny, they did not want to see him rewriting the legislation wholesale. They made clear that they would not accept a mere "motherhood" bill along the lines Penny had envisioned in the previous Congress. The essence of that approach had been proposed by Howard Berman in 1985 and rejected by the earliest incarnation of the family leave coalition. To fall that far back would not only forfeit the support of AARP and others, it would also betray the vision of the bill put forward by its original legal theorists. Lichtman and Lenhoff, backed by several feminist law school professors, had argued for the medical leave paradigm as a way out of the "special treatment" trap. They had not come this far to dive deliberately back into that trap now.

Penny could see he would not rally anyone to that cause, nor to the Hatch-Stenholm alternative of preference in rehiring. The coalition had also been stretched to its limit on the exemption threshold (fifty employees), so suggestions of moving that threshold to a hundred were received coldly. But Penny sensed some give in the leave length. By shortening the leave length and having fewer weeks for medical conditions than for new parenthood, Penny thought the coalition could demonstrate realism and flexibility. They could prove, in his words, that "they were more interested in getting a law than in embarrassing Bush."

At a glance the shortened leave for medical situations seemed likely to set off the alarms at AARP, where Pollak had stood such vigilant watch over the elder care and spousal provisions. But Pollak, like Penny himself, had concluded that the bill had two chances: Either it had to attract a huge majority in the House or it had to bluff the White House into believing it might. For Pollak, too, the key was not in the number of employees or weeks but in getting the law on the books and having it apply to the entire family. She considered almost everything else negotiable.

That did not make Pollak an automatic advocate for Penny proposals, however. The bargaining went back and forth before settling at eight weeks for new birth or adoption and six weeks for everything else.

In his effort to make the bill look different to members who might switch if given an excuse, Penny was getting well down into the weeds. For example, the small-business exemption (fifty employees) in HR 2 counted only a firm's employees within a seventy-five-mile radius of its main facility; Penny proposed shortening the radius to fifty miles, allowing a few more companies at the margin to escape the mandate. He also thought medical leaves should require a second doctor's opinion, and that employers should have some say in scheduling intermittent leaves. And he wanted to structure enforcement around an administrative law model (similar to that used in the Fair Labor Standards Act) rather than give each complainant a right to private action (as in civil rights cases). Pollak was open to this, having had negative experiences with the latter.

Not everyone in the coalition was eager to do business with Penny. He was not in good odor with the unions, some of which wanted to deal and some of which saw more political value in another veto standoff in 1992, which would be Bush's reelection year. There were also groups that felt the bill had been compromised too much already and would lose all meaning if trimmed further. The National Organization for Women, for example, had pulled out in protest of the bill's diminishing coverage and lack of paid leave. But most of the inner circle that functioned as the coalition's executive committee was intrigued with the possibility of reaching two-thirds through the services of this converted opponent.

From his side, Penny soon saw Pollak as "driving the bandwagon for the compromise." She was a major asset not only because she was among the coalition's most seasoned Hill lobbyists but also because the AARP was by now shouldering much of the cost of the coalition's efforts (including for the printing and delivery of its literature and mailings). Her voice was always heard in the strategy sessions, the gatherings that took place weekly during the session and daily when the bills were moving. This was a more pragmatic and savvy cadre than at the start, pared down from more than two dozen participants to fewer than ten. If they needed to soften the bill again and lobby for a package of amendments, most were willing. But they placed one condition on the transaction: Penny had to sell it himself to the main cosponsors and committee chairmen in the House.

Penny tried. At first, he thought he might be getting through to Schroeder, who did not dismiss him out of hand. Pat Williams, deputy whip for labor issues as well as the chairman of the critical subcommittee, was willing to give Penny a hearing. Roukema, however, had no interest in the Minnesotan's compromise, beginning with his deep reduction in medical leave (down from a dozen weeks in HR 2 to just six). It had been the medical provision that had cemented Roukema's support for the issue years earlier, and she saw no reason to devalue it now. She got on the phone to Clay and told him she was standing her ground. It was just what Clay wanted to hear. He had no use for Penny, and he had no faith in Penny's promised votes.

Late in October, however, with the thrill of the Senate passage still fresh, everyone involved on the House side felt a tremendous eagerness to follow suit. There had to be a way to get over the top. Bonior was willing to "whip" the Penny package to gauge its potential. His soundings turned up far fewer votes than needed, but at least the compromise came somewhat closer than HR 2. Bill Ford then talked to the support coalition people on his own and received the distinct impression that they had cast their lot with Penny. He conveyed this impression to some of the staff people involved, who came to think the deal was all over but the formalizing of the legislative language.

On November 2, Lenhoff and her husband left on a long-arranged trip to see his father in Israel. She got on the plane believing the compromise was at hand. Each night she placed an international call back to her office. "Do we have a deal with Penny?" she would ask. And each night staff lawyer Helen Norton would wait in the office after hours to take the call and dutifully answer: "No, not yet."

For a time, confusion reigned. Clay got word at one point that Bill Ford had met with the support coalition and thrown his weight behind the Penny compromise. Briefly, Clay wondered if he was somehow being cut out, sandbagged. But how could he be? He had been a cosponsor since 1986 and he was chairman of one of the two main committees of referral. After touching base with Ford, Clay made sure everyone understood that the bill sponsors and committee chairmen were in charge. They would decide what would go to the floor and when.

"There comes a time when you're going to the floor when the whole thing is really up for grabs," staffer Fred Feinstein said. "You're trying to juggle fifteen different things." Among the distractions was the confusion on the part of some staff and lobbyists about the role of Feinstein himself. Some thought he still worked for Clay, and that talking to Feinstein counted as communication with Clay. But Feinstein had always been responsible to the chairman of the Labor-Management Relations Sub-committee, which meant he had been working for Williams since the end of 1990 (when Clay became chairman of Post Office).

Some in the coalition were pressing the members for a vote on Penny's amendments. Why did there need to be 290 hard votes to signal override capability? Why not get to 280 and trust the dynamics of the floor action to take over? After all, the leadership could always get five or six votes one way or another in the final minutes. When Jim Wright of Texas was Speaker, the leadership had stopped clocks and performed other near miracles to win the close ones.

But did Penny have even 280? Some liberal Democrats who liked the bill the way it was were grumbling about their votes being taken for granted at the base of Penny's pyramid. In the week after Lenhoff left for Israel, Patsy Mink of Hawaii announced she would not vote for Penny's substitute and that she would abandon the bill if his version passed. Pat Schroeder quickly announced she was with Mink. The vote was unraveling. "It was all hanging by a thread," recalled Feinstein. "I went home that Wednesday night [November 6] feeling that the whole thing had just collapsed."

The great lunge at two-thirds had come up short. Clay and Roukema refused to negotiate further with Penny, directly or indirectly. Ford and Clay told leadership they wanted to go to Rules the following week and seek to have the substance of the Bond-Dodd compromise from the Senate declared in order as an amendment in the nature of a substitute.

For the first time in the six-year history of the family leave effort there were serious recriminations within the advocates' camp. The unhappiness was far more widespread than it had been when Marian Wright Edelman blew up at Dodd for giving family leave precedence over child care in the fall of 1988.

The key House members were angry. They did not understand how the coalition could have become so enamored of the Penny alternative, or how they themselves could have been confronted with something like a *fait accompli*. They did not understand how Penny could have penetrated this far onto their turf when he had no more than 270 votes in his pocket. They were unhappy with Penny, with other members who had worked with him and with the support coalition. And there was plenty of ire left over for the staff. "We should have seen it coming," said Feinstein. "We should have warned them."

Pollak was angry, too, as were others in the coalition. Many outside backers still believed they were making sacrifices for the sake of passing a bill, and they had come to believe the votes would be there if the Penny deal went through. They believed the principles of the issue were intact in the compromise and the price was within reason. They saw the members as inflexible, letting their dislike of Penny supersede their interest in the bill. But Clay kept asking the same questions: What had the White House, the House Republican leadership or the business lobbies ever promised in return for the changes in the bill? Would the business lobbies stop "scoring" the vote (using it as a basis for their annual scorecard on each member) or ease off in their opposition? "Has the White House promised to sign this?" he would ask. "What do the Republicans in the House say?" And when he heard the coalition's answers Clay would shake his head and say: "You're compromising with no one but yourselves."

In the end, no one knew for certain how many votes there may have been for Penny's compromise. Penny himself guessed about 280, which surely would have raised eyebrows at the White House. But others involved never saw more than 270 votes. Dodd made scores of phone calls to House members testing the appeal of Penny's specifics and never felt the effort was close to reaching two-thirds. Why bother with Penny, Clay would ask, when we can get into the 260s or 270s without him? In retrospect, Clay contended that the distraction of Penny's effort had cost the bill its shot at two-thirds; he thought votes that might have been wooed another way were sealed off when Penny's play fell short and feelings were hurt all around.

"We were very upset because we had wanted a compromise," Pollak would say later. "But we would never have gotten to 290, and that was what Clay was telling us and he was right. We were negotiating with ourselves, and we never got a business to support the bill because of a compromise."

Lenhoff, who had agonized about it all from half a world away throughout the crucial ten days, later looked back and said, "It was the members of Congress who said no, and to their credit, they were right."

THE BILL WENT TO THE Rules Committee the following Tuesday, November 12. Leadership had agreed to bring the bill to the floor and amend it to look like the Senate-passed bill. Rules would also allow Stenholm to offer the preference-in-rehiring substitute that Hatch had tried in the Senate. Otherwise, there would be no amendments. Bill Goodling, the ranking Republican on Ed and Labor, would be left to decide what kind of recommittal motion he wanted.

Among those frozen out was Nancy Johnson, a Connecticut Republican and a cosponsor of HR 2. She had asked to offer an amendment that would have attached Stenholm's rehiring provisions to the bill as an addendum, not a substitute. Florida Republican Michael Bilirakis was denied the opportunity to offer his own bill on family leave—which combined preference in rehiring with various tax incentives for employers to grant leave—in whole or in part. And Illinois Republican Harris W. Fawell, a longtime opponent of the bill, wanted to amend it with regard to employees of the House itself. The bill said House staff who felt denied their rights could go through the usual House Office of Fair Employment Practices, but it barred them from carrying their case to the federal courts as private sector employees could.

Fawell was joined by several other Republicans in protesting the exclusion of this amendment. While it seemed relatively peripheral, the underlying intent was to highlight the Capitol Hill habit of exempting itself from workplace laws. And when Fawell got out on the floor to object to the rule, he quickly linked his amendment to the larger scandal then looming—the overdrafts at the House bank.

These distractions notwithstanding, the Democrats took the floor on November 13 with a strong feeling of momentum. Williams noted that over the years the issue had been on the Hill, three House committees had held seventeen days of hearings and eleven separate markups. Pat Schroeder alluded to "the message we got loud and clear from the voters on Tuesday," referring to results in several statewide elections on November 5—including Harris Wofford's upset win in a Senate contest in Pennsylvania on a platform of health care and other domestic policy reforms.

The most telling words of the day, however, were the names on the substitute to be offered: Bart Gordon and Henry Hyde, two heroes of the 1990 battle whose return in 1991 signified the bill's enduring beachhead among southern Democrats and social conservative Republicans.

The rule was approved along party lines and the House resolved itself into the Committee of the Whole so as to consider amendments.

One can tell immediately whether the House is in session as the House or as the Committee of the Whole by checking the placement of the mace, a symbol inherited from Roman custom via the British House of Commons. The mace is a bundle of ebony rods bound in silver with a silver ball and a silver eagle on top. It usually stands on a high pedestal by the Speaker's desk. When the House sits as the Committee of the Whole, the mace is moved to a lower pedestal. (The current mace was made in 1841 to replace the one burned by the British troops who sacked the Capitol in 1814.)

Most of the arguments aired that Wednesday afternoon in November had been worn smooth. Relatively few members actually came to the floor to debate, submitting written statements for the record instead. Among the more notable contributions of this kind was that of Republican Olympia Snowe from Maine, who had been a gradual but firm convert to the bill in the mid-1980s when she was cochair of the Congressional Caucus for Women's Issues. She tweaked the Democrats for taking eight months to bring the bill from committee to the floor ("We brought our troops back from the Persian Gulf faster"). Her central message, however, was that family leave was working just fine in her state, a "predominantly small-business state," where it applied to firms with as few as twenty-five employees. Problems that had been predicted had not materialized, Snowe said; "the ogre was much tamer than previews had claimed."

The statements of November 13 came primarily from supporters, but the opposition was represented as well. Tom DeLay, a Texas Republican, noted how disingenuous the advocates were to claim low costs for unpaid leave and then heap praise on the paid leave policies of other countries. "Passing this bill puts us on a slippery slope to closing exemptions and mandating paid leave," he said.

Penny, a prominent participant in the floor debate in 1990, quietly submitted a written statement this time around. He said he supported the Gordon-Hyde language (which was the Senate's Bond-Dodd language) as "a step in the right direction" but that he would still oppose HR 2 even after that step had been taken. He said that addressing the problems of work and family meant being "sensitive to the employer community" as well. "I must add for the record," Penny concluded, "that the proponents of this measure have gone a long way to try to accommodate my concerns. We were very close to reaching agreement on a compromise which would have improved the bill and might have secured enough votes to override a veto."

Among the last statements submitted that day was one from Howard Berman of California, who spoke of the issues at hand, the Dodd-Bond deal and the Gordon-Hyde substitute, as well as the basic need for leave policy. Berman modestly omitted any reference to his own seminal role in the issue's development in the mid-1980s.

THE TWO SUBSTITUTES RULES HAD declared in order (Stenholm and Gordon-Hyde) were to be considered under "king of the mountain" rules, a contemporary procedure first used in the House in 1982. Under this rubric, the House meeting as the Committee of the Whole considers a succession of amendments "in the nature of a substitute," each of them tantamount to a separate bill. Substitutes essentially strip everything from the committee-reported bill and replace it with the text of the amendment, which usually repeats most of the committee-reported bill with certain alterations embedded at various points. This has several political and parliamentary advantages. Chief among the latter is the elimination of the "bigger bite" amendment by which opponents of a bill might otherwise seize and enlarge upon any change made on the floor. But the more profound appeal of the procedure is that it allows members to vote for or against a succession of alternatives, building an instant record on the bill both pro and con—secure in the knowledge that only their last vote will really count.

A given member could say he favored family leave and point to a vote for Stenholm's substitute, and the same member could say he opposed mandates and point to a vote against Gordon-Hyde or against final passage. When the House plays "king of the mountain," members may vote for as many or as few of these substitutes as they like. But whichever substitute is approved last is the only one left alive when the Committee of the Whole rises and the House of Representatives proper votes on final passage.

On November 13 the House took up Stenholm's substitute first. The Texas Democrat argued that his plan gave everyone far more flexibility by allowing new parents up to six years of leave (and those with medical needs two years), with the privilege of preferential rehire available at any time during that period. That would enable employers to plan their workforce needs, Stenholm said, and give families far more time to be together. "And unlike HR 2," he added, "it does not lead down the slippery slope to paid leave and other new categories of mandated benefits."

Ford and Clay each spoke briefly on the substitute, saying it made no provision for emergency situations of short duration and that a stated preference in rehiring at the employer's discretion was no guarantee of a job. Schroeder took the floor and said Stenholm's alternative might sound wonderful if "you came to this Congress on a turnip truck and you are really, really easily spun around." She called it a "fig leaf" but said she was thankful to have it, because it proved members knew it was "dangerous" to oppose family leave outright when the workplace had "changed so radically."

Shortly before four-thirty the House voted on Stenholm. The Texan picked up thirty-one votes from Democrats, mostly from members of the Conservative Democratic Forum, an informal group of about fifty that grew up around Stenholm in the early days of the Reagan era. But he did not do as well as might have been expected among Republicans, fifty-six of whom voted against his substitute. This number included most of the forty-eight Republicans who would later vote for Gordon-Hyde and the thirty-five who would vote for the bill on final passage. But it also included some hard-core conservatives such as Dick Armey, who saw Stenholm's idea as a lesser evil than HR 2, but in the end an evil.

The weakness of the vote for Stenholm's alternative reflected in part the lack of any effective lobbying by organized outsiders. The Chamber of Commerce had shown interest in the preferential rehiring idea, but had not pressed hard on its behalf. The most active lobbies, the NFIB and the participants in the CARE coalition, had concluded that Stenholm's provisions still constituted a mandate and an unacceptable constraint upon employers. But there was also a sense of futility about the Stenholm debate because the "king of the mountain" procedure was in effect. Stenholm's substitute could have passed with three hundred votes and still not mattered because it would be followed by another substitute that, if adopted, would replace it—top to bottom—as though it had never existed. And so on with the next substitute, and the next.

On this occasion, of course, there was to be just one more substitute considered, the recycled Senate bill in the guise of Gordon-Hyde. And everyone on the floor knew that this substitute was going to be adopted last and become the active text of HR 2. Debate on it began immediately after the vote on Stenholm, but the speeches said less about the amendment at hand than about the general merits of family leave. After Gordon had detailed the changes of the Bond-Dodd language and suggested they should be enough to allay the fears of business, Henry Hyde took the floor. "As one who shares a conservative vision for our society," he said, "I don't think my support for family leave is aberrational, but rather that it's consistent with traditional family values."

Most floor speeches in the House sound canned; Hyde's remarks stood out for their freshness. He waxed passionate in bemoaning "the assault on the family from every direction." He tossed off axioms, such as "Capitalism with a human face is an imperative, not an imposition." And while he agreed that government should not intrude, he shifted rhetorical gears by referring not to government but to law. "The law is also a teacher," he said. "And the lesson that family leave teaches is that children and parents aren't always the last consideration."

After that, the few remaining speeches were largely superfluous. Bill Goodling reminded his colleagues that the bill before them was scarcely a compromise at all, doing nothing to alter the bill the Senate had passed in October. Majority leader Richard Gephardt gave a brief reprise of his speech from 1990, touching on the story of his own son's cancer.

Then they voted, and the green lights seemed suddenly to be everywhere, running up and down the big boards on the chamber's south wall. The Gordon-Hyde substitute was winning big. It picked up four Democratic votes in Alabama and seven in Georgia. In Oklahoma, all four Democrats voted for it (including NFIB-friendly Dave McCurdy) and brought along Republican Mickey Edwards, usually a conservative hotspur.

On the numerical tote board, the ayes tumbled quickly past 200 and on past 250. When the number moved past 280, someone at the floor table surrounded by members and staff shouted, "We're there!" The final total was 287–143, one vote over two-thirds (of all present and voting). Only twenty-eight Democrats had voted against Gordon-Hyde, most of them from the South but seven from the North (Bob Carr of Michigan and Les Aspin of Wisconsin among them). On the other side, nearly fifty Republicans had been willing to buck their party's majority, many of them reassured not only by Hyde's remarks but by his name on the amendment. Others had felt liberated by the tacit agreement passed along by some of the business lobbyists that they would not "score" the vote on Gordon-Hyde. That tactic had allowed some fence-sitters a pro vote before they voted against final passage.

But most of the Republicans stuck with their leaders and opposed the substitute. There had been no retreat by the main business coalition or by the NFIB, which had seen no daylight in the Dodd-Bond language in the Senate and saw no more in it in the House. With the amendments considered, the Committee of the Whole rose, the mace was moved, and the Republicans got their built-in last hurrah: a motion to recommit the bill to committee.

In this instance Goodling moved to recommit with instructions that the bill be reported back as an eight-week unpaid leave for the parents of a newborn or newly adopted child. This was close to the old moms-only concept Howard Berman had urged in 1984 and that Penny had tried to bring to the floor in 1990. But proposing this approach in a motion to recommit reduced it to a pro forma protest by the minority party, and as such it packed no punch. Roukema gave a brief exegesis on the origin of the full-family approach and a sharp critique of the alternative at hand ("It says yes to mama and no to all the other workers that also need this care") and the motion was dumped by a lopsided 312–119. (Most Democrats rally to the party standard as a matter of course on motions to recommit.)

The House proceeded immediately to vote on final passage of HR 2 as amended by Gordon-Hyde. But when the votes had been counted, shortly after six o'clock, the euphoria of an hour earlier was forgotten. On final passage, only thirty-five Republicans stayed with the bill while forty-eight Democrats deserted it. The result was a vote of 253–177. And while that represented a solid improvement over the 237 votes for HR 770 in 1990, it fell more than thirty votes shy of two-thirds. For a moment, the gap between the 287 vote and the 253 seemed incomprehensible, but the explanation was not difficult to find. While the business lobby had not exactly given members a pass on Gordon-Hyde, they had made clear that the vote on final passage mattered more. That gave nearly three dozen members a way to play Solomon and divide the baby, voting yes on Gordon-Hyde and no on HR 2.

"Members wanted to be on record voting for something," said CARE's Tavenner, "but they did not want it to become law."

THROUGHOUT THAT AFTERNOON, while the House debated and voted, Lenhoff was fidgeting on a plane crossing the Atlantic Ocean. She landed at Dulles Airport at about the time of the vote on the Stenholm substitute. As the Committee of the Whole debated Gordon-Hyde, Lenhoff and her husband were encountering baggage difficulties. She went to a pay phone and called the House Democratic cloakroom. Were they on the bill? Yes. Had they voted on Gordon-Hyde? Not yet. Lenhoff and her husband got their bags and caught a cab outside in a cold, late-autumn rain. As they rode through the gray Virginia countryside that separates distant Dulles from the capital, Lenhoff wished there were a radio equivalent of C-SPAN. By the time they got across the Potomac, it might all be over.

Lenhoff got out of the cab at 14th and Pennsylvania, two blocks from the White House. Her husband went home with the bags while she caught another cab heading east to the Capitol. Once inside the building and past the security monitors she raced toward the House chamber, despairing when she noticed how few people were around. It must be over. There could not still be votes coming if so few people were in the hallways. She turned around and headed for the Senate side, wondering about the fate of the civil rights bill then still hanging in the balance. And then around the corner and walking straight toward her came Judith Lichtman and Helen Norton from her office, with Joel Packer of the National Education Association and others in tow.

"What happened?" she gasped.

"You missed it," they said in chorus.

They were happy, it seemed, still buoyed by the big vote for Gordon-Hyde. But they were also sobered by the final passage vote. Lenhoff's face fell when she heard it. It sounded so low, after the weeks of negotiating with Penny, visualizing 260 and 270, and dreaming of 280 or more. There had been such great joy over 237 votes in 1990, when the bill was still struggling to earn respect. But now their sights were set so much higher. They were trying to override a president who had yet to be overridden in either chamber. And to fall this far short, this late in the game, was disheartening—and more so, the more they thought about it.

13.

To the White House
Once Again

THROUGH THE FIRST THREE YEARS of George Bush's presidency, White
House conversations about family leave bills tended to be short. Chief of
Staff John Sununu, the former governor of New Hampshire, generally
took the view that such a mandate would become law only over his dead
body. Bush himself did not officially speak to the issue except in the text
of his 1990 veto message.

When Hill Republicans tried to negotiate the issue with White House
people they trusted they heard that family leave was "an Oval Office
decision." Yet when they tried to make their case in that office, they were
rebuffed—not once, but repeatedly. Roukema was the first to importune
the White House on behalf of the bill, and she was increasingly incensed
by the lack of a response. "We never got a foot in the door over all those
years," she said, recalling the letters and phone calls from herself, Kit
Bond, Henry Hyde, Gerald Solomon, and other conservative backers of
the bill. Roukema tried an end run by calling up her former House
colleague Lynn Martin, now secretary of labor, but Martin, too, refused
to discuss the subject.

Dodd also tried "every door and window" at the White House. One
avenue he explored was his relationship with Dan Quayle. Dodd had
always believed Quayle to be interested in family leave as a policy ques-

tion and cognizant of its value as a political issue. They had talked about it as far back as 1988 when Quayle was an active participant on the Senate Labor Committee and, for a time, a potential bridge to committee Republicans. Years later Dodd still believed he might have gotten Quayle's vote at the bill's maiden markup in the Senate in July 1988 had Quayle not been under consideration for the national ticket at the time.

The bill's advocates even took the highly unusual liberty of writing directly to the first lady, Barbara Bush, soliciting her intercession on behalf of family leave. They thought Mrs. Bush would be sympathetic, given her well-known devotion to children's causes and family issues.

In the end, however, nothing worked. Much of the blame for Bush's isolation from the issue tended to settle on Sununu, who often served as the heat shield between Bush and displeased Republicans who did not wish to speak ill of the president. Sununu was unalterably opposed to the family leave bills he saw on the Hill, but in this he was no different from the White House staff in general.

For a while it looked as though Sununu would fall from grace after using official cars and planes too liberally; but he survived that. Then in the fall of 1991 a stunning Democratic win in a Pennsylvania senatorial race made it clear that public unhappiness over the deteriorating economy was worse than anyone in the White House had realized. The president himself might be in jeopardy in a year. The administration needed a scapegoat, and on December 3 the unpopular Sununu resigned.

Once again, the advocates of family leave saw reason to hope. With a new chief of staff in place, there might be a new attitude toward the social agenda. Sununu's successor, Transportation Secretary Samuel K. Skinner, was associated politically with Illinois's Republican Governor Jim Thompson, a party moderate. Skinner himself was known for skill in negotiating and crafting agreements. Surely now, at the very least, the issue's advocates could have a fair hearing.

Sununu's letter of resignation came less than three weeks after HR 2 had passed the House, where it was still being "held at the Speaker's desk." Unlike the 1990 legislation, which both chambers passed in identical form, the bills passed by the House and Senate in 1991 had slight differences, enough to necessitate a conference committee. Thus, the final formal detail in the House action of November 13 was a request for a conference with the Senate on S 5, which, technically speaking, was the legislative vehicle the House had actually passed (after first substituting the text of its own, newly amended HR 2). Normally, the leadership in each chamber would have appointed conferees shortly after final passage. But neither Speaker Foley nor majority leader Mitchell did so after a week or even two weeks. And they still had not done so when Sununu was cleaning out his desk at the White House in December.

No one had any doubt about who the conferees would be or what they would decide. The chairs and senior members of the relevant committees and subcommittees are chosen more or less automatically (as are the ranking members and a few other senior members of the minority from those panels). Occasionally, the party leaders wrangle with committee leaders over how many conferees should be named and how far down in the ranks to reach for participants. Getting on the conference committee can be of enormous importance to individuals with heavy stakes in the details of complex bills, such as the 1986 tax overhaul or the revision of the Toxic Waste Superfund or the Clean Air Act. But in the case of family leave, scarcely any suspense surrounded the handful of minor differences between the bills, so appointment to the conference would be little more than a routine chore.

But Speaker Foley and majority leader Mitchell were in no hurry to initiate the conference. They wanted to allow time for a possible negotiation with the White House through back channels. And if no deal could be struck, they preferred to place the bill before the president at the moment when a veto would get maximum media attention: as close to Election Day as possible.

So 1992 BEGAN WITH THE FAMILY LEAVE bill in limbo and the White House under somewhat new management. Shortly after occupying the small office next to the Oval Office, Skinner met with Nick Calio, the former presidential liaison to the House. Calio had left the administration in 1991 to join a prestigious lobbying firm founded by Ken Duberstein, who had been Ronald Reagan's last chief of staff. Skinner offered Calio the job of assistant to the president for legislative affairs, succeeding Fred McClure, who had just retired. Calio accepted and in January returned to the White House as the president's chief lobbyist on the Hill.

Calio's earlier stint on the White House staff had begun in 1989, when he was part of McClure's original stable of lobbyists. Previously, Calio had been vice president for government relations at the National Association of Wholesaler-Distributors, where he had been Mary Tavenner's boss and had helped set up the CARE coalition in 1987. A dapper and compact dynamo of a man, Calio was known for the ease with which he moved among the Hill's various tribes and factions. He was close to Dick Cheney, the House GOP whip who became secretary of defense in

March 1989. But he prided himself on a good working relationship with Ways and Means Chairman Dan Rostenkowski and other pivotal Democrats as well.

Calio specialized in tax and budget issues in the early months of the Bush presidency, as the president pressed for budget cuts and a reduction in the marginal tax rate on capital gains. But he also found himself pulled away to deal with the likes of child care, the minimum wage, unemployment compensation, civil rights and a range of other labor and social policy squabbles. In 1989 his shop had consisted of three professionals (at the level of special assistant to the president) and three staff assistants, and with this crew he had covered the House and all its committees on the full range of issues, foreign and domestic. Now he was back with responsibility for both House and Senate.

Also brought aboard at the White House that winter was Linda Tarplin, who traded in her title as a deputy assistant secretary for legislation in the Department of Health and Human Services for the equally prolix title of special assistant to the president for legislative affairs in the Senate. Tarplin had specialized in human services issues such as child care, which was how she had met her husband, Rich Tarplin, who was staff for Chris Dodd on child care as well as family leave. The two had become acquainted in 1989 through long hours of negotiating from opposite sides of the table on child care. "We figured out pretty early that we could not discuss politics if the relationship was going to go anywhere," Rich Tarplin later said. Remarkably, their conflicting views of public policy were subordinated to their mutual interest in each other and they were married in 1990—the year Bush's first veto of family leave was sustained in the House.

Linda Tarplin's new duties for Calio included S 5, but the bill presented little immediate challenge. Despite the hopes of many family leave advocates, the Skinner regime showed no more interest in bargaining than had its predecessor. Calio tried to accommodate the House Republicans who kept clamoring to meet with the president. He was able to sit Roukema down with Skinner, but Roukema would remember that meeting as elliptical and unsatisfying. Skinner refused to let Hill Republicans meet directly with the president on the issue.

THE ONLY DECISION THE ADVOCATES of family leave could make on their own at this juncture was the timing of the next veto. For a time that winter, the sponsors in the House and Senate considered a strategy some referred to as "stick it to him twice." It would be possible to conference the two versions of the bill and then clear the conference report in a matter of days. So why not do so shortly after the second session of the 102nd Congress convened in January? Then, after Bush's expected veto had been sustained in the House, there would be time for committees to meet in both chambers and mark up yet another iteration of family leave.

The new bill could then be brought back to the floor and advertised as yet another compromise, another display of cooperativeness on the part of Congress. If Bush vetoed the bill again, he would look more unreasonable and unyielding than ever. And surely this last veto could be put off until the end of the session, scant weeks before the election. At a minimum, the political value of the bill would be maximized. And if the machinations moved Bush to sign the bill or negotiate a deal, then so much the better.

This hardball strategy had great appeal for some of the outside supporters and inside sponsors, especially on the House side. But the leadership was less enthusiastic. Election years constrict the calendar in both chambers, as many bills ripen for floor action all at once and the impending election makes members eager to adjourn. If a recycled family leave bill were to collide with appropriations bills and other must-pass legislation in the fall, it might not find its proper hour. If passed in the final weeks, it might be subject to the pocket veto—a practice originated by Andrew Jackson in the 1830s and used by presidents at odds with Congress ever since.

The president normally has ten days to sign or veto a bill before it becomes law without his signature. But if Congress is not in session when the ten-day period elapses, the unsigned bill dies. If Congress were to pass a recycled family leave bill in time to avoid such a happenstance, it would need the cooperation of Senate Republicans. But would such cooperation be forthcoming? Or would a twice-around strategy destroy the procedural truce that Mitchell and Dole had struck in twice voice-voting the bill?

As a practical matter, even talking about such things put off the bill's Republican advocates. Roukema, already well out of step with her GOP colleagues on the issue, wanted no part of a plot to embarrass her party and its president. The same could be said for Bond, whose cooperation had given Dodd the upper hand in the Senate. (Bond, for his part, favored the idea of holding the bill at the desk, too, but for a rather different reason: He hoped it would allow time for someone at the White House to have a change of heart.)

"We had a bipartisan group together by that point," one House staff member said. "So it had to be: 'Please, Mr. President' and not 'In your face, you fool.' "

Substance arguments also militated against forcing Bush to veto the bill twice in one Congress. Further compromises in the bill would need to be carefully calibrated. Merely cosmetic changes might be dismissed by the more skeptical news media, easing the desired pressure on Bush and possibly backfiring on Democrats (whose motives would seem baldly partisan). But any significant compromise—such as shorter leave periods or weakened penalties—would be difficult to retract if and when another bill needed to be drafted in the next Congress.

All these arguments having been weighed, Bill Clay sent a memo to Bill Ford on February 25 regarding family leave. As one committee chairman to another, Clay was informing Ford that efforts to avert a veto through some form of negotiated settlement had been fruitless. At this point, Clay wrote, family leave was of more value to congressional Democrats as an issue in the fall 1992 campaign than as a live policy option. Clay had decided it was best to put the bill on Bush's desk just once and to do it in September.

The failure to reach a truce on family leave was probably less a matter of intransigence on either side than it was a symptom of political weakness on both sides. While Sam Skinner had been reorganizing the White House and supporters of family leave had been assessing their options, George Bush had been having a bad time in the courts of public opinion. His approval rating had dropped from its near-90 peak in mid-1991 to a decidedly mortal 55 percent. Worse yet, the supposedly invulnerable incumbent had watched two opponents arise to challenge him from the right. One was conservative commentator Pat Buchanan, a former speechwriter for Richard Nixon and communications director for Ronald Reagan. Buchanan had been one of several conservative opinion makers who had never accepted Bush as Reagan's successor. In fact, Buchanan's views owed less to Reagan than to Barry Goldwater, the 1964 GOP presidential nominee, who Buchanan said had "the purer vision."

The other rival keeping Bush awake was Ross Perot, the billionaire businessman from Dallas who had dabbled in politics in his idiosyncratic fashion for more than twenty years. The glib and aphoristic Perot was talking about launching an independent candidacy for president and paying the bills for it himself, and he was attracting a following.

Most political observers remained convinced that Bush would be the party's nominee in 1992 and the winner in November, but polls showed Buchanan doing surprisingly well in New Hampshire, the traditional site of the nation's first presidential primary. And when that state voted on February 18, Bush won—but with just 53 percent of the Republican vote. With this sudden chill upon him, Bush could ill afford to be seen abandoning his party's conservative core on any issue as noticeable as family leave.

But if the White House was staving off humiliation, Congress was suffering from extraordinary institutional anemia as well. Not only were individual members under investigation or indictment for various infractions, but the entire House was under scrutiny because of questionable practices at its internal bank. Members had for years enjoyed the use of accounts into which their paychecks were automatically deposited. Members could write drafts on these accounts, and they could write overdrafts as well—without penalty. The General Accounting Office had become increasingly critical of the bank because it allowed members access to future paychecks in this manner, in effect writing themselves interest-free loans against their future salary. The GAO had for years been threatening to release information about the scope of the abuse, and in September 1991 it did so. The GAO reported that 8,331 such overdrafts had been written during a twelve-month period of 1989–90.

Relatively few members had abused this privilege significantly, but the brouhaha over "bounced checks" and "check kiting" knew no bounds. When the Democratic leadership tried to limit the damage by exposing only the most egregious offenders, they only succeeded in worsening the crisis. In April 1992 the House would release the full list of all 325 current or recent members who had at least one overdraft. Embarrassment over the incident contributed to a rash of retirements from the House that year: the sixty-five members who voluntarily left their seats at the end of the 102nd Congress were the most to do so in any year since World War II.

RETIREMENTS WERE BOTH A CAUSE and a symptom of the political ferment of 1992. In every even-numbered year elections are held for every seat in the House and one-third of the Senate. But some election years instill more fear than others because periodic shake-ups are built into the system. The quadrennial election for president tends to engage public attention, which by itself generates instability in the electoral process. But 1992 was also the first election year to follow the census of 1990, and every decennial census produces an upheaval in congressional politics because of reapportionment and redistricting.

The Constitution requires that the seats of the House be reallocated every ten years to reflect the relative populations of the states. This process was eased in the nineteenth century by the steady expansion of the House (it began in 1789 with just sixty-five seats). But after the turn of the century, the consensus was that the body had grown unwieldy. After much wrangling, the number of seats was fixed at 435, where it has remained since. So states that lose population or grow more slowly than the national average see one or more of their seats in the House apportioned to other states. The 1990 census took three seats from New York and two each from Pennsylvania, Michigan, Illinois and Ohio. The big gainers were once again the Sun Belt states: Texas added three seats, Florida four and California seven.

Each reapportioned seat automatically means one fewer incumbent and one new member. But the destabilizing effect does not end there. Reapportionment also begets redistricting, which requires each state legislature to redraw the lines that define the congressional districts in that state so as to equalize their population. The idea of leveling districts' populations is not explicit in the Constitution, but it has been the subject of a series of Supreme Court decisions in recent decades.

The Court has also required legislatures to draw maps that concentrate racial minorities in districts where they can dominate the vote and elect representatives of their own choosing. Given all the bench law on redistricting, the split-party control of many state legislatures and the power many governors have to veto the new map, the process often leads to an impasse or a lawsuit that empowers a federal court to draw the electoral map. Either way, the undertaking is fraught with uncertainty for an incumbent, who may find his or her district divided up among several others or altered to favor the other party.

When the presidential and census cycles coincide, the effects can be far-reaching. In the twentieth century they fell together every twenty years from 1912 to 1992. In four of these five, the voters installed a new party in the White House. And in three of those four, the voters also changed the party in control of at least one chamber of Congress.

In 1992 this double whammy was complicated further by the unsettled electoral circumstances in the Senate. The GOP campaigned, at least initially, on the hope of recapturing the majority it had lost in 1986. But the Democrats had at least as good a chance of building their strength to sixty, the supermajority level at which they could limit floor debate without any crossover votes from the minority (a level of dominance neither party had achieved since the 1970s).

Given all this volatility, 1992 promised to be a triple witching hour for incumbents on Capitol Hill. And there was yet another dimension of change in 1992, one likely to be the most enduring. Women were taking a more prominent role in politics. For years, women had voted in greater numbers than men. But in 1992 women were more likely than ever before to become candidates themselves.

This last consideration was an enormous boon for family leave. Not only was the issue a natural weapon for women candidates, but it became a hoop through which countless male candidates could be made to jump. It was also useful for Democrats under assault by advocates of "family values," a phrase generally used by social conservatives to cover a panoply of issues from school prayer to abortion, pornography and homosexual activism. Conversely, family leave offered political shelter of a different sort for a dozen Republicans in the Senate and roughly forty in the House who voted for it. Some antiabortion conservatives used it as proof of their concern for women forced to choose between work and motherhood. Others saw it as a chance to demonstrate their independence from "big business" or their connection with the everyday problems of working families, particularly young households.

The voter appeal of any particular bill is a constant factor in the calculations of Congress. Some critics of the institution argue that members respond only to party leaders, interest groups and financial contributors. But when lobbyists talk about members, they almost immediately refer to the politics of their states and districts. Thus, when Donna Lenhoff of the Women's Legal Defense Fund heard that Kit Bond was interested in working with Dodd on a compromise, she immediately thought of Harriett Woods, the former lieutenant governor of Missouri who had nearly beaten Bond in the 1986 election. Was Bond thinking that Woods would want a rematch in 1992? Bond's career had been a catalog of close elections, and he expected no less in seeking reelection to the Senate. As it turned out, Bond's opponent in 1992 would not be Woods, but it would be a woman. And Bond's pivotal role in the family leave saga would help him balance his record on gender politics (including his vote to confirm Clarence Thomas) and pull out another narrow victory.

When virtually every officeholder is a nervous officeholder, virtually every issue is a campaign issue. So it was natural for family leave's lead sponsors, committee chairs and Democratic Party leaders to discuss how best to use the yeasty issue to their political benefit in 1992. The answer was obvious: Force the president to cast an unpopular veto and he may choose to make a deal. The question was, when would it be best to pull the trigger? Once the "stick it to him twice" scenario had been discarded, the consensus was to follow Clay's advice and wait for the fall.

• • •

IN THEIR FRUSTRATION, THE supporters of family leave often looked upon the White House as resolute and impenetrable. But from the perspective of those within it, or those relying on it, the White House could seem a fragile fortress indeed. That was why Calio and the various business lobbies kept a worried watch over the 195 members who had voted to sustain Bush's first veto of family leave in July 1990. A few of these had not returned for the 102nd Congress, retiring or meeting defeat (none for reasons visibly related to family leave). But the great majority were back and still committed to supporting the president—including nearly all of the fifty-seven Democrats who had resisted their own leaders' effort to override in 1990.

Calio and the business lobbies knew they needed to hold only about 150 of their votes to sustain a veto. Even so, they were wary. It would send the wrong message if the president's margin of victory were to narrow appreciably. Any defections would be publicized, possibly creating an undertow that could drag their vote down unexpectedly.

Calio was a business lobbyist by profession and a fiscal policy specialist. But he also had a keen sense of realism in the performance of his job. And over the years he had watched the family leave issue grow from a wispy cloud on the horizon to a thunderhead capable of causing real damage. Even as he wrapped up the vote to sustain the first veto in 1990, he was thinking about the need for a successor strategy. At some point, as Tavenner liked to put it, members were going to want something to be for.

Calio had always questioned how sincere some of the Democrats were about the substance of the issue, suspecting they were more interested in the issue for its political value. "It was a good woman's issue," he said. "It allowed Democrats to portray Bush as insensitive to women." Still, if for that reason alone, Calio suspected that someday there would be a table with pots of coffee, legal pads and people from his shop in shirtsleeves sketching out a deal with congressional staff.

Calio had his staff research the alternatives that had been offered in Congress and within the executive branch as well, including the idea of granting tax breaks to small companies that permitted family leave. But none ever broke out from what Calio called "the embryonic sac." The most obvious alternative, a moms-only bill or a mom-and-pop bill for birth and adoption only, was broached in White House discussions but went nowhere. Once again, the mantra was: "A mandate is a mandate is a mandate."

In fact, the most serious conversations toward a compromise during the Bush presidency took place not in 1992 but in the spring of 1990, shortly before the first House vote on HR 770. "We had discussions with people on the Hill in 1990 at a time when we weren't sure how our votes were stacking up," Calio said. "And that, frankly, is the only time when the notion of developing an alternative had any resonance with some people in the White House. But discussion was limited even at that time."

Whatever impulses Skinner or Calio may have had in early 1992, there seemed no room to move. Buchanan's primary challenge made it all but impossible for Bush to backtrack on his veto threat, given that the president's previous compromises on taxes, the minimum wage and civil rights were the fuel powering Buchanan's campaign. The issue was not salient on the Democratic side, either, as all the major contenders for the nomination supported it.

It was clear that, come the fall campaign, the Democrats would be coming after Bush on family leave. But that knowledge was not having the desired effect at the White House. "They were not willing to deal," said a disappointed Bond. "I think the president is just plain wrong on this."

WITH NO COMPROMISE IN SIGHT, THE Democrats held the ball for the last shot. Senate conferees were not named until the last week of July, when the leadership announced the appointment of the five most senior Democrats on Senate Labor (including Kennedy and Dodd) and the three most senior Republicans (Hatch, Kassebaum and Coats). A week later the House leadership named twenty Democrats and fourteen Republicans from three committees (Ed and Labor, Post Office and House Administration) to conference on the various titles or major segments of the bill. The majority was led by Clay, Ford and Schroeder, the minority by Goodling, Petri and Roukema.

Prior to a conference, staff for the relevant House and Senate committees prepare side-by-side comparisons of the bills at issue, highlighting the differences. The primary responsibility for this usually devolves on committee staff accountable to the leader of the conference delegation from each chamber (in this case, Kennedy and Clay). But committee staffs often work together across party lines, chamber allegiances and committee jurisdictions. Staff may also hold preconference negotiating sessions to identify sticking points and expedite negotiations between the members themselves. Conferences usually meet in public, at least at the end of the process, to vote on the compromises members have already agreed to in private meetings.

It was not difficult to predict the direction of the conference. Every

Democrat was a supporter of the Dodd-Bond language, while the Republicans—outnumbered from the start—included such supporters as Roukema and Coats. The conferees needed just one meeting on August 5 to ratify the staff work already done and compose the differences between the two versions.

The Senate bill had a provision by which employers could recapture health insurance premiums paid for employees on leave who never returned to work. The House had no such provision, and the Senate conferees did not insist on theirs. Score one for the House, and for the backers of the bill. The Senate also defined an employee as someone who had been on the payroll for the previous twelve months and had worked 1,250 hours. The House said only that a worker must be employed for at least twelve months on something other than a temporary or intermittent basis. Once again the Senate receded.

In one interesting conflict the Senate had referred to leaves taken "because of the birth of a son or a daughter" while the House had added the clause: "and in order to care for such son or daughter." The Senate accepted the change, which was made when opponents of the bill suggested that noncustodial or absentee fathers might abuse the privilege of leave-taking for other purposes. It had been suggested in debate that even rapists might claim the leave upon the birth of a child so sired.

While the senators had agreed to apply the provisions of the bill to Senate employees, the House bill applied them to both the Senate and House. The Senate bill said an employer could require an employee to substitute vacation or paid sick leave ("accrued annual leave") for some of the weeks within the twelve-week period of unpaid leave. But the House bill provided for such substitution only when requested by the employee, and the House carried the day.

Similarly, the two chambers had slight differences in their definition of a parent for purposes of elder care. They resolved these by saying an employee could have leave to care for a biological father or mother or a person who had been the legal equivalent ("in loco parentis"). Where the Senate had defined a "serious health condition" as an "illness, injury, impairment or physical or mental condition," the House had prefaced that list with the word "disabling." But the House conferees did not insist on this limiting modifier, so it was dropped in the conference report. The Senate bill said employers could seek recertification of employee health conditions "on a reasonable basis." The House went along with this but specified that such recertification had to be at the employers' own expense.

The most common means of resolving conflicts in conference is to split the difference. This is typical, for example, in reconciling discrepancies between House and Senate appropriations bills. But it is not always appropriate for harmonizing less quantitative conflicts. In such cases, when a clear majority of conferees favor a stronger or weaker bill, that majority may simply outvote the other conferees. If they press their advantage too far, of course, they risk seeing the House or Senate reject the conference report (which either kills the bill or restarts the conference). In the case of family leave, it was possible for its supporters to prevail on every substantive question.

The report of the conference agreement (HR Report 102-816) was filed with the House (which had technically passed the bill after the Senate and requested the conference) on August 10. The next day, August 11, Mitchell sought and received unanimous consent to consider the report. But the unanimous consent agreement did not include a recorded vote on the family-leave conference report. Dodd wanted a recorded vote this time, hoping to prove that the bill's two-thirds support in the chamber was real and to build a fire under both the House and the White House.

But Dole dug in his heels. If Kennedy and Dodd pressed for such a vote, there would be extended debate in a week when the Senate expected to wrap up its summer work prior to the Republican National Convention. As it was, three separate pieces of legislation backed by both parties' leaders would be stalled short of passage in the Senate that week, foiled in each case by the procedural maneuvers of a single Republican senator. To avoid becoming the fourth victim, Dodd gave up on having a recorded vote, and the conference report on family leave cleared the Senate on August 11 by unanimous consent.

The House did not act on the report as quickly because doing so might have placed the bill on the president's desk just before the three-week August recess began. This would have allowed Bush to pocket veto the legislation—ignoring it for ten days while Congress was not in town. If Congress is not meeting when the ten-day period has lapsed, the bill dies as if successfully vetoed; Congress cannot return a week later to revive it. Although Congress has disputed the president's power to pocket veto during a recess (as opposed to an end-of-session adjournment), the House leadership decided this was not the moment to risk a court's interpretation of that dispute.

Two days later, on August 13, Bush took the podium in the White House press room to announce that Skinner was being replaced as chief of staff by Secretary of State James A. Baker 3rd. The move surprised no one, as Bush was trailing Bill Clinton by nearly 20 percentage points in the polls and needed to shake up his campaign effort. Skinner had come to the White House to heal wounds opened by Sununu and to preside over a presumably smooth nomination process. He was supposed to shield Bush from internal squabbles and help him raise his batting average on the Hill. But what had seemed a practical agenda had proven unmanageable, and some on staff grumbled about Skinner's lack of real authority or his reluctance to use what he had.

When Baker arrived in the White House on August 23, accompanied by a staff team of his own from the State Department, he was appalled at the pile of unresolved issues in domestic policy, including family leave. Completely irrespective of the merits of the bill at hand, Baker could not understand why the issue had been allowed to fester this long. He expressed similar feelings about other social matters, including the ban on medical or scientific research performed using fetal tissue. "Baker at the end very much wanted to find a way out of it, to make a deal," recalled Tom Scully, the deputy to Richard Darman, the director of the Office of Management and Budget (OMB), assigned to domestic issues. "He thought we were all nuts to still be fighting on family leave."

The House was due back from recess on September 9 and the word was that Rules would consider the conference report that same day. On September 7, Calio sent a memo to Bob Zoellick, Baker's right-hand man at State, who had transferred with him to the White House. The issue was "whether the president can moderate his opposition to family and medical leave legislation." In the memo Calio recited the elements of the bill and reviewed the state of play, with the conference report already cleared in one chamber and poised to clear that week in the other. He noted that the White House was "not in a position to reopen the conference at will" and that it had "never developed a substitute or supported an alternative, as we did, for example, on child care."

Calio offered Zoellick three courses of action. One was to "change our position and sign the bill." Calio thought this would get as much bad press as another veto, but he added that the bill "could dissipate as a campaign issue if we sign." This having been said, Calio leaned back the other way and noted that "we would have a lot of repair work to do with our small business allies."

A second option was simply to veto the bill and "articulate forcefully our reasons." This was something that Calio and many of the administration's defenders were fully prepared to do. "However, if we go this route, we need to give POTUS [internal administration acronym for president of the United States] a concise and clear statement that he can/will use," Calio advised.

The third option was to reissue the veto threat but offer some positive

alternative that encouraged private employers to adopt friendly policies
for family leave. This could take the form of a tax incentive, such as the
50 percent cost write-off for employee leaves proposed by Senator Larry
Craig, a Republican from Idaho. Alternatively, the White House might
embrace the preferential rehire approach of Stenholm and Hatch. Neither the Sununu nor the Skinner regime had taken a position on this
idea, but it was regarded as a mandate by the small-business lobby.

A meeting ensued on the issue in Zoellick's office, with Baker on hand
along with Darman, Calio and Scully. The consensus was that the first
option looked too much like a political deathbed conversion. "We were
too locked in to just sign the bill," said Scully later. "Baker wanted us to
come up with something more credible." But not the Stenholm-Hatch
approach, which had been drubbed already in floor votes in both chambers. The third option was deemed the most plausible, with some version
of the tax incentive to be formalized as quickly as possible. Calio went to
work with Bob Grady from the Treasury Department, and Scully went to
work on "talking points" to sell the idea.

On September 9 the House Rules Committee processed the conference report (HR Report 102-816) for swift clearance on the floor the
following day. Even though the law had already been passed once by the
whole House, the conference report constituted a new question for debate and needed a rule of its own to order consideration on the floor.
Such rules are generally quite simple, as conference reports are not subject to floor amendment. On September 10 the vote approving the rule
was a bracing 329–71. By contrast, the vote to approve the report itself
was a limp 241–161, with more than 30 members not voting. More than
one-fourth of all the votes against the report (42) were cast by Democrats.
On this basis, it appeared certain that the president's promised veto
would be sustained.

The bill was now officially before the president, who would issue his
veto on September 22. But in the meantime, on Wednesday the six-
teenth, the White House unveiled the results of the combined effort of
the Department of the Treasury, the Office of Legislative Affairs and the
OMB. It was a tax incentive plan, and it was touted as a Republican
alternative to S 5. Loosely based on the bill offered by Idaho's Senator
Craig (S 841), the Bush plan allowed a refundable tax credit to businesses
that granted up to twelve weeks of leave. The credit would be equal to 20
percent of the employee's wages, and it would apply to all businesses with
up to 500 employees (larger firms were assumed to have their own plans).
Craig was delighted to endorse the president's version, calling it a "posi-

tive environment" for "synergy" between employees and employers, "coming together to craft the individual program."

Roukema called the president's plan "a very transparent ploy, coming in at the end." She said the tax plan might be a fine addendum to a family and medical leave policy but that it was no substitute for one. It addressed the same array of family crises, but it provided no guarantee of a job for those in crisis. Moreover, it applied only to hiring entities that paid taxes, so it had no effect on governments or nonprofit institutions. Dodd said the president's plan was simply not serious. And even Dick Armey, who had no use for family leave in the first place, allowed that the timing of this new plan was "unfortunate."

Nevertheless, the president's effort did give the Republicans something to talk about on the floor the following week when Bush's veto arrived. Bush's veto message concentrated on his objections to mandates, much as it had in 1990. But this time Bush could also mention his own plan and ask Congress to consider it seriously in 1993.

Mitchell got a time agreement on September 23 to debate and vote on the veto override on the following day. In that debate Dole repeatedly held aloft a copy of the tax plan, asking: "What about the president's plan?" But it was clear from the lack of interest that the White House had missed its moment of opportunity. "If we had come out with this same plan six months earlier, it might have been a bill," said Scully.

Dole had one other argument that September that he had not used before. It was that the presidential election was six weeks away and the GOP should not be overriding its embattled incumbent president. After all, without a Republican in the White House, Republicans would feel far less important in the Senate. But the appeal to team spirit rang hollow, in part because two dozen Republican senators were already contemplating a vote to override Bush's veto of a cable television reregulation bill.

The Senate overrode the veto of S 5 with two votes to spare, 68–32. Fourteen Republicans voted to override, even though Ted Stevens of Alaska, a late convert to S 5, turned around and voted to sustain. David Boren, an Oklahoma Democrat who had never voted for the bill itself, voted for the override and told Dodd on the floor that he would vote for the bill in the next Congress.

Two days later the House began to debate the motion to override but did not get to a vote before quitting for the weekend. On September 30, the final day of the month and the fiscal year, the House confirmed the vote counters' predictions, mustering just 258 votes for the override. With eight members not voting, that meant the bill was twenty-seven votes shy of two-thirds. Once again, forty-two Democrats voted to sustain, while thirty-eight Republicans were ready to override.

The House vote trumped the Senate vote because both chambers must agree to override. Bush had won another round, but he did so in the shadow of a larger, impending contest. Bill Ford alluded to that shadow in the brief debate on the override motion, warning the Republicans that this might be the last time they would see the bill in so moderate a form. "I promise you, I'll put a good bill on President Clinton's desk and he'll sign it," Ford said.

Part Five

ENACTMENT:
THE 103RD CONGRESS
(1993)

14.

A New Day

ON JANUARY 20, 1993, BILL CLINTON delivered the first inaugural address given by a Democrat in sixteen years. The speech tended toward the simple, built as it was on such ideas and phrases as "make change our friend" and "the world is more free but less stable." Clinton spoke of families and children several times and compared social conscience and legislation to "the way families provide for their children." He also spoke of an end to the "era of deadlock and drift." Clinton made no specific mention of family leave or any other issue, but for the advocates in the audience none was necessary. The new president had been speaking to their issue when it counted most—in his campaign.

The campaign of 1992 was the first in which family leave had figured significantly. There had been talk of the issue in 1988, when Democratic presidential nominee Michael Dukakis endorsed the idea. But at the time of that earlier presidential campaign, Congress had yet to pass a family leave bill and candidate George Bush had yet to show himself averse to one. In 1990, when the midterm congressional elections were held, a family leave bill had been passed but vetoed. Family leave was an issue only in scattered races.

In 1992, however, the family leave veto came in September, and the dramatic effort to override that veto continued until just five weeks before

Election Day. Moreover, unlike 1988, family leave in 1992 was an issue of clear difference between the two presidential candidates—Bush had twice vetoed it, Bill Clinton had pledged to sign it—and that made it a defining issue between the parties.

The political effect of that issue was hard to measure with precision, but it was palpable for many Republicans. One who had given it some thought was Tom Scully, the White House aide who had been around for the last gasp of attempted compromise on the issue. "I still thought it was something of a bogus issue, not something employees were that eager to have," Scully said. "On the other hand, Republicans were idiots to make such a big fight of it."

Clinton had been vocal in support of family leave, beginning in his primary campaign. The new first lady, Hillary Rodham Clinton, had many friends among the leaders of the family leave coalition, most especially Marian Wright Edelman of the Children's Defense Fund. And one of Clinton's closest aides, George Stephanopoulos, had worked the bill in the House in 1990 when he was chief floor assistant to majority leader Richard Gephardt.

But family leave gained its greatest prominence in the campaign when Clinton picked Tennessee Senator Albert Gore Jr. as his vice-presidential running mate. Media biographies of Gore featured the story of his six-year-old son being struck and nearly killed by a car outside a ballpark in Baltimore. The boy had spent weeks in a hospital with his parents at his bedside. In accepting his nomination at the July convention in Madison Square Garden, Gore told the story so affectingly that even the press rows were hushed. "When you've seen your reflection in the empty stare of a boy waiting for a second breath of life," said Gore, "you realize that we weren't put here on earth to look out for our needs alone."

In subsequent weeks, as Clinton and Gore toured the country by bus, they found this poignant story had entered the national consciousness. They found their call for family leave had become one of their best applause lines. Gore also reprised his Garden performance on the floor of the Senate that September, just before the vote to override Bush's veto of S 5. Taking a rare break from the campaign to participate, Gore was again at his best in recalling his son's accident and convalescence. And then he surprised many in the chamber (and the far wider audience watching on C-SPAN) by revealing that, during those weeks in the hospital, Bush had called repeatedly to ask how the boy was doing. Gore said that proved to him that the president cared, that he knew what suffering with a child was all about (one of the Bushes' daughters had died in childhood). On that basis, Gore said, he felt sure the president wanted to sign the bill.

In the campaigns of 1992, "you just don't get it" became a political refrain, a catchphrase of general utility that was particularly apt for mocking old-fashioned attitudes or candidates. Democratic pollster Celinda Lake liked to say that family leave was a leading indicator of whether a given candidate "got it" or not. She said it measured a candidate's awareness of the changing worlds of home and work. And it was a particularly useful issue for the women who had been nominated for the Senate in 1992 by the Democrats in ten different states.

"I don't think anyone voted for female candidates because of family leave directly, or you'd be hard-pressed to find many, anyway," Scully would say. "But besides abortion there was this general perception of insensitivity and this was part of that, part of the background noise."

In Illinois, the Democrats nominated an African-American Cook County (Chicago) official, Carol Moseley-Braun, and in Washington State they backed a junior state legislator, Patty Murray, who campaigned as "the mom in tennis shoes." In California, the Democrats had nominated not one but two women. One was Congresswoman Barbara Boxer, who had been among the first members pushing for a post-maternity leave bill in the mid-1980s (along with her in-state colleagues Howard Berman and George Miller). Boxer had since been among the most fiery debaters on behalf of the Clay-Schroeder-Roukema bills, and she was matched in November against a conservative southern California TV commentator noted for his atavistic attitudes on social questions.

California Democrats had also nominated Dianne Feinstein against appointed Republican Senator John Seymour, who had consistently opposed family leave. Seymour had been the senator chosen to introduce Bush's tax-incentive plan as an amendment to S 5 in September 1992 (and the only senator to miss the override vote that same month).

In November 1992 all four women were elected, joining Democrat Barbara Mikulski of Maryland and Republican Nancy Landon Kassebaum to raise the number of women in the Senate to six (double the previous record high).

Together, the two major parties nominated an unprecedented 106 women for the House in 1992 and elected forty-eight (including Eleanor Holmes Norton, the nonvoting delegate from the District of Columbia). Of the twenty-nine women in the last Congress, all but two had sought reelection in 1992 and all but three of these had been reelected. They were joined by twenty-four first-time winners, including five from California and four from Florida. The new House would have two-thirds again as many women as ever before, and for the first time more than half the state delegations would include at least one woman.

Three senators who had voted against family leave (Alan Dixon of Illinois, Seymour and Republican Robert Kasten of Wisconsin) had been replaced by solid supporters. Only one supporter, Terry Sanford of North Carolina, had been replaced by an opponent. On the House side, proponents hoped to have the votes of all twenty-four freshman women (each of whom, Democrat and Republican alike, had campaigned in favor of abortion rights) and most of the eighty-six freshman men as well.

DURING THE CAMPAIGN SEASON ITSELF the family leave coalition broke into its constituent parts to participate in whatever ways their tax status permitted. Some of the participant groups, such as the National Women's Political Caucus and Emily's List (a fundraising group whose acronym stands for Early Money Is Like Yeast), were chartered as campaign organizations. The labor unions, of course, carried on their usual campaign activities: giving money to candidates through their political action committees (PACs), urging members to vote for certain candidates and providing campaign workers as well.

For such groups, the threat to withhold donations is often as potent a lobbying tool as the offer to donate. Some Democrats who had failed to support family leave found their usual founts of cash somewhat less bountiful in 1992. Bob Carr of Michigan, who was being outspent that fall by a self-financing Republican millionaire named Dick Chrysler, raised more than $500,000 from PACs while other colleagues were raising $1 million or more. With his traditional labor sources pinched, Carr went to business groups to try to make up the difference. But his success in this regard was mixed, and he was outspent that fall by more than $400,000. He won by fewer than 4,000 votes.

Many of the other family-leave coalition groups were organized under Section 501.c(3) of the Internal Revenue Code, which bars tax-exempt nonprofit organizations from direct involvement in elections. The Women's Legal Defense Fund, for example, could not raise money for or give money to candidates, provide staff to candidates or furnish "opposition research" on members who had voted against family leave. They could offer nothing other than what was already publicly available in their literature and handouts, including Donna Lenhoff's invaluable compendium of personal stories compiled over the years. These family anecdotes, many of which had been entered into the *Congressional*

Record, would stand candidates in good stead in making their stump speeches. Apart from that, the WLDF could also direct inquiries to other groups within the coalition that could provide more help.

Some similar restrictions applied to the business lobbying groups as well, although each of them had long ago set up separate PACs that could collect and distribute money on behalf of friendly candidates. Family leave was sufficiently disturbing to some business groups that they considered cutting off PAC funds to some of the Republicans they usually helped. High on the list were Marge Roukema and Kit Bond, the GOP drivers of family leave in the House and Senate, respectively.

In the end, however, the business groups had little leverage over Roukema or Bond. The former faced only a token opponent in her 1992 reelection campaign, and Bond had already amassed a huge campaign treasury by Missouri standards. Moreover, Bond's Democratic opponent was a liberal St. Louis city councilwoman who posed no threat to his support among businesspeople—family leave or no. The senator was so positioned that his handling of the issue helped him on the one hand and did him no real harm on the other.

ON ELECTION NIGHT, NOVEMBER 3, the presidential results were known early and the media coverage made much of the "Year of the Woman." But there was also a sobering side to the results from the standpoint of family leave. While the number of women in the House was increasing by two-thirds, the overall orientation of the chamber was moving to the right. Despite Bush's ouster the GOP picked up a net of ten seats, the best showing in the House by the party of a defeated president in exactly one hundred years. Although the Senate races exhibited no corresponding trend, the Democrats felt a pang of disappointment over the ones that got away. On election night, for a few hours, the majority appeared close to sixty seats (enough to invoke cloture with a united caucus). To achieve this Democrats had to win all three of the races that were too close to call at midnight on the East Coast. In the end they lost all three.

While these results could scarcely be called disappointing, they did fall short of the dream scenario for advocates of family leave. This would make a difference when the sponsors, supporters and other interested parties began to debate the scope and character of the family leave bill to be introduced (and presumably passed) in the new Congress. Although there would surely be majorities in the House and Senate to pass family leave in the form approved by the last two Congresses, a substantially stronger bill might be another matter.

So Lenhoff was back in the game as of December after being on the sideline throughout the fall. In September, just four days before Bush had vetoed S 5, Lenhoff and her husband had received the telephone call they had been hoping for. The baby they had been waiting to adopt had been born, and they were to come to the hospital right away—in Alabama. They would need to stay near the hospital for two weeks while their new daughter, Sonya, recovered from birth complications and while the adoption was processed by state authorities. Back in Washington, Lenhoff continued her leave through the fall, taking care of Sonya and watching the campaign unfold on C-SPAN. On December 1 she returned to WLDF on a reduced schedule (a form of leave that would soon be controversial with respect to the family leave bills in the 103rd Congress).

In Lenhoff's absence that fall, more of the day-to-day contact with the coalition was performed by Lichtman, who had served as a kind of unofficial chairman of the board since the coalition's inception. A longtime civil rights lawyer and feminist advocate, Lichtman had founded the WLDF in the early 1970s and built it into one of the three or four most important lobby-and-litigation forces in its field. She had known some of the operatives in Clinton's campaign for more than a decade, and it was easy to stay in touch casually through the network of feminist lawyers and community activists in Washington.

More generally, however, the coming of the Clinton administration was a disquieting moment for the capital. The city and its political culture had grown accustomed over the previous dozen years to the cool and conventional efficiency of conservative Republicans in the White House. The arrival of the Arkansas contingent in the weeks following the election reminded capital veterans of the Georgian invasion that accompanied newly elected "outsider" Jimmy Carter sixteen years earlier.

The style of the transition team prefigured that of the new administration: hardworking and serious but poorly organized, often ad hoc and occasionally chaotic. All administrations have moments when they are at loose ends. Under the new regime, though, such moments seemed to be more frequent.

Family leave was fortunate, however, in that several key players in its support coalition were about to move into jobs in the new administration. Geri Palast, the head of the Service Employees International Union and a family leave backer since the beginning, was about to take over the congressional and intergovernmental affairs office at the Department of Labor.

Similarly, at the Department of Health and Human Services, one of the top jobs was going to Jerry Klepnei, a longtime champion of the bill as head of the public employees union, the American Federation of State, County and Municipal Employees (AFSCME). As the new assistant secretary of the largest department in the federal government, Klepner would also install Rich Tarplin of Dodd's staff as his associate.

RIGHT AFTER THE ELECTION, SOME IN the coalition had spoken of going back to the bill that had preceded the Dodd-Bond compromise, or to the thirty-five-employee threshold for small-business exemption, or to the four-month leave. Some even wanted to bring back Pat Schroeder's HR 2020 from the spring of 1985 (twenty-six weeks of leave, all businesses with five or more employees). Within the family leave coalition of more than 250 supporting organizations, there were some who thought it time to propose paid leave.

Lichtman liked the idea of a stronger bill. After all, she liked to point out, the Civil Rights Act of 1991 applied to businesses with more than fifteen employees and the Fair Labor Standards Act covered everything but mom-and-pop stores. But Lichtman also liked the idea of swift passage and enactment, both for the symbolism and for the assurance. Let the thing lie around for a few months, she thought, and there was no telling what might get in the way. She was even concerned that this relatively simple legislative concept might get caught up in the coming proposals for health care reform. "There was never any serious discussion of going back to the early versions of the bill," she said later. Schroeder herself discouraged talk of a return to the pristine condition. "We decided it was better to get this done now," Schroeder said. "We could see the [new] administration had a lot of things on their plate."

Bill Ford, who would be returning as chairman of the House Education and Labor Committee, had ended the veto debate in September by saying he was ready to put "a good bill" on the president's desk early in 1993. Elsewhere he was quoted talking about fashioning "a real bill" on family leave—a phrase variously interpreted to mean anything from longer leaves to paid leaves.

But when he got back to Washington in January, Ford told reporters that Clinton had called him in Michigan and made clear he wanted to go with the bill that Bush had vetoed. That would heighten the contrast between administrations and prove the government was working again. On January 5, swearing-in day for the new Congress, Ford got a letter from Mack McLarty, who was to be the new White House chief of staff.

It praised the bill as passed in the previous Congress and said Clinton was committed to "signing family and medical leave legislation early in his administration." Underlining the point, McLarty said Clinton hoped Ford would "introduce legislation early in the session and move forward quickly to final passage." Translation: no new issues, no new hang-ups, move it. And Ford, who had spent nearly thirty years on the Hill building a reputation as a team player, did so. "If that's what Bill Clinton wants, we'll give it to him," Ford said.

But if no one else took the idea of a tougher bill too seriously, the NFIB took it seriously enough. NFIB lobbyist Mary Reed, for example, presumed that Bill Ford would redraft the bill in January "to make it worse." Participants in the CARE core group were talking strategies and possible alternatives. Some of Bill Goodling's Ed and Labor staff broached the idea of yet another compromise, one that would take the essence of Charlie Stenholm's six-year preference in rehiring and extend it further. There was talk of House GOP leader Bob Michel offering a version of the tax credit proposed by Bush late in the 1992 session.

But in the end no such effort was mounted. The NFIB had done another poll over the winter and received questionnaires back from about 10 percent of its 600,000 members. Those responding were 6 to 1 against any form of mandated family leave policy. Even if NFIB had wanted to negotiate a bill it found less onerous, its own supporters had made that all but impossible.

At this juncture, the ever-enterprising Tim Penny renewed his conversations with colleagues with regard to family leave. Still interested in the legislation and still hankering to shape its final form, he put in postelection telephone calls to some of the same Clinton transition people the coalition had been talking to. But Penny got back a firm "thanks but no thanks" from the Clinton staff. The president-elect wanted to move the bill in its most recent form, he was told.

The House leadership had its say in this decision as well. Speaker Foley later reflected that "presenting essentially the same legislation to the House was proper." He acknowledged the argument that, with the White House once again in Democratic hands, congressional Democrats ought to "improve" their bill by "eliminating the compromises and some of the changes that were made" earlier in pursuit of a two-thirds majority. But as an institutionalist and a man of judicial temper, Foley tended to respect the handiwork of preceding Congresses. Preserving the bill as previously passed was an act of "good faith," he said, adding as a clincher: "The president supports this view."

The consensus having been reached then that the bill should return to the floor substantially unchanged from 1992, the House leadership agreed to designate family leave as HR 1, marking the completion of its transformation from ugly duckling to swan.

THE POSTELECTION MONTHS WERE A TIME of accelerating activity for Fred Feinstein, who was contemplating a job in the administration (he would eventually be named general counsel of the National Labor Relations Board) while still working for Pat Williams at the Labor-Management Relations Subcommittee. Feinstein had hooked up early with the transition team, particularly Clinton economics adviser Derek Shearer and Robert Reich, who would soon be named the successor to Lynn Martin as secretary of labor.

Feinstein already had been reviewing the family leave bill line by line with the Legislative Counsel's Office and lawyers from the Department of Labor. He could not help feeling bemused by the sudden rush. Now it was time to write the permanent bill—title, section and paragraph. "Every year we had scrubbed it, but we had never scrubbed it with the expectation that it would become law as written," he said. Now that it mattered most, time was suddenly of the essence.

Yet with all the sudden pressure, Feinstein also noticed with satisfaction that the bill was no longer assigned to the most junior lawyer in the Legislative Counsel's Office. He was now dealing with that office's most senior labor law expert. And instead of being sent veto threats from the Labor Department, he was getting calls from its solicitor and being asked to help prepare the secretary's committee testimony.

The decision to stick with the 1992 model of family leave did not preclude tinkering with it a bit. Feinstein and the Labor scrubbers spotted one change of substance they thought essential. They wanted employees to be able to take leave by reducing their daily or weekly schedules—to take unpaid time off in increments of hours—so as to care for family members or get medical treatment for themselves. But providing this "reduced schedule leave" option to professional employees ran afoul of existing Labor Department regulations. The department had interpreted the Fair Labor Standards Act to say that salaried workers given time off by the hour without pay would have to be treated as hourly workers for other purposes under the act (including overtime pay).

This was obviously a land mine the staff did not wish to step on, so they fashioned a "technical change" to the bill that revised the Labor Department regulations. This revision did not appear in either HR 1 or

S 5 as printed, but it was made part of the bill by committee action in both the House and the Senate. Republicans did not object in either chamber at the committee level, but revision would come back to haunt the sponsors on both floors.

THE HOUSE AND SENATE OFFICIALLY convened the 103rd Congress on January 5. The members were sworn in and the traditional ceremonies performed to establish the authority of the leaders. The House follows the swearing-in with a formal vote for Speaker, with every member of either party voting for that party's leader (meaning that the real contest for the job takes place beforehand in the majority party's closed caucus). This is the one vote of the year in which party discipline is absolute, meaning that to vote for the rival party's candidate for Speaker is to leave the party.

Having been elected Speaker for the third time, Tom Foley of Washington was escorted from the floor to the Speaker's desk by Jennifer Dunn, a freshman Republican woman from his home state of Washington. By tradition, the Speaker is escorted by the senior member of the minority from his state, but with the near shutout the GOP had suffered in her state in 1992, freshman Dunn was the only Washington Republican in the House. Having completed this quaint exercise in civility, however, the House immediately fell to wrangling over the highly partisan issue of voting status for delegates.

In addition to its 435 members, the House of Representatives includes five other people who represent U.S. citizens living in Guam, Puerto Rico, American Samoa, the District of Columbia or the U.S. Virgin Islands. These delegates had for some years been voting in committee but not on the floor of the House. In December 1992, Eleanor Holmes Norton, the delegate from the District of Columbia, convinced her colleagues in the House Democratic Caucus that these delegates should also vote on the floor when the House was meeting as the Committee of the Whole (whether their votes made a difference or not). The Democrats moved to change the House rules accordingly.

The Republicans saw it quite differently, however, insisting the Constitution granted votes in the House only to "members chosen . . . by the people of the several states." The debate was unusually fierce for swearing-in day. But just before submitting the rule to a vote, the Democratic leaders added a wrinkle. If the delegates' votes decided an issue in the Committee of the Whole, that issue would have to be voted on again separately by the regular House. With that modification, the new rule passed the House on a party-line vote. Republicans immediately vowed to force double votes whenever delegates voted in the Committee of the Whole. Sitting in the hopper that same afternoon was the first bill on which that vow would be tested: HR 1, the Family and Medical Leave Act of 1993.

THE NEW FAMILY LEAVE BILL WAS introduced by Bill Ford and thirty-four original cosponsors on swearing-in day. The number of cosponsors would swell to 170 prior to passage, including thirteen Republicans and the chamber's lone independent, Bernard Sanders of Vermont. Once again the bill was referred to the same three committees and once again it began the steeplechase to the floor, through subcommittees and full committees, hearings and markups and Rules. But this time it would cover the course even faster than in the previous two Congresses, hurtling through in a matter of days. Congress traditionally adjourns for several weeks in January while committees organize and members get their sea legs. But in 1993, eager to pounce on the new president's agenda, the new Congress stayed in session and began markups before the month was out.

On Wednesday, January 27, the House Ed and Labor Committee marked up HR 1 (having held a brief hearing on the bill in Pat Williams's Labor-Management Relations Subcommittee the previous day). Bill Goodling of Pennsylvania, the ranking member who had been politically uncomfortable defending the position of Presidents Reagan and Bush in earlier Congresses, faced a simpler task now. With the bill prewrapped for signature by a Democratic president, Goodling would simply lead the opposition in defeat. He himself offered five amendments at the markup, and the Republicans had nine other ideas for modifying, delaying or derailing the bill. All these suggestions were rejected by voice vote.

Goodling's amendments tended to receive more serious treatment than those of other members. One of his would have exempted any employee whose absence would cause "substantial and grievous economic injury" to the company or "substantial endangerment to the health and safety of other employees or the public." The Democrats said this tracked over the top 10 percent exemption already in the bill and smacked of a loophole opening. The amendment lost on a 27–13 vote.

Goodling did slightly better when he proposed that the bill designate as "health care providers" only those so licensed by the state. On that language he was able at least to unite the Republicans. But his best-crafted amendment may have been the "cafeteria plan," which neatly encapsulated the overall Republican approach. It would have allowed employers to satisfy the requirements of the act by making family leave available as one option within a "cafeteria-style benefit plan." The idea was to "allow employees to choose which benefit package best suits their needs," sacrificing some portion of their vacation or other benefits for family leave coverage. Roukema opposed this idea, as did all the Democrats.

Roukema's bid for bipartisanship on the committee was slightly weakened in the 103rd Congress, as Republican ally Scott Klug had forsaken the panel for a slot on the Energy and Commerce Committee. But she could still look to Susan Molinari of New York. Molinari voted for some of the Republican amendments on January 27, while Roukema held fast against all but state licensure.

The only amendment approved that day was Williams's substitute text of the bill that incorporated the technical fixes and Fred Feinstein's revision to Labor Department rules on reduced-schedule leave. The votes of Roukema, Molinari and the twenty-seven Democrats together sent the bill to the floor on a 29–13 motion to report.

The two lesser committees of referral, with jurisdiction over narrow sections of the bill applying to federal employees (Post Office and Civil Service) and congressional employees in particular (House Administration), reported their sections by voice vote later on the same day that Ed and Labor held its markup. On the Senate side, Ted Kennedy and Chris Dodd had brought the bill through Senate Labor a day earlier. The new president had been in office for exactly one week, and family leave already had completed its journey through the committee process in both chambers.

AFTER THE MARKUP ON JANUARY 27, Feinstein and other committee staff worked nightly until 3 or 4 A.M., slapping together the committee report. In this instance, the package of bill text, cost estimates, minority views and legislative history ran to eighty-eight pages. "We'd all worked on bills that became law before, but never within a week," Feinstein said later. The leadership had set February 2 as the bill's date with the Rules Committee.

Prior to that meeting, the sponsors sat down with Rules Chairman Joe Moakley of Massachusetts to discuss the fate of HR 1. The mood was relaxed, even jovial. But with enactment now a certainty, the details of the bill would constitute reality in the making. Goodling would come to Rules with a fistful of the amendments he had offered in committee— and perhaps more. There might also be some requests from the likes of Tim Penny or John LaFalce, the chairman of the Small Business Committee.

The sponsors were not asking for a closed rule that precluded any and all floor amendments (although some supporters would have thought it a good idea). But the Ed and Labor staff was especially concerned that Rules be on the lookout for a Goodling amendment on reduced-schedule leave. There had been no such amendment offered in committee, but Feinstein was still worried.

Presumably, the Democratic leadership had the votes to nix any floor amendments it found truly noxious. But what the sponsors worried about was the sneak attack at the margins—the apparently minor amendment, the seemingly innocuous and niggling notion that would prove irresistible to swing-voting members. The Republicans would want to do what they could to dull the bill's edge, and they might find votes among Democrats interested in bowing to business constituents on at least a roll call or two.

The sponsors thought this had been made clear enough in their confab with Moakley. On Tuesday, February 2, they came to Rules and watched as Moakley killed all but three of the thirty amendments various members sought to have declared in order. But to their surprise, they also saw Moakley smile upon Goodling and allow him three amendments he wanted, including one on reduced-schedule leave. No one seemed quite sure whether signals had been confused or whether the leadership felt secure enough in its vote counts to give Goodling his shot. But it was done, and it could not be undone. "So we had to grit our teeth and say let's just beat him on the floor," said Feinstein with a shrug.

ON FEBRUARY 3, DURING THE NOON hour, the rule was introduced on the floor by Bart Gordon, a familiar champion of family leave in the past two Congresses and a Rules Committee member. It included a waiving of the usual three-day layover rule by which no bill can be taken up until the committee report has been filed and three days have passed. It also limited to three the number of amendments to be in order, all to be offered by Goodling, with one motion to recommit.

Jamie Quillen of Tennessee, the seventy-seven-year-old ranking member on Rules, made his usual appeal for an open rule. He conceded that the House had debated family leave in similar form five times (and voted five times), but he reminded the body that 110 freshmen members elected in November (more than one-fourth of the total body) had not. The rule was approved 259–164.

The Committee of the Whole then proceeded to consider the bill itself, as amended in committee and reported to the floor. Ninety minutes of debate were to be controlled by Ford and Goodling, another ninety by Clay and John Myers (ranking member of Post Office), and twenty minutes by the chairman and ranking member of House Administration. For the rest of the afternoon, speakers came to the well to register their support and opposition.

Fred Grandy of Iowa was heard from again, but this time he had plenty of company. Among his Ed and Labor confreres on the floor were Dick Armey of Texas and John Boehner of Ohio. Armey quoted the country singer Clint Black's line "Ain't it something what a heart can convince a mind." Boehner, one of the conservative backbenchers known as the "Gang of Seven," was remarkable in his rhetorical exertions. "America's business owners are a resilient bunch," Boehner said, "but let there be no doubt, HR 1 will be the demise of some. And as that occurs, the light of freedom will grow dimmer."

But the most striking opposition speeches may have been the relatively brief ones delivered by the three female Republicans elected for the first time in November 1992. All three were supporters of abortion rights and had been thought likely to cross over on family leave, along with Roukema, Molinari and most of the other Republican women. But they stood with their party leaders instead, and all three—Dunn of Washington, Deborah Pryce of Ohio and Tillie Fowler of Florida—were sharply critical of the bill. Dunn called herself "a woman who is concerned about our economy," called the bill "anti-woman and anti-business" and argued it would make employers reluctant to hire women of child-rearing age.

Months later Schroeder recalled those speeches with bitterness. "Their very first vote [and] they voted against family leave," she said. "And they not only voted but they took to the floor and did a number on it. Even if you have to vote no, why give the speech?" To counter the impression conveyed by these speeches, the Democrats saw to it that each of their twenty-one freshmen women came to the floor to speak for the bill.

Roukema was especially disappointed that, after years of trying to turn her party's old guard around on the issue, she could not even make her case successfully to the GOP freshmen. Not one of the forty-three new Republicans spoke on behalf of the bill. And only two, Michael Huffington and Steve Horn of California, would vote for it (Huffington also inserted a written statement in the record saying the law should never apply to small business and leaves should never be paid).

Shortly after seven o'clock that evening, Ford and Goodling wrapped up the day's debate. "The three hours and twenty minutes today was for

the purpose of having everybody come down and be seen on television,"
said Goodling. "The next hour and forty-five minutes will be for purposes
of trying to perfect the legislation." Goodling had the three amendments
that Rules had declared in order brought to the floor for debate that
evening. The first was the cafeteria-plan alternative he had proposed in
committee. It was briefly debated and defeated 244–187. Newt Gingrich,
the Republican whip, immediately rose to enter a statement in the record
noting that the "actual" vote among "states that have been admitted to
the Union" was 239–187 (excluding the votes of the five delegates).

Goodling next proposed his exemption of employers where leave
would cause economic injury or endangerment. It was advertised as an
adaptable alternative to the bill's existing one-size-fits-all exemption for
the top 10 percent of payroll. Dan Glickman, a Democrat from Wichita,
Kansas, rose to say that lots of medium-sized businesses had truly essential technical people who were not among their best-paid employees. But
Ford was dismissive. "If the employee was truly essential," he said, "he
should be receiving top salary." The debate was limited to twenty minutes
by the rule, and the lateness of the hour might have limited members'
interest in new arguments. The vote came shortly after eight-thirty, and
the amendment was defeated 238–185.

But Goodling had saved his best pitch for last. The third amendment
came shortly before nine o'clock, and it required that any plan for reduced schedule or intermittent leave be subject to employer approval.
Having spotted the new language on reduced-schedule leaves, Goodling
thought he might have the wedge to separate the sponsors from much of
their majority. He felt sure the Republicans would not vote to allow
employees to fashion their own leave schedules without employers having their say, and he thought he might pull over a big chunk of the
Democratic middle as well.

"I would like to have total attention," Goodling said, startling some of
his colleagues on the floor. "Because this is something that has never
been debated before, never been discussed before, never been part of
any legislation that people have voted for or against."

Goodling told the House that the reduced schedule meant "an employee could now set his or her work schedule" to consist of four hours a
day or six or whatever pleased the employee. "This right is obviously
more expansive than the concept of intermittent leave," he argued. "The
concept of a reduced leave is simply too broad to turn over to the yeas or
nays of a health care provider and certainly not without some intelligent
consideration of what we are doing here."

Prior versions of the bill had required employer approval of intermittent leaves, so Ford had a challenge before him in persuading his colleagues this was no more than a technical fix. He said there was not much a parent could do when a pediatrician said, "I want that kid every Monday for the next five weeks," especially if the doctor's office was fifty miles away. Ford said the altered language was "a difference without a distinction." And he begged his colleagues not to be "fooling around at this time of night with this kind of 'how many angels can dance on the head of a pin' attack on this bill." Before yielding, Ford took the calculated risk of mentioning that the Senate had already rejected an amendment similar to Goodling's—a dicey observation given the traditionally hostile reaction some House members have to anything that smacks of the Senate.

Ford's rhetorical bluff did not work. As soon as the green and red lights began winking on, it was clear Goodling had struck pay dirt at last. All forty Republicans who later would vote for HR 1 itself voted for Goodling's amendment. The Democratic leadership had whipped the vote furiously all afternoon and into the evening, but eighteen Democrats who would later vote for the bill saw Goodling's amendment as their chance to moderate their position. Goodling prevailed by a vote of 223–209, and the managers of the bill had egg on their faces.

Moments later the underlying amendment (the committee substitute) that had been before the Committee of the Whole was put to a vote (as modified by Goodling). It passed 269–163, and the committee rose. But because the delegates had voted in the Committee of the Whole on Goodling's amendment, Gerald Solomon of New York immediately demanded a roll call vote of the regular House (excluding the delegates). The amendment passed again by a vote of 221–204.

There remained the matter of a motion to recommit, which Harris Fawell of Illinois made "with instructions." In this instance, the instructions were to allow congressional employees who did not receive satisfaction from internal personnel proceedings to take the House itself to court. The motion was debated very briefly and defeated along party lines, 253–175.

It was nearly eleven o'clock when Speaker Foley announced the rejection of the recommittal motion and asked for a voice vote on final passage. The ayes were louder, but as always on matters of any importance, the Republicans demanded a recorded vote. The tally was 224 Democrats, 40 Republicans and independent Bernard Sanders of Vermont in favor, 134 Republicans and 29 Democrats (21 of them from the South) opposed. The 265-vote total improved somewhat on the 258 the House had reached in attempting to override Bush's veto the previous September. The bill picked up two supporters net among Republicans and five among Democrats, reflecting the influx of new faces more than any changing of minds. But even so, the closeness of the two tallies showed how little, not how much, the 110 freshmen had changed the House.

According to the usual procedure, majority leader Gephardt immediately moved to reconsider the vote. Ford moved to lay that motion on the table. The motion to reconsider a vote is a long-standing feature of parliamentary rules. It is offered immediately following the announcement of the results. And once the motion to reconsider has been made and "laid on the table" (killed), the vote in question becomes final and cannot be reversed at any time.

In practice, this amounts to sewing up the incision after an operation. And as a matter of course and convenience, it is usually agreed to by unanimous consent or by voice vote. But on this occasion the Republicans' deputy whip, Robert Walker of Pennsylvania, wanted to make a show of his party's displeasure over the delegate-voting issue and other grievances. So even as the chamber was rapidly emptying, Walker demanded a division of the House (also called a standing vote because members vote by standing to be counted). No record is made of how each member votes, but the procedure is more precise and less subjective than a voice vote. On this occasion the motion to reconsider was killed by a vote of twenty-one ayes and fourteen noes. It was a ragged and unceremonious end to the evening, but at least it settled the matter.

Ford then offered the benediction, the request for unanimous consent to allow the clerk of the House to make corrections to section numbers, punctuation and cross-references in the engrossment (official reprinting) of the bill. This is absolutely standard, and it offers a poor target for obfuscation in any event. Walker was apparently finished for the night and no objection was heard to Ford's request.

Family leave had passed the House.

15.

The Final Act

ON THE SENATE SIDE, THE FAMILY leave team of Dodd, Bond and Kennedy came to the 103rd Congress with little left to conquer. They had already achieved a two-thirds Senate majority on behalf of the bill in the last Congress. They could even claim bipartisan support in the end, as exactly one-third of the Senate Republicans voting had joined to defy President Bush's veto in September 1992.

Bond, in particular, remained eager to press the bill home. He was delighted with the decision not to rewrite the bill or change its parameters, a decision underscored when the Senate leadership once again reserved the number S 5 for the bill (which was not officially introduced until January 21). Preserving the essential text from 1991 (referred to by many as the "Bond language") enabled Bond to maintain the middle-road rationale he had been preaching ever since. After having fought bitterly with the business lobbies for eighteen months, Bond seemed intent on vindication; he not only wanted to see the bill become law, he also wanted to see the Senate vote go so high that the controversy would be consigned to memory.

The new S 5 had its hearing before Senate Labor on January 22, one day after its introduction and just two days after President Clinton's inauguration. Testimony would be taken from the new Labor secretary, economist Robert Reich, on the same day he took his oath of office. In preparing for his first hearing as a cabinet member, Reich would rely on his assistant for intergovernmental and congressional affairs, Geri Palast, who as an official of the Service Employees International Union had been active for years in the family leave coalition. Palast made sure Reich not only had a statement on the bill but a full head of steam on the issue as well.

The hearing was a victory lap for the bill and an obligatory bore for the opposition. Real resistance to the bill in the Senate had long since dwindled to rhetorical flag-waving, and the minority members on Senate Labor were not in a mood to prolong the exercise. Hatch, who was still on the committee, had stepped aside as its Republican leader (or "ranking member") to take the equivalent position on the Judiciary Committee. By sheer seniority, the ranking designation would have gone to Strom Thurmond, the Senate's most senior member of either party, who had celebrated his ninetieth birthday the previous month. But Thurmond had not been on Senate Labor as long as Nancy Landon Kassebaum of Kansas (and he preferred to be ranking member on Armed Services). Although he had no special status on Senate Labor, Thurmond retained an interest in its issues and in early 1993 Bond tried hard to get him to support family leave.

Thurmond was a legendary figure in the Senate, a onetime segregationist who had run for president in 1948 on the "States' Rights Democrat" ticket and later led the first wave of southern Democrats defecting to the party of Lincoln. In his later years Thurmond was known for moderating his views on race, marrying a beauty queen less than half his age and continuing to father children into his seventies (his nickname among colleagues for years was "Sperm Thurmond"). But by the 1990s Thurmond was divorced and slowed somewhat by his age. His youngest daughter had diabetes (prompting him to deviate from the antiabortion line to oppose the Reagan-Bush ban on fetal tissue research).

Bond believed he could reach his senior colleague when he testified at the Senate Labor hearing on January 22. Thurmond listened intently and told Bond he liked the changes that had been made and might reconsider his position. That prompted reporter Jill Zuckman, who covered family leave for *Congressional Quarterly*, to quiz Bond in the hallway after the hearing. What changes, she asked, was Thurmond talking about? Wasn't the new S 5 the same bill as the old S 5? Bond rolled his eyes and pantomimed a stage blow to Zuckman's head. "Don't tell him that," he said.

If Bond felt he could reach Thurmond, Dodd had thought for years he could break through to Kassebaum. Outsiders often presumed Kassebaum to be a moderate-to-liberal Republican, if only because she was a woman and a supporter of legal abortion. But while she cast a high-profile vote against her party occasionally, she usually voted with it, especially on matters affecting business.

Kassebaum had rebuffed Dodd's importuning on family leave since the 1980s, and it was no different when she took the first chair next to Kennedy in 1993 on the minority side of the Senate Labor dais. "I always feel like the skunk at the picnic on this issue," she said. "But I feel it is wrong for us to mandate benefits."

Kassebaum felt herself tugged in two directions by her own history. She had raised four children but also pursued a career on the business side of local broadcasting. She had sympathy for families and small enterprises alike. And none of the arguments she heard on the Hill affected her as much as the urgings of her own daughter, Linda Johnson, who had two children and a job as a pathologist at the Walter Reed Army Hospital (Johnson was joined in her support for family leave by two Kassebaum daughters-in-law). "We discussed it until we realized we'd discussed it to death," the senator said.

With the January 22 hearing committed to the record, Kennedy scheduled the bill's markup for the following Tuesday, January 26. This, too, would be a largely pro forma affair. Kassebaum would decline to offer any amendments for the minority in committee, adding that she would "save [her] ammunition for the floor." While Kassebaum could count on three of the other six Republicans on the panel (Hatch, Thurmond and newcomer Judd Gregg of New Hampshire), two others were cosponsors of the new S 5 (Jim Jeffords and Dan Coats) and a third planned to vote for it (Dave Durenberger). The full committee vote to report the bill favorably would be 13–4. One of the news photographs of the markup showed Dodd and Kennedy in a hearty handshake, with Michelle Pollak of the AARP beaming at them from the background.

ON JANUARY 28, JUST TWO DAYS AFTER Kennedy and Dodd had wrapped up their committee work on the new S 5, George Mitchell went to the floor to propound a unanimous consent agreement to proceed to family leave the following Tuesday, February 2. This was a rush job of the sort few senators had ever seen. But the Democrats' intent was to make family leave the monument over gridlock's grave, and Mitchell was dutifully doing his part. He figured he would need time for at least one cloture petition to ripen. Beyond that, he knew that "must-pass" bills in the

Senate become magnets for loose proposals of all kinds. And there was one such "rider" that Mitchell feared in particular.

Mitchell's main worry was that the Senate Republicans would use S 5, the first train leaving the station in 1993, as a vehicle for a challenge to President Clinton on the issue of gays in the military. If a hostile amendment were attached to the bill, family leave would no longer be a clean demonstration of the new cooperation between the branches. Were such an amendment attached, family leave could not even be signed into law by the new president.

Many Democrats bemoaned the emergence of gay rights at the forefront of the new administration's agenda. The lead items were supposed to be family leave and action on the economy. Clinton had spoken of lifting the military's gay ban as far back as October 1991, and when the issue had surfaced during the campaign it had attracted relatively little attention. In the first week after the inauguration, however, the proposed change suddenly dominated the news and played as if it had been utterly unexpected.

Republicans said that if Clinton lifted the ban by executive order (it had been enforced by Pentagon fiat since World War II), they would seek to restore it by writing it into law. It appeared that the Senate, at least, would have to debate the issue and confront the new president. The issue was not germane to family leave, of course, but the Senate's rules allow nongermane amendments of all kinds. Even if unsuccessful on the floor, such riders may gain media notice and score points with certain constituencies. And this particular issue had already had tremendous press, handing Republicans their first chance to embarrass the fledgling administration on policy.

Then on Friday, January 29, Clinton reached an agreement with conservative Democrats by which any substantial and permanent change in the military policy toward gays would be delayed six months. The compromise was endorsed by Sam Nunn of Georgia, the chairman of the Senate Armed Services Committee and his party's longtime leader on defense issues. But Dole and the cadre of social conservatives within his caucus were already committed to testing the will of the Senate on this issue at their first opportunity, so negotiations went on through the last weekend of January. And so did the preparations for the last family leave battle in the Senate.

In maneuvering to minimize the disruption, Mitchell had some high cards of his own. He had more than enough votes for cloture on S 5 if it came to that, and he knew Dole was loath to have his party be seen as stalling a popular bill in the first two weeks of a presidency.

With frantic effort that kept Kennedy's and Dodd's staffs working into the wee hours each night, the committee report for S 5 had been written and printed in time to be sitting on each of the one hundred senators' desks on the morning of February 2. Shortly after eleven o'clock Dodd took the floor and delivered a speech he clearly relished. He immediately tied his seven-year-old bill to the three-month-old election results. "One hundred and four million Americans stepped into polling stations across this country to cast their ballots . . . they all had one thing in common: they were sick and tired of politicians who prefer partisanship to leadership."

Dodd reprised his now-familiar reference to Sisyphus, the mythological figure condemned to an eternity of pushing a rock up a mountain and watching it roll back down. All the pieces were falling into place. "We trust," chimed in Kit Bond, "the boulder will not roll down again."

Dodd had a good time informing the Senate that the National Retail Federation's executive committee had endorsed S 5 the previous day. "The Family and Medical Leave Act is what government should be about," Dodd intoned. "It is what the American voters have sent us here to do."

Kennedy added his remarks, being sure to include a previously unused example of another family pauperized when the illness of a child made it hard for both parents to keep their jobs. He then ceded the floor to friendly senators wishing a place in the chorus. All four of the Senate's new Democratic women—Boxer, Murray, Feinstein and Moseley-Braun —made family leave the occasion for their first major policy speeches on the floor. Their presence in the chamber, and the sudden emergence of the issue on the national stage, seemed to be parts of the same whole.

At half past noon that day, each party held its weekly "policy luncheon" where, as usual, the main topic was politics. These sessions are held in small dining rooms just off the Senate floor and are invariably closed to nonsenators, most especially the press. But individual senators typically file out of the dining room and report the proceedings to the nearest reporter.

The word from the Republican lunch on February 2 was that Jesse Helms and others of the party's right wing had insisted on tackling the military ban on homosexuals regardless of Clinton's January 29 compromise. On the floor shortly thereafter, Helms thundered his defiance, denouncing the lifting of the gay ban as "the No. 1 priority of the homosexual political movement," an assault on the armed forces as "the last bastion of traditional morality in this country."

The words that mattered that Tuesday afternoon, however, were passing between Mitchell and Dole as they tried to work out a schedule and a format for the issues at hand. There would have to be some accommodation made for Helms and others who wanted to vote on the gay ban. Meanwhile, half a dozen Republicans, including Kassebaum and Dole himself, stood ready with amendments they wanted to offer to S 5.

In midafternoon Mitchell and Dole made a joint appearance on the floor to inform the Senate of their progress. Mitchell formally directed a question to Dole regarding the gay-ban amendment. Dole said there would be no amendment from his side on that subject that day. Negotiations were still going on, Dole said, and the minority might ask for a break in the family leave debate to consider "a freestanding piece of legislation" on the gay ban. He said he did not "want anyone to have the impression we might be holding up the family leave bill, even though I would not mind doing that." Dole got a chuckle from the other senators on the floor for this remark, to which he added: "But I think this bill will finally pass. I know the senator from Connecticut [Dodd] will be happy when that day comes."

And so the debate continued that afternoon, with interested senators shuttling from the floor to the cloakrooms to Mitchell's office. Representatives of the family leave coalition had moved from the Senate Reception Room, where they had stood watch in previous Congresses, to the more comfortable and honorific venue of the vice president's office. This space, which had been off-limits to them during the Bush years, when it was sometimes headquarters for their rivals, now belonged to Al Gore. Through Gore and Kennedy, it was loaned to the likes of Donna Lenhoff, her allies and, briefly, her mother.

In January, when inauguration day had kicked off two weeks of hearings, markups, debates and floor votes, Lenhoff's mother came to Washington from Chicago to help care for newly adopted Sonya while Lenhoff spent twenty hours a day on the final push for family leave. During the final Senate debate Lenhoff's mother came to see her in the Capitol and found her stationed by the telephone in the borrowed Gore office. Not long thereafter, Kennedy swept into the room and found Lenhoff's mother sitting in a chair. The woman was so startled at the sight of someone so famous that she leaped to her feet and stood at attention.

FAMILY LEAVE WAS AGAIN THE FIRST item of business on Wednesday, with a time agreement in place for debate and votes on several amendments. First up was Larry Craig's latest version of his 20 percent tax credit, which he had spent much of the previous day promoting on the Senate floor. His amendment was tabled (killed) 67–33 on the first notable Senate roll call of the 103rd Congress.

There would follow two amendments by Senator Slade Gorton of Washington dealing with key employees and the length of notice given by leave-taking employees. The first would be tabled by voice vote and the second by a vote of 60–40.

Senator Charles Grassley of Iowa, a late participant in the debate in 1991, offered some ideas on arbitration procedures as an alternative to lawsuits and Labor Department proceedings. These found favor with Republicans and conservative Democrats alike and came close to passing (the tabling motion was agreed to 53–47). It was a far more successful thrust than Kassebaum's revival of the basic Goodling "cafeteria plan" alternative, which was sunk 63–36.

After two other amendments had been debated and defeated, Mitchell and Dole came to the floor together to report on their negotiations. Mitchell said: "Senator Dole made one suggestion to me; I made a suggestion to him. We have consulted with various of our colleagues on both sides. As of this moment we do not have an agreement." Taking his turn, Dole said there were still a number of amendments to family leave, including "two meritorious amendments" of his own: "I know I will receive sympathetic consideration," Dole said, "before they are killed."

Talks between the two party leaders were apparently at an impasse. And after suggesting the absence of a quorum, Mitchell, in anticipation of a filibuster, proceeded to file his cloture petition signed by sixteen senators—all Democrats, led by Dodd and Kennedy.

Mitchell's filing this petition was a defensive preparation for a battle he preferred not to fight. He still hoped the debate on family leave would not reach the artificial and dilatory phase that is a filibuster. If it did not, there would be no need to vote on cloture. But Mitchell in that week was maneuvering with two purposes in mind. He wanted Dole to agree to an exact time limit on the family leave debate, and he also wanted Dole to agree to a two-stage vote on the gay ban.

If the gay ban were brought to the floor as a freestanding issue with one up-or-down vote on homosexuals in the military, the president might well be embarrassed. But if moderate Democrats and Republicans were first given a middle-course alternative to vote on, they might be willing to give the president a face-saving break.

· · ·

WHILE THE MAIN SOURCE OF ANXIETY at that moment was the gay-ban amendment, Dodd and his staff were still concerned about pending challenges to the substance of their bill. The Senate had come close to approving Grassley's amendment on arbitration procedures, and there had been forty-two votes for an amendment offered by John Danforth of Missouri (a supporter of family leave) that would have referred complaints under the bill to a mediator. It was possible that an amendment still lurked in the underbrush that might bite them.

Dodd had always come to the floor fearing certain amendments that might undermine the family leave consensus. When a bill has just enough votes to pass, or just enough for cloture, any amendment can be a killer—tilting the balance of the bill and tearing the careful weave of its support. Dodd had worried about moms-only amendments that would be hard to vote against. He had worried about amendments that would trim the bill Penny-style and stir a backlash among the hard-core supporters. In 1991, when Dodd was erecting a shaky two-thirds majority for the first time, even the slightest adjustment to the balance threatened to bring his edifice crashing.

In 1993, Dodd again came to the floor mindful of the land mines. Tarplin sat by him again each day, occupying the "side chair" Senate rules allow for one staff member per senator. On his lap Tarplin held his dark blue notebook bulging with every important document on family leave back to 1987. It also contained talking points to fend off any amendment ever offered or threatened. But by 1993, Dodd knew all the material as well as any staff member. And he was especially ready for amendments regarding the cost of the bill to employers.

Cost had been a slippery element of the debate over family leave from the beginning. Initially, it was an issue almost entirely for opponents of the mandate. But in time, and with the accumulation of studies that argued their side, advocates of family leave began raising cost issues themselves. Cost estimates varied wildly, and two of the figures used most often in the eight-year debate defined its polar opposites: One was the $20 billion cost tossed out by the U.S. Chamber of Commerce in the mid-1980s (later adjusted down to $16 billion and then to $2.5 billion) and the other was the comparatively minuscule estimate of about two cents per covered worker per day, derived from the earliest General Accounting Office study done for Dodd in 1987.

This latter figure struck Dole as an absurd calculation, and he had mocked it in past floor debates. With Hatch and many other Republicans, Dole had long argued that the GAO was refusing to confront reality, ignoring all the ancillary costs of personnel changes and productivity loss. But to some degree, the argument never recovered from the hyperbole of the earliest Chamber of Commerce estimates.

Now, with the bill on the verge of passage, Dole was having one last swipe both in earnest and in jest. He meant to expose what he saw as a false cost estimate, but he also meant to tweak Dodd. For all his angry talk on the floor of the Senate, Dole has a convivial side more often seen in private. He had long been chummy with the Connecticut Democrat in particular. Dole and Dodd had joshed each other about the "two-cent amendment." On the morning of February 4, Dole came down the aisle in the Senate to find an index card resting on the lectern that stood on his desk. Two pennies were taped to the card, which read: "In hopes you can be persuaded not to offer your amendment."

Dole did offer the cost cap, however, and he pressed it with all the glowering seriousness he could muster. If Dodd was serious about two cents per day, Dole said, then let employers be exempt once their costs had exceeded $7.30 per worker per year (two cents multiplied by 365 days). In rebuttal, Dodd readily admitted the GAO itself had raised its figure to $9.50 in its more recent study, but suggested that three cents a day was not much more crushing than two. Moreover, he argued that some companies, such as Aetna Life Insurance, had found a net saving from family leave because it required fewer new hires and less training. In the end, it was apparent that the rest of the Senate was ignoring this joust. Dole allowed his $7.30 cap to be snuffed by voice vote.

Dole's second amendment also dealt with cost. Instead of a cap, it sought to exempt businesses from the mandate until the federal government provided tax credits or other subsidies to offset the cost of compliance. This amendment was also debated and tabled, this time on a recorded vote of 67–31.

SHORTLY THEREAFTER, MITCHELL AND Dole took the floor to propound their long-awaited unanimous consent agreement dealing with all the issues at hand. It soon became apparent that the combination of Dodd's two-thirds majority and Mitchell's ripening cloture petition had brought the Republicans around. Dole would offer his amendment codifying the gay ban. But Mitchell would then offer a second-degree amendment to Dole's amendment. That would give conservative and moderate Democrats something to vote *for* before they cast the unavoidable vote against the ban itself. There would also be four full hours of debate so that each individual who felt so burdened could explain his or her vote on the floor.

Mitchell made another tactical move of considerable acuity when he let Nunn handle the debate against the gay-ban amendment. Nunn had been around on the gay-ban issue before, partly because he had been targeted for protests in the 1980s. Nunn's credentials as a hawk were well established, and he served as the unofficial chairman of the unofficial caucus of southern Democrats. Coincidentally, he was also a late convert to family leave, having come aboard after long lobbying by the Nine to Five chapter in Atlanta. The gay-ban debate proceeded along predictable lines, with Helms leading the charge on the right and several Democrats arguing that the ban should be lifted. Some were surprised when Mitchell, stepping out of his customary role, delivered one of the more impassioned pleas himself. He spoke of the need to "lift our sights and our hopes and our votes above appeals to division, above appeals to the worst that is in our people, above all the discrimination and the prejudice and the anxiety and the fear that is being created in this debate."

But most of the senators who spoke described positions somewhere between the poles. And in that sense it was clear Mitchell's main contribution had been in shaping the issue for floor consideration. Through the days of negotiation with Dole, he had borne in mind the need to have two votes and the need for a rationale that would serve conservative Democrats and moderate Republicans alike. And most remarkably of all, he had cut the deal so as to dispose of the matter for a period of months. Part of the agreement by which he and Dole had agreed to proceed on the gay ban (and so to the final vote on family leave) stipulated that there could be no further floor action on the gay-ban issue until July 15, the date to which Clinton had deferred his own efforts to lift the ban.

The debate proceeded throughout the afternoon and into the evening, covering both Dole's amendment and Mitchell's. Some Republicans denounced Mitchell's second-degree amendment as a "political fig leaf," and so it was. It said the Pentagon should review the policy and report to Congress, and that the Senate Armed Services Committee should hold hearings. But it was a nonbinding "sense of the Congress" resolution, a format the Senate uses when it wishes to skirt an issue it cannot resolve or refuses to address.

However transparent it may have been, the tactic worked. It worked so well that when it came time to vote, Dole struck his tent and signaled his colleagues not to vote against Mitchell's sense of the Congress resolution (to avoid the appearance of a defeat). The Senate then moved directly to a vote on Dole's amendment to S 5, which essentially said Clinton could not lift the ban without submitting the change in policy to

Congress in the form of a bill. "No more mumbo jumbo, no parliamentary sleight of hand," Helms had said. "The only amendment before the Senate today that will prevent the overt entry of homosexuals into the Armed Forces of the United States is the Dole amendment."

But Helms could count, and he could see he was about to lose. With Mitchell's amendment adopted and Nunn standing firm in favor of the six-month deferment, all but two Democrats were willing to vote against Dole's amendment and take whatever heat that vote might generate (the two holdouts were the Alabama delegation: Howell Heflin and Richard Shelby). Moreover, seven Republicans crossed over to join the majority, making the final vote to table Dole's amendment an authoritative 62–37.

WITH THE GAY-BAN AMENDMENT ROUNDLY rejected, Dodd was within arm's reach of his final vote and victory. There remained only the issue of reduced leave scheduling (sometimes referred to as paydocking because it put nonhourly workers off the payroll for periods of unpaid leave). The Goodling amendment that Bill Ford had failed to spike in the House was offered in the Senate by Republican Hank Brown of Colorado. Brown made much the same argument Goodling had, but he found his audience less interested. With the gay-ban issue finessed and the family leave coalition looking unbeatable, Brown seemed only to be prolonging the evening. The vote to table his amendment was 59–39.

The battle was effectively over. Dole gave up and allowed a recorded vote on final passage at last. While the senators filled the well to vote, the usual milling became a round of handshakes and claps on the back for Dodd. The vote itself was a triumph: S 5 was passed with 71 ayes to just 27 nays. Conservative Democrat David Boren of Oklahoma, true to his word from the end of the last session, voted for the bill.

Dodd made the floor speech that put the ribbon and the bow on the package. After expressing his thanks to colleagues—Kennedy, Mitchell, Bond, Coats, Ford—he let the credits roll for some minutes while he cited his own staff and those of others. He also tipped his hat to Lichtman, Lenhoff and Helen Norton of the Women's Legal Defense Fund by name, before submitting for the record a list of 250 other organizations.

But before going to bed for the night, Congress needed to perform one more legislative trick to make the leadership, the committee chairmen, the White House and the sponsors and supporters of family leave all happy. They needed to clear the bill for immediate signature by the president.

As matters stood, the two chambers had passed different bills. The

Senate version had Mitchell's compromise on the gay ban and language on intermittent leave that the House had deleted (by passing Goodling's amendment). Normally, one chamber or the other would declare a "stage of disagreement" and request a conference to compose the discord. But the congressional leaders were interested in demonstrating how fast they could accomplish things, and they did not want to slog through the several phases of a conference committee (naming conferees, getting them together, writing a conference report and having it cleared by each chamber). The word from the White House was that the new president would clear his schedule and sign the bill the very next day if Congress could deliver it overnight.

There was a way to do that, but it involved keeping the Senate and House in session late so as to pass identical bills. First, the Senate had to take up HR 1, the document passed by the House the previous day. As a technical matter, formally acting on the House's bill would facilitate consideration of the legislation in that chamber. But to preserve the Senate's own version, it was also necessary to strike virtually all the text of HR 1 and substitute the text of S 5 as amended and passed by the Senate.

All this could be accomplished in a matter of minutes in a nearly empty Senate chamber thanks to the foresight of the leadership. All the necessary motions—to proceed to HR 1, to strike its existing language and to substitute the Senate's—had been embedded in the unanimous consent agreement Dole and Mitchell had devised earlier in the week. So Mitchell could stand virtually alone on the Senate floor and request unanimous consent for each of his motions, knowing that no objection would be heard.

On the other side of the Capitol, the House had remained in session awaiting the return of its bill. The Rules Committee had quickly approved a "self-executing rule" by which a single vote of the House would accept the Senate version of HR 1. That would eliminate any need for a conference and thereby clear the legislation for the president's signature. But this would also mean acceding to the Senate's version of the bill and not insisting on any of the House's amendments because what was being called HR 1 was now a shell containing the substance of the other chamber's bill. Several Republicans who had objected to this procedure in the Rules Committee earlier in the evening went straight downstairs to continue their protest on the House floor.

Floor debate began shortly after ten o'clock and the Republicans began making their case. Some objected to a minor amendment Dodd had added by voice vote defining the term "spouse." Some objected to the absence of the Goodling amendment, which had been offered unsuccessfully in the Senate as the Brown amendment. And several objected, most vociferously, to the Mitchell language on gays in the military. House conservatives immediately sought to use the Mitchell "sense of the Congress" language as a means to attach amendments of their own that would otherwise fail the House's test of germaneness.

Among the procession of Republicans protesting late that Thursday night was Bob Dornan, a former actor and talk-show host from southern California who occasionally filled in as guest host for radio commentator Rush Limbaugh. Dornan said he felt that it must be time to go Christmas shopping because the Democrats were running the House as if the year-end close of a session were at hand.

But the protests were in vain. It was late, and the House leaders knew they had the votes to wrap it up. When deputy whip Walker tried to move the House into a Committee of the Whole (so as to debate and record votes on amendments to the Senate version), Speaker Foley and the majority rebuffed him. The Democrats did not want to play by Committee of the Whole rules, which would have prolonged the wrangle and permitted a vote on the gay-ban compromise.

Shortly before midnight, there was a motion to "call the previous question"—ending debate and forcing a vote. It was approved 227–172, with 31 members not voting. Thereafter the House acted on the resolution offered up by the Rules Committee earlier that night, which had the effect of accepting the Senate-passed HR 1. It passed 247–152 with 31 members not voting.

The House and Senate had passed identical bills. There would be no conference. The formal documents (the "enrolled bills") would be produced overnight and signed by the officers of each chamber early Friday—en route to the Rose Garden.

IT WOULD BE THE FIRST BILL SIGNING IN THE Clinton White House, and the evidence of inexperience was everywhere. The hastily drafted invitation list did not exactly match the pass list given to White House security. The White House staff did not have copies of the final roll-call tally sheet to distribute as souvenirs. Neither did they have pens with Clinton's name on them, a staple in bill-signing ceremonies. So Clinton had to use ordinary pens, inscribing part of his signature with each one before handing it to one of the honorees gathered behind him as he signed the bill.

There was also the last-minute debate about speeches. Invited to speak were Foley and Mitchell. Also addressing the assemblage were Dodd and Kennedy and their counterparts from the House: Bill Ford, Bill Clay and Pat Williams, all of whom the White House would need in legislative battles to come. All the members who spoke were men. No time was found for Pat Schroeder, who had introduced the first bill and given the issue its first real visibility on the Hill. Neither was the microphone offered to Marge Roukema, the Republican whose conversion to the cause of family leave not only helped it pass in the House but also prefigured its final compromise. Schroeder and Roukema stood by at the ceremony with prototypical resignation. Rank-and-file members, women in particular, become accustomed to the hierarchy of congratulations in Congress. But in this case the two women remembered how some of the men in the Rose Garden that day had once regarded family leave as a lightweight distraction to more serious legislative business.

One of two women to speak at the ceremony was Judith Lichtman (the other was Vicki Yandle, a Georgia mother who had lost her job when her daughter developed cancer). Lichtman spoke of two purposes in asserting herself. One was to remind all present that the Women's Legal Defense Fund had been very much present at the creation of the family leave issue—dating back to the Pregnancy Discrimination Act of 1978 and to the first stirrings of legislation on the leave issue in 1985. "There was this notion of the bill as a labor bill," she later said. "Sometimes that amused me and sometimes it annoyed me in the extreme. Because we believed that the women's movement and feminists had really provided the leadership within the support coalition for this bill—and we didn't want the fact that smart politicians and bright insider players from those [other] communities had come aboard to obscure that."

Lichtman's second purpose was to address one of the great frustrations with which activists often struggle: the lack of public appreciation for what they do. "Women in America don't know and can't figure out what the feminist movement has done for them," Lichtman said. "In the case of family leave, we saw a need and created a public policy that would make an everyday difference in people's lives. That idea was very important to me. The message was that the feminist movement cares about working families."

THE DOCUMENT LAID BEFORE THE president that afternoon of February 5 would go into the books as PL 103-3, meaning it was the third public law enacted in the 103rd Congress. Ahead of it in line were two minor matters: the continuation of Secret Service protection for the former vice president and his wife, and an adjustment to the pay and benefits available within the Office of the Secretary of the Treasury.

As cleared for the president's signature, the family leave law closely resembled the bill crafted by Dodd and Bond and their staffs in the spring and summer of 1991. That bill, in turn, owed a great deal to the House compromise of the previous Congress, engineered by Jim Jeffords and Marge Roukema in the Ed and Labor Committee as far back as 1989.

The Family and Medical Leave Act of 1993 entitled employees to twelve weeks of unpaid time off to care for a newborn or newly adopted child, for a seriously sick child, spouse or parent, or for the employee's own serious medical condition. During the leave the employee's benefits were to be continued (including health insurance) and upon return the employee would be guaranteed the same position or its equivalent with no loss of seniority. Excluded from coverage were businesses with fewer than fifty employees (within a seventy-five-mile radius) and employees who had worked fewer than 1,250 hours for their current employer within the previous twelve months. The bill applied to public sector employees, including federal employees and (under separate rules) the employees of Congress itself. But an affected business could exempt individuals in the top 10 percent of its payroll if it could show that the absence of these employees would cause the business "substantial and grievous economic injury."

The bill as passed included an intermittent leave provision by which employers could temporarily transfer an employee taking such leave to another position that better accommodated it—so long as the alternative position carried equivalent pay and benefits and the employee in question was qualified for it.

Beyond these fundamentals, the text of the bill included various detailed instructions as to the "legislative intent" of its authors. These would be translated into regulations over the next several months by officials of the Labor Department. And these regulations would be subject to further adjustment and interpretation by the courts. For example, the bill spelled out the certification an employee would need in order to qualify, including second and third medical opinions (to be paid for by the employer, with the third opinion being final).

The bill included provisions for substituting paid leave for part of the twelve-week allowance, including the substituting of vacation or sick days accrued. Employers would be required to supplement the paid weeks with unpaid weeks only up to an aggregate total of twelve full weeks' leave. Businesses were allowed to require periodic reports from employees on leave as well as thirty days' advance notice of foreseeable situations that might require leave (such as childbirth). But employers were explicitly prohibited from interfering with an employee's right to take unpaid leave through coercion, intimidation or threat.

MANY ADMINISTRATION OFFICIALS CLEARLY related to the signing as a kind of watershed, a second inaugural. Photographs from that day in the Rose Garden would crop up as instant icons on the walls and desks of staff officials and advocates of the bill. Tarplin also had framed on his wall his copy of S 5, autographed with personal thanks by Bill Clinton. Lenhoff had on display a tally sheet from a late Senate vote on the bill and a photograph of herself wrapped in a dark overcoat and a pair of sunglasses with turquoise frames, meeting the Clintons in the Rose Garden.

Howard Paster, now the chief White House lobbyist on the Hill, had a picture of the signing ceremony in his office as well. Within a week of the signing he would show it to Tim Penny, to whom he added a none-too-subtle message of "wish you could have been there."

Fred Feinstein had labored in the House Ed and Labor Committee's backrooms and sat in the back-row chairs set for staff for a dozen years, waiting for the chance to see a major bill signed into law. He got that chance with family leave, and he enjoyed the thrill to the maximum. "It was almost sublime," he said.

But the descent from the mountaintop began quickly. The evening news programs showed the signing ceremony, and the Saturday papers carried the story, many on page one. But the big story from Washington that Friday would not be family leave but the botch that had been made of Kimba Wood's appointment as attorney general. Had the signing ceremony been delayed until Monday or Tuesday, there might have been a round of Sunday stories (summing up the congressional action and pointing toward the signing) and a second round of stories pegged to the Rose Garden ceremony. As it happened, the coverage was compressed into a Friday night–Saturday morning cycle, the least watched and least read cycle of the week. The added competition from the Kimba Wood debacle merely sealed the story's unkind fate.

The relationship between family leave and the news media had once had aspects of romance. But the bloom had been off that rose long before the bill reached the Rose Garden. At first, the story had lent itself to warm prose and pictures of families: moms nuzzling infants or sitting anxiously at hospital bedsides. Most of the reporters assigned to cover the bill were women, not a few of whom either had or planned to have children. And while these reporters did not necessarily lose their objectivity in covering the bill, most of them came to the issue with more personal understanding than was common among the members of Congress.

The relationship between the sponsors and reporters never entirely soured, but the sense of urgency required to sustain media interest seemed lost after the failure to override in 1990. The bill's subsequent passages were not accorded nearly the same coverage, and the individual reporters seemed numbed by the repetition of hearings and markups in each successive Congress. Having managed to hook their editors and producers on the story once, they seemed to have downgraded its news value on each successive cycle. Once burned, twice shy. The average reporter on Capitol Hill was reluctant to tout family leave again until it was certain to become law.

Some true believers among the bill's advocates were surprised at the way the coverage fell off after 1990 and disillusioned with the altered tone of the coverage. The bill had been "watered down," the stories said, stressing the statistic about the exemption of 95 percent of all businesses and often not making clear that approximately 40 percent of all employees in the country worked for the other 5 percent of companies. From a strategic standpoint, however, there was value in the turnaround of the press. Lenhoff liked to say that every time a news report referred to the bill as having been compromised, the purpose of the compromise was realized and reinforced. "It hurt us to see it referred to as 'watered-down,' but it helped with the members," she would say.

THE MEDIA, HOWEVER, WERE NEVER as important to the fate of family leave as they or their critics may have thought. By far the most effective forces in this regard were the ideas, arguments and pressures brought to bear by the individual members (pro and con) and by the coalitions supporting and opposing the bill. The advocates prevailed in part by having a more compelling message—helping families in need—that could be readily communicated. They prevailed also because in committee and in floor debate they stuck to that message and did not become distracted by the appeal of specific amendments or alternatives.

The opponents' case suffered in part because they had to concede and pay obeisance to the desirable nature of family leave. But beyond that, their objections to the mandate were at times tainted by contradiction. Opponents would label the bill unnecessary because, as Jamie Quillen of Tennessee once put it, "93 percent of the small-business people already have this and 33 states have their own laws." Yet they would characterize a federal mandate for family leave as somehow uniquely devastating. "We saw the issue as: how big should the federal government be?" said Nick Calio of the Bush White House. But however important that question might be, it was not easy to convey against the images of mothers and fathers at their children's bedsides. And no one knew that better than Calio.

At the same time, the single most effective organization on either side of eight years of family leave lobbying was probably the NFIB. From the first involvement of the group in the late years of the Reagan administration until the House vote sustaining Bush's second veto in 1992, lobbyists for the small-business group were ubiquitous and indefatigable.

The NFIB knew exactly what it was fighting against in the family leave debate. Motley saw family leave as the first part of "a new wave of quasi-social business legislation where business is asked to take on more and more of the social costs. We were set on stopping the first one or making its passage as painful as possible."

In terms of cost, Motley readily admitted, family leave was a minor matter. "It's an inconvenience," he said, "mandating something businesses are doing on their own." But once such a pattern of mandates had been established, Motley believed, it would be the precedent for such mandated benefits as employee health insurance. "We felt we had to die on that line," he contended. "It was literally do or die for us." Lichtman would mull this over months later and say: "They were not wrong."

But what set the NFIB apart from the Chamber of Commerce and the other large organizations was its ability to generate persuasive testimony from its constituent army, in person, on the phone and in countless telegrams and mailings. When the NFIB solicited letters from its membership, it went first to its field offices (one in each of the fifty state capitals) and then to prominent members of the group who had personal relationships with members of Congress. These individuals would be expected to call or write personal notes. Then there were the mass mailings to the organization's 600,000 members, which could produce enormous outpourings of return mail addressed to individual House and Senate offices. And then there were the random personal contacts that the NFIB encouraged their members to make. "Our members are really everywhere," Mary Reed, an NFIB lobbyist in the later years of the family leave fight, liked to say. "The Ford dealer who sells a member a car, the barbershop where he gets his hair cut and the place where he drops his laundry off."

But while the NFIB was hard to beat, the coalition supporting family leave grew steadily stronger and more savvy until passage of the legislation was inevitable. By making common cause with antiabortion conservatives, the basic core of feminists and labor liberals had performed the essential trick that turns ideas into laws. They surrounded the opposition and minimized it. The day Henry Hyde took the floor in the House to speak for family leave, the issue was essentially decided.

If the sponsors and support groups were the dynamic forces, their product was shaped as well by the institutional constraints of Congress itself: the need for legislative language, the multilevel committee process, the gatekeeping role of the leadership, the pitfalls of floor consideration, the necessity of doing it all in one chamber and then doing it all again in the other—and, finally, the imperative of obtaining the president's signature.

Meeting all these tests is like working the combination to a lock on a vault. But it is more than that. Because the human dynamics of lawmaking not only produce a product, they also create the product in the process. "If we had not been there," Mary Tavenner said of her CARE coalition, "family leave would have passed as written. We made them change it. The bill became more and more 'reasonable' until inevitably some businessmen were neutralized."

Many serious-minded people regard this characteristic of government as a flaw, a persistent impurity. But in functioning lawmaking bodies, the ideal and the pragmatic are not mutually exclusive values.

In reflecting on the family leave fight, Pat Schroeder tended to pine for the purer bill she had introduced in 1985. But Chris Dodd did not. In his last floor speech on family leave he quoted Ted Kennedy saying the best ideas he had seen in thirty years in the Senate had all taken time to become law. Months later, reflecting on it all in his capital hideaway office (in a space where Daniel Webster once aged his wines), Dodd added: "The best ideas are better because they take time. They are better thought out. We have a better sense of balance and a better sense of what we're doing. Maybe the best ideas should take a little more time."

Epilogue

(Updated for the Paperback Edition)

THE EARLY POSTENACTMENT HISTORY of the Family and Medical Leave Act in 1993 defied both the high hopes of the law's advocates and the dire predictions of its adversaries. The bill did not unleash a great wave of leave-taking among eligible employees, nor did it prompt the passage of other, larger pieces of social legislation. At the same time, the new law did not notably disrupt the conduct of business, nor did it lead to a host of new mandates upon the private sector.

President Clinton was pleased to talk about family leave, making it a fixture of his addresses to Congress (including his first two State of the Union speeches) and public discussions of his record. Marking the second anniversary of the law's effective date in 1995, Clinton told a national radio audience about a father in Port Lavaca, Texas, who had been able to leave work to be with his daughter for the month before she died of leukemia.

Other Democratic leaders made family leave a facet of their stock stump speeches, often citing anecdotes of its use. One was Chris Dodd, father of family leave in the Senate, who took on the title of general chairman of the Democratic Party in 1995. Dodd sometimes referred to a telegram he had received from a sergeant at the Pentagon. The sergeant had a brother dying of AIDS and their mother in Connecticut had wanted to take time off from her job so her son could die at home. Because of the bill, the sergeant said, his mother could take twelve weeks and keep her job.

But if such stories were set aside, it was hard to show just how much difference the law might be making. The Family and Medical Leave Act of 1993 created a commission to study and report on the new law's effects on employers and employees. The unpaid commission consisted of two senators, two House members and eight other individuals appointed by the leaders of the House and Senate (with the cabinet secretaries of labor and of health and human services as nonvoting members). Among the private individuals named by the Democrats was Donna Lenhoff of the Women's Legal Defense Fund. Among those named by the Republicans was Mary Tavenner, the founder of the Concerned Alliance of Responsible Employers coalition.

The act took effect on August 5, 1993 (six months after the president's signature), and the first commission meeting took place three months later. Although the law provided no specific funding, the commission had the support of Labor Secretary Robert B. Reich and was able to hire a small staff and conduct two surveys of business reaction. The commission also held field hearings in San Francisco, Chicago and Washington. At one hearing, a spokesperson for Bell Atlantic said employees were systematically abusing the "intermittent leave" feature of the law and complicating life for the giant communications firm's personnel office. Similar complaints from businesses surfaced in *The Wall Street Journal*. But on the whole, testimony from business groups lacked the old fire and brimstone of the days when the law was just a bill.

The Conference Board, a New York–based commercial research organization, said its survey found that 70 percent of businesses had experienced "little or no difficulty" in complying with the new law. The Society for Human Resource Management, oriented toward personnel directors, said that the law created administrative problems but that a majority of businesses had found it possible to comply (about half with the aid of a lawyer or other consultant). The Labor Policy Association reported that its survey of businesses found 73 percent had experienced a positive impact from the law or no impact at all. The testimony of these groups generally reinforced the data from academic studies done earlier by the University of Michigan and the University of California at Berkeley.

In fact, the central impression was of a law that was fulfilling neither the dreams nor the traumas that had been conjured in the process of its enactment. Many eligible workers were simply unaware of the new benefit. But even where awareness was relatively high, use of the new law remained low. Employees in the main were unable or unwilling to take substantial periods of leave without pay. Many proponents of family leave would have been only too pleased to revisit the pay issue in a new bill in the next Congress. But by 1995 the atmosphere for labor legislation on Capitol Hill had chilled once again.

Within eighteen months of the law's effective date, Congress would be under new management, following the election of Republican majorities to both the House and the Senate in November 1994. Thereafter, Capitol Hill would undergo a change of attitude and agenda. The new House was being run by the new Speaker, Newt Gingrich of Georgia, who had helped to lead opposition to family leave from the first time it came to the floor in 1990. At Gingrich's side were Majority Leader Dick Armey and Majority Whip Tom DeLay, two Texans elected in 1984 who had fought family leave since its first introduction in committee in their freshman term.

The new House agenda included an explicit assault on "unfunded mandates," by which the federal government made state and local governments and private businesses take on responsibilities without providing any help with the costs. Family leave was high on the list of such mandates, and there was talk of an effort to repeal the law outright. No such effort took active form in the first session of the 104th Congress, in part because so much else was happening on the regulatory front. But Democratic supporters of the program seemed almost eager to have family leave challenged. "Make my day," said Pat Williams, the Montana Democrat who had helped pass family leave in the House.

FAR FROM HAVING HERALDED A NEW ERA, family leave found itself a lonely monument to the social agenda with which many feminist and labor activists had begun the 103rd Congress. There were other domestic achievements for the Clinton administration: a deficit-reducing budget, two rounds of gun control and a law creating a pilot program for national service. But the soaring hopes raised in the Rose Garden that warm day in February had set expectations far higher.

If the Clinton administration's early actions proved disappointing for many supporters, they were nonetheless galvanizing for many opponents. The compromise on gays in the military was a case in point. While it generally displeased homosexual-rights activists, it was widely perceived as a deep bow to an interest group and portrayed as a crippling blow to Clinton's credentials as a centrist "New Democrat." The administration failed to pass a "stimulus package" in 1993 but was criticized nonetheless for tax-and-spend profligacy. And the passage of a waiting-period requirement on handgun sales (the Brady bill) and a ban on some assault weapons prompted the gun lobby to raise more money and mobilize more votes for congressional candidates than ever before.

The political consequence was a decisive defeat for Democrats in the midterm elections of 1994. Republican majorities were elected to both the Senate and the House for the first time since the election of 1952. In the Senate, the new class elected in November 1994 consisted of eleven Republicans and not one Democrat (the first such class since the popular election of senators began). In the House, Republicans gained a net of fifty-two seats by winning most of the vacancies and knocking off thirty-four Democratic incumbents. No Republican incumbent who sought reelection to either the House or Senate was defeated.

The early months of 1995 were a time of seat scrambling and scene shifting in Washington, especially in the House, where the Democratic hegemony had held through four full decades. Eager to signal a new era, the House Republicans let it be known that they were under new management. Robert H. Michel of Illinois, the GOP leader since 1980, retired and gave way to Gingrich. The newly empowered generation promptly killed several standing committees and changed the names of several others.

Among those eliminated entirely was the Post Office and Civil Service Committee, one of the committees to which family leave had been referred. Had the Democrats retained control, the new chair of Post Office would have been Pat Schroeder (who would decide in 1995 to retire after twelve terms). The other two committees that handled family leave in the House had their names changed. Education and Labor became the Committee on Educational and Economic Opportunities, while the House Administration Committee became the House Oversight Committee.

The renamed Ed and Labor Committee would be gaveled to order by an old hand, Bill Goodling of Pennsylvania. And in the chair of its old Labor-Management Relations Subcommittee (now called the Employer-Employee Relations Committee) would be Tom Petri of Wisconsin, a veteran of the family leave debate from its inception.

As the enemies of family leave were raised up, its Democratic advocates were forced to stand aside. Bill Ford, the chairman of the Ed and Labor Committee who came late to the issue but pushed it hard when he arrived, retired rather than seek reelection in 1994. Bill Clay, the long-time family leave sponsor who had hoped to succeed Ford, found himself the ranking member of the minority instead.

Republican friends of family leave, however, prospered along with their party. Marge Roukema was third in seniority on Goodling's committee, but chose to chair a subcommittee of the Committee on Banking and Financial Services instead. Henry Hyde, the senior statesman of the GOP old guard whose timely affirmation had been pivotal for family leave's first floor victory, became chairman of the House Judiciary Committee. Gerald Solomon, the Rules Committee Republican who had fought against the rules for family leave but voted for the bill, became the new chairman of the Rules Committee.

The new House would be missing many of the faces familiar to those who had followed family leave. Minnesota Democrat Tim Penny, weary after years encamped in no-man's-land, retired to a public relations firm based in Minneapolis. Michigan Democrat Bob Carr, one of the most vociferous Democrats opposing family leave, ran for the Senate and lost. Iowa Republican Fred Grandy, another tough floor fighter against the bill, lost a bid for governor. And Maine Republican Olympia Snowe, a cautious but steadfast supporter of family leave, captured the seat George Mitchell vacated in the Senate.

Far less renaming and reshuffling went on in the Senate, where party control had changed hands more often and where power struggles tend to be more individual in nature. But here, too, change was evident. George Mitchell retired rather than seek a third full term. Bob Dole, marking his tenth anniversary as the Senate Republican leader, was once again the majority leader (as he had been in 1985–86), and he was also actively organizing yet another campaign for president in 1996. Chris Dodd staged a brief campaign for Senate Democratic leader in November 1994, losing by a single vote. Ted Kennedy was replaced as chairman of Senate Labor and Human Resources by Republican Nancy Kassebaum, the Kansas senator who had agonized over her vote against family leave. Kit Bond became chairman of the Small Business Committee, Orrin Hatch took the reins at Judiciary.

FAMILY LEAVE'S LEGISLATIVE LIFE was long enough to endure several changes of political season on Capitol Hill. When the issue first appeared in the 98th Congress, Democrats nursed hopes of political success in 1984. But by the time the first family leave bill was introduced a year later, Ronald Reagan had carried forty-nine states in winning reelection and the conservative cause seemed to be carrying all before it. Just two years later the Democrats would retake the Senate and begin overriding Reagan's vetoes. George Bush would win the White House in 1988, rise to a record high in the Gallup poll in 1991 and plunge all the way to defeat in 1992. The Democrats would have a banner year almost nationwide at Bush's expense, then suffer their worst defeat in half a century in 1994.

In all this ebb and flow, and despite the changes, the underlying forces and structures of the Congress—the committees and caucuses, the legislative strategies and floor tactics—remain much the same. Even after a dramatic role reversal between the parties, the human dynamic of conflict and compromise continues.

Congress is best perceived by taking the long view. It has its roots in the political thought of the 1700s, and its traditions derive from two full centuries of conflict. Yet it continues to adapt to the diversity and dissonance of a modern nation of a quarter of a billion people. The Congress of any given moment naturally seems inadequate next to our nostalgic notions of its past or idealized visions of its potential. But Congress has always had most of the virtues and vices it has now, in varying degrees, and it probably always will. It is weak, in one sense, because it is a human institution, designed to remain close to the urgings and entreaties of the people it serves. But this same characteristic is what makes it a representative institution, and that is ultimately its source of strength and legitimacy.

Glossary

Amendment. A motion to alter, delete or augment any or all of a bill or resolution being considered in committee or on the Senate or House floor. A first-degree amendment applies to the bill or resolution itself, a second-degree amendment modifies a first-degree amendment, and a third-degree amendment modifies a second-degree amendment. This relationship between proposed changes is called the "amendment tree."

Amendment in the Nature of a Substitute. As the name implies, this is a motion to strike all the language of a given bill or resolution and replace it with new (or largely new) language from beginning to end. Such amendments, called substitutes, may represent fresh starts or they may incorporate a number of smaller changes scattered throughout the existing text of a bill or resolution. Substitutes are often offered in committee by the chairman ("the chairman's mark") or by other members. The substitute format is also used on the floor.

Calendar. In addition to referring to the calendar of months and days, this term refers to the waiting queues of bills and other matters ready for floor action. The Senate uses a Calendar of General Orders and an Executive Calendar (for treaties, appointments and other business for the president). The House has five calendars, including a Consent Calendar for noncontroversial matters and a Union Calendar for revenue and spending matters.

Cloakrooms. The siderooms off the floor where members can relax and talk to one another in private during sessions. There is a cloakroom for each party in each chamber, and each has staff who keep track of the business on the floor for the benefit of the members and other interested parties.

Closed Rule. A rubric for debating a bill on the House floor under which amendments will not be in order unless offered by the committee reporting the bill. Revenue bills and tax code changes approved by the Ways and Means Committee have often been debated under closed rules.

Cloture. A limit on further debate regarding a particular proposal in the Senate—in effect, a means to cut off a filibuster. Under Senate Rule XXII (as amended), cloture limits additional debate to thirty hours. When a cloture petition signed by sixteen senators has been filed, the yeas and nays are called for on the second calendar day thereafter. Cloture requires three-fifths of the full Senate, or sixty votes if there are no vacancies.

Committee of the Whole.   Parliamentary mode of procedure used routinely to consider and vote on amendments to bills. Once common to both chambers, it is now used exclusively in the House. It facilitates floor proceedings because it requires only 100 members to do business rather than a full quorum of 218 and it limits the range of floor motions available. All bills taken from the Union Calendar (affecting revenue or spending) must be considered in the Committee of the Whole (full name: Committee of the Whole House on the State of the Union).

Committee Report.   Issued alongside the printed version of a bill following approval of the bill or resolution in committee, this report includes the text of the bill itself, plus explanatory material, the legislative history of the bill and the dissenting views of committee members who opposed it.

Conference.   A meeting of members from each chamber to resolve differences in the House and Senate versions of a bill on the same subject.

Conference Committee.   The members appointed to a House-Senate conference by the leaders of their respective chambers. The conferees, as they are also known, represent both parties and all committees to which the bill at issue has been referred.

Conference Report.   The product of a conference committee which is returned to the floor of each chamber for debate but which cannot be amended. When chambers have approved the conference report by simple majority vote, the measure (or bill) is said to have been cleared. It then needs only the president's signature to become law.

Continuing Resolution.   A joint resolution of the House and Senate by which governmental programs have their spending authority extended for a given period of time in the absence of a regular appropriations bill. The "CR" became a major legislative vehicle, embodying authorization for various program changes, when the normal passage of appropriations bills ground to a halt in the 1980s.

Engrossed/Enrolled.   When a bill is passed by one chamber, the official copy of its final text as amended is called the engrossed bill. When a bill has been passed by both chambers in identical form (with or without the work of a conference), the final official copy presented to the president on parchment is called the enrolled bill.

Filibuster.   In the Senate, an extended debate or use of dilatory tactics by which one or more senators refuse to yield the floor or to proceed to formal consideration or voting on the matter at hand. The term dates from the mid-1800s (it is Dutch by way of the Spanish) and was originally used in the House, but the practice was common from the earliest days of the Senate.

Hold.   Senators are said to have "placed a hold" on a particular bill or resolution when they ask their party leader to inform them prior to any further action on that measure. The placing of a hold signals that a given senator will not accept a unanimous consent agreement on that measure and may plan to filibuster it. The tactic has special value in that party leaders traditionally do not divulge which senators have placed holds on which bills.

Hopper. The wooden box near the desk of the clerk of the House into which members place new bills for introduction. Bills at introduction are often referred to as being "in the hopper" or as freshly "dropped."

"King of the Mountain." A floor procedure in the House by which the Committee of the Whole considers a series of amendments in the nature of a substitute. The adoption of any such amendment serves to eradicate the adoption of all predecessors. Thus the last substitute amendment approved becomes the bill.

Markup. The formal session at which a committee or subcommittee debates, amends and votes to report legislation that has been referred to it. Markups are rarely held if the chairman does not feel sure of a majority vote to report the legislation favorably. But chairmen can never entirely control the committee proceedings, nor predict how every amendment will fare. After markup, committee staff produce a committee report for the floor. At that point the leadership begins the process of deciding whether and when to bring the bill in question to the floor.

Motion to Proceed. In the Senate, the official act of bringing a bill or resolution to the floor for consideration. The motion is debatable, and it may be the occasion for a filibuster.

Open Rule. A plan for consideration of a bill on the floor of the House under which members may submit as many amendments as they wish within the general rules of the House (including the germaneness rule that requires amendments to be relevant to the bill at hand).

Party Caucus/Conference. Strictly speaking, a caucus is any group of like-minded legislators who meet to plan tactics and strategy in either chamber. The most important caucuses are those of the two parties: the Republican Conference in both chambers, the Senate Democratic Conference and the House Democratic Caucus. These groups meet before a new Congress convenes to elect the leaders in both chambers, organize the committees and approve procedural rules. They also meet regularly throughout the session.

Pocket Veto. The president's constitutional power to prevent a bill from becoming law without returning it to Congress for further action. Normally, a bill the president has not returned within ten days (not counting Sundays) becomes law without his signature. But if Congress is not in session when the ten days have lapsed, the president cannot return the bill and it dies.

Reading. Parliamentary tradition and House and Senate rules require that bills and resolutions be read aloud three times before a final vote. In practice, however, the bill text is rarely read on the floor. The Senate allows bills to be read "by title only." House rules follow this procedure for the first and third readings but require a full second reading, which is usually dispensed with by unanimous consent of the members present.

Reconsideration. A motion that can be made once after passage of a bill or resolution. It is usually offered immediately after passage. By moving to reconsider and immediately killing the motion (by "laying it on the table"), the bill's managers foreclose any future effort to revisit its passage.

Recorded Vote. A vote in which members are recorded as yeas, nays or present but not voting. Such votes are common in both committee and floor consideration. On the House floor, such votes are taken by electronic device. In the Senate, each senator announces his or her vote to the Senate's recording clerk.

Report Language. The additional material added to a committee report to explain or elaborate upon the actual text of a bill. This material may clarify the intent of the bill's sponsors and supporters and is often important to administrators writing regulations to enforce a law or to judges attempting to interpret and apply it.

Rules. The permanent rules of the House and Senate are rooted in parliamentary tradition, constitutional guidelines and generations of precedent. Each body also has a Rules Committee, although the Senate version generally deals with internal administration rather than floor procedure. The House Rules Committee devises elaborate scenarios for floor consideration of bills, including each amendment that will be in order. These rules then take the form of a resolution that must be adopted by the House prior to debate on a bill.

Sense of the Senate/Congress. A resolution expressing the sentiments of the body (or its majority) with regard to any given question. It has no force of law, carries no commitment to action and is often adopted as an alternative to an actual legislative proposal.

Time Agreement. In the Senate, a unanimous consent agreement setting an outside limit on debate on a particular bill or resolution, specifying which amendments will be allowed and how long each will be debated. Time agreements usually say when votes will be taken on the amendments and on the underlying legislation.

Unanimous Consent. Literally, the agreement of every member of the body to permit something to happen on the floor. Strictly speaking, the term "unanimous" refers only to those members present in the chamber at the time consent is requested. But as a practical matter, in the Senate the leaders of both parties routinely notify the offices of all members in advance of requests for unanimous consent. In this case, the request serves as advance notice of the leadership's plans for floor consideration. The unanimous consent agreement in this sense serves the function that the Rules Committee does in the House.

Veto. The president's constitutional power to prevent a bill from becoming law. The president returns the bill in question to the originating chamber with a written statement of his objections called a veto message. If Congress is in session at the time the bill is returned, it can attempt to revise the legislation to meet the president's objections or attempt to override the veto. An override requires the support of two-thirds of those present and voting in each chamber.

Voice Vote. A method for taking a vote when the outcome is expected to be obvious. It is often used in committee or on the floor of the House. A member may object to this procedure, which is also referred to as the yeas and nays, and ask for a division (also known as a standing vote because members stand to be counted) or a recorded vote.

Whip. As a verb, the term refers to leaders lobbying the members of their own party; "to whip a vote" is to work the rank and file on behalf of a given measure. As a noun, the term refers to a specific office in the party power structure, an office that stands just below the majority leader or minority leader in each chamber. Besides cajoling colleagues, the whip conveys information from the rank-and-file membership to the leaders. In the House of the 1980s and early 1990s, the majority whip was assisted by chief deputy whips, a floor whip, several deputy whips, "zone whips" and a host of at-large whips. The entire "whip operation" included more than ninety members.

Whip Count. The vote estimate the whip delivers to the party leadership prior to the consideration of a major bill on the floor. Such counts may determine whether a bill is brought to the floor at all.

A Note on Sources

MOST OF THE SOURCES FOR THIS narrative account of family leave and its legislative history are evident within the text itself. In a few cases, noncontroversial comments have been attributed to unnamed sources in the interest of expediency. In some instances, background information has been drawn from interviews with former staff members who were only willing to share their recollections anonymously.

Family leave surfaced as an issue in 1984, the year I came to Washington for the Congressional Fellowship program sponsored by the American Political Science Association. Throughout the decade described, I have been concerned with Congress as an APSA Fellow, a staff member in the House and Senate, and since 1987 as a reporter and editor for *Congressional Quarterly*. This book and its descriptions of Capitol Hill—its people, procedures and customs—are rooted in personal experience.

The specific legislative history of family leave, however, is drawn from a variety of sources. These begin with the *Congressional Record* and the accumulated documents, records, notes, files and reports of the several House and Senate subcommittees to which the successive bills were assigned.

In addition, I conducted more than sixty interviews with members and their staffs in the House and Senate, as well as in the White House and in the various lobbying organizations that lined up for and against the bill. In this regard, I was especially well served by the cooperation of the chief sponsors of the legislation in both chambers. In the House, I relied in particular on Congresswoman Pat Schroeder, Democrat of Colorado (sponsor of the original family leave bill in 1985 and cosponsor of every bill thereafter), and Congresswoman Marge Roukema, Republican of New Jersey (cosponsor of the later bills and ranking Republican on the Labor-Management Relations Subcommittee of the House Education and Labor Committee). In the Senate, the main mover was Senator Christopher J. Dodd, Democrat of Connecticut, the original sponsor of family leave in his chamber and later the chairman of the Children, Family, Drugs and Alcoholism Subcommittee of the Senate Labor and Human Resources Committee. Also highly informative were some of the legislation's chief adversaries, including Republican Dick Armey and Democrat Tim Penny in the House.

But the most detailed recollections of events inside and outside the process itself came from the staff members who worked on the bill year after year, and from the proponents and opponents who lobbied for and against family leave for nearly a decade. Among the staff, I am especially beholden to Fred Feinstein, then the staff counsel for the Labor-Management Relations Subcommittee of Education and Labor in the House, Andrea Camp of Congresswoman Schroeder's staff and Rich Tarplin, who was Senator Dodd's lead staff person on the bill from the 100th Congress to the Rose Garden signing ceremony. All these staff veterans provided access to their voluminous files on family leave in all its phases.

Especially helpful in establishing the bill's early history were Sherry Cassedy and Anne Radigan, staff members for the Congressional Caucus for Women's Issues (Radigan's 1988 monograph on the early versions of the family leave bill was published by the Women's Research and Education Institute). Jill Kagan and Nancy Reder, both former House staff members, provided a virtual library of material from the period before family leave legislation was first formally introduced as a bill.

Among advocates of family leave, the group that picked up the issue most immediately and held on most firmly was the Women's Legal Defense Fund, led by Judith Lichtman with Donna Lenhoff as the issue's chief counsel. Both were most generous with their time and information. Also invaluable were the recollections of participants from the Children's Defense Fund, the American Association of Retired Persons, the National Conference of Catholic Bishops and the AFL-CIO.

Among the many adversaries of the legislation who shared their experiences on this issue, the two whose contributions were most useful were Mary Tavenner, organizer of the CARE coalition against the bill, and John Motley of the National Federation of Independent Business. Mike Resnick of the National School Boards Association supplied a wealth of detail on the issues of concern to his group. Among those who shared their recollections of family leave as an issue for the White House, Nick Calio, special assistant to President George Bush for legislative affairs, was especially persuasive and illuminating.

Index

AARP (American Association of
    Retired Persons):
    and child care, 133
    and elder care, 78, 118, 157, 165,
        225
    and HR 2, 224, 225–26
    and HR 770, 152, 157–59
    and HR 925/S 2488, 78, 118
    and HR 4300, 66
    mythical power of, 157
    and spousal care, 157, 165, 205,
        225
ABC bill (Act for Better Child Care),
    120–21, 122, 151, 159–60
abortion, 57, 60, 92, 155, 244, 257,
    258, 268, 290
Ackerman, Gary L., 174
ACLU (American Civil Liberties
    Union), 32
ADA (Americans with Disabilities
    Act), 195–96
Adams, Brock, 108, 134
Addams, Jane, 21
Adminstration Committee, 101, 139,
    140, 142, 148, 203, 246, 294
AFL-CIO, 56, 57, 63, 106, 152, 162,
    220–21
AFSCME, 154, 261
Albert, Carl, 170
amendments:
    "bigger bite," 231
    as killers, 279–80

and king of the mountain, 231–32
in markups, 45
and media, 275
in the nature of substitute, 100, 231
American Academy of Pediatrics, 119
American Association of Retired
    Persons, see AARP
American Civil Liberties Union, 32
American Federation of State, County
    and Municipal Employees
    (AFSCME), 154, 261
American Federation of Teachers,
    138
American Samoa, 264
Americans with Disabilities Act
    (ADA), 195–96
appropriation bills, 111–12
Armed Services Committee, 37–38
Armey, Dick, 251, 293
    and HR 1, 268
    and HR 2, 206, 232
    and HR 770, 140, 167, 176
    and HR 925, 93, 99–101
    and HR 4300, 62, 65, 68
Aspin, Les, 233
Association of Junior Leagues:
    conference of, 40, 42, 43, 46
    and narrow vs. broad focus, 78, 158
    in support coalition, 29, 66, 106, 152

Baker, Howard H., Jr., 81
Baker, James A., 3rd, 144, 249

Bartlett, Steve, 206
  and HR 770, 167, 168, 171, 176, 179,
    180, 182, 196
  and HR 925, 99–101
  and HR 4300, 62, 63, 65, 68
Bentsen, Lloyd M., 187
Berman, Howard:
  and California state law, 18, 19, 21,
    45, 80, 179
  and genesis of bill, 18–21, 23, 29,
    30–34, 136, 224, 257
  and HR 2, 231
  and HR 2020, 38–41, 54, 59
  and moms-only concept, 23, 224, 234
  and S 249, 89
Bernardin, Joseph Cardinal, 156
Biaggi, Mario, 65
Bilirakis, Michael, 229
Biller, Moe, 63
Black, Clint, 268
Boehlert, Sherwood L. (Sherry), 62,
    177
Boehner, John, 268
Bond, Christopher S. (Kit), 134, 156,
    158, 206, 295
  and compromise, 207–10, 272; *see
    also* Dodd-Bond compromise
  and PAC funds, 259
  and S 5, 204, 216, 236, 240, 246, 273
Bonior, David, 161–64, 168, 220, 221,
    222, 224, 226
Boren, David L., 251, 282
Bork, Robert H., 99
Boxer, Barbara, 38–41, 59, 257, 276
Bradley, Bill, 187
Brady, Mary Del, 88
Bravo, Ellen, 154–55
Brazelton, T. Berry, 40, 46, 50, 64, 89
Brown, Hank, 282, 284
Buchanan, Pat, 241–42, 246
Buckley, James L., 81–82
Budget Act (1974), 44
Bumpers, Dale, 187
Burns, Conrad, 193
Burton, Phil, 18, 30
Bush, Barbara, 193, 195, 237
Bush, George, 81, 107, 112, 120, 149,
    239, 256–57, 295–96
  approval ratings of, 203–4, 241
  vs. Congress, 145–46, 150, 186
  and deal making, 159, 246
  and family leave, 125, 138, 175, 194–
    196, 206–7, 236, 255
  and Gulf War, 203, 205

inauguration of, 129–30, 145
  and minimum wage bill, 114–15,
    145, 149–50, 153, 159, 246
  and plant-closing bill, 144
  and primaries, 242, 246, 249
  and tax incentive plan, 250–51, 262
  and veto, 123, 146, 150, 182, 191,
    194–97, 202, 214, 236, 246, 248–
    251, 255–56
business community:
  and amendments to bill, 117
  and family leave, 83–86, 94, 163
  and mandates, *see* employers
  and social legislation, 289
  see also small business
Byrd, Robert C., 76, 111, 129, 185
  background of, 113
  and Dole, 112–13, 114
  and minimum wage bill, 114–16
  and S 2488, 120–23, 132

California:
  Attorney General's Office, 32
  Chamber of Commerce, 18
  state law, 18, 19, 21, 45, 80, 179
  support for bill from, 40–41
California Federal Savings and Loan
    Association (Cal Fed), 17–18, 19,
    21, 22, 32, 45–46, 54, 61, 80
Calio, Nick, 167, 189, 238–39, 245–46,
    249–50, 289
Canada, child care in, 27–28
capital gains tax, 145–46, 150–51, 186
Carberry, John Cardinal, 156
CARE (Concerned Alliance of
    Responsible Employers), 85–86,
    100, 137, 238
  and HR 1, 262
  and HR 700/S 345, 139, 166–67, 189
Carr, Bob, 167, 169, 170, 233, 258, 294, 295
Carter, Jimmy, 186, 260
Cassedy, Sherry, 29, 31, 32, 40–41
Catholic Conference, U.S., 29, 57, 78,
    155–57, 159, 176, 177
Chafee, John H., 122, 215, 216
Chamber of Commerce, U.S.:
  and compromises, 217
  cost estimates by, 86, 88, 121, 207,
    279–80
  and hearings, 88
  influence of, 151
  and Lamp, 64, 84, 100, 212
  as opposed to bill, 61–62, 85, 100,
    191, 197, 223

Champlin, Steve, 162, 165, 173, 181
Chandler, Rod, 65
Cheney, Dick, 146, 238–39
child care, 23–29, 228
  ABC bill, 120–21, 122, 151, 159–60
  and cost of bill, 121
  hearings on, 25–29, 32–34, 37, 40
  at home, 27–29
  and media, 33, 53–54
  as S 5 (1989), 133, 159–60, 189
  support for, 90, 132–34, 144
  for working parents, 25–28, 33, 95
child labor laws, 109
child pornography ("kiddle porn"),
    119–20, 123
Children, Family, Drugs and
    Alcoholism Subcommittee, 58,
    75, 76, 87, 131, 134–36
Children, Youth and Families, Select
    Committee on, 23–29, 32–34, 39,
    202–3, 208
Children's Caucus, 75
Children's Defense Fund, 78, 133, 152
Chrysler, Dick, 258
Citizens for a Sound Economy, 197
Civil Rights Act, (1964), 19, 21–22, 45,
    113
Civil Rights Act (1991), 220, 246, 261
civil rights bill (1990), 196
Civil Service Subcommittee, 47
Clay, William L., 52, 204, 210, 291
  and HR 1, 268, 285
  and HR 2, 203, 205, 222–23, 226–28,
    232, 241, 246
  and HR 770, 130, 136–37, 139, 154,
    167, 169, 173, 175, 180
  and HR 925, 77, 78, 83, 86, 87, 93,
    94, 95, 97, 100, 102
  and HR 2020, 47, 51, 54–55, 56, 57
  and HR 4300, 58, 59–60, 63, 64–65,
    67–68, 153
Clay-Jeffords compromise, 66–68
Clay-Schroeder bill, *see* Family and
    Medical Leave Act
Clinton, Bill, 11, 37, 249, 255, 260,
    261–62, 291, 293
Clinton, Hillary Rodham, 256
cloture, 115–16
  and S 2488, 117, 122
Coal Employment Project, 29
Coats, Daniel R.:
  and genesis of bill, 28, 33
  and S 5, 208, 211, 216, 246–47, 274
  and S 345, 134, 141

Cochran, Thad, 108, 109, 122, 190,
    193, 213–14
Coelho, Tony:
  and HR 925, 124, 125, 143–44
  and majority whip, 94, 105, 143,
    161
  resignation of, 148, 149
  and whip task forces, 105, 143, 162
Cohen, William S. (Bill), 215, 216
committee reports:
  as base for new bill, 131
  and floor consideration, 69, 70
  language clarified in, 57–58
  Report 99–699, 70
committees:
  assignments to, 18–19, 47, 79
  bills softened in, 62, 165
  conference, 104–5, 149–50, 246
  formal referral to, 43–44
  hearings in, 25–29, 44–45, 46–47,
    64–65
  in House, 44
  and landmark legislation, 44
  legislation identified with, 56
  markups in, 45, 64–69
  multiple referral to, 44
  reports of, 57–58, 69, 70, 131
  right of referral to, 43–44
  standing, 44, 294
  witnesses before, 26–28
  see also specific committtees
Compensation and Employee Benefits
    Subcommittee, 47
Concerned Alliance of Responsible
    Employers, *see* CARE
conference committees, 104–5
  for HR 2/S 5, 149–50, 237–38, 246–
    248
  splitting the difference in, 247–48
conference reports, HR Report 102–
    816, 248–50
Congress:
  adjournment of, 69, 70, 77
  vs. Bush, 145–46, 150, 186
  calendars in, 240
  cloakrooms of, 166, 187
  committee assignments in, 18–19,
    47, 79
  ebb and flow of, 296
  employees of, 68, 101, 139–40, 142,
    207, 229, 266, 270, 286
  institutional anemia in, 242
  institutional constraints of, 290
  legislative process in, *see* legislation

Congress (*cont.*)
  new kinds of members in, 154
  opening ceremonies in, 264
  reapportionment and redistricting
    in, 242–43
  sense of, 284
  and veto, 83
  women in, 244, 257–58, 259
  see also House of Representatives;
    Senate
Congressional Black Caucus, 59
Congressional Caucus for Women's
  Issues, 34, 40, 59, 92, 230
Congressional Record, 43
Conte, Silvio, 59
Cooper, Jim, 62, 85, 223
Craig, Larry E., 250–51, 277–78
Cranston, Alan, 23, 117, 189, 209
Crockett, George, 59

Dailey, Sharon, 155
D'Amato, Alfonse M., 137, 216
Dammann, Julie, 204
Danforth, John C., 122, 137, 156, 216,
  279
Darman, Richard, 249–50
day care, *see* child care
"Dear Colleague" letters, 43, 59–60
DeConcini, Dennis, 58
DeLay, Tom, 71, 230, 293
Dellums, Ronald V., 38, 59
Democratic Leadership Council
  (DLC), 37, 124
Democrats:
  "boll weevils" in, 92, 150–51
  in midterm elections, 294
  party platform of, 111
  and Reagan, 36–37, 295–96
  and Rules Committee, 143
  and Senate leadership, 76
  and social legislation, 82–83, 111,
    114, 255, 293
Derrick, Butler, 223
Dickinson, Bill, 142
Dirksen, Everett McKinley, 81
discrimination:
  against women, 19, 20–23
  and equal-treatment bill, 21, 30, 45
  in House committees, 38
  racial, 21–22
District of Columbia, 257, 264
Dixon, Alan J., 156, 258
DLC (Democratic Leadership
  Council), 37, 124

Dodd, Christopher J., 58, 129–30,
  236–37, 290, 291, 295
  and child care, 132–34, 228, 239
  and elder/spousal care, 158
  and HR 2, 228
  and "road show" hearings, 89, 94, 104
  and S 5, 202, 204, 206–11, 213–15,
    223–24, 240, 246, 248, 251, 266,
    272, 274, 276–78, 280, 282–85
  and S 249, 75–76, 77–78, 79–82, 83,
    86–91, 103–10
  and S 345, 130–36, 141–42, 160,
    183–85, 187–93, 195, 197
  and S 2488, 106–9, 110, 116–23
  and tax incentive plan, 251
Dodd, Thomas J., 81–82
Dodd-Bond compromise, 207–11, 214,
  215, 217, 224, 227, 230–34, 247,
  261
Dole, Elizabeth, 193, 203
Dole, Robert J. (Bob), 53, 76, 196,
  295
  background of, 113–14
  and Byrd, 112–13, 114
  and S 5, 206, 212–14, 217, 248, 251,
    275, 277–83
  and S 249, 84
  and S 345, 141, 188, 190–93
  and S 2488, 121–23
  and voice vote, 240
Domenici, Pete V., 133–34
Donahue, Tom, 63
Dornan, Robert K. (Bob), 284
Downey, Tom, 151
Dreyfuss, Richard and Jeremie, 89
Duberstein, Ken, 238
Dukakis, Michael S., 110–11, 112,
  117, 124, 125, 146, 255
Duncan, John J., 60
Dunn, Jennifer, 264, 268
Durenberger, David F., 122
  and S 5, 206, 207, 211, 213, 215–17,
    274
  and S 345, 134, 141, 142

Edelman, Marian Wright, 133, 228,
  256
Education and Labor Committee, 294
  and genesis of bill, 30, 34, 286
  and HR 1, 261–62, 265, 266
  and HR 2, 202–3, 206, 229, 246
  and HR 770, 130, 139–40, 142, 168
  and HR 925, 78, 84, 94, 97, 99–103,
    123

and HR 2020, 44, 50–51, 54–55, 56, 57
and HR 4300, 60, 62, 63, 65, 66–68, 70
Labor-Management Relations Subcommittee, 30, 47, 136
Labor Standards Subcommittee, 34, 47
old guard in, 62
and plant-closing bill, 51–52
Young Turks in, 62, 99–100
Edwards, Don, 31
Edwards, Mickey, 233
elder care, 78, 95, 106, 118, 157–58, 165, 185, 225, 247, 286
Emily's List, 258
employees:
benefits of, 29, 64, 88–89, 95, 136, 247, 266, 269, 286
of Congress, 68, 101, 139–40, 142, 207, 229, 266, 270, 286
key, 210–11
rights of, 22–23, 30, 40
temporary, 88, 207
employers:
mandates for, 28, 29, 39, 42, 134, 173, 174, 195–96, 251, 262
penalties to, 210
engrossed/enrolled bills, 150, 193–94
Equal Employment Opportunity Commission, 22
Equal Rights Amendment, 20–21
Ethics Committee, House, 148
Europe, child care in, 27–28, 30, 155, 173

Fair Labor Standards Act, 46, 55, 109, 119, 225, 261, 263
Family and Medical Leave Act (1986):
Clay-Jeffords compromise on, 66–68
committee report on, 68
floor consideration of, 69–71
as HR 4300, 58–72
markup on, 66–69
open rule for, 71–72
as Parental and Medical Leave Act, 58–66
and Rules Committee, 71–72
small-business exemption in, 67
support coalition for, 66, 69
title of, 66
Family and Medical Leave Act (1987):
amendments to, 100–102
cosponsors of, 94, 98

hearings on, 87
as HR 925, 76–78, 86 87, 92 103, 107, 123–25
introduction of, 86
markups on, 93–94, 98, 100–103
revisions needed for, 94–97
support coalition for, 77–78, 86, 97
Family and Medical Leave Act (1989):
amendments to, 140–41, 164–71
cosponsors of, 130
floor consideration of, 164–81
floor vote on, 181, 201
as HR 770, 130–31, 136–41, 142–44, 152–59, 161–82, 184–85, 194–97
introduction of, 130
markups of, 139–40
modified open rule for, 168–69
provisions of, 130–31
substituted for S 345, 184–85, 202
timetable for, 131
and veto, 182, 194–97, 202
vote-counting for, 165, 246
Family and Medical Leave Act (1991):
amendments to, 205, 206, 227–34
cosponsors of, 227
final passage vote on, 234–35
floor consideration of, 227–34
as HR 2, 202–6, 219–35, 237–38
and HR Report 102–816, 248–50
"king of the mountain" rules for, 231–32
markups of, 205–6
movement of, 202–3, 204–6
Penny in, 219–28, 230–31, 234
power players for, 202
provisions of, 247
vote-counting for, 227–28, 234
and votes to override, 227, 235, 251–52
Family and Medical Leave Act (1993):
amendments to, 266–67, 269–70
background of, 12–13
commission for study of, 292
committee report on, 266–67
cosponsors of, 265
epilogue on, 291–96
floor consideration of, 267–71
genesis of, 17–34
as HR 1, 261 64, 265–71
markups to, 265–66
motion to reconsider, 271
passed by House, 271
as PL 103–3, 284–87
provisions of, 286–87

Family and Medical Leave Act (1993)
    (*cont.*)
  signing ceremony for, 11, 284–85,
    287
  substituted for S 5, 283–84; *see also*
    Parental and Medical Leave Act
    (1993)
  summary of, 12
  voice vote on, 270–71
Family Employment Security Act
    (FESA):
  compensation in, 29–30, 39, 40
  as genesis, 30–34
  length of, 29
  support group for, 30–32, 34, 37,
    38–39, 46
family leave:
  and abortion, *see* abortion
  and child care, *see* child care
  and compensation, 29–30, 39, 40,
    42, 43
  cost estimates for, 86, 88, 89–90,
    96–98, 101, 121, 173, 207, 279–80
  and elder care, 78, 95, 106, 118,
    157–58, 165, 185, 225, 247, 286
  and employee benefits, 29, 64, 88–
    89, 95, 136, 247, 266, 269, 286
  employer mandate for, 28, 29, 39,
    42, 134, 173, 174, 195–96, 251, 262
  genesis of bill on, 17–34
  idea vs. issues of, 288–89
  initial legislative steps of, 42–45
  length of, 29, 95–96, 118–19, 165,
    225–26, 231–32, 261, 286
  and media, 83, 89, 193, 201–2, 210,
    287–88
  minimum labor standard in, 95, 224
  narrow vs. broad focus of, 23, 30–
    31, 32, 33, 38–41, 46, 49, 78, 95,
    104, 109, 130, 152–59, 179, 224
  as national issue, 117, 256
  as nondiscriminatory, 23, 95
  opposition to, 70, 82–86, 163
  as PL 103–3, 284–87
  political potential of, 153–54
  post-leave reinstatement in, 95, 286
  preferential rehire in, 217, 224, 229,
    231–32
  and presidential campaign, 110
  reduced-schedule, 267, 269–70, 282
  and spousal care, 106, 157–58, 165,
    205, 225, 286
  state laws on, 18, 19–22, 45, 80, 95,
    205

  support for, *see* support coalition
  and tax incentive plan, 250–51, 262,
    277–78
  see also parental leave; *specific
    legislation*
family vlaues, 233, 244
Fawell, Harris W., 48–49
  and HR 1, 270
  and Hr 2, 229
  and HR 770, 175, 197
  and HR 4300, 63, 65, 68
Fazio, Vic, 176–77
federal workers:
  and congressional staff, 68, 101,
    139–40, 142, 207, 229, 266, 270,
    286
  and HR 2, 205
  and HR 770, 173
  and HR 925, 105
  and HR 2020, 45, 47
Feinstein, Dianne, 257, 276
Feinstein, Fred, 287, 294
  and genesis of bill, 30, 31
  and HR 1, 263, 266, 267
  and HR 2, 227, 228
  and HR 770, 136, 138–39, 152, 157,
    162, 166, 173, 179, 181, 198
  and HR 925, 95, 96, 106, 125
  and HR 2020, 46, 48, 54–57
  and HR 4300, 57, 66, 67
feminists, *see* women
Ferraro, Geraldine A., 26, 38
FESA, *see* Family Employment
    Security Act
FESA Group, 30–32, 34, 37, 38–39,
    46
filibuster, 114, 115–16, 188, 190, 211–
    212
Fish, Hamilton, Jr., 59
floor consideration, 69–72, 79, 187,
    190
  amendments in, 71
  criteria for, 69
  gatekeepers to, 69–70, 164
  under open rule, 71–72
  see also Rules Committee
Foley, Thomas S., 285
  and conference committee, 238
  and House speaker, 148, 149, 168,
    262–63, 264, 270, 284
  and override votes, 150, 197
Ford, Gerald R., 99
Ford, Wendell H., 202, 209–10,
    213

Ford, William D., 51–52, 63, 64, 65, 220, 222, 294
and HR 1, 261–62, 265, 268, 270, 282, 285
and HR 2, 202, 206, 222–23, 226–27, 232, 241, 246, 252
and HR 770, 130, 154
Foreign Affairs Committee, 19
Fowler, Tillie K., 268

Gallaher, Mark, 156
Gallup, George, Sr., 203
Garland, Lillian, 17–18, 19, 45, 54, 61, 80
gays in military, 275, 276–77, 278–79, 281–82
General Accounting Office:
and cost estimates, 88, 89–90, 96–98, 101, 173, 207, 279–80
and House bank overdrafts, 242
General Electric v. *Gilbert*, 22
General Foods, 46
Generous Dianne, 84
Gephardt, Richard A., 149, 150, 169, 176, 233, 256, 271
Gergen, David, 198
Gingrich, Newt, 62, 146–47, 172, 174, 269, 293, 294
Glickman, Dan, 269
Gold, Marty, 189
Goldwater, Barry, 241
Gonzalez, Henry B., 59
Goodling, Bill, 99, 103, 294
and cafeteria plan, 265–66, 269, 278
and HR 1, 262, 265, 267, 268–70
and HR 2, 206, 229, 233, 234, 246
and HR 770, 140, 168, 176
and reduced-schedule leave, 267, 269–70, 282, 283
Gordon, Bart, 163, 165, 178–79, 213, 267
Gordon-Hyde substitute, for HR 2, 230–33, 234–35
Gordon-Weldon substitute, for, HR 770, 165–66, 167, 168, 170, 173, 177, 178, 179–80, 181, 183, 184
Gore, Albert, Jr., 256–57, 277
Gorton, Slade, 278
Grady, Bob, 250
Cramm, Phil, 56
Gramm-Rudman-Hollings bill (PL 99–177), 53, 55–56
Grandy, Fred, 168–69, 171, 173–76, 268, 295

Grassley, Charles E., 278–79
Gray, William II., 3rd, 149, 150, 161–162, 171, 173, 174, 220
Green, Bill, 59
Gregg, Judd, 274
Guam, 264
Gulf War, 203, 205
Gunderson, Steve, 68, 102, 155, 196, 205

Hager, Susan, 64
Hamilton, Martha Ditto, 135–36
Harkin, Tom, 108, 216
Hart, Gary, 58, 77, 81
Hatch, Orrin G., 59, 273, 295
and child care, 133, 190
and preferential rehiring, 221, 224, 229, 250
and S 5, 207–8, 213–14, 217, 224, 246, 274, 279
and S 249, 75, 82, 90–91, 104
and S 345, 134–35, 190, 193
and S 2488, 108, 109, 120
Hatfield, Mark O., 216
Hawkins, Augustus F. (Gus), 51–52, 151, 202
and HR 770, 139
and HR 925, 98, 100, 101, 102
and HR 4300, 60, 63, 65, 66, 68
Hayes, Charles A., 48, 63
Hébert, F. Edward, 38
Heflin, Howell, 282
Helms, Jesse, 276–77, 281, 282
Henry, Paul 68
Hill, Anita, 212–13
Hollings, Ernest F., 56
Holloway, Clyde, 175
hopper, bills dropped into, 42
Horn, Steve, 268
Houghton, Amo, 167, 169, 171, 175
House of Representatives:
Administration Committee, 101, 139, 140, 142, 148, 203, 246, 294
Armed Services Committee, 37–38
bank overdrafts of, 229, 242
bills introduced in, 42–43
clerk of, 271
committees in, 44
as Committee of the Whole, 172, 230–34, 264–65, 267–71
division of (standing vote), 271
Education and Labor Committee, 30, 62
Ethics Committee, 148

House of Representatives (*cont.*)
floor debate in, 79
Foreign Affairs Committee, 19
and House Resolution 388, 169
HR 1, Family and Medical Leave
Act (1993), 261–64, 165–71
HR 2, Family and Medical Leave
Act (1991), 202–6, 219–35, 237–
238
HR 2, minimum wage (1989), 144,
145, 148, 149–50, 153, 159, 162,
174
HR 284, Roukema's substitute bill
(1987), 83, 93
HR 770, Family and Medical Leave
Act (1989), 130–31, 136–41, 142–
144, 152–59, 161–82, 184–85,
194–97
HR 925, Family and Medical Leave
Act (1987), 76–78, 86–87, 92–103,
107, 123–25
HR 2020, Parental and Disability
Leave Act (1985), 42–51, 53–58
HR 4300, Family and Medical Leave
Act (1986), 58–72
and HR Report 102–816, 248–50
Interior Committee, 38
Judiciary Committee, 19
and king of the mountain, 231–32
legislation introduced in, 42–43,
54
mace, placement of, 230, 234
majority caucus in, 43, 150
majority leader of, 114
majority whip in, 105, 143–44
number of seats in, 243
party discipline in, 264
Post Office and Civil Service
Committee, 44, 294
reapportionment and redistricting
in, 242–43
retirements from, 242
right of referral in, 43–44
Rules Committee, *see* Rules
Committee
Select Committee on Children,
Youth and Families, 23
Speaker of, 43–44, 70, 164, 264
standing vote (division) of, 271
Steering and Policy Committee, 18–
19, 69–70, 164
Union Calendar of, 164
votes tallied in, 172
votes to override veto, 197–98

voting status for delegates, 264–65,
269, 270, 271
Ways and Means Committee, 151
whip task force in, 105, 143, 162, 167
Huffington, Michael, 268
Humphrey, Gordon, 108, 109, 141
Hussein, Saddam, 203
Hyde, Henry J., 156, 290, 295
and HR 2, 230, 233, 236
and HR 770, 177–78, 179, 181,
194

Interior Committee, 38
Iran-Contra scandal, 76, 98, 112

Jackson, Andrew, 240
Japan, family leave in, 173
Jeffords, James M., 52, 107, 140, 286
and Clay-Jeffords compromise, 66–
68
and HR 925, 83, 95, 98, 99, 100, 102,
103
and HR 4300, 65, 66, 67, 68, 77
and S 5, 208, 216, 274
and S 345, 141, 142
Jenkins, Ed, 178–79
job protection, 19
job reinstatement, 95, 286
preferential rehiring, 167, 217, 221,
224, 229, 231–32, 234, 250, 262
Johnson, Liberia, 49
Johnson, Linda, 274
Johnson, Lyndon B., 19
Johnson, Nancy L., 97, 229
Judiciary Committee, House, 19
Junior Leagues, *see* Association of
Junior Leagues

Kamerman, Sheila, 26–27, 28, 40,
50
Kassebaum, Nancy Landon, 81, 134
257, 273–74 , 295
and S 5, 246, 277, 278
and S 345, 141
Kasten, Robert W., Jr., 258
Keating, Charles H., Jr., 189
Kemp, Jack, 146
Kennedy, Edward M. (Ted), 183, 187,
194, 277, 290, 295
and minimum wage bill, 115, 122
and S 5, 202, 207–8, 213–15, 246,
248, 266, 272, 274, 276, 278, 285
and S 249, 76, 80, 81, 82, 83, 89, 90,
91

and S 345, 130, 136, 141, 142, 184–
185, 187–88, 192, 193
and S 2278, 58
and S 2488, 108, 120
Kennedy, Patrick, 89, 207
Kerrey, Bob, 216
key employees provision, 210–11
King, Martin Luther, 3rd, 89
king of the mountain, 231–32
Klepner, Jerry, 154, 261
Klug, Scott L., 206, 266

labor:
    campaign activities of, 258
    and election year, 225
    and genesis of bill, 29, 32
    and HR 770, 152–55, 159, 162
    and HR 2020, 39, 46, 56
    and HR 4300, 39, 46, 56, 60, 63–64,
        71, 153
    minimum standard, 95, 224
    and minimum wage, 115, 144, 153
    PACs of, 258
    pros and cons of, 155
    and social legislation, 144, 150
    and super seniority issue, 57
Labor and Human Resources
        Committee:
    and S 5, 272–74
    and S 249, 75, 76, 80, 82, 84, 90–91,
        104, 131
    and S 345, 130, 136, 140, 141–42, 148
    and S 2278, 58–59
    and S 2488, 118
Labor-Management Relations
        Subcommittee, 294
    and HR 1, 265
    and HR 2, 204–5, 227
    and HR 770, 130, 136, 139, 140
    and HR 925, 87, 93–94, 95
    and HR 2020, 30, 47, 48, 54
    and HR 4300, 63–64, 65
Labor Standards Subcommittee, 34,
        47, 63, 87
LaFalce, John J., 223, 267
Lake, Celinda, 257
Lamp, Virginia, 61, 64, 84, 86, 100,
        212
landmark legislation, committee
        referrals of, 44
Landon, Alfred, 81
Law, Bernard Cardinal, 156
leadership, of majority party, 69–70,
        142–43

League of Women Voters, 21, 32
legislation:
    and adjournment, 69, 70, 77
    amendment in the nature of
        substitute for, 100, 231
    amendments as killers to, 279–80
    appropriations, 111–12
    cleared for president's signature,
        150, 193–94
    and cloture, 115–16
    committee identification of, 56
    committee reports on, 57, 69, 70
    companion bills for, 58, 70, 77–78
    conference committees for, 104–5,
        149–50, 246
    corrections to, 271
    cosponsors of, 43, 55–56, 69, 70, 71
    double standard in, 20
    drafting committee for, 20
    engrossed/enrolled, 150, 193–94
    financing of, 40
    floor consideration of, 69–72, 79
    full reading of, 67
    hold placed on, 211–12
    industry/interest association with, 56
    intent of, 286
    interpreted by courts, 286
    introduction of (House), 42–43, 54
    introduction of (Senate), 58–59, 76,
        79–80, 86
    landmark, 44
    language of, 31, 57
    and majority whip, 143–44
    markups of, 64–69, 102
    and media, 56
    motions to recommit, 169, 234
    motions to reconsider, 271
    moving of, 44, 54
    multiple identities of, 55–56
    narrow vs. broad focus of, 38–41
    numbers assigned to, 42
    and open rule, 71–72, 168
    outside advocates of, 56
    parliamentary tradition for, 43
    and president's agenda, 56
    process of, 43–45, 77
    redesign of, 58
    roll call vote on, 215–16
    rules for, 164
    softened in committee, 62, 165
    stages of active consideration of,
        44
    substance or effect of, 55
    suspension calendar for, 71

legislation (*cont.*)
  three-day layover rule, 267
  time needed for passage of, 183,
    227, 290, 295
  timing of, 40, 47, 69, 144, 190, 244,
    263
  unanimous consent agreement for,
    187, 192, 211–12
  and veto, *see* veto
  voter appeal of, 244
  whip task force for, 105, 143, 162,
    167
Legislative Counsel, Office of, 31
Lenhoff, Donna, 40, 152–53, 258, 260,
    277, 287, 288, 292
  and AARP, 157, 158
  and FESA Group, 30, 38
  and genesis of bill, 19–23, 29, 30–
    34, 54
  and HR 2/S 5, 204, 214, 216, 224,
    226, 227, 229, 234–35
  and HR 770, 152, 166
  and HR 925, 86, 106
  and HR 2020, 46
  and HR 4300, 66
Letterman, David, 145
Lichtman, Judith, 289
  and bill signing, 285
  and genesis of bill, 29, 33, 34
  and Junior Leagues, 40
  and stronger bill, 261
  and support coalition, 86, 152, 182,
    214, 224, 235, 260
Limbaugh, Rush, 284
lobbying, lobbyists:
  Catholic, *see* Catholic Conference
  by Chamber of Commerce, 61–62,
    151, 212
  effectiveness of, 151, 232, 289–90
  and genesis of bill, 22, 29, 32
  opposition to bill from, 60–62, 70,
    82–86, 163, 191, 195, 197
  support for bill from, 29, 41; *see also*
    support coalition
  and tax status, 258–59
  threat to withhold donations by, 258
  "typical drill" of, 84
  and votes on final pasage, 234
  votes rated by, 92–93, 163, 228, 233–
    234, 245

McCain, John, 216
McClure, Fred, 150, 238
McCurdy, Dave, 221, 233

McGrath, Raymond, 177
McKernan, John R., Jr., 68
McKinney, Stewart B., 60
McLarty, Thomas F. (Mack), 261–62
Madigan, Ed, 146
majority party, leadership committee
    of, 69–70, 142–43
majority whip:
  House, 105, 143–44
  Senate, 117, 187, 209
  task forces of, 105, 143, 162, 167
  and "whipping the bill," 143
Mansfield, Mike, 190
markups, 64–69, 102
  amendments in, 45
  proxies for, 64–65
Marriott, Dan, 25–26, 33
Martin, Lynn, 181, 194, 203, 205, 236,
    263
Matsunaga, Spark, 108
media:
  and amendments, 275
  and bill-signing ceremony, 11
  and child care, 33, 53–54
  and family leave, 83, 89, 193, 201–2,
    210, 287–88
  and Gingrich "special orders," 146–
    147
  and HR 925, 97–98, 103
  and HR 2020, 53, 61
  and legislation, 56
  and Rule XXII, 115–16
  and veto, 83, 238, 241
  and voice vote, 191, 192
  and Year of the Woman, 259
Merchants and Manufacturing
    Association, 18
Metzenbaum, Howard M., 104, 106,
    108, 185
Michel, Robert H. (Bob), 262, 294
Mikulski, Barbara A., 108, 257
Miller, George, 80
  background of, 24
  and genesis of bill, 23–29, 32–34, 37,
    46, 257
  and HR 2, 202–3
  and HR 2020, 38, 59, 63, 163
Mineta, Norman, 105, 124, 125, 144,
    152
minimum labor standard, 95, 224
minimum wage bill:
  and Bush, 114–15, 145, 149–50, 153,
    159, 246
  and cloture, 116, 122

conference report on, 149–50
and filibuster, 115–16
as HR 2, 144, 145, 148, 149–50, 153, 159, 162, 174
and labor, 115, 144, 153
and motion to proceed, 114–15
and veto, 150
and wage differential, 157
Mink, Patsy, 227
Mitchell, George J., 129, 185–88, 189–192, 212, 281, 295
and HR Report 102–816, 248
and S 5, 202, 209, 211, 213–14, 217, 238, 251, 274, 275, 277, 278, 280–285
and Thomas nomination, 212, 214
and voice vote, 240
Moakley, John Joseph (Joe), 71, 166–169, 266–67
Molinari, Susan, 175, 206, 266, 268
Mondale, Walter F., 38
Montana, family leave in, 21
Morella, Connie, 173
Moseley-Braun, Carol, 257, 276
motherhood issue, narrow focus of, 21, 23, 40–41, 78, 224, 234, 279
motions to recommit with instructions, 169, 234
motions to reconsider, 271
Motley, John, 289
and HR 2/S 5, 208
and HR 770/S 345, 135–36, 166, 182, 188, 191
and HR 925/S 249/S 2488, 84, 86, 90–91, 100, 103, 118, 125
and HR 2020, 60–61
Moynihan, Daniel Patrick, 58, 81
Murkowski, Frank H., 216
Murphy, Austin J., 47, 48, 49, 63
Murray, Patty, 257, 276
Muskie, Edmund S., 186
Myers, John T., 48, 50, 268

National Association of Manufacturers, 84, 88, 151
National Association of Wholesaler-Distributors (NAW), 82, 167, 223, 238
National Association of Women Business Owners, 88
National Association of Working Women (Nine to Five), 78, 124, 154–55, 281

National Council of Jewish Women, 66, 106, 152
National Education Association, 138, 214
National Federation of Independent Business (NFIB):
and HR 1, 262
and HR 2, 223, 234
and HR 770/S 345, 135, 166, 189, 197
and HR 925/S 249, 84, 91, 100, 103, 125
and HR 2020, 60–61
influence of, 151, 289–90
polls taken by, 61, 86
Sentinel of Small Business awards from, 92–93, 163
National Organization for Women, 32, 41, 105, 225
National Restaurant Association, 85
National Retail Federation, 85, 223, 276
National Retail Merchants Association, 85
National School Boards Association (NSBA), 102, 136–39
National Women's Law Center, 32
National Women's Political Caucus, 32, 258
New Deal, 61
New York School Boards Association, 137
NFIB, *see* National Federation of Independent Business
Nickles, Don, 122
Nine to Five, 78, 124, 154–55, 281
Nixon, Richard M., 37
Norton, Eleanor Holmes, 257, 264
Norton, Helen, 226, 235
NSBA (National School Boards Association), 102, 136–39
Nunn, Sam, 155, 187, 275, 281–82

Oakar, Mary Rose, 48
O'Connor, John Cardinal, 156
O'Grady, Jane, 66, 153–54, 162, 220–221
O'Neill, Thomas P., Jr. (Tip), 71, 76, 84, 143, 146–47, 157
open rule:
in floor consideration, 71–72
modified, 168–69

Packer, Joel, 214, 235
Packwood, Bob, 105, 135, 216

PACs, 258, 259
Palast, Geri, 260, 273
Parental and Disability Leave Act
    (1985):
  committee referrals of, 44–45
  cosponsors of, 51, 59
  hearings on, 46–50, 53
  as HR 2020, 42–51, 53–58
  introduction of, 43
  provisions of, 42, 57
  revisions in, 46,58
  sidetracking of, 54, 61
  title of, 58
Parental and Medical Leave Act
    (1986):
  cosponsors of, 58–60, 63
  hearings on, 63–65
  as HR 2020/4300, 58–66
  markups on, 65–66
  opposition to, 61–62
  revisions in, 65–66
  as S 2278, 58–59
  support coalition for, 66
Parental and Medical Leave Act
    (1987):
  child care added to, 120–22
  and cloture, 121–23
  combining with kiddie porn bill,
    119–20
  cosponsors of, 87, 89
  floor consideration of, 116–23
  hearings on, 86–90
  introduction of, 83, 86
  markup of, 107, 110
  move to recommit with instructions,
    120, 121
  national attention to, 123
  revisions of, 109, 117–19, 122
  as S 249, 75–76, 77–78
  as S 2488, 106–9, 116–23
  support coalition for, 118, 131
  vote-counting for, 117, 119, 122
Parental and Medical Leave Act
    (1989):
  cosponsors of, 130
  floor consideration of, 184–93
  hearings on, 134–36
  HR 770 substituted for, 184–85, 202
  introduction of, 130
  markups on, 136, 140, 141–42
  provisions of, 130–31
  as S 345, 130–36, 141–42, 183–93
  sense of the Senate resolution on,
    141–42

timetable for, 131–32
voice vote for, 190–92
vote-counting for, 132, 133–34, 188–
    191, 213–17
Parental and Medical Leave Act
    (1991):
  amendments to, 207, 213, 215–17
  floor consideration of, 213–18, 219
  and HR Report 102–816, 248
  markups on, 207–9
  power players for, 202
  provisions of, 247
  as S 5, 202, 206–18, 219, 237
  and veto, 214
  voice vote for, 217
  votes to override, 218, 251, 255–56
Parental and Medical Leave Act
    (1993):
  amendments to, 275, 276–84
  Bond language in, 272
  clearing for signature, 282–84
  committee hearings on, 272–74
  final passage of, 282
  floor consideration of, 281–82
  and gays in military, 275, 276–77,
    278–79, 281–82
  HR 1 substituted for, 283–84; see
    also Family and Medical Leave
    Act (1993)
  party leader negotiations on, 278
  as S 5, 272–83
  unanimous consent agreement on,
    274, 280
  and votes for cloture, 274–75, 280
parental leave, 27–29, 38–50, 77–78,
    93
  and abortion, 57, 60
  broadened support for, 63
  initial legislative steps of, 42–45
  as motherhood bill, 40–41
  opposition to, 61–62, 70
  see also family leave; specific
    legislation
Parker, Mike, 124, 167, 169
Paster, Howard, 287
Paul, Alice, 20–21
Pell, Claiborne, 108, 134
Penny, Timothy J., 287, 295
  background of, 221–22
  and HR 1, 262, 267
  and HR 2, 219–28, 230–31, 234
  and HR 770, 140, 150, 167, 168,
    174–75, 178, 180, 203
  and HR 925, 102, 124

Pepper, Claude D., 71, 83, 149
Perot, Ross, 241
Personnel and Police Subcommittee, 142
Petri, Tom, 49, 205, 246, 294
PL 103–3, Family and Medical Leave Act (1993), 284–87
  provisions of, 286–87
  signing ceremony, 11, 284–85, 287
plant-closing bill, 51–52, 54, 144–45, 174
pocket veto, 240, 248
Pollak, Michelle, 118, 119, 157–58, 204, 214–15, 226, 228, 274
Poole, Lorraine, 48
pornography, child, 119–20, 123
post-leave reinstatement, 95
Post Office and Civil Service Committee, 294
  and HR 1, 266
  and HR 2, 203, 205, 246
  and HR 770, 130, 140, 142, 168, 173
  and HR 925, 87, 94, 103, 105, 123
  and HR 2020, 44, 45, 47, 50–51, 55
  and HR 4300, 63, 64–65, 68
POTUS, use of term, 249
Pregnancy Discrimination Act (1978), 19—22, 285
president:
  agenda of, 56
  legislation cleared for, 150, 193–94
  and veto, 150, 188, 190–91, 194, 244
Pryce, Deborah, 268
Puerto Rico, 264

Quayle, J. Danforth (Dan), 28, 114, 141, 208
  and S 5, 236–37
  and S 249, 91, 104, 107
  and S 345, 195
  and S 2488, 108, 109
Quillen, Jamie, 169–70, 267, 288–89

race:
  discrimination on basis of, 21–22
  and redistricting, 243
Radigan, Anne, 29, 31, 32, 40–41
Reagan, Ronald, 20, 23, 24, 38, 112
  and Democrats, 36–37, 295–96
  inauguration of, 35–36
  and minimum wage, 114–15
  and plant-closing bill, 143
  programs cut by, 62
  and Republicans, 36

  second term of, 98–99
  and Senate, 76, 111, 146
  and veto, 83, 98, 111, 119, 123
Real, Manuel L., 19, 20–22, 23, 40, 45–46, 80
reapportionment and redistricting, 242–43
reduced-schedule leave, 267, 269–70, 282, 283
Reed, Mary, 262, 289
Reich, Robert B., 263, 273, 292
Renwanz, Marsha, 87, 88, 89–90, 106
Republicans:
  bill opposed by, 181
  bill supported by, 180, 194, 206–8, 213
  "gypsy moths" in, 92
  in midterm elections, 294
  and Reagan, 36
  in Senate, 79
Resnick, Mike, 102, 136–39, 140–41
Reuther, Alan, 32
Ridgewell's, 20
Roberts, Barney, 174
Rogers, Will, 145
Roosevelt, Franklin D., 203
Rose Charlie, 203
Ross, Susan Deller, 20, 21, 29, 32
Rostenkowski, Dan, 105, 151, 239
Roth, William V., Jr., 216
Roukema, Marge, 286, 295
  background of, 92
  and HR 1, 266, 268, 285
  and HR 2, 204, 205, 206, 210, 226, 227, 234, 240, 246–47
  and HR 284, 83, 93, 97
  and HR 770, 130, 139, 140, 155, 157, 164, 174, 175, 177, 194, 195
  and HR 925, 95–98, 100–103, 123
  and HR 4300, 63, 64, 65, 66, 67–68
  and PAC funds, 259
  and small business, 92–93
  and White House, 236, 239, 251
Rowland, John, 177
Rudman, Warren B., 56
Ruff, Jackie, 131
  and S 5, 204, 211
  and S 345, 132, 135, 191
Rules and Administration Committee (Senate), 187, 209
Rules Committee (House), 143, 149, 163
  and floor consideration, 69–70, 71, 100, 106, 166, 250
  and HR 1, 266–67

Rules Committee (House) (*cont.*)
and HR 2, 227, 229–30
and HR 770, 164, 166, 168
and HR 4300, 71–72
and HR Report 102–816, 250
and open rule, 168
self-executing rule in, 283
Rule XXII, 115–16

Saiki, Patricia, 181, 207
Sanders, Bernard, 265, 270
Sanford, Terry, 258
Schneider, Claudine, 97, 181
Schroeder, Pat, 204, 210, 261, 290, 294
and genesis of bill, 26, 29, 31, 34
and HR 1, 268, 285
and HR 2, 226, 227, 229, 232, 246
and HR 770, 130, 170–71, 180, 181–
182, 198
and HR 925, 76–77, 78, 83, 93, 94,
96–98
and HR 2020, 37–38, 41–43, 45, 46–
51, 54–55, 57, 60, 63, 82, 96, 153,
224, 261
and HR 4300, 58, 59
and plant-closing bill, 51–52, 54,
143
Schwartz, Janis, 21
Scully, Tom, 210, 249–50, 256, 257
"Select Kids," *see* Children, Youth
and Families, Select Committee
on
Senate:
Appropriations Committee, 185
Armed Services Committee, 275
Children, Family, Drugs and
Alcoholism Subcommittee, 58,
75, 76
Children's Caucus, 75
cloture in, 115–16
committee seats apportioned in, 79
Democratic leadership in, 76, 295
electoral circumstances in, 243
extended debate in, 188
filibusters in, 114, 115–16, 188, 190,
211–12
floor consideration in, 79–80, 187,
190
Labor and Human Resources
Committee, 58–59, 75, 76, 80, 82,
104
legislation introduced in, 58–59, 76,
79–80, 86
majority leader in, 114, 186, 295

majority whip in, 117, 187, 209
minority leader in, 186–87
motion to proceed in, 114–15
president pro tempore of, 76, 185
and Reagan, 76, 111, 146
Republicans in, 79
roll call vote in, 215–16
Rules and Administration
Committee, 187
Rule XXII in, 115–16
S 5, child care (1989), 133, 159–60,
189
S 5, Parental and Medical Leave Act
(1991, 1993), 202, 206–18, 219, 237
S 249, Parental and Medical Leave
Act (1987), 75–76, 77–78, 79–82,
83, 86–91, 103–10
S 345, Parental and Medical Leave
Act (1989), 130–36, 141–41, 155–
156, 183–93
S 2278, Parental and Medical Leave
Act (1986), 58–59
S 2488, Parental and Medical Leave
Act (1987), 106–9, 110, 116–23
sense of the Senate resolution, 141–
142
time agreements in, 187
unanimous consent in, 187, 192
unlimited debate in, 187
voice vote in, 159–60, 190–92
vote to override veto, 251, 255–56
Service Employees International
Union, 153, 154, 260, 273
sex discrimination, 19, 20–23
sexual harassment, 212–13
Seymour, John, 257, 258
Shearer, Derek, 263
Shelby, Richard C., 282
Simon, Paul, 108, 156
Simpson, Alan K., 120
Sisyphus, 276
Skinner, Samuel K., 237, 238, 239,
241, 246, 248–49, 250
Slaughter, Louise M., 168, 169, 170
Sloan, John, Jr., 90–91
small business, 49, 60, 211
bill opposed by, 64, 91, 135
and cost estimates, 207
exemptions for, 29, 64, 65, 66, 67,
77, 86, 93, 95–96, 118, 125, 137–
138, 165, 178, 224, 225, 261, 286
lobbying by, 22, 70
and Roukema, 92–93
Sentinel awards of, 92–93, 163

Small Business Committee, 223, 267
Smith, Christopher H., 60, 156
Smith, Howard W., 69
Smith, Lamar, 177
Smith, Virginia, 188
Snowe, Olympia, 31, 59, 97, 175, 230, 295
social legislation, 63, 80
  and business, 289
  and Democrats, 82–83, 111, 114, 255, 293
  and genesis of bill, 23–26
  and labor, 143–44, 150
  new era of, 13, 29
  in public vs. private sector, 61
  and Reagan, 24
  unresolved issues in, 249
Solomon, Gerald, 170, 181, 236, 270, 295
Sombrotto, Vince, 63
South Carolina, 49
Speaker of the House:
  and floor consideration, 70, 164
  formal vote for, 264
  and right of referral, 43–44
Specter, Arlen, 58, 87, 88, 90, 122, 215, 216
Specter, Joan, 48, 50, 87
spousal care, 106, 157–58, 165, 205, 225, 284
Stafford, Robert, 107, 108, 109, 122, 141
state laws:
  on family leave, 18, 19–22, 45, 80, 95, 205
  and federal legislation, 60
Steering and Policy Committee, 18–19, 69–70, 164
Stenholm, Charles W., 181
  and amendments, 168–69, 180
  and HR 1270, 217
  and preferential rehiring, 167, 217, 221, 224, 229, 231–32, 234, 250, 262
Stennis, John, 76
Stephanopoulos, George, 256
Stevens, Ted, 216, 251
Stockman, David, 62
Sununu, John, 167, 194–95, 236, 237–238, 249, 250
super seniority issue, 57
support coalition:
  costs of, 26

as "family leave coalition," 86, 260, 290
FESA Group, 30–32, 34, 37, 38–39, 46
for HR 2/S 5, 204, 211, 214, 215–17, 224, 226–28, 235, 277
for HR 770, 152–59, 165–66, 175–176, 181, 194
for HR 925/S 2488, 77–78, 86, 97, 118, 131
for HR 4300, 66, 69
and tax status, 258–59
Supreme Court, U.S.:
  and appeals process, 22
  Bork nomination to, 99
  and Cal Fed appeal, 45, 54, 61, 80
  and civil rights, 196
  General Electric v. *Gilbert* in, 22
  and redistricting, 243
  Thomas nomination to, 212–13
suspension calendar, 71
Symms, Steven D., 122

Tarplin, Linda, 239
Tarplin, Rich, 239, 261, 287
  and S 5, 204, 207, 211, 214, 279
  and S 345, 131, 132, 135, 138, 140–141, 158, 184, 189, 191
  and S 2488, 106–9, 111, 116, 117–119, 123
Tauke, Tom, 67, 68
Tavenner, Mary, 82–86, 100, 123, 137, 223, 238, 290, 292
  and HR 2/S 5, 210–11, 234, 245
  and HR 770, 139, 163, 166–67, 188–189, 191, 197
tax incentive plan, 250–51, 262, 277–278
Tax Reform Act (1986), 70
Taylor, Gene, 65
Thomas, Clarence, 212–13, 214
Thompson, Jim, 237
three-day layover rule, 267
Thurmond, Strom:
  and S 5, 273–74
  and S 249, 75, 88
  and S 345, 193
  and S 2488, 108, 109, 119–20, 121, 123
time agreements, 187
Title VII, 22
Tower, John, 145, 146, 147, 186
Twain, Mark, 145

unanimous consent agreement (UC),
    187, 192, 211–12
  on HR Report 102–816, 248
  on S 5, 280, 283
"unfunded mandates," 293
Union Calendar, 164
unions, *see* labor
United Auto Workers, 32
United Mine Workers, 46, 153, 154

veto:
    and Bush, 123, 146, 150, 182, 191,
      194–97, 202, 214, 236, 246, 248–
      251, 255–56
    and media, 83, 238, 241
    options, 249–50
    pocket, 240, 248
    and president, 150, 188, 190–91,
      194, 244
    and Reagan, 83, 98, 111, 119, 123
    timing of, 239–41, 244
    votes to override, 197–98, 202
    votes to sustain, 245
Virgin Islands, U.S., 264

Walker, Robert S., 177, 271, 284
Waters, Maxine, 19, 21
Waxman, Henry A., 33–34, 80
Ways and Means Committee, 151
Webster, Daniel, 290
Weicker, Lowell P. Jr., 104, 107, 108,
    109, 122, 141
Weiss, Ted, 59
Weldon, Curt, 163–64, 165, 167, 168,
    179–80, 213
    see also Gordon-Weldon substitute
Wellstone, Paul, 207
whip, *see* majority whip
White House Conference on Small
    Business, 60
Williams, Pat, 13, 227, 229, 263
    and HR 1, 265, 266, 285
    and HR 2, 203, 204–6, 226
    and HR 770, 162–63, 171–72, 203
Williams, Wendy:
    and genesis of bill, 20, 29, 32, 45
    and HR 2020, 48–50
    and Junior League, 40

Wisconsin, family leave in, 154
witnesses:
    academic experts, 26–27, 40, 46, 50
    adversarial, 64
    broadened spectrum of, 63–64, 135
Wofford, Harris, 229
women:
    in Congress, 244, 257–58, 259
    Congressional Caucus for Women's
      Issues, 34, 40, 59, 92, 230
    discrimination against, 19, 20–23
    issues for, 38, 257, 276, 290
    National Women's Political Caucus,
      32, 258
    networks of, 260
    and public policy, 285
    and schism of feminists, 41
    and sexual harassment, 212–13
    and special-vs.-equal debate, 20–23
    in workforce, 22, 25, 48, 63
    Year of, 259
Women's Legal Defense Fund
    (WLDF), 19–20, 29, 133, 152,
    258–59, 260, 282, 285
Wood, Kimba, 287
Woods, Harriett, 244
workforce:
    and changing worlds of, 257
    and child care, 25–28, 33, 95
    double standard for, 20–23
    and employee rights, 22–23, 30
    parents in, 27–29, 33
    women in, 22, 25, 48, 63
Wright, Jim, 82, 144, 163–64
    and congressional pay raise, 147–48
    and opposition to bill, 125
    resignation of, 148–49
    and Rules Committee, 143
    as Speaker, 76, 84, 94, 124, 129, 227

Yandle, Vicki, 285
Year of the Woman, 259
"yuppie welfare" bill, 140, 153–54,
    179

Zigler, Edward, 27–28, 87
Zoellick, Bob, 249, 250
Zuckman, Jill, 273